My Little Monster

10

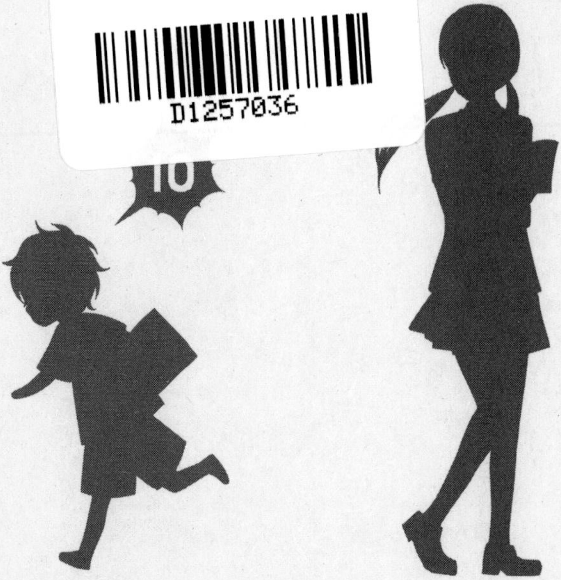

Robico

CONTENTS

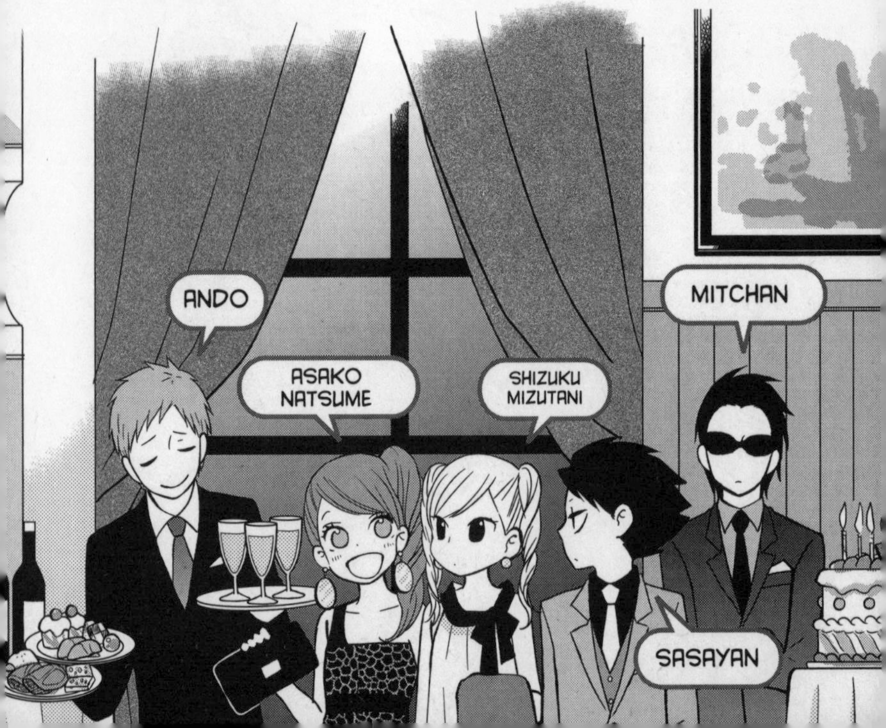

MITCHAN
SHIZUKU MIZUTANI
ASAKO NATSUME
ANDO
SASAYAN

STORY

When Shizuku Mizutani does a favor for problem child Haru Yoshida, who sat next to her in school, he develops a huge crush on her. Attracted to his innocence, she eventually falls for him, too, but when she asks him out, he inexplicably turns her down. After that, the couple repeatedly fail to find themselves on the same page as they eventually move on to their second year of high school. Now Haru has confessed his love, and the two are finally an official couple. At first, Shizuku doesn't really feel like anything is different, but as they spend their entire summer vacation together, she realizes how nice it is to be with the one you love. But apparently something has gone wrong in the Yoshida family—will this event drive a wedge between Shizuku and Haru?!

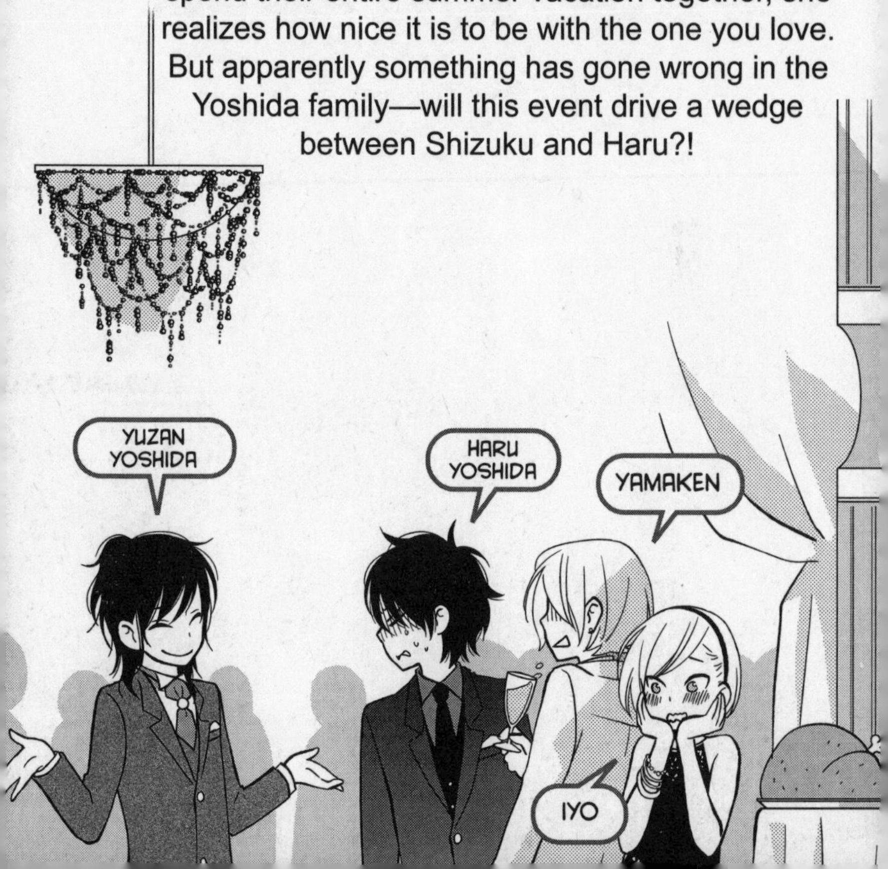
YUZAN YOSHIDA
HARU YOSHIDA
YAMAKEN
IYO

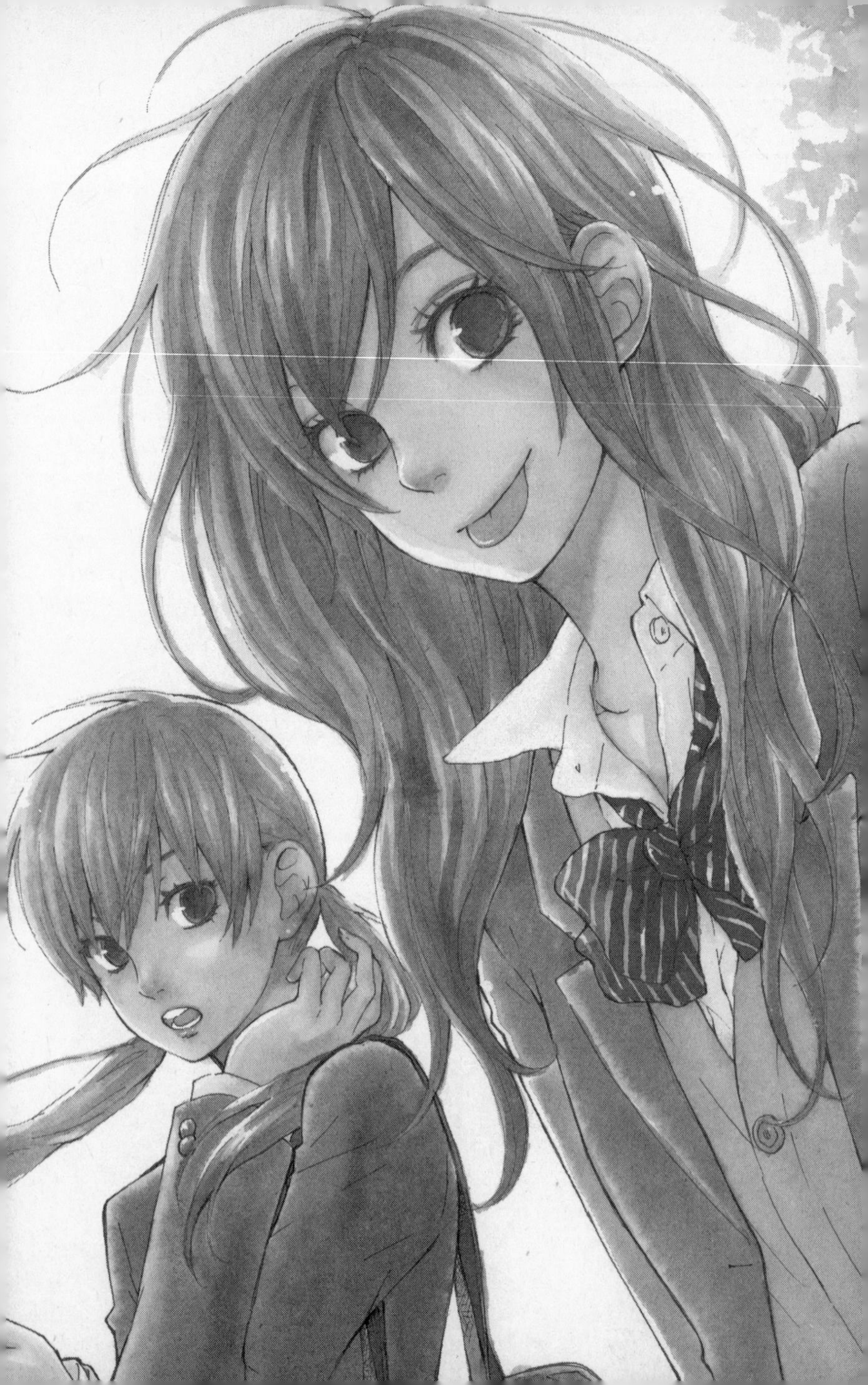

CHAPTER 37: THE YUZAN-SAN STORY

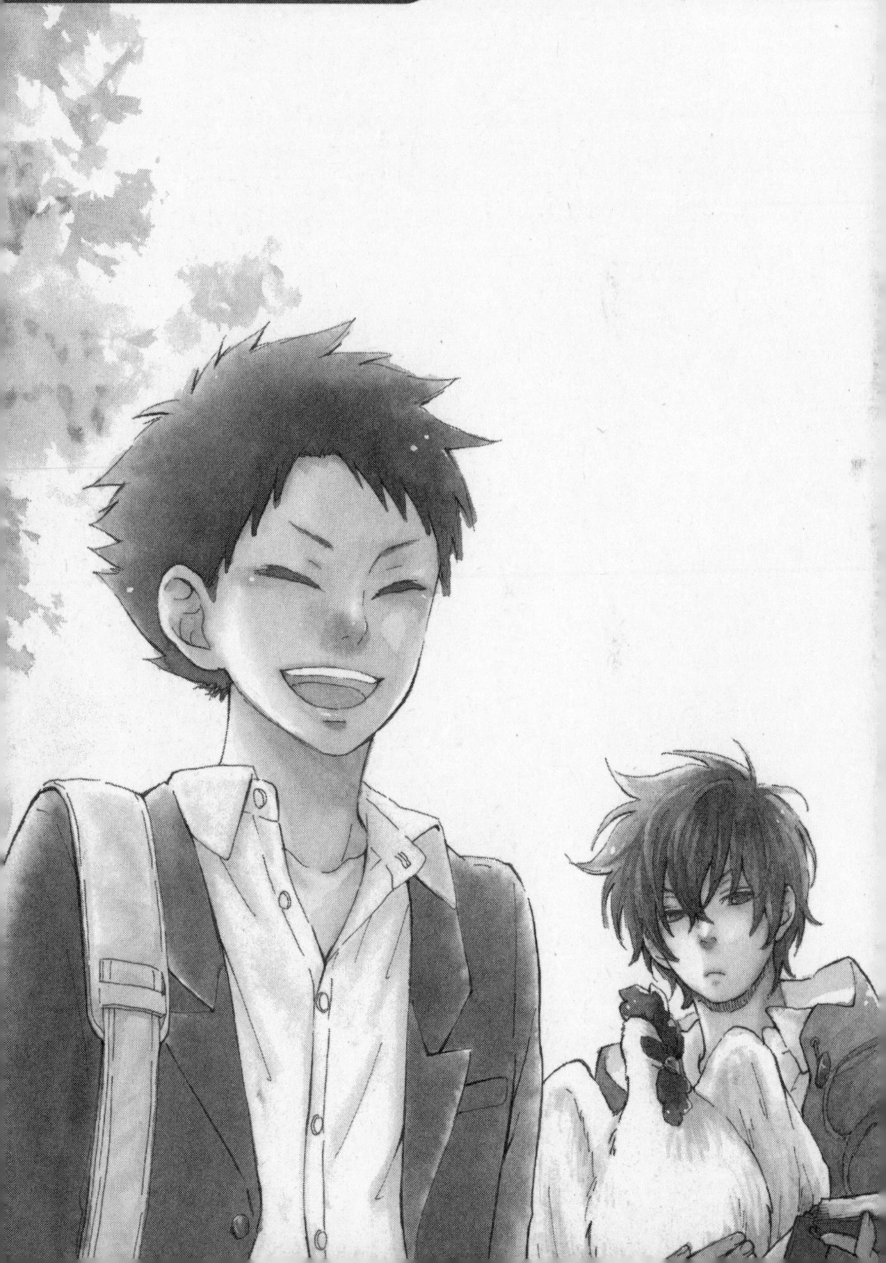

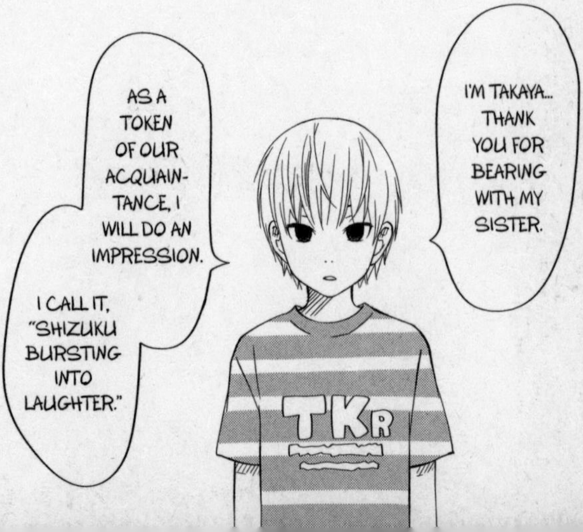
I'M TAKAYA... THANK YOU FOR BEARING WITH MY SISTER.
AS A TOKEN OF OUR ACQUAINTANCE, I WILL DO AN IMPRESSION.
I CALL IT, "SHIZUKU BURSTING INTO LAUGHTER."
TKR

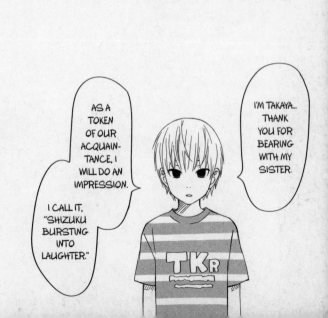

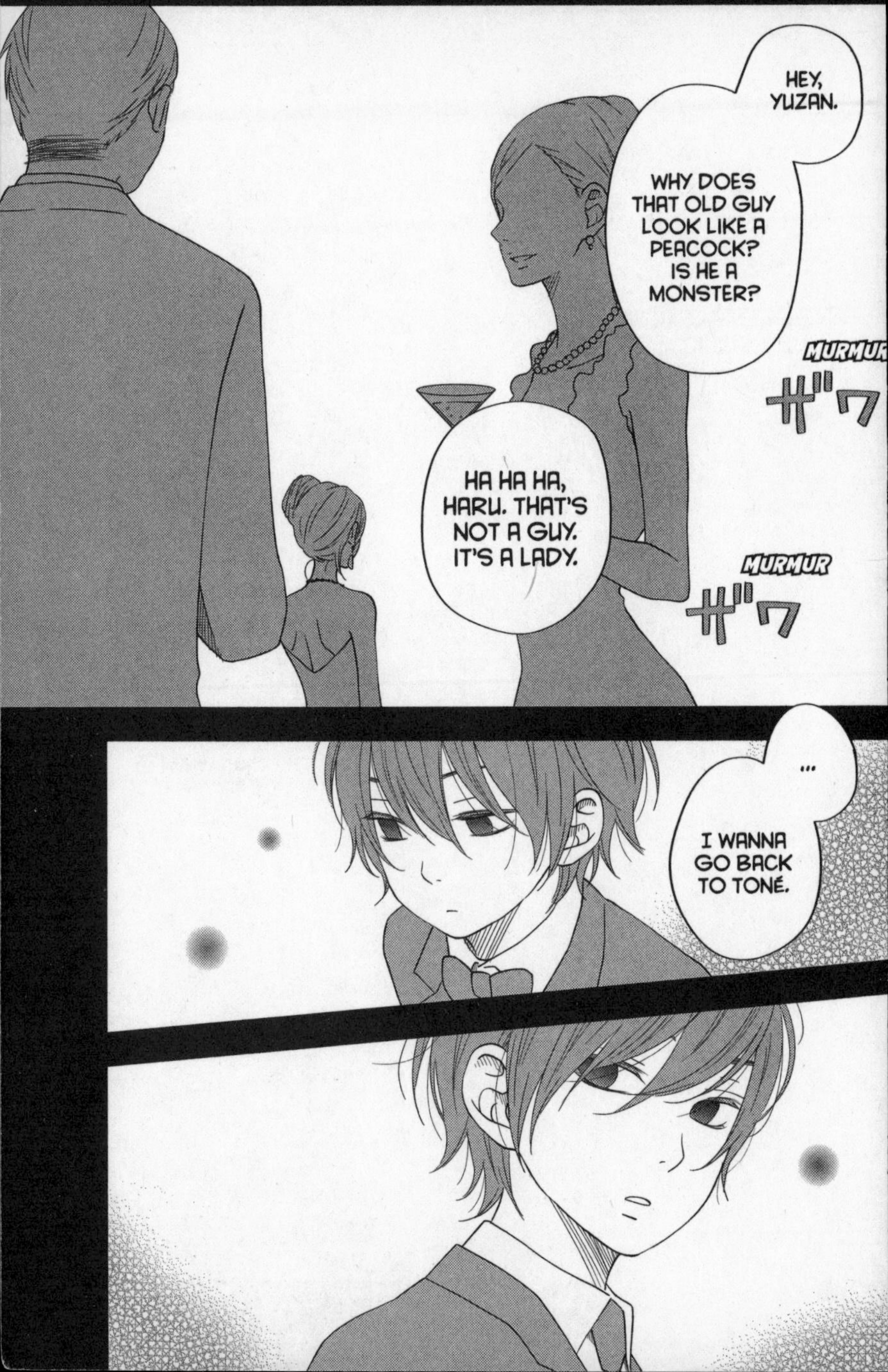
HEY, YUZAN.
WHY DOES THAT OLD GUY LOOK LIKE A PEACOCK? IS HE A MONSTER?
MURMUR
ザワ
HA HA HA, HARU. THAT'S NOT A GUY. IT'S A LADY.
MURMUR
ザワ
...
I WANNA GO BACK TO TONÉ.

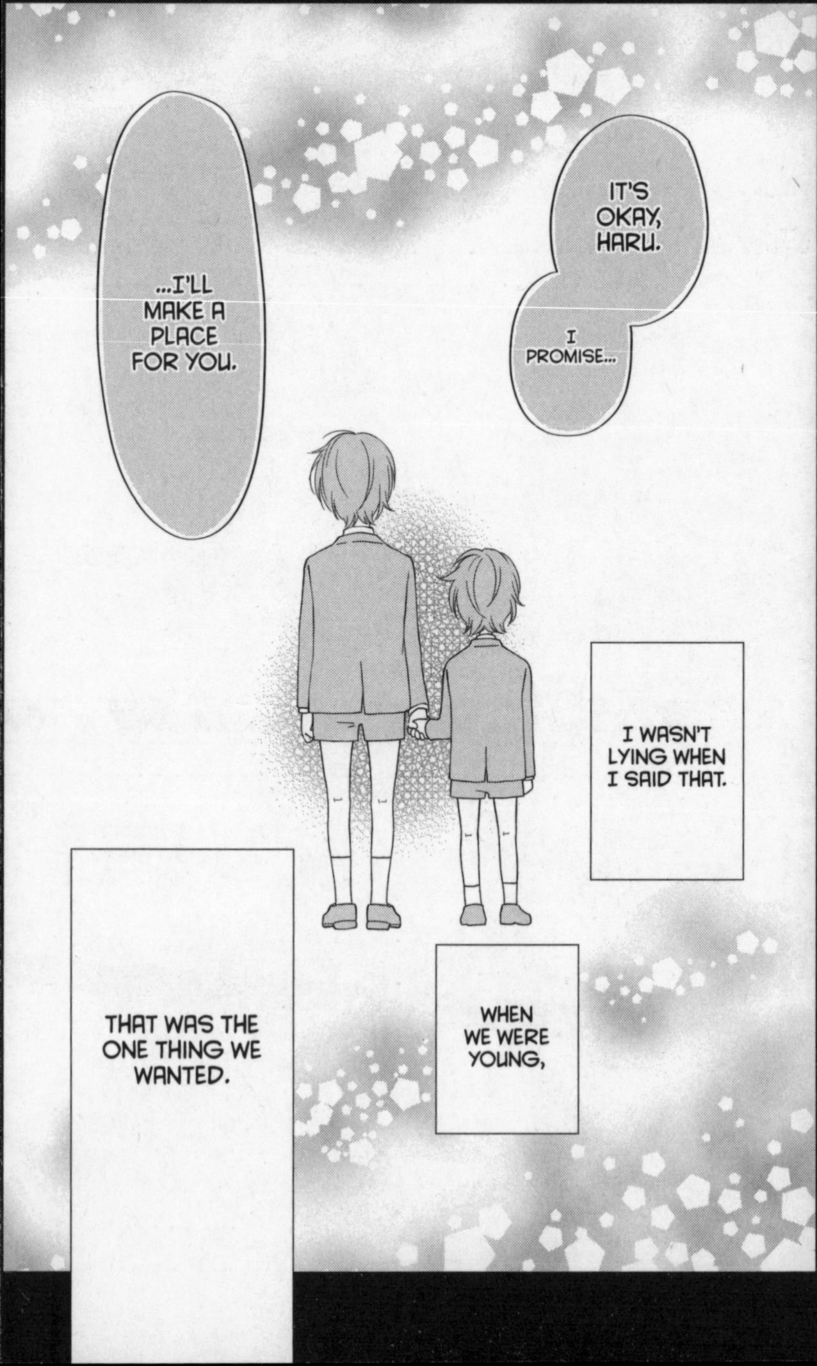
IT'S OKAY, HARU.
I PROMISE...
...I'LL MAKE A PLACE FOR YOU.
I WASN'T LYING WHEN I SAID THAT.
WHEN WE WERE YOUNG,
THAT WAS THE ONE THING WE WANTED.

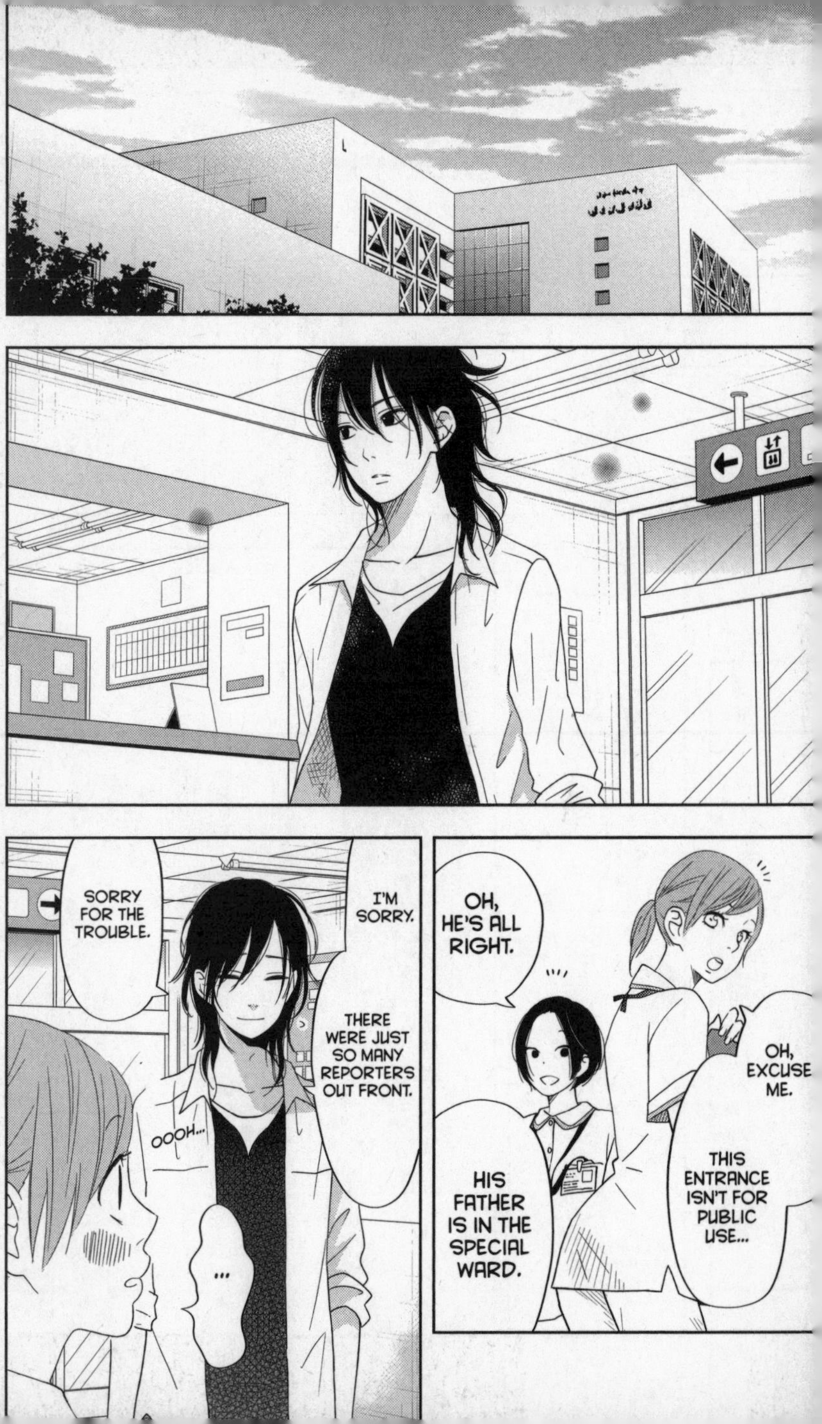
OH, EXCUSE ME.
THIS ENTRANCE ISN'T FOR PUBLIC USE...
OH, HE'S ALL RIGHT.
HIS FATHER IS IN THE SPECIAL WARD.
I'M SORRY.
THERE WERE JUST SO MANY REPORTERS OUT FRONT.
SORRY FOR THE TROUBLE.
OOOH...
...

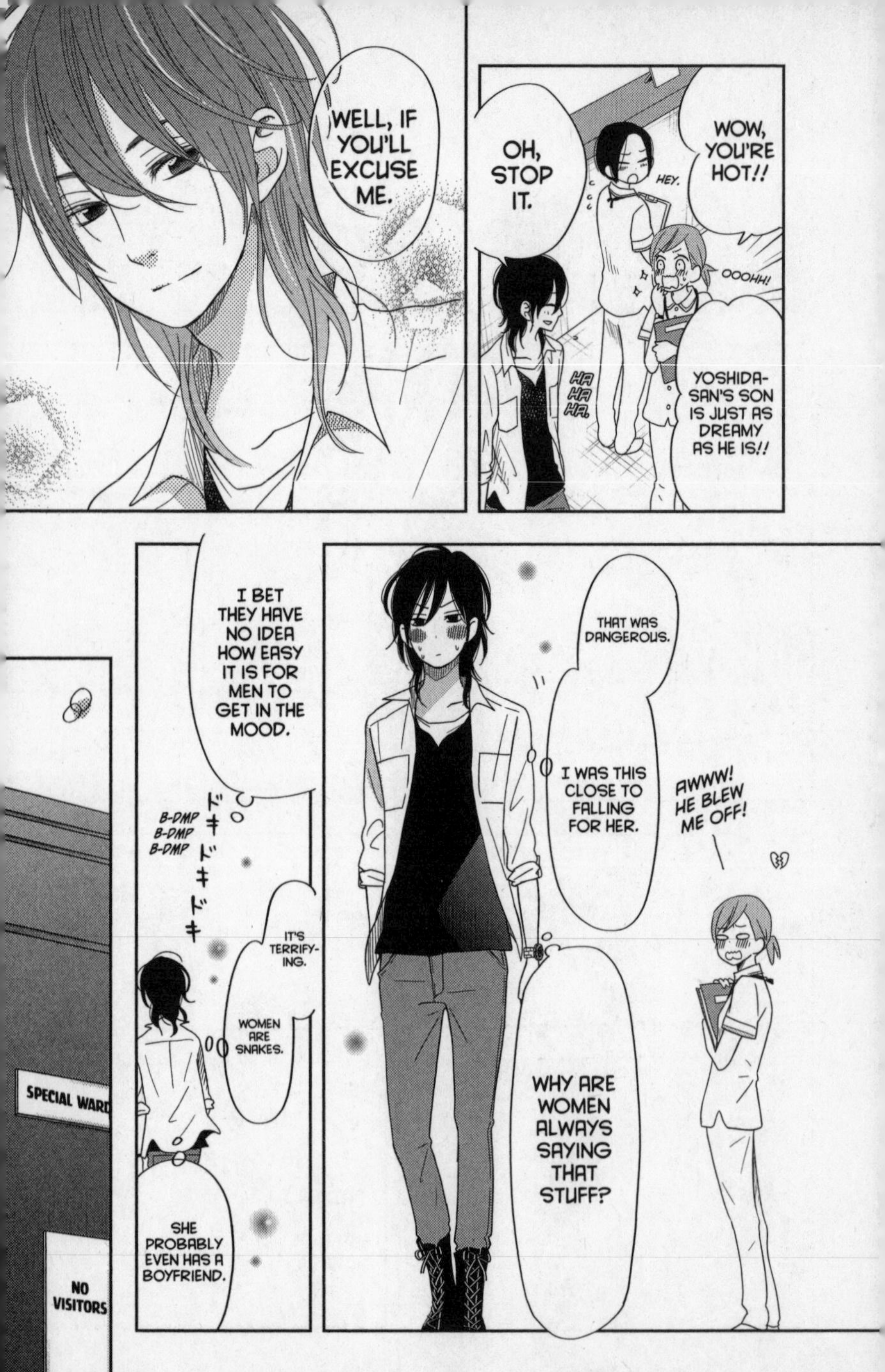
WOW, YOU'RE HOT!!
HEY.
OH, STOP IT.
OOOHH!
YOSHIDA-SAN'S SON IS JUST AS DREAMY AS HE IS!!
HA HA HA.
WELL, IF YOU'LL EXCUSE ME.
THAT WAS DANGEROUS.
I WAS THIS CLOSE TO FALLING FOR HER.
AWWW! HE BLEW ME OFF!
WHY ARE WOMEN ALWAYS SAYING THAT STUFF?
I BET THEY HAVE NO IDEA HOW EASY IT IS FOR MEN TO GET IN THE MOOD.
ドキドキドキ
B-DMP B-DMP B-DMP
IT'S TERRIFYING.
WOMEN ARE SNAKES.
SHE PROBABLY EVEN HAS A BOYFRIEND.
SPECIAL WARD
NO VISITORS

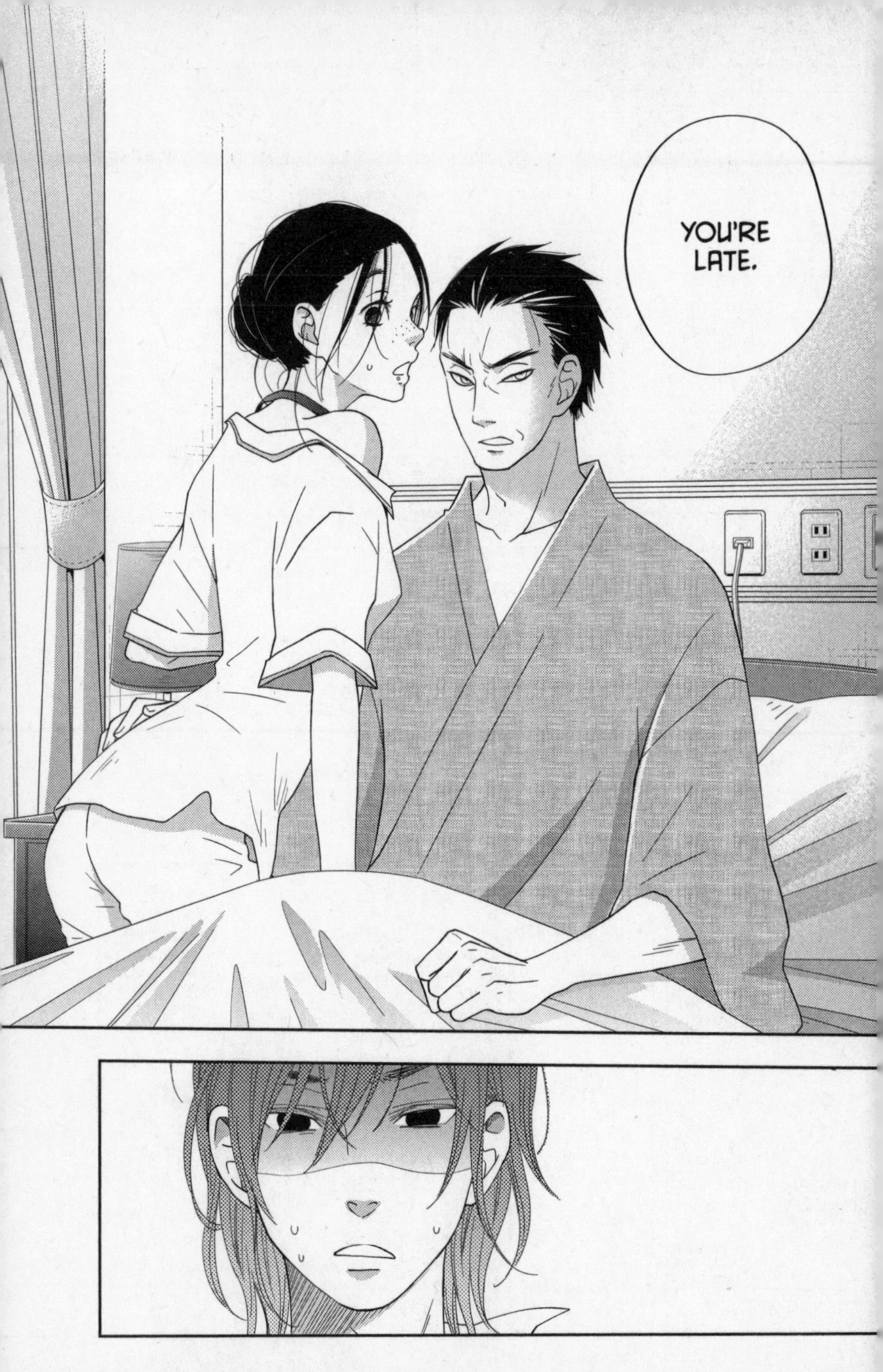
YOU'RE LATE.

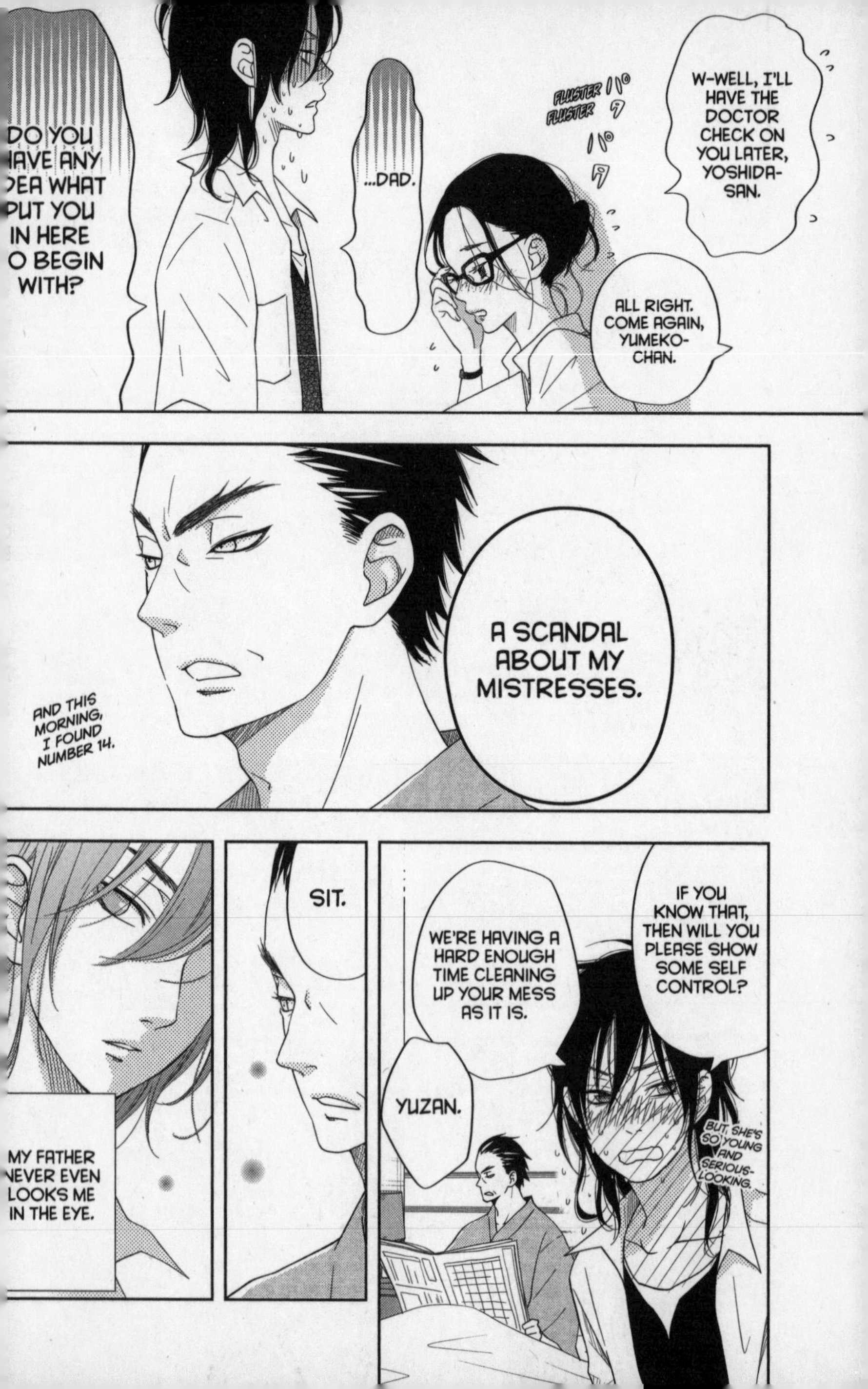
W-WELL, I'LL HAVE THE DOCTOR CHECK ON YOU LATER, YOSHIDA-SAN.
FLUSTER FLUSTER
ALL RIGHT. COME AGAIN, YUMEKO-CHAN.
...DAD.
DO YOU HAVE ANY DEA WHAT PUT YOU IN HERE O BEGIN WITH?
A SCANDAL ABOUT MY MISTRESSES.
AND THIS MORNING, I FOUND NUMBER 14.
IF YOU KNOW THAT, THEN WILL YOU PLEASE SHOW SOME SELF CONTROL?
WE'RE HAVING A HARD ENOUGH TIME CLEANING UP YOUR MESS AS IT IS.
BUT, SHE'S SO YOUNG AND SERIOUS-LOOKING.
YUZAN.
SIT.
MY FATHER NEVER EVEN LOOKS ME IN THE EYE.

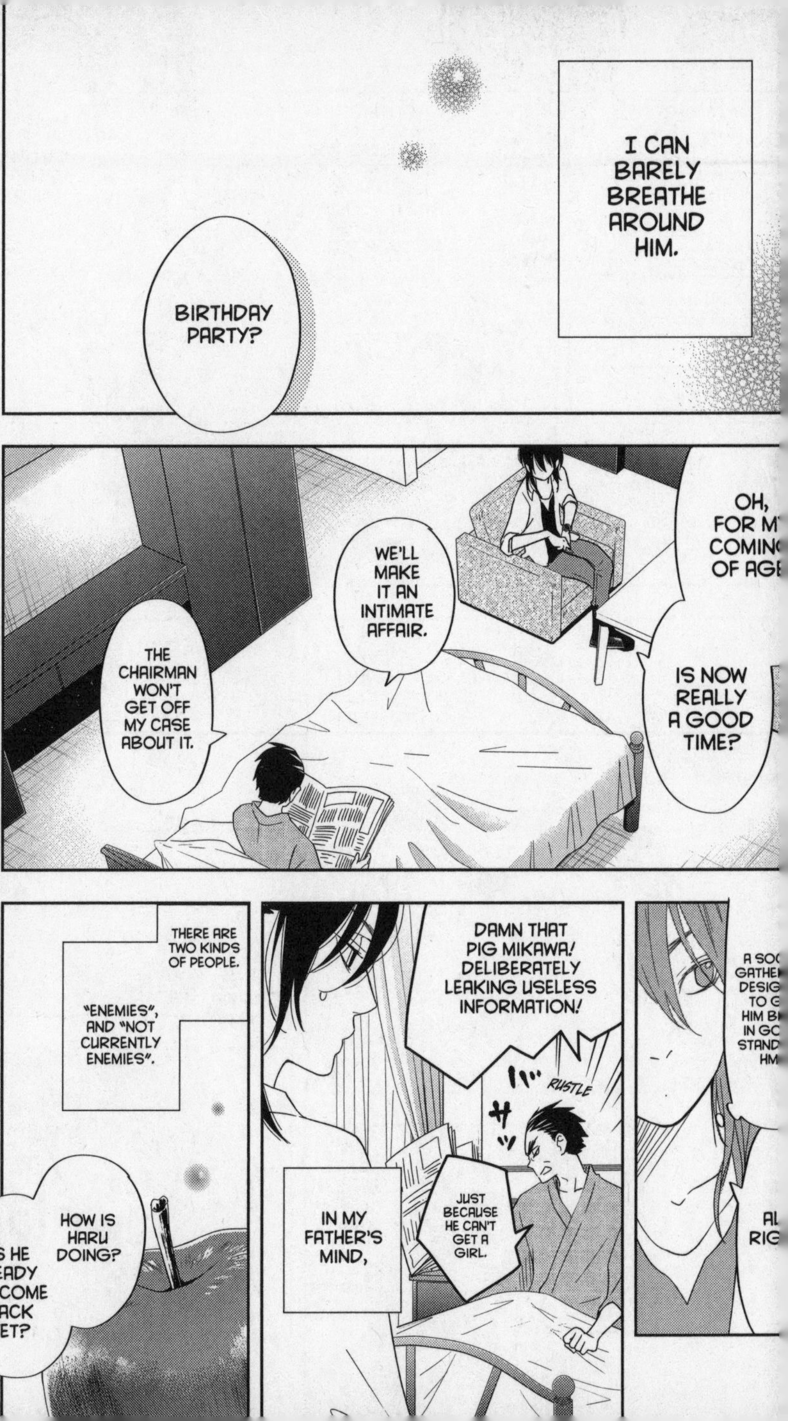
I CAN BARELY BREATHE AROUND HIM.
BIRTHDAY PARTY?
OH, FOR M COMIN OF AG
IS NOW REALLY A GOOD TIME?
WE'LL MAKE IT AN INTIMATE AFFAIR.
THE CHAIRMAN WON'T GET OFF MY CASE ABOUT IT.
A SOC GATHE DESIG TO G HIM B IN GO STAND HM
AL RIG
DAMN THAT PIG MIKAWA! DELIBERATELY LEAKING USELESS INFORMATION!
RUSTLE
JUST BECAUSE HE CAN'T GET A GIRL.
IN MY FATHER'S MIND,
THERE ARE TWO KINDS OF PEOPLE.
"ENEMIES", AND "NOT CURRENTLY ENEMIES".
HOW IS HARU DOING?
IS HE READY TO COME BACK YET?

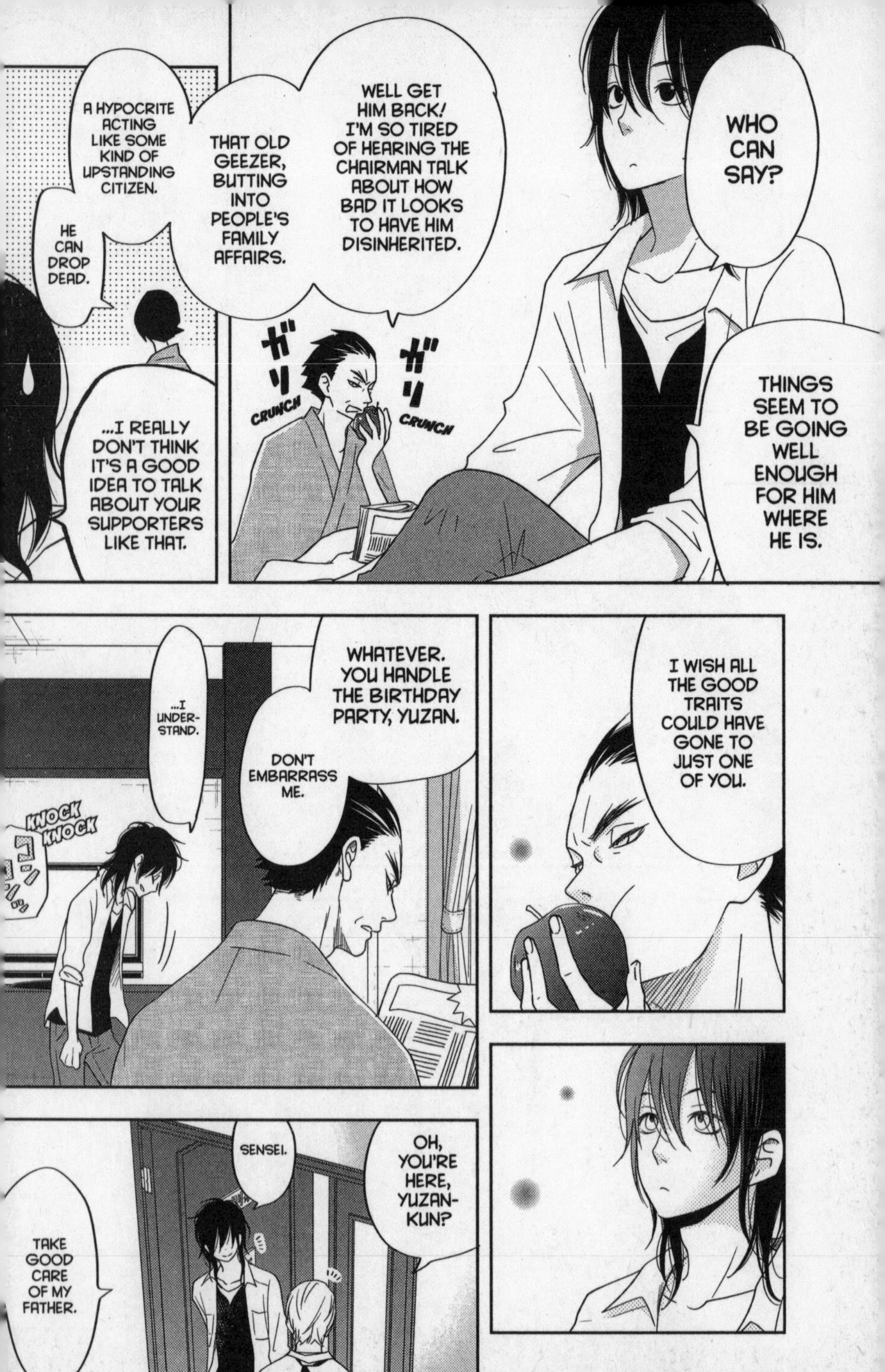
WHO CAN SAY?
THINGS SEEM TO BE GOING WELL ENOUGH FOR HIM WHERE HE IS.
WELL GET HIM BACK! I'M SO TIRED OF HEARING THE CHAIRMAN TALK ABOUT HOW BAD IT LOOKS TO HAVE HIM DISINHERITED.
THAT OLD GEEZER, BUTTING INTO PEOPLE'S FAMILY AFFAIRS.
CRUNCH
CRUNCH
A HYPOCRITE ACTING LIKE SOME KIND OF UPSTANDING CITIZEN.
HE CAN DROP DEAD.
...I REALLY DON'T THINK IT'S A GOOD IDEA TO TALK ABOUT YOUR SUPPORTERS LIKE THAT.
I WISH ALL THE GOOD TRAITS COULD HAVE GONE TO JUST ONE OF YOU.
WHATEVER. YOU HANDLE THE BIRTHDAY PARTY, YUZAN.
DON'T EMBARRASS ME.
...I UNDER-STAND.
KNOCK KNOCK
OH, YOU'RE HERE, YUZAN-KUN?
SENSEI.
TAKE GOOD CARE OF MY FATHER.

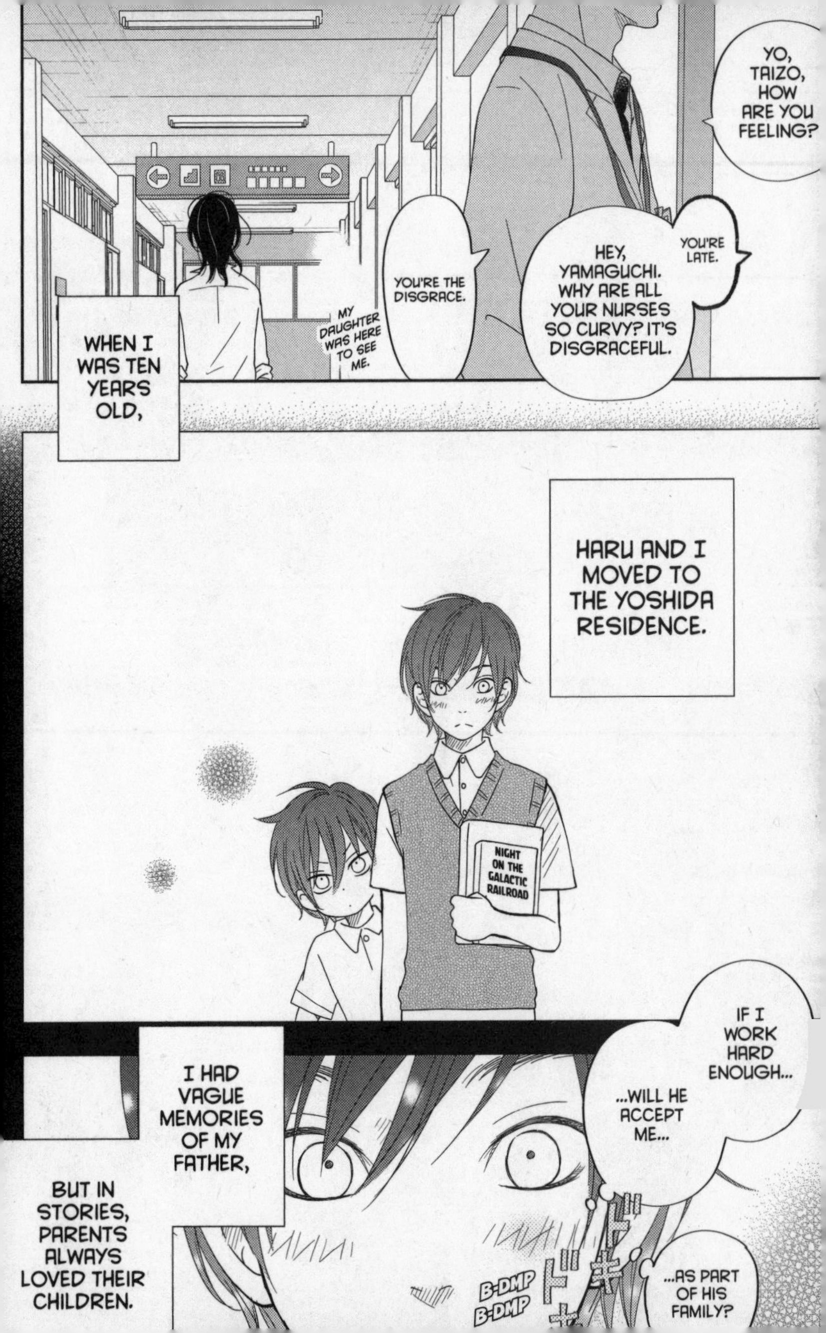
YO, TAIZO, HOW ARE YOU FEELING?
YOU'RE LATE.
HEY, YAMAGUCHI. WHY ARE ALL YOUR NURSES SO CURVY? IT'S DISGRACEFUL.
YOU'RE THE DISGRACE.
MY DAUGHTER WAS HERE TO SEE ME.
WHEN I WAS TEN YEARS OLD,
HARU AND I MOVED TO THE YOSHIDA RESIDENCE.
NIGHT ON THE GALACTIC RAILROAD
IF I WORK HARD ENOUGH...
...WILL HE ACCEPT ME...
...AS PART OF HIS FAMILY?
B-DMP B-DMP
I HAD VAGUE MEMORIES OF MY FATHER,
BUT IN STORIES, PARENTS ALWAYS LOVED THEIR CHILDREN.

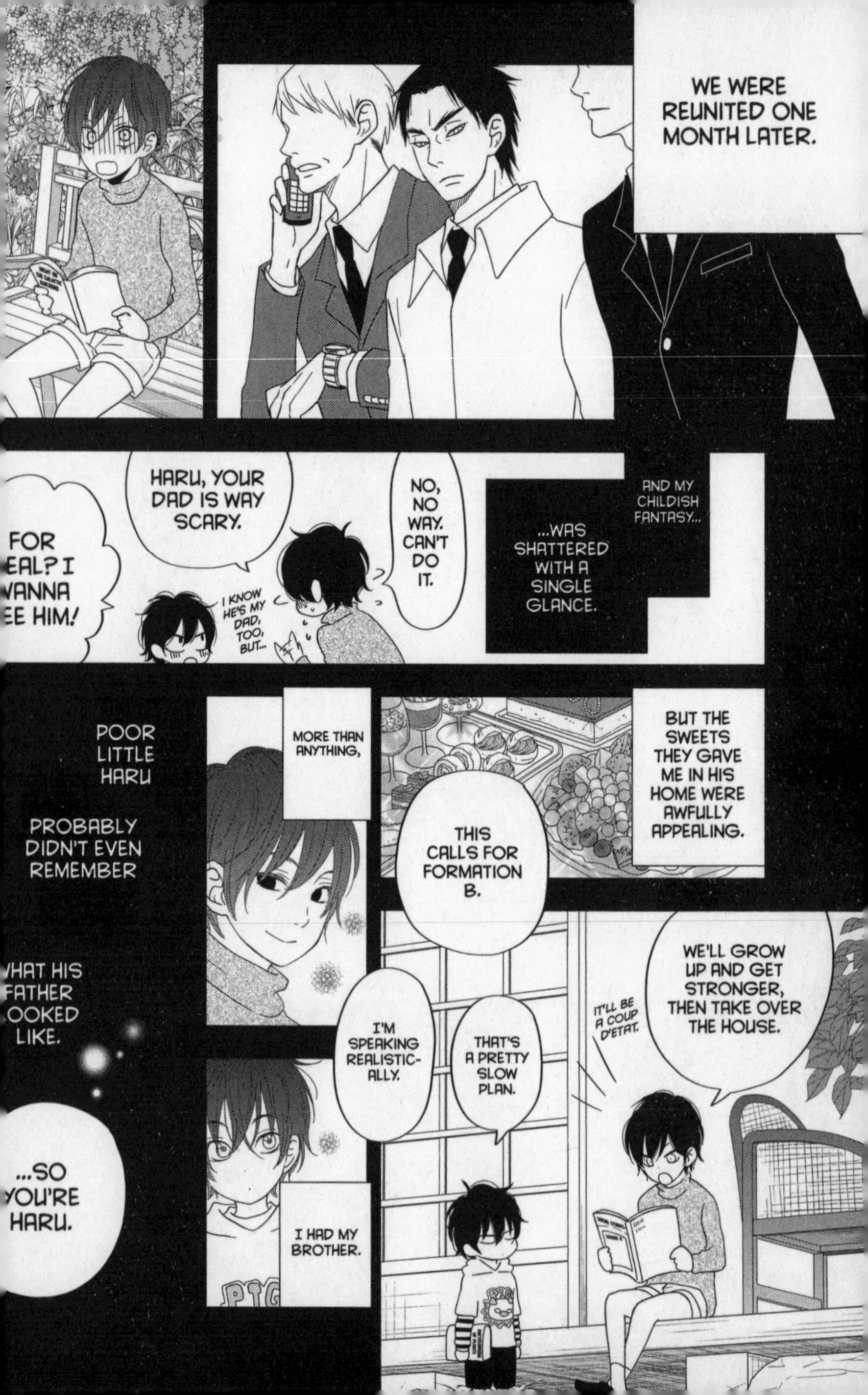
WE WERE REUNITED ONE MONTH LATER.
AND MY CHILDISH FANTASY...
...WAS SHATTERED WITH A SINGLE GLANCE.
NO, NO WAY. CAN'T DO IT.
I KNOW HE'S MY DAD, TOO, BUT...
HARU, YOUR DAD IS WAY SCARY.
FOR EAL? I VANNA EE HIM!
BUT THE SWEETS THEY GAVE ME IN HIS HOME WERE AWFULLY APPEALING.
MORE THAN ANYTHING,
THIS CALLS FOR FORMATION B.
WE'LL GROW UP AND GET STRONGER, THEN TAKE OVER THE HOUSE.
IT'LL BE A COUP D'ETAT.
THAT'S A PRETTY SLOW PLAN.
I'M SPEAKING REALISTIC-ALLY.
I HAD MY BROTHER.
POOR LITTLE HARU
PROBABLY DIDN'T EVEN REMEMBER
HAT HIS FATHER OOKED LIKE.
...SO OU'RE HARU.

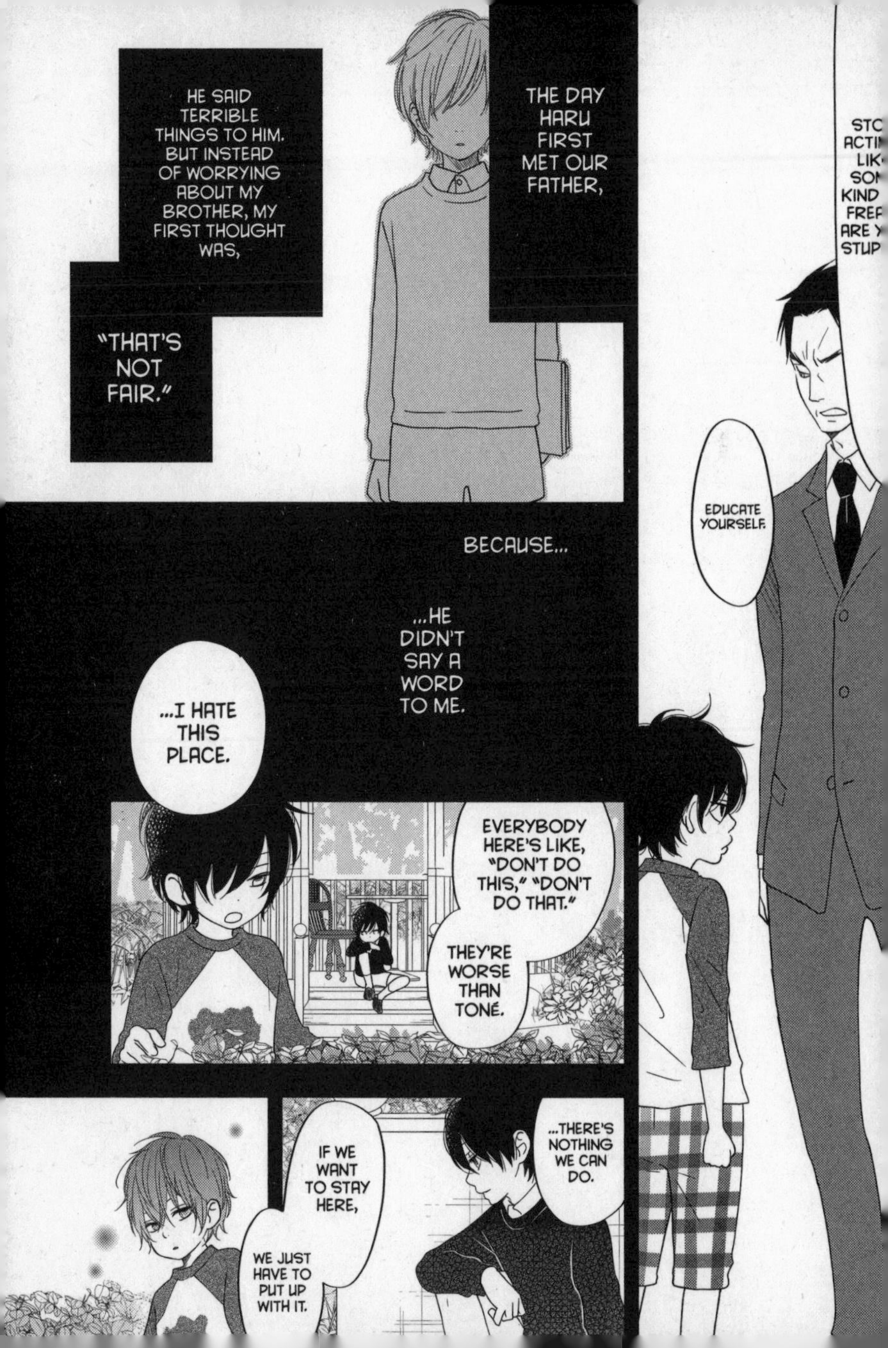
EDUCATE YOURSELF.
THE DAY HARU FIRST MET OUR FATHER,
HE SAID TERRIBLE THINGS TO HIM. BUT INSTEAD OF WORRYING ABOUT MY BROTHER, MY FIRST THOUGHT WAS,
"THAT'S NOT FAIR."
BECAUSE...
...HE DIDN'T SAY A WORD TO ME.
...I HATE THIS PLACE.
EVERYBODY HERE'S LIKE, "DON'T DO THIS," "DON'T DO THAT."
THEY'RE WORSE THAN TONÉ.
...THERE'S NOTHING WE CAN DO.
IF WE WANT TO STAY HERE,
WE JUST HAVE TO PUT UP WITH IT.

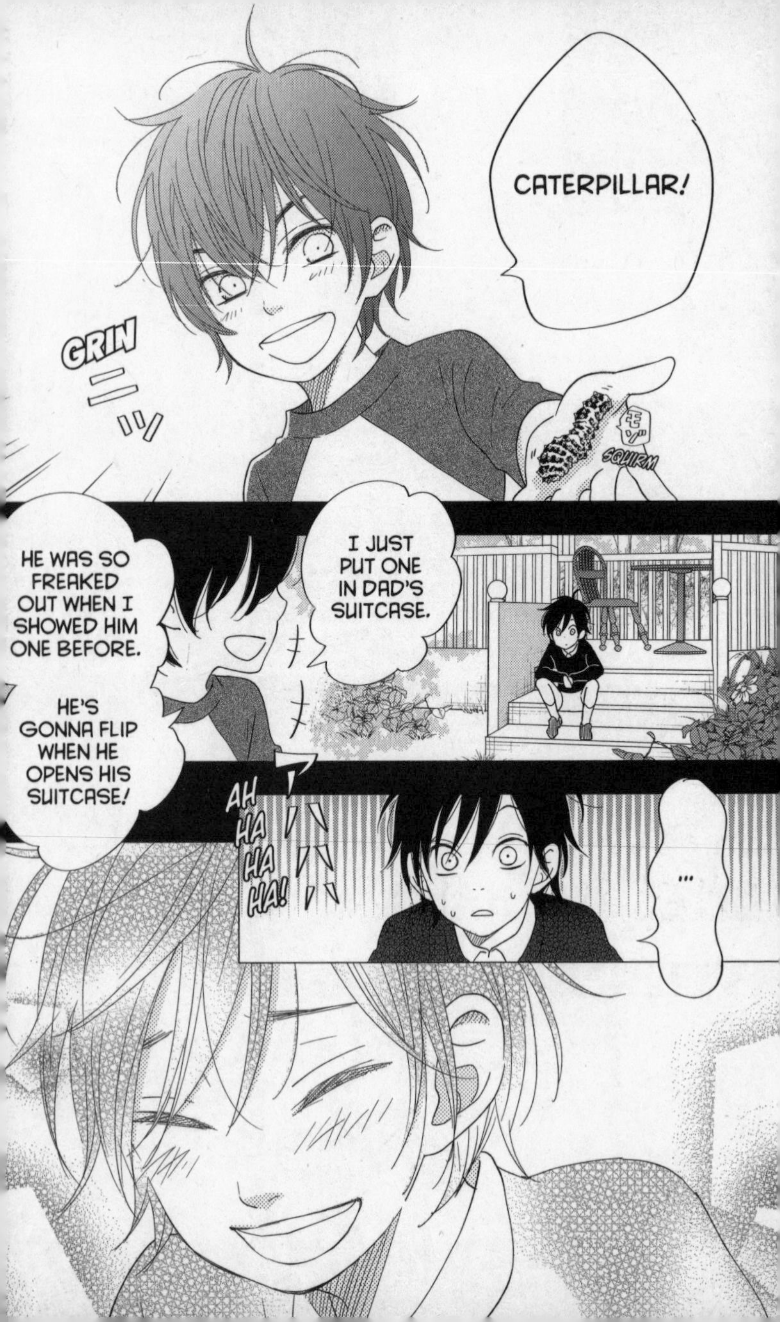
CATERPILLAR!
GRIN
SQUIRM
I JUST PUT ONE IN DAD'S SUITCASE.
HE WAS SO FREAKED OUT WHEN I SHOWED HIM ONE BEFORE.
HE'S GONNA FLIP WHEN HE OPENS HIS SUITCASE!
...
AH HA HA HA!

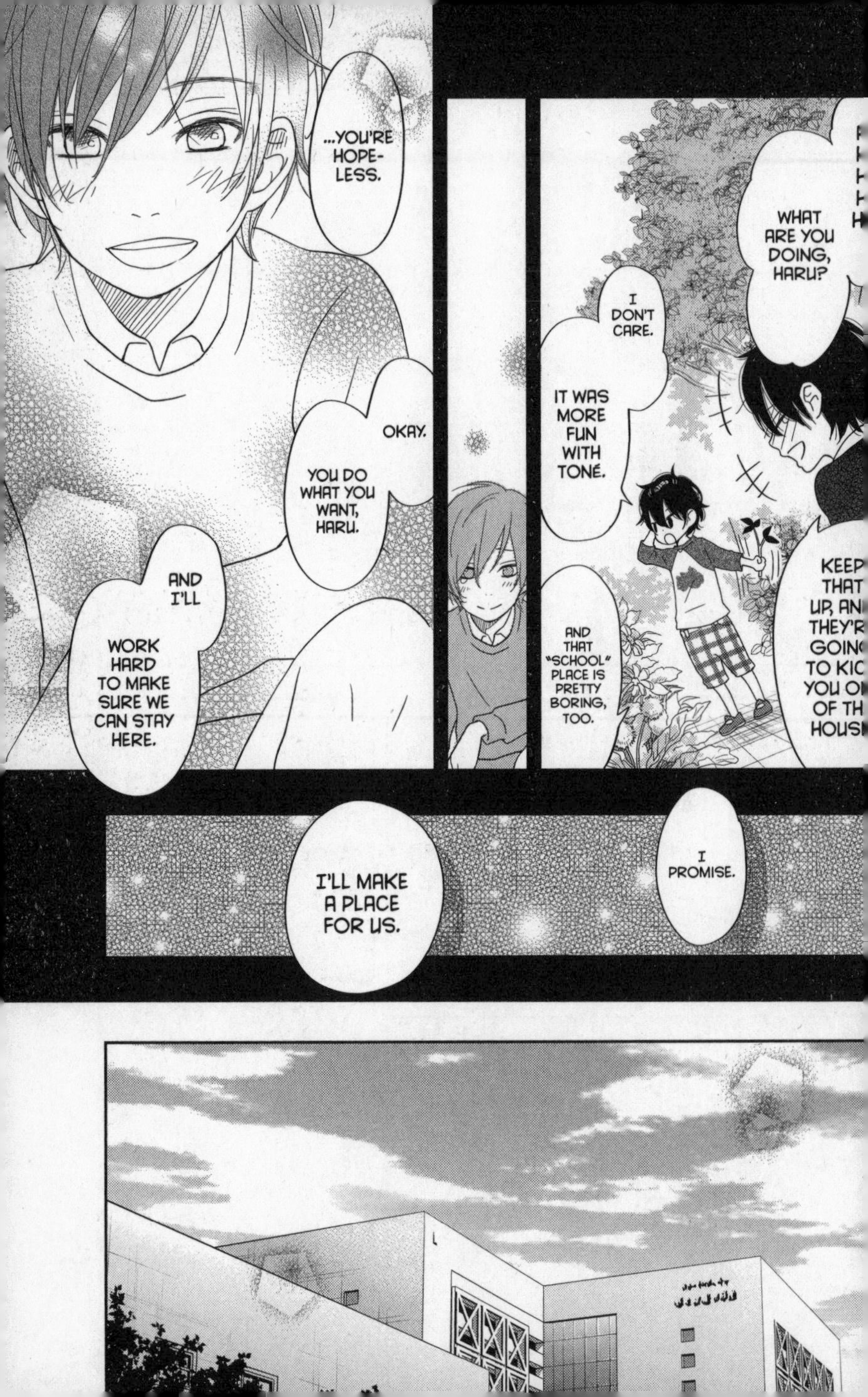
WHAT ARE YOU DOING, HARU?
KEEP THAT UP, AN THEY'R GOIN TO KIC YOU O OF TH HOUS
I DON'T CARE.
IT WAS MORE FUN WITH TONÉ.
AND THAT "SCHOOL" PLACE IS PRETTY BORING, TOO.
...YOU'RE HOPE-LESS.
OKAY.
YOU DO WHAT YOU WANT, HARU.
AND I'LL
WORK HARD TO MAKE SURE WE CAN STAY HERE.
I PROMISE.
I'LL MAKE A PLACE FOR US.

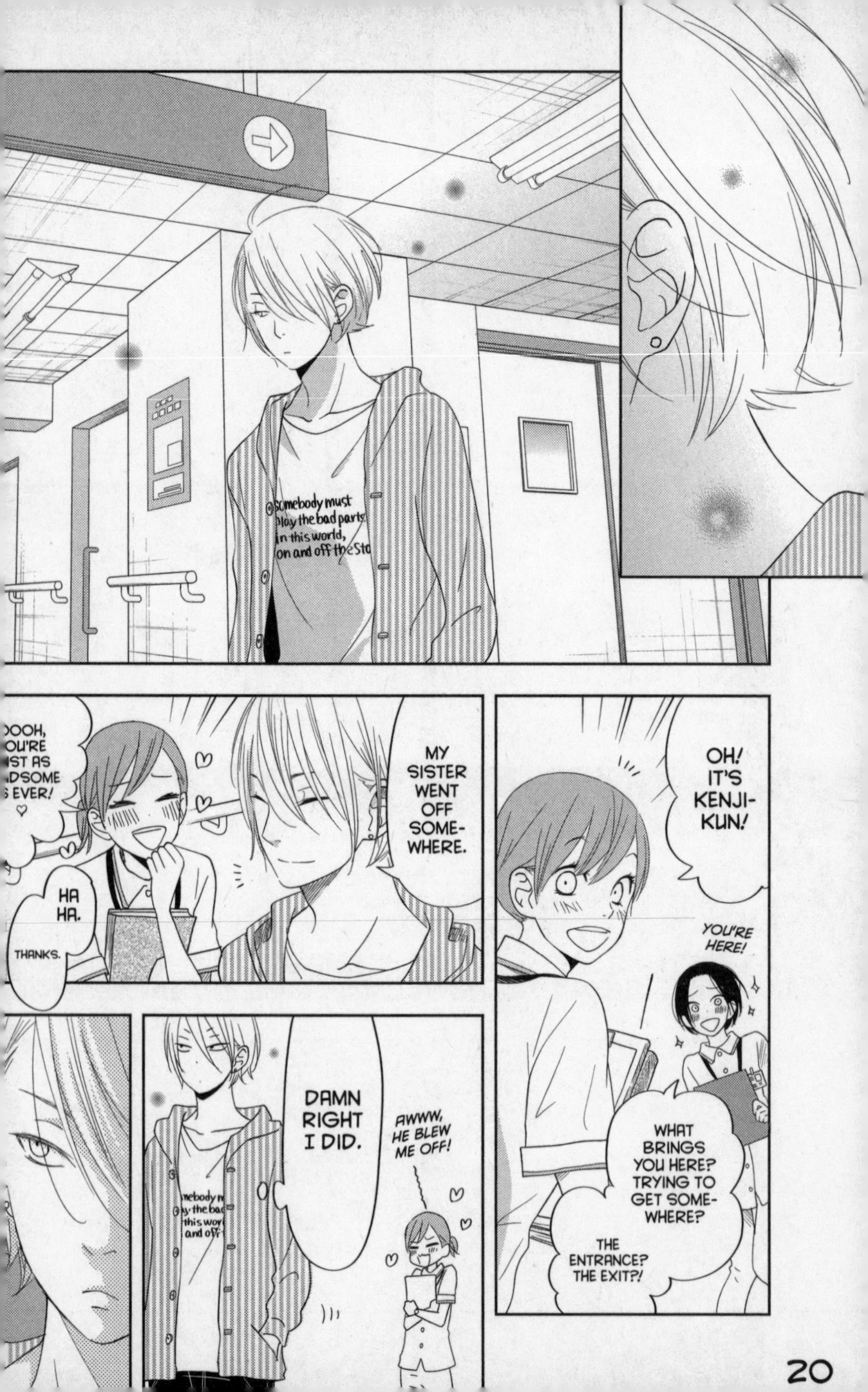
Somebody must play the bad parts in this world, on and off the Sta
OH! IT'S KENJI-KUN!
YOU'RE HERE!
WHAT BRINGS YOU HERE? TRYING TO GET SOME-WHERE?
THE ENTRANCE? THE EXIT?!
MY SISTER WENT OFF SOME-WHERE.
OOOH, OU'RE ST AS ADSOME S EVER!
HA HA.
THANKS.
DAMN RIGHT I DID.
AWWW, HE BLEW ME OFF!

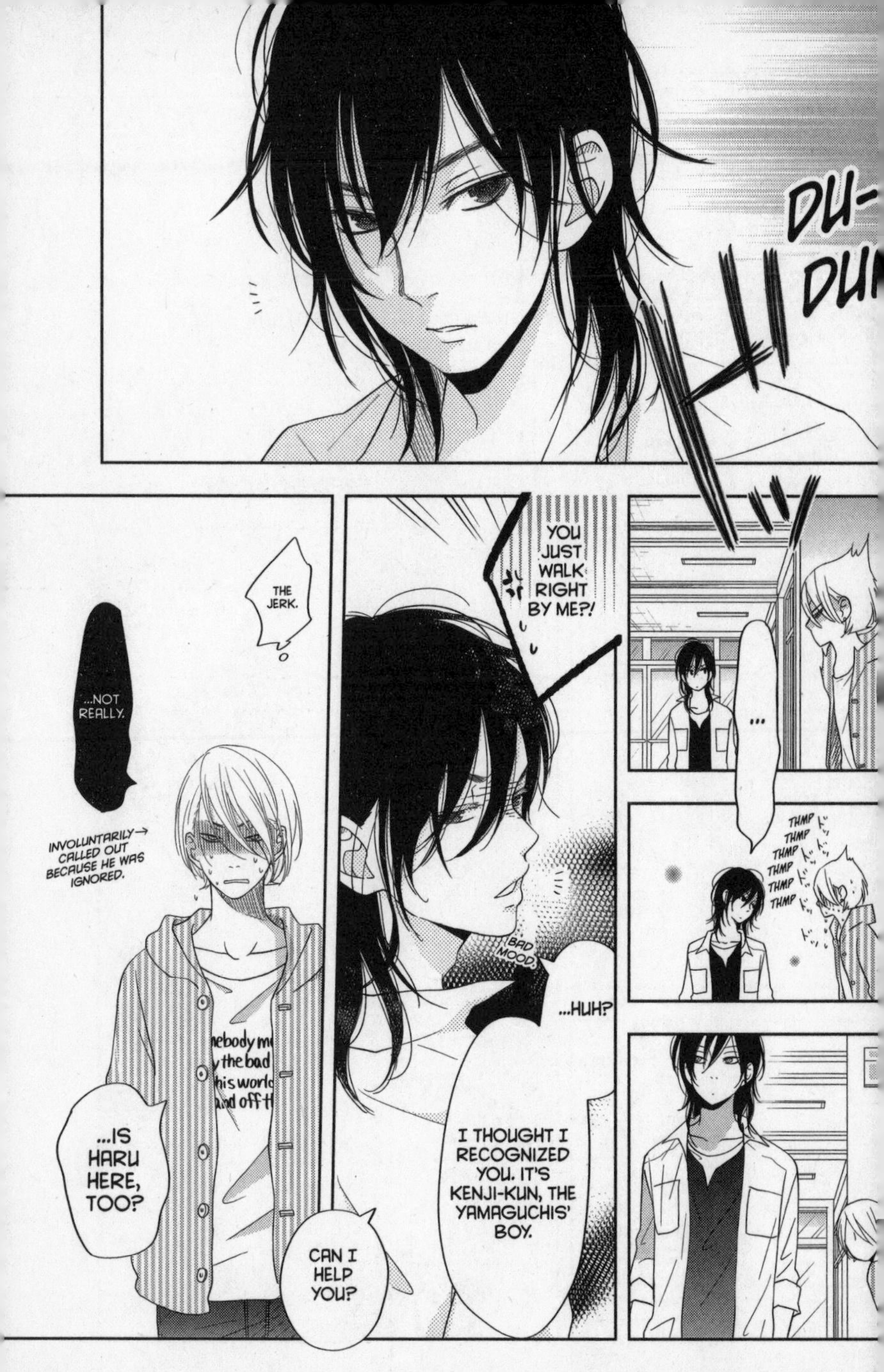
DU-
DU
...
THMP THMP THMP THMP THMP THMP
YOU JUST WALK RIGHT BY ME?!
BAD MOOD.
...HUH?
I THOUGHT I RECOGNIZED YOU. IT'S KENJI-KUN, THE YAMAGUCHIS' BOY.
CAN I HELP YOU?
THE JERK.
...NOT REALLY.
INVOLUNTARILY→ CALLED OUT BECAUSE HE WAS IGNORED.
...IS HARU HERE, TOO?

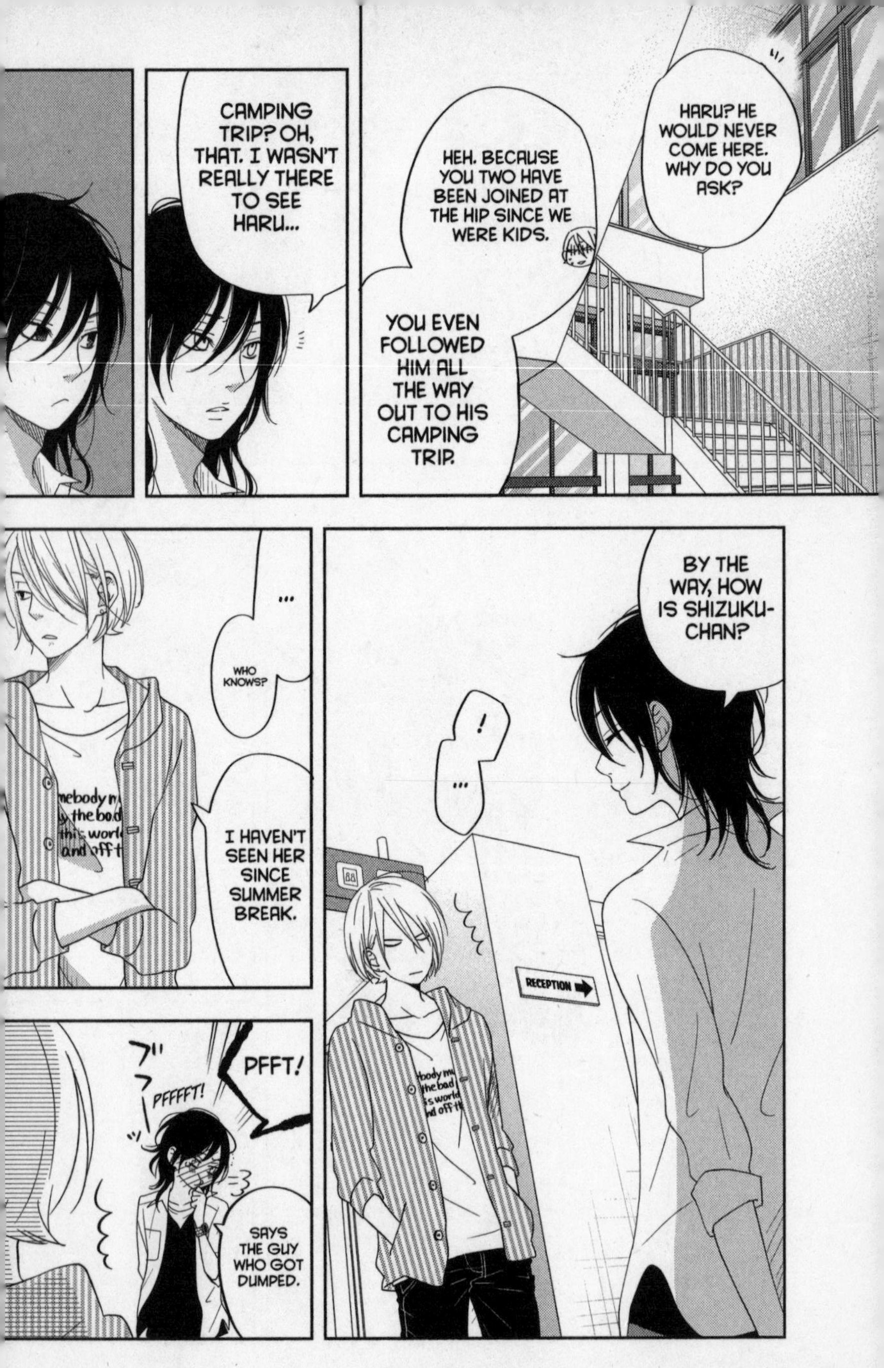
HARU? HE WOULD NEVER COME HERE. WHY DO YOU ASK?
HEH. BECAUSE YOU TWO HAVE BEEN JOINED AT THE HIP SINCE WE WERE KIDS.
YOU EVEN FOLLOWED HIM ALL THE WAY OUT TO HIS CAMPING TRIP.
CAMPING TRIP? OH, THAT. I WASN'T REALLY THERE TO SEE HARU...
BY THE WAY, HOW IS SHIZUKU-CHAN?
!
...
RECEPTION
...
WHO KNOWS?
I HAVEN'T SEEN HER SINCE SUMMER BREAK.
PFFT!
PFFFFT!
SAYS THE GUY WHO GOT DUMPED.

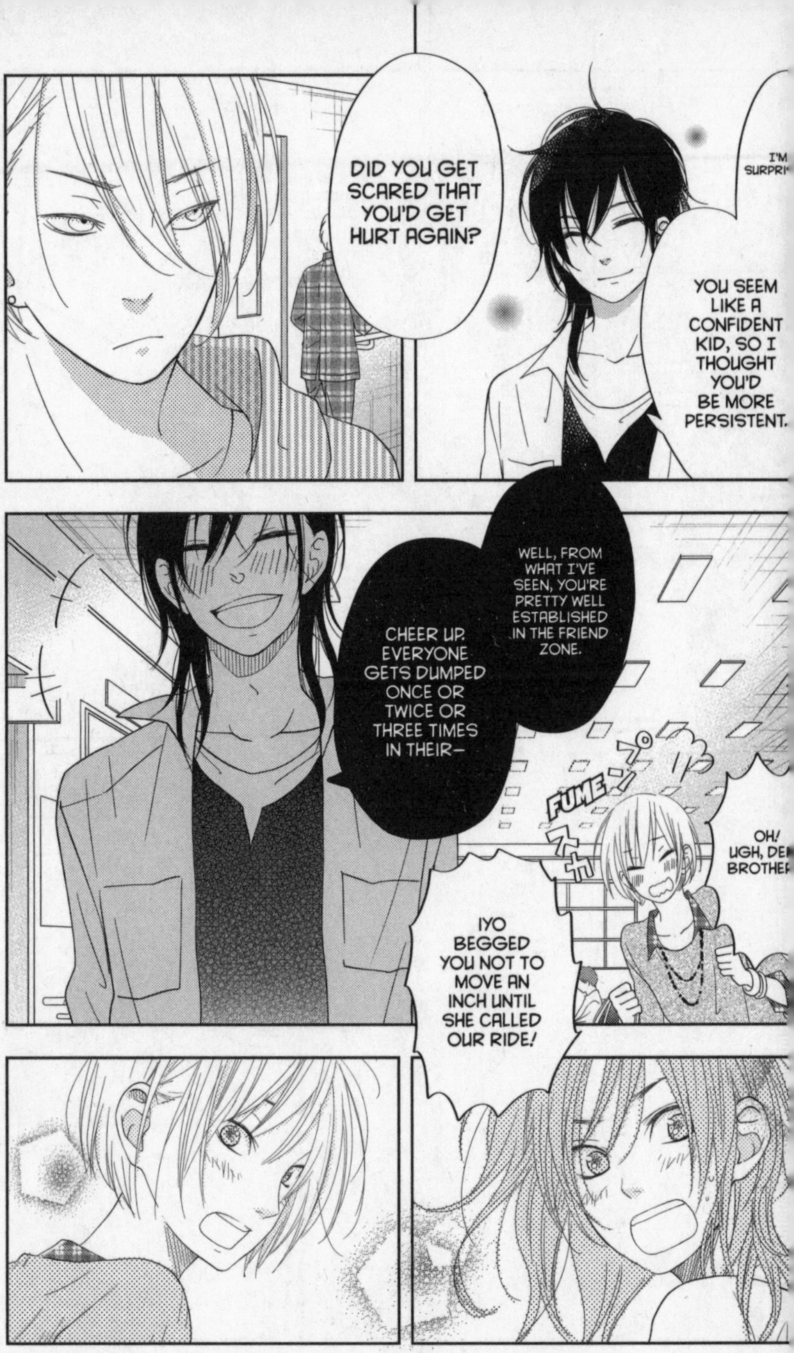
I'M SURPRI
YOU SEEM LIKE A CONFIDENT KID, SO I THOUGHT YOU'D BE MORE PERSISTENT.
DID YOU GET SCARED THAT YOU'D GET HURT AGAIN?
WELL, FROM WHAT I'VE SEEN, YOU'RE PRETTY WELL ESTABLISHED IN THE FRIEND ZONE.
CHEER UP. EVERYONE GETS DUMPED ONCE OR TWICE OR THREE TIMES IN THEIR—
FUME
OH! UGH, DE BROTHER
IYO BEGGED YOU NOT TO MOVE AN INCH UNTIL SHE CALLED OUR RIDE!

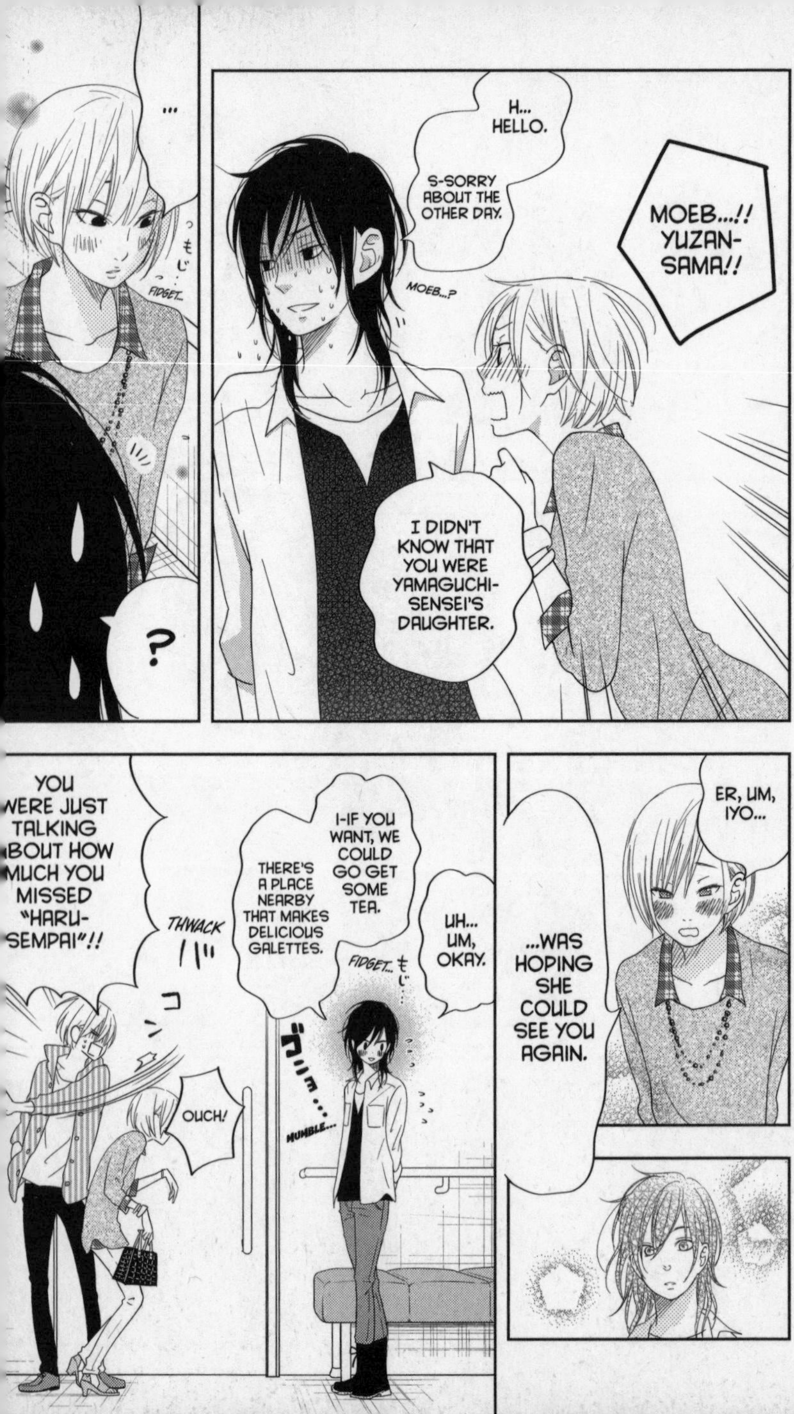
MOEB...!! YUZAN-SAMA!!
H... HELLO.
S-SORRY ABOUT THE OTHER DAY.
MOEB...?
I DIDN'T KNOW THAT YOU WERE YAMAGUCHI-SENSEI'S DAUGHTER.
...
もじっ
FIDGET...
?
ER, UM, IYO...
...WAS HOPING SHE COULD SEE YOU AGAIN.
I-IF YOU WANT, WE COULD GO GET SOME TEA.
THERE'S A PLACE NEARBY THAT MAKES DELICIOUS GALETTES.
UH... UM, OKAY.
FIDGET... もじ
HUMBLE...
YOU WERE JUST TALKING ABOUT HOW MUCH YOU MISSED "HARU-SEMPAI"!!
THWACK
OUCH!

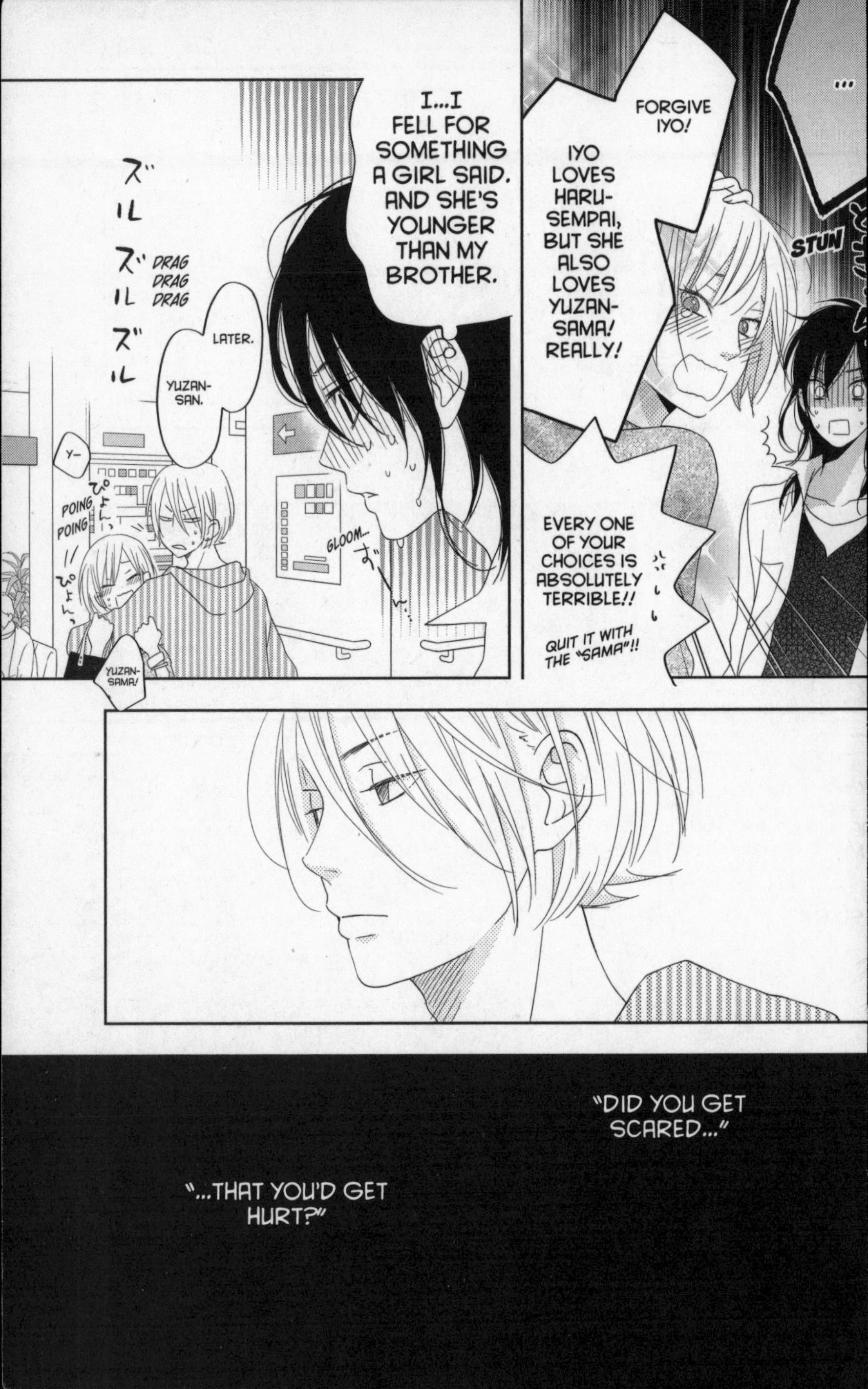
...
FORGIVE IYO!
IYO LOVES HARU-SEMPAI, BUT SHE ALSO LOVES YUZAN-SAMA! REALLY!
STUN
EVERY ONE OF YOUR CHOICES IS ABSOLUTELY TERRIBLE!!
QUIT IT WITH THE "SAMA"!!
I...I FELL FOR SOMETHING A GIRL SAID. AND SHE'S YOUNGER THAN MY BROTHER.
GLOOM...
LATER.
YUZAN-SAN.
ズルズルズル
DRAG DRAG DRAG
Y-
POING POING
YUZAN-SAMA!
"DID YOU GET SCARED..."
"...THAT YOU'D GET HURT?"

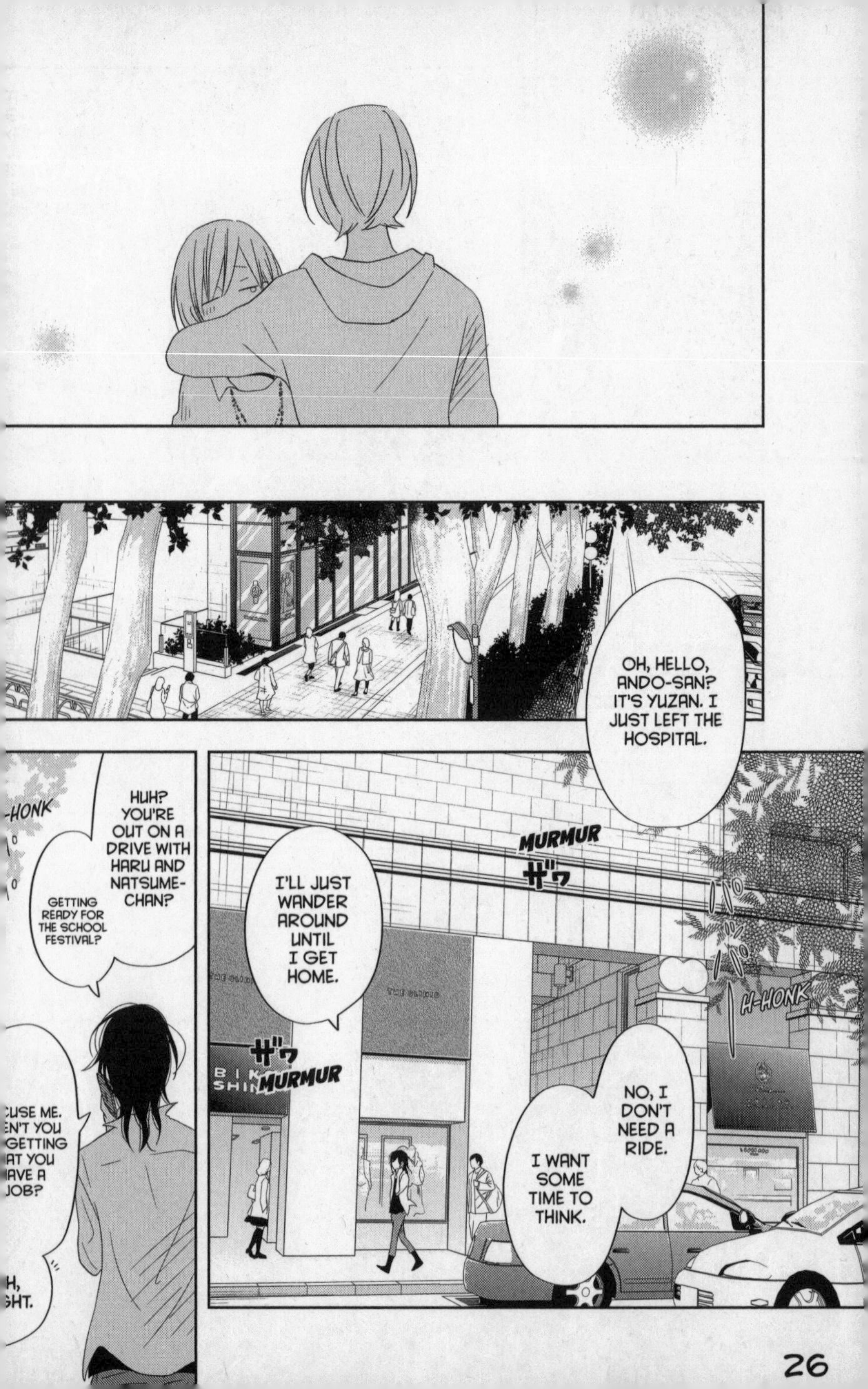
OH, HELLO, ANDO-SAN? IT'S YUZAN. I JUST LEFT THE HOSPITAL.
MURMUR
ザワ
パ
パ
H-HONK
NO, I DON'T NEED A RIDE.
I WANT SOME TIME TO THINK.
I'LL JUST WANDER AROUND UNTIL I GET HOME.
ザワ
MURMUR
-HONK
HUH? YOU'RE OUT ON A DRIVE WITH HARU AND NATSUME-CHAN?
GETTING READY FOR THE SCHOOL FESTIVAL?
CUSE ME. EN'T YOU GETTING AT YOU AVE A JOB?
H, GHT.

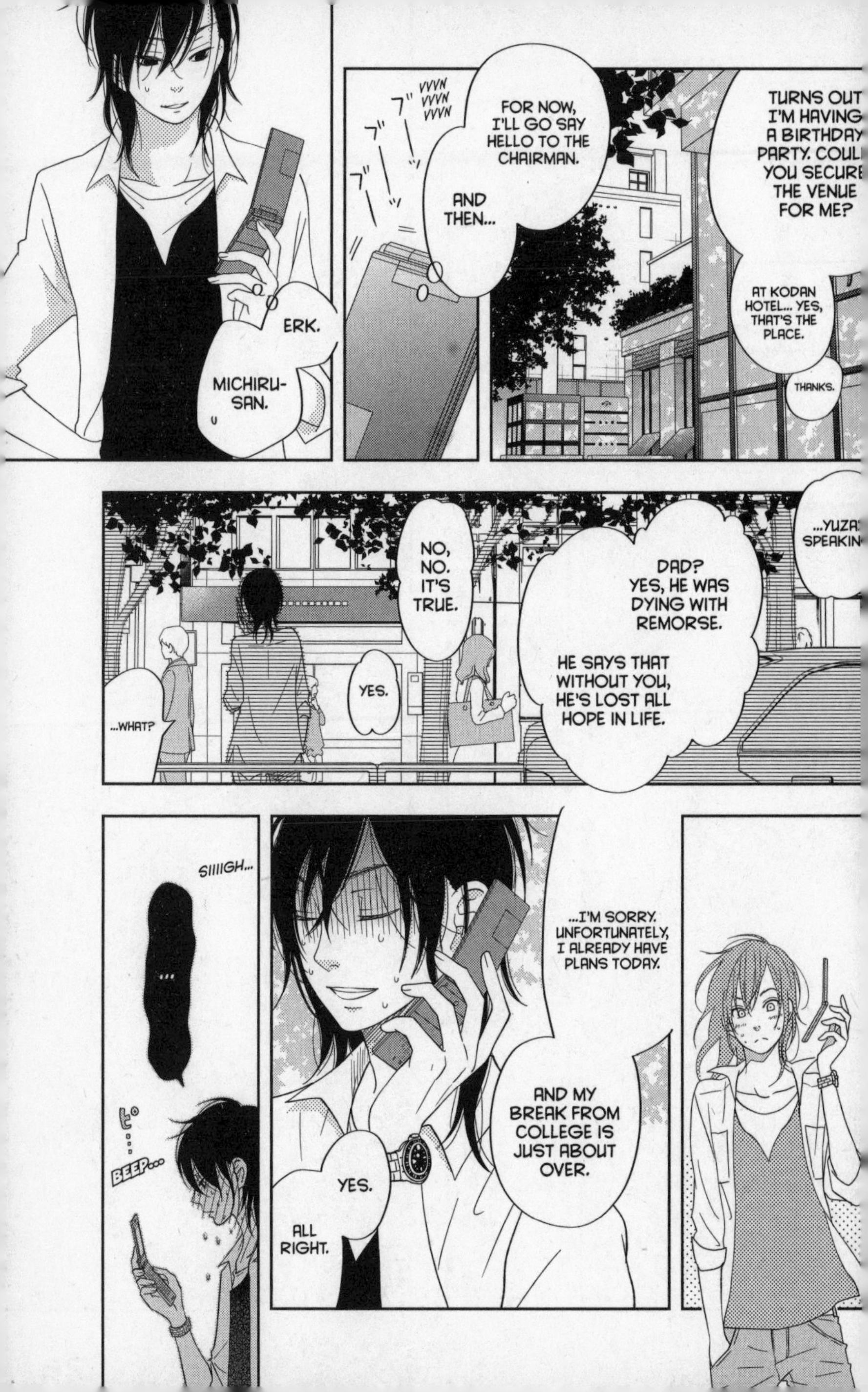
TURNS OUT I'M HAVING A BIRTHDAY PARTY. COUL YOU SECURE THE VENUE FOR ME?
AT KODAN HOTEL... YES, THAT'S THE PLACE.
THANKS.
VVVN VVVN VVVN
FOR NOW, I'LL GO SAY HELLO TO THE CHAIRMAN.
AND THEN...
ERK.
MICHIRU-SAN.
...YUZA SPEAKIN
DAD? YES, HE WAS DYING WITH REMORSE.
HE SAYS THAT WITHOUT YOU, HE'S LOST ALL HOPE IN LIFE.
NO, NO. IT'S TRUE.
YES.
...WHAT?
...I'M SORRY. UNFORTUNATELY, I ALREADY HAVE PLANS TODAY.
AND MY BREAK FROM COLLEGE IS JUST ABOUT OVER.
YES.
ALL RIGHT.
SIIIIGH...
...
BEEP...

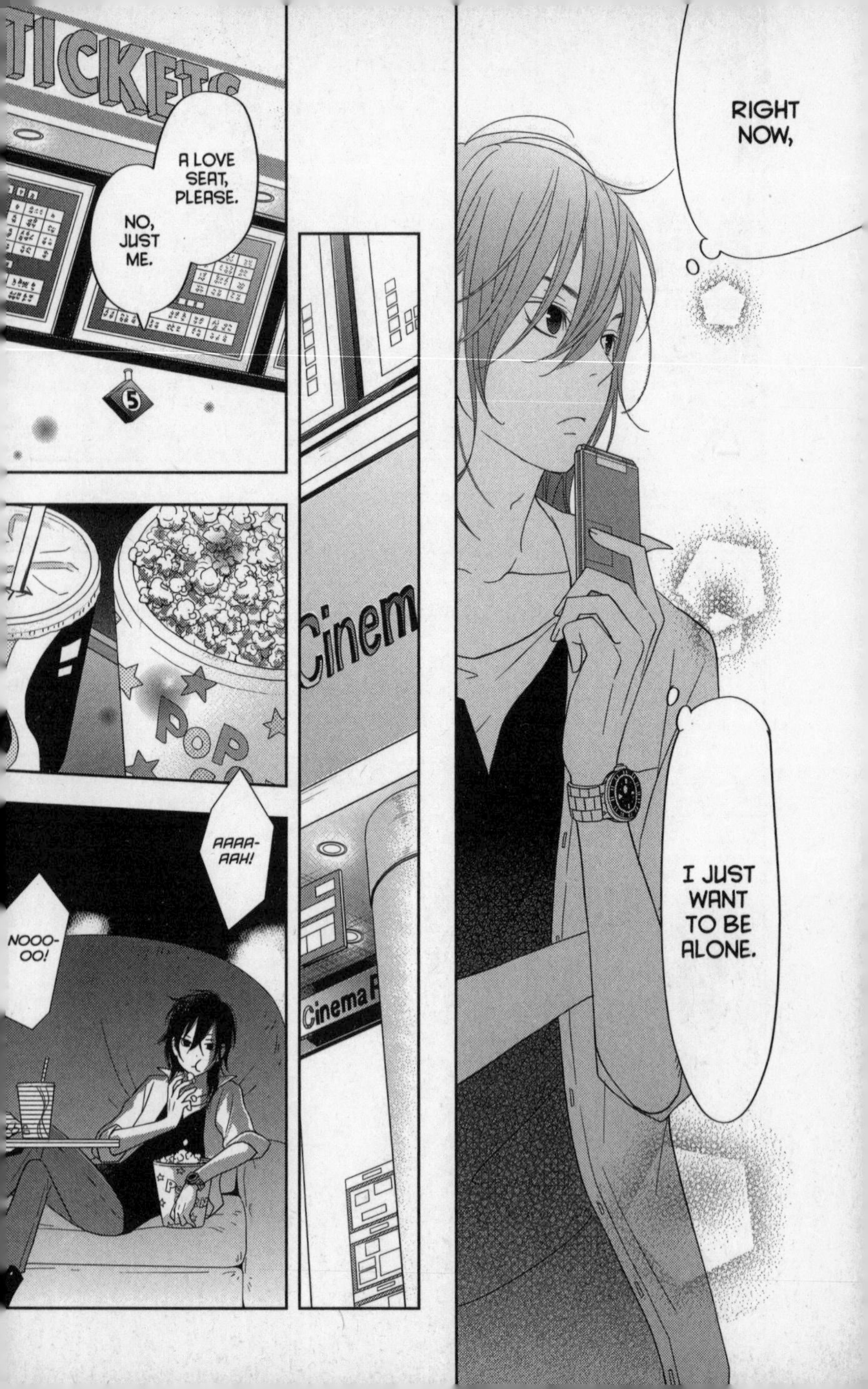
RIGHT NOW,
I JUST WANT TO BE ALONE.
A LOVE SEAT, PLEASE.
NO, JUST ME.
AAAA-AAH!
NOOO-OO!

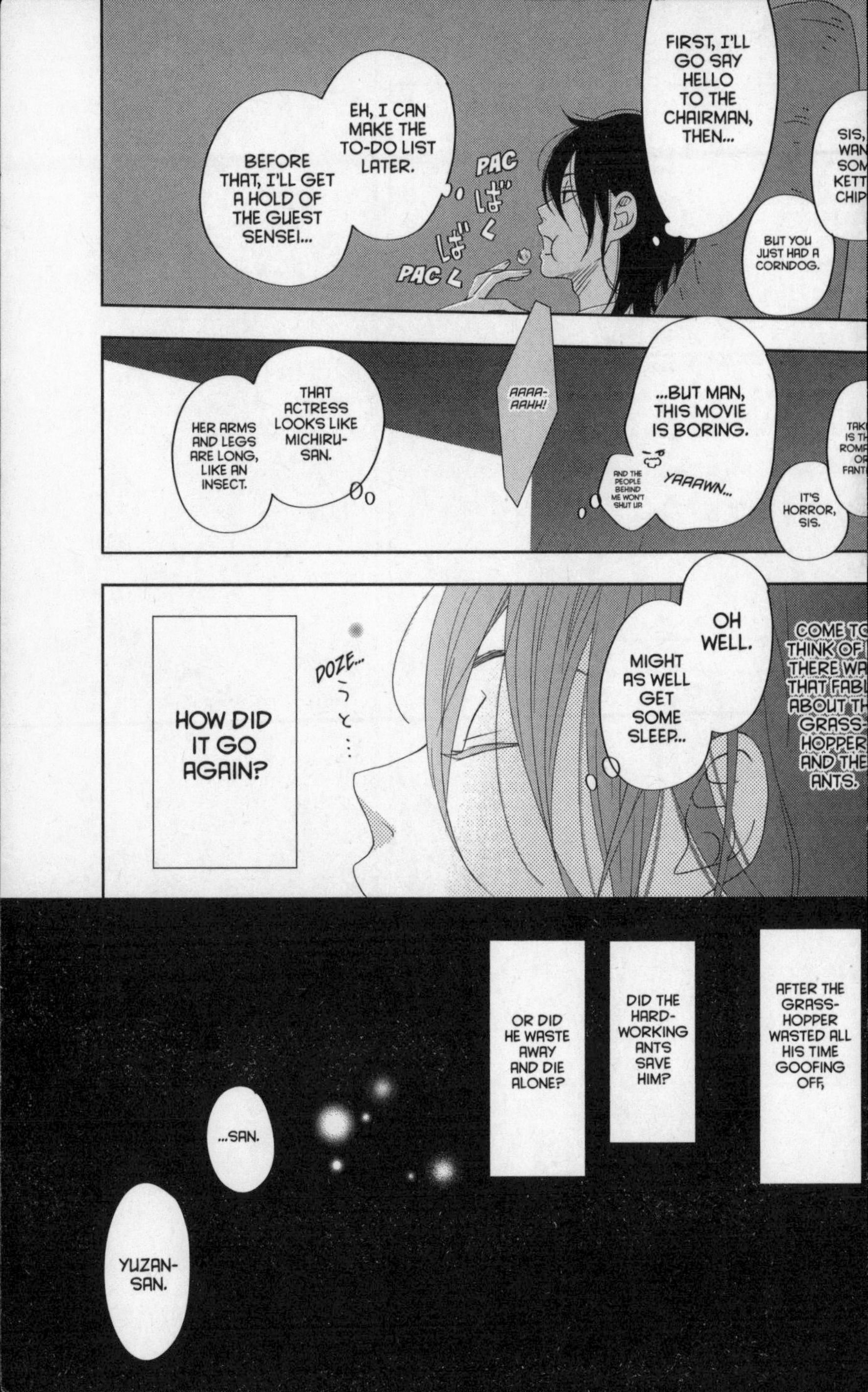
BUT YOU JUST HAD A CORNDOG.
FIRST, I'LL GO SAY HELLO TO THE CHAIRMAN, THEN...
PAC PAC
EH, I CAN MAKE THE TO-DO LIST LATER.
BEFORE THAT, I'LL GET A HOLD OF THE GUEST SENSEI...
IT'S HORROR, SIS.
...BUT MAN, THIS MOVIE IS BORING.
YAAAWN...
AND THE PEOPLE BEHIND ME WON'T SHUT UP.
AAAA-AAHH!
THAT ACTRESS LOOKS LIKE MICHIRU-SAN.
HER ARMS AND LEGS ARE LONG, LIKE AN INSECT.
OH WELL.
MIGHT AS WELL GET SOME SLEEP...
DOZE...
HOW DID IT GO AGAIN?
AFTER THE GRASS-HOPPER WASTED ALL HIS TIME GOOFING OFF,
DID THE HARD-WORKING ANTS SAVE HIM?
OR DID HE WASTE AWAY AND DIE ALONE?
...SAN.
YUZAN-SAN.

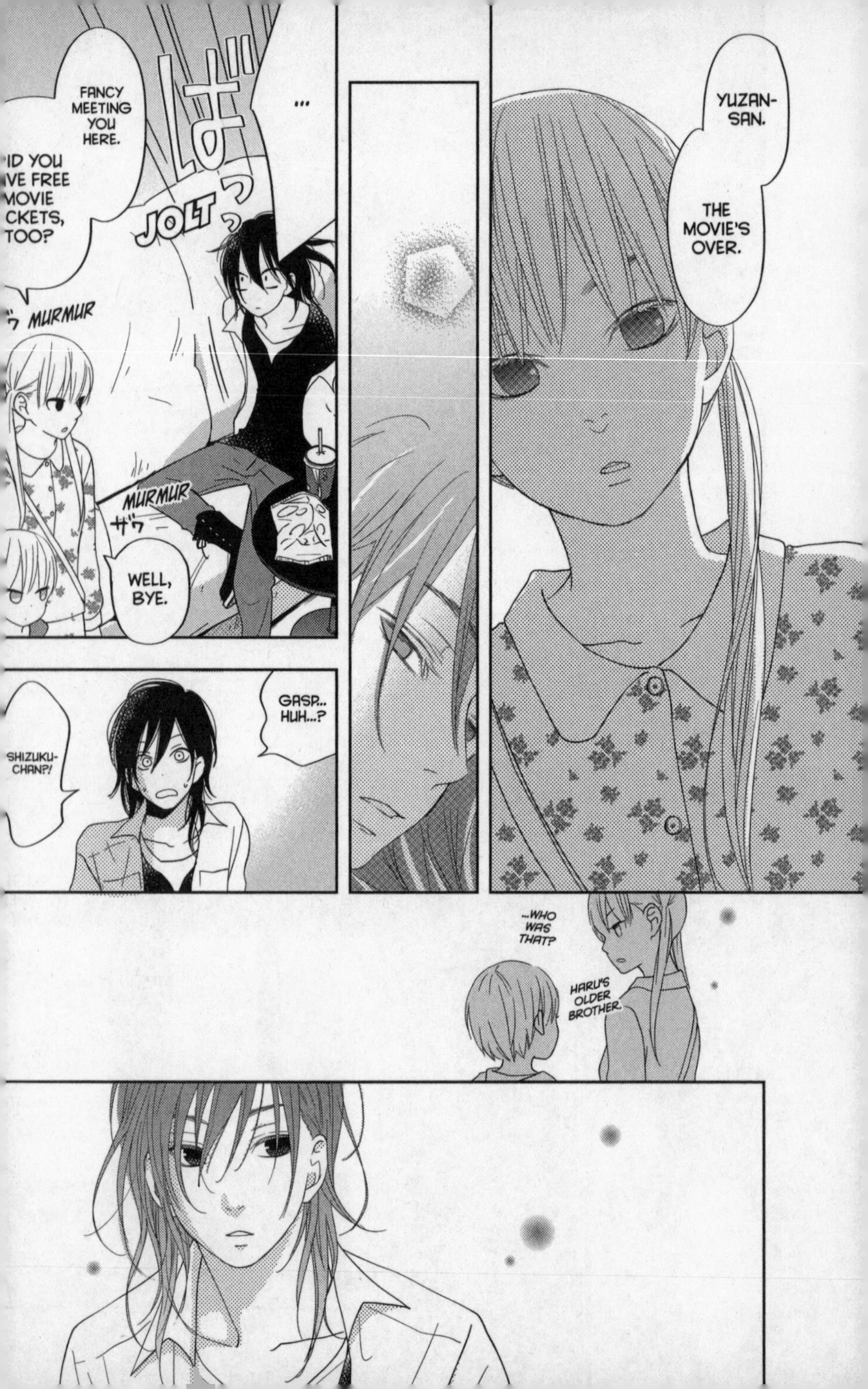

YUZAN-SAN.
THE MOVIE'S OVER.
...
JOLT
FANCY MEETING YOU HERE.
ID YOU VE FREE MOVIE CKETS, TOO?
MURMUR
MURMUR
WELL, BYE.
GASP... HUH...?
SHIZUKU-CHAN?!
...WHO WAS THAT?
HARU'S OLDER BROTHER.

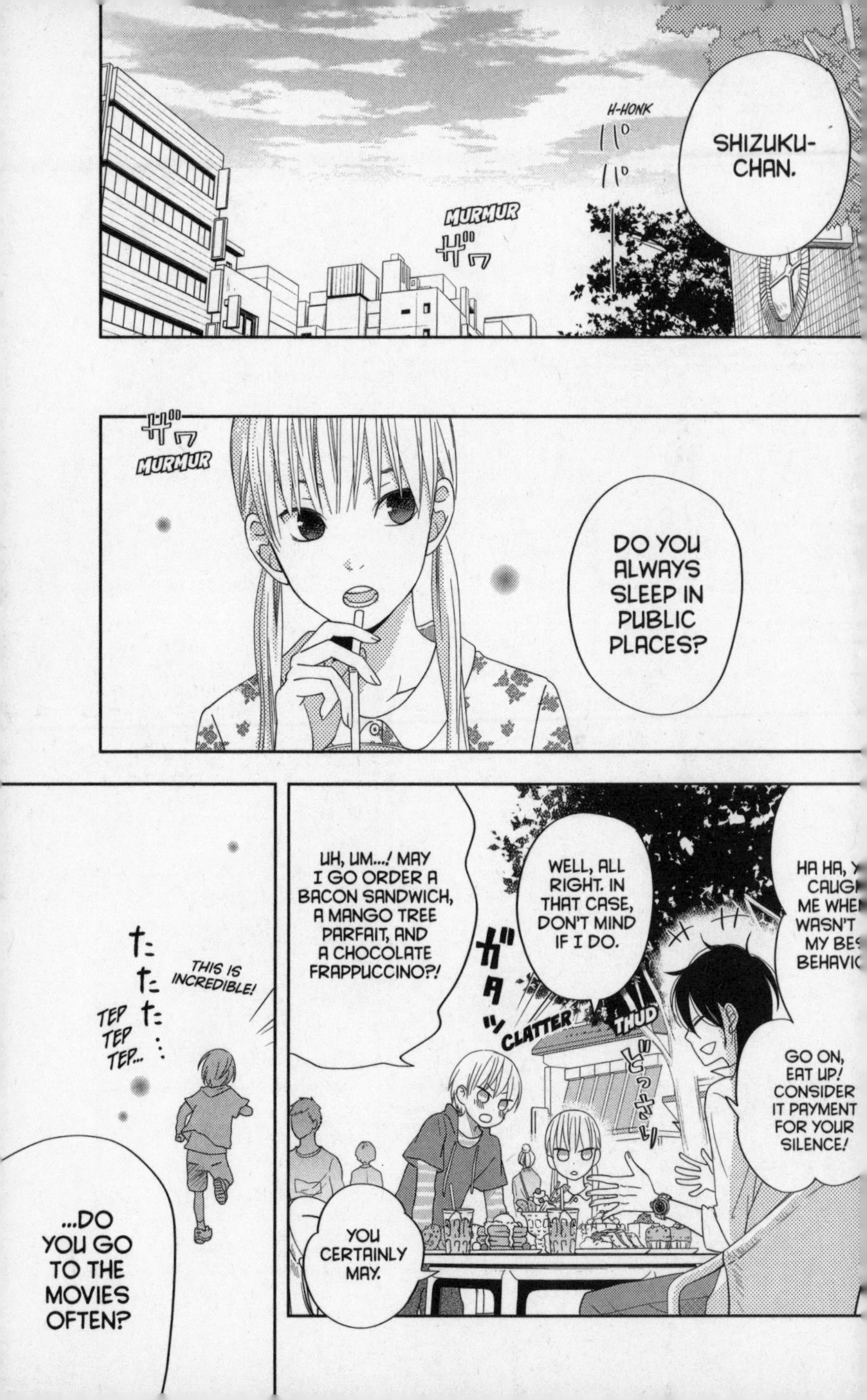
SHIZUKU-CHAN.
H-HONK
MURMUR
MURMUR
DO YOU ALWAYS SLEEP IN PUBLIC PLACES?
HA HA, Y CAUG ME WHE WASN'T MY BE BEHAVI
GO ON, EAT UP! CONSIDER IT PAYMENT FOR YOUR SILENCE!
THUD
WELL, ALL RIGHT. IN THAT CASE, DON'T MIND IF I DO.
CLATTER
UH, UM...! MAY I GO ORDER A BACON SANDWICH, A MANGO TREE PARFAIT, AND A CHOCOLATE FRAPPUCCINO?!
YOU CERTAINLY MAY.
THIS IS INCREDIBLE!
TEP TEP TEP...
...DO YOU GO TO THE MOVIES OFTEN?

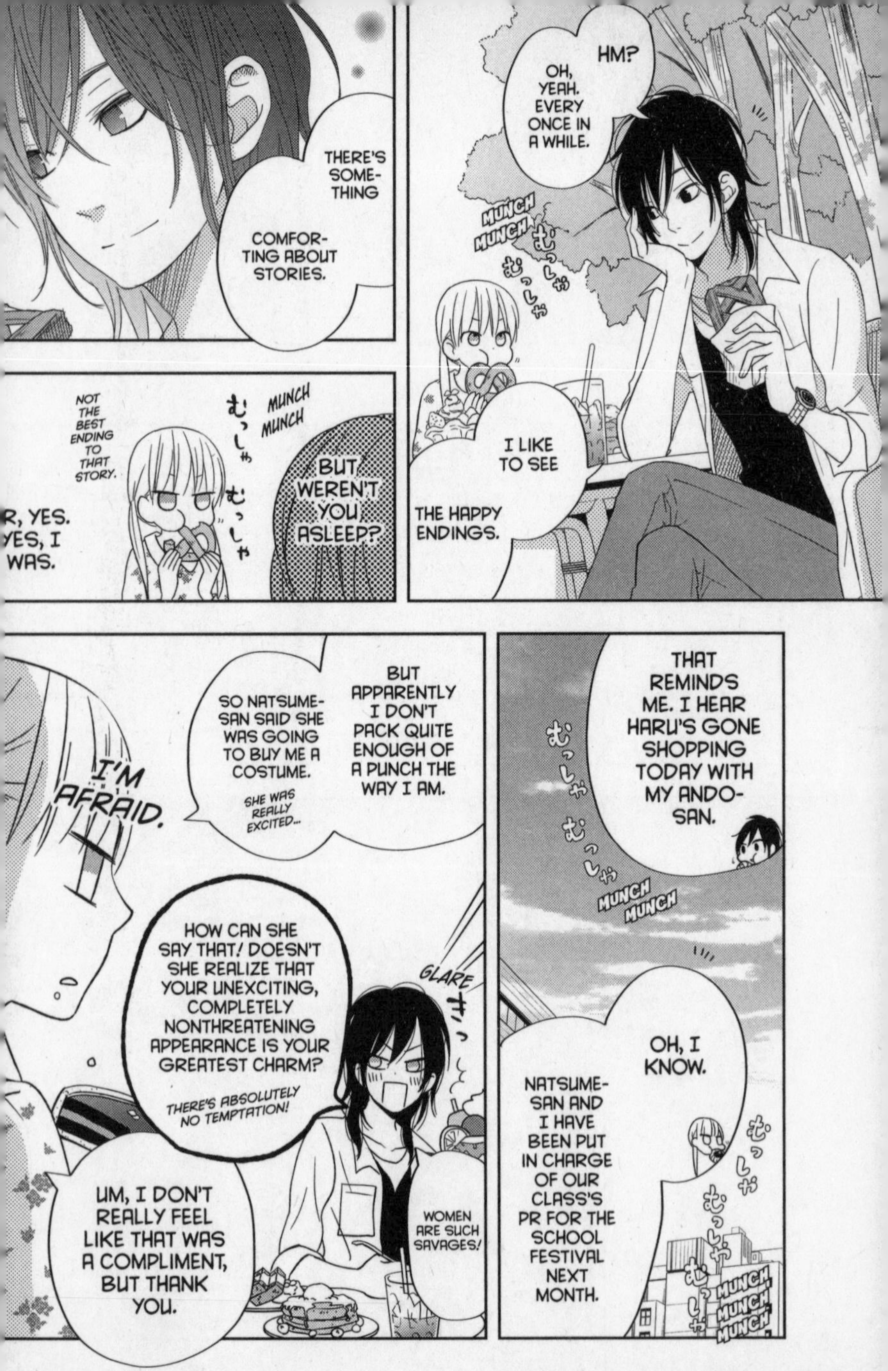
HM?
OH, YEAH. EVERY ONCE IN A WHILE.
MUNCH MUNCH
むっしゃ むっしゃ
I LIKE TO SEE THE HAPPY ENDINGS.
THERE'S SOME-THING COMFOR-TING ABOUT STORIES.
BUT WEREN'T YOU ASLEEP?
MUNCH MUNCH
むっしゃ むっしゃ
R, YES. YES, I WAS.
NOT THE BEST ENDING TO THAT STORY.
THAT REMINDS ME. I HEAR HARU'S GONE SHOPPING TODAY WITH MY ANDO-SAN.
むっしゃ むっしゃ
MUNCH MUNCH
OH, I KNOW.
NATSUME-SAN AND I HAVE BEEN PUT IN CHARGE OF OUR CLASS'S PR FOR THE SCHOOL FESTIVAL NEXT MONTH.
むっしゃ むっしゃ むっしゃ
MUNCH MUNCH MUNCH
BUT APPARENTLY I DON'T PACK QUITE ENOUGH OF A PUNCH THE WAY I AM.
SO NATSUME-SAN SAID SHE WAS GOING TO BUY ME A COSTUME.
SHE WAS REALLY EXCITED...
I'M AFRAID.
GLARE
きっ
HOW CAN SHE SAY THAT! DOESN'T SHE REALIZE THAT YOUR UNEXCITING, COMPLETELY NONTHREATENING APPEARANCE IS YOUR GREATEST CHARM?
THERE'S ABSOLUTELY NO TEMPTATION!
WOMEN ARE SUCH SAVAGES!
UM, I DON'T REALLY FEEL LIKE THAT WAS A COMPLIMENT, BUT THANK YOU.

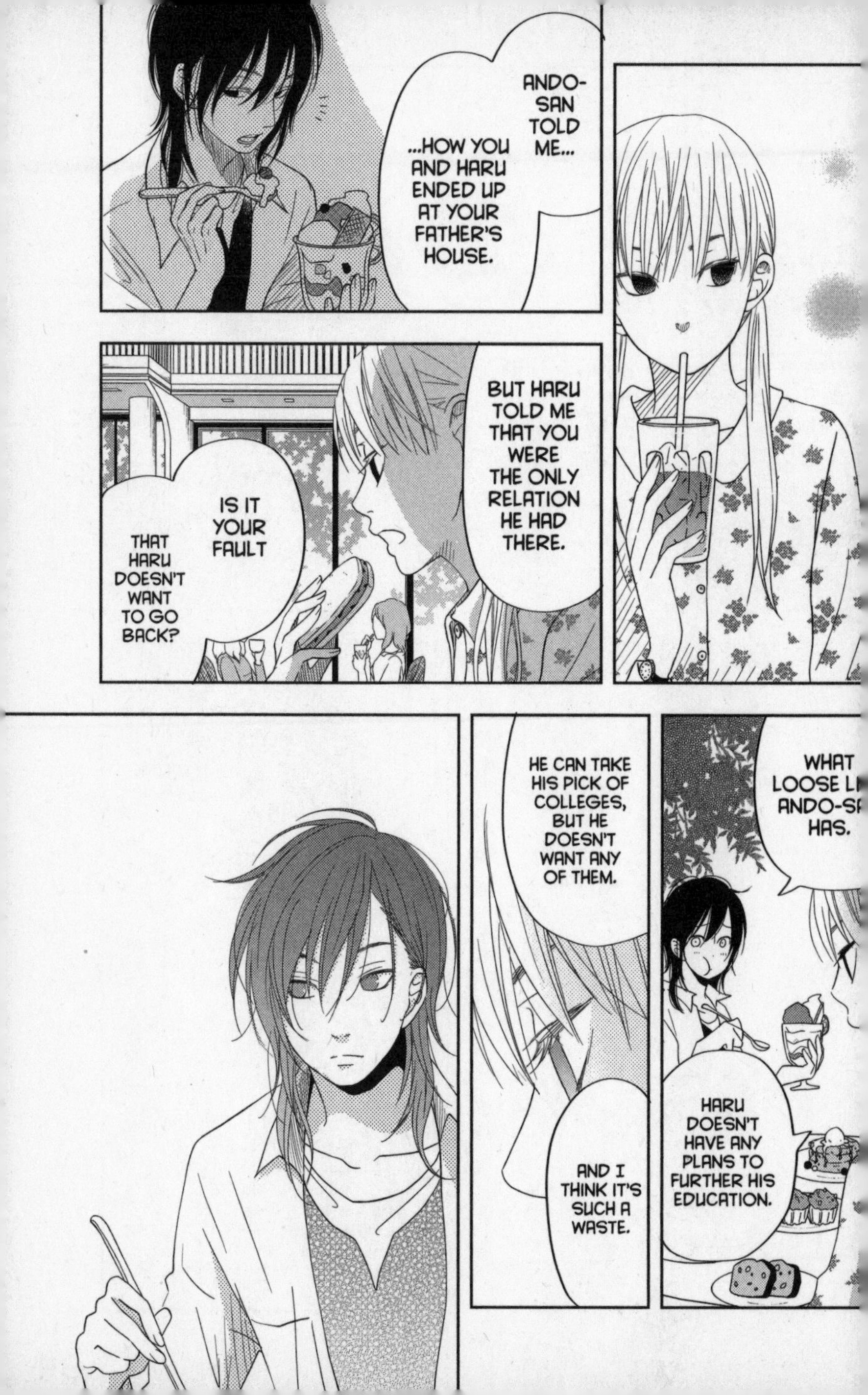
ANDO-SAN TOLD ME...
...HOW YOU AND HARU ENDED UP AT YOUR FATHER'S HOUSE.
BUT HARU TOLD ME THAT YOU WERE THE ONLY RELATION HE HAD THERE.
IS IT YOUR FAULT
THAT HARU DOESN'T WANT TO GO BACK?
WHAT LOOSE LI ANDO-SA HAS.
HARU DOESN'T HAVE ANY PLANS TO FURTHER HIS EDUCATION.
HE CAN TAKE HIS PICK OF COLLEGES, BUT HE DOESN'T WANT ANY OF THEM.
AND I THINK IT'S SUCH A WASTE.

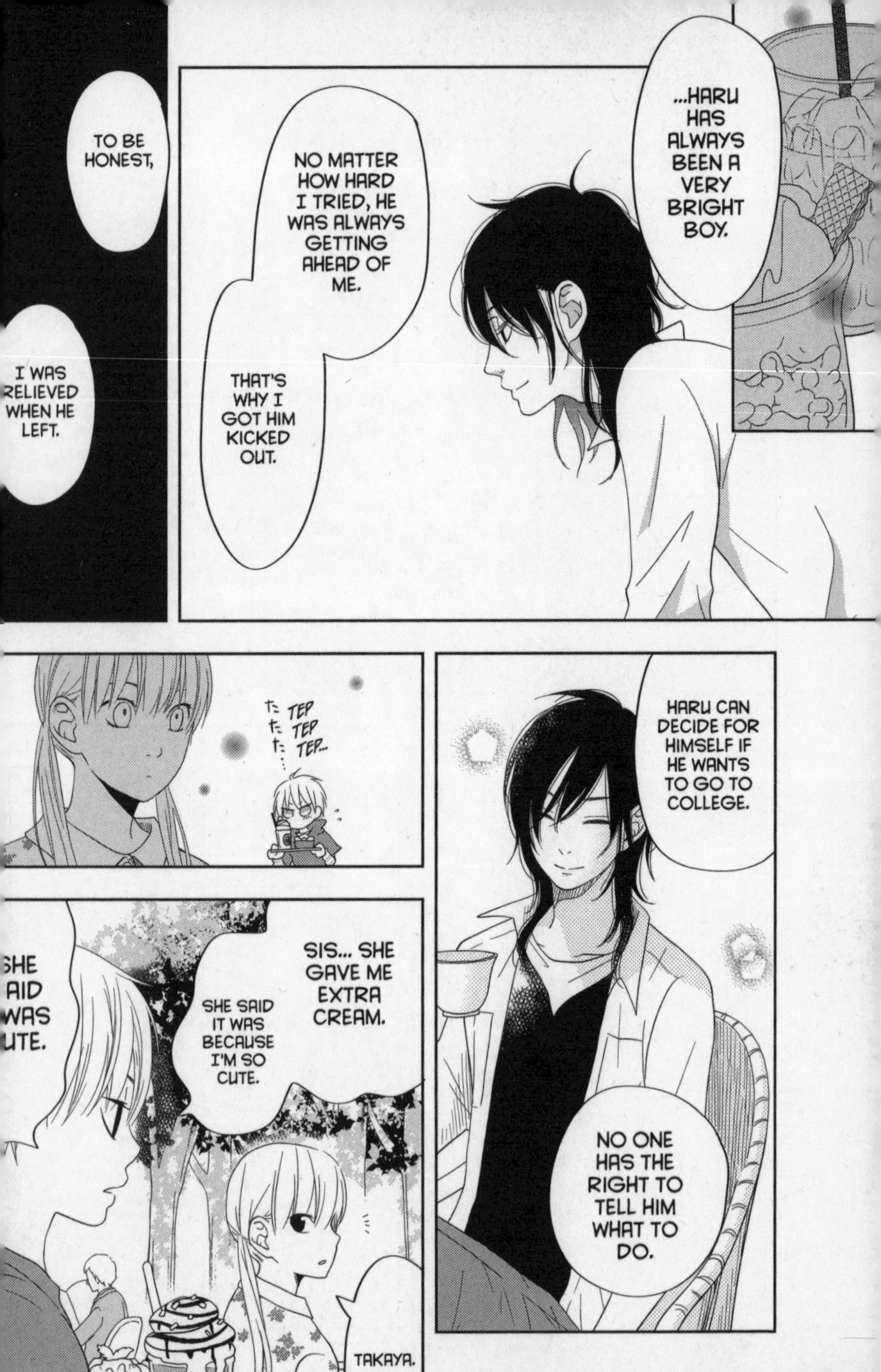
...HARU HAS ALWAYS BEEN A VERY BRIGHT BOY.
NO MATTER HOW HARD I TRIED, HE WAS ALWAYS GETTING AHEAD OF ME.
THAT'S WHY I GOT HIM KICKED OUT.
TO BE HONEST,
I WAS RELIEVED WHEN HE LEFT.
HARU CAN DECIDE FOR HIMSELF IF HE WANTS TO GO TO COLLEGE.
NO ONE HAS THE RIGHT TO TELL HIM WHAT TO DO.
たたた TEP TEP TEP...
SIS... SHE GAVE ME EXTRA CREAM.
SHE SAID IT WAS BECAUSE I'M SO CUTE.
TAKAYA.

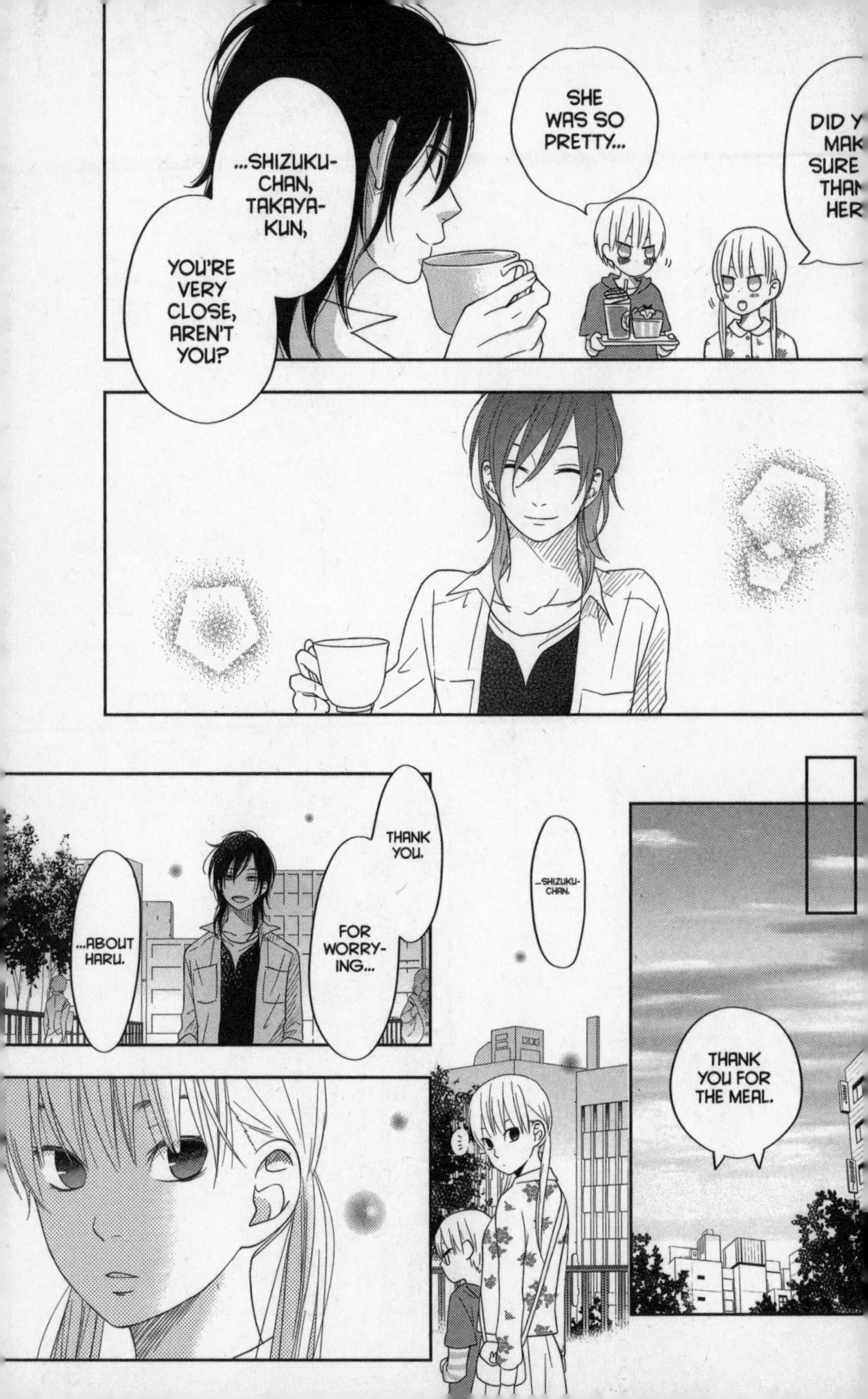
DID Y MAK SURE THAN HER
SHE WAS SO PRETTY...
...SHIZUKU-CHAN, TAKAYA-KUN,
YOU'RE VERY CLOSE, AREN'T YOU?
THANK YOU FOR THE MEAL.
...SHIZUKU-CHAN.
THANK YOU.
FOR WORRYING...
...ABOUT HARU.

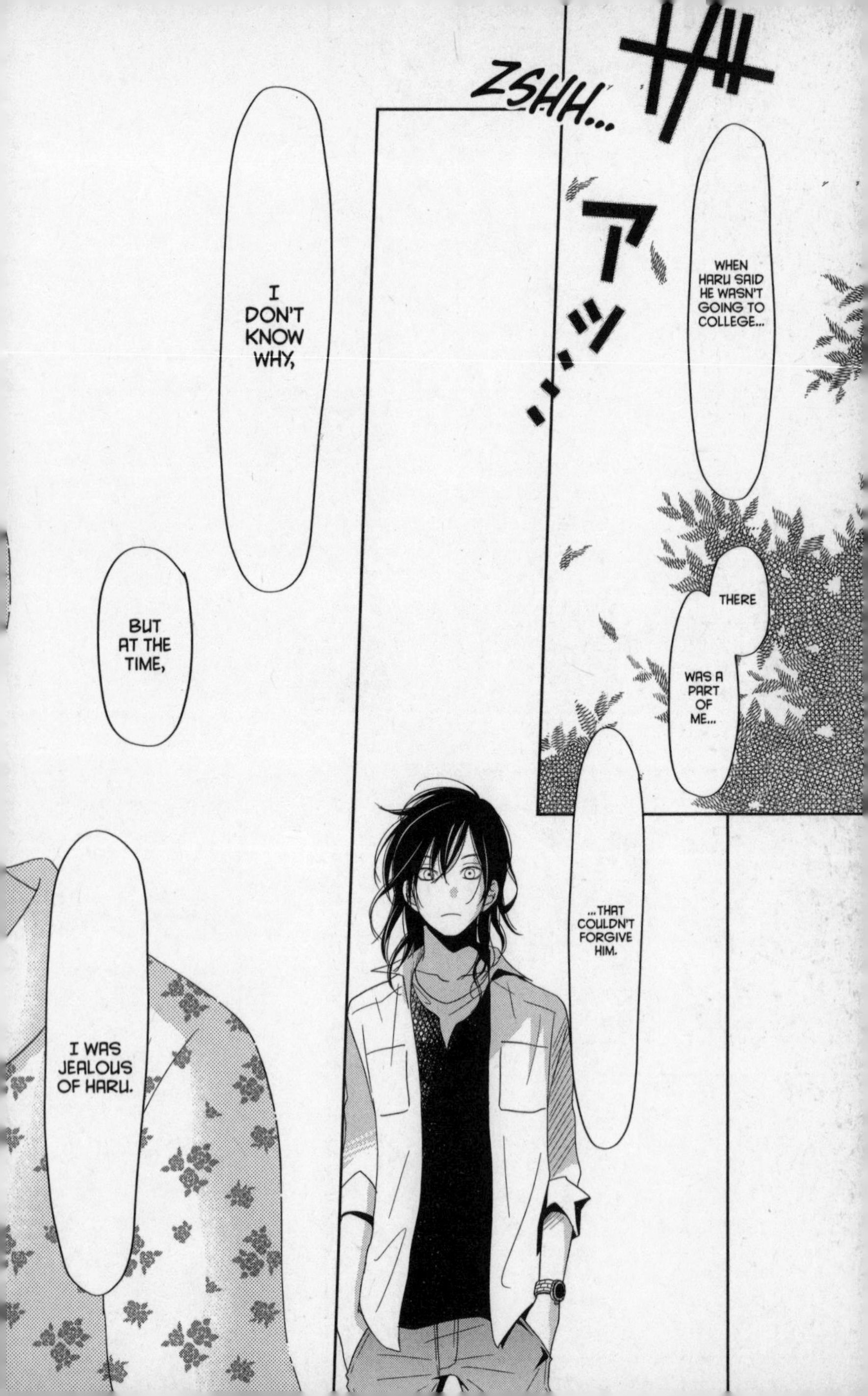
ZSHH...
WHEN HARU SAID HE WASN'T GOING TO COLLEGE...
THERE
WAS A PART OF ME...
...THAT COULDN'T FORGIVE HIM.
I DON'T KNOW WHY,
BUT AT THE TIME,
I WAS JEALOUS OF HARU.

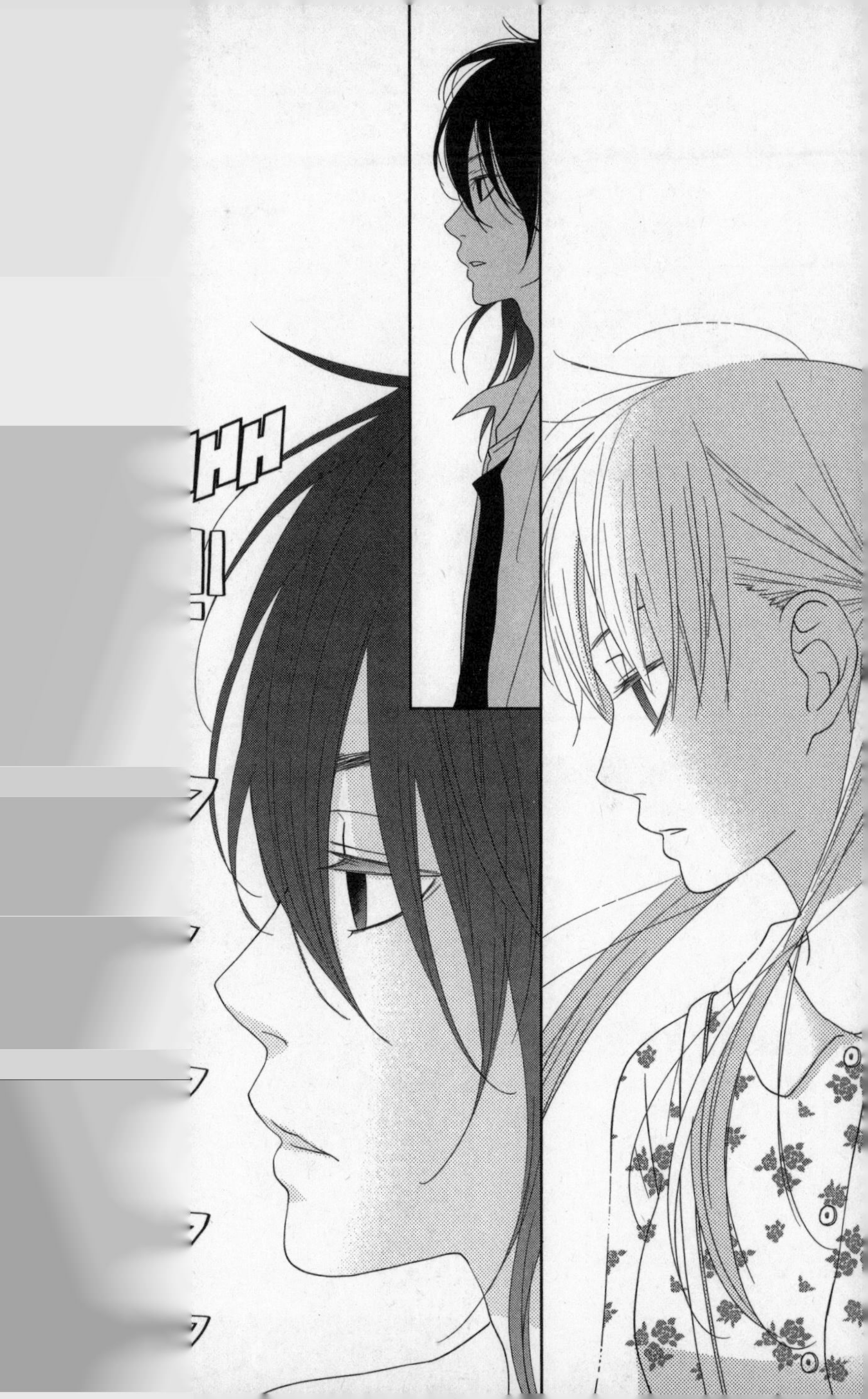
HH
!!

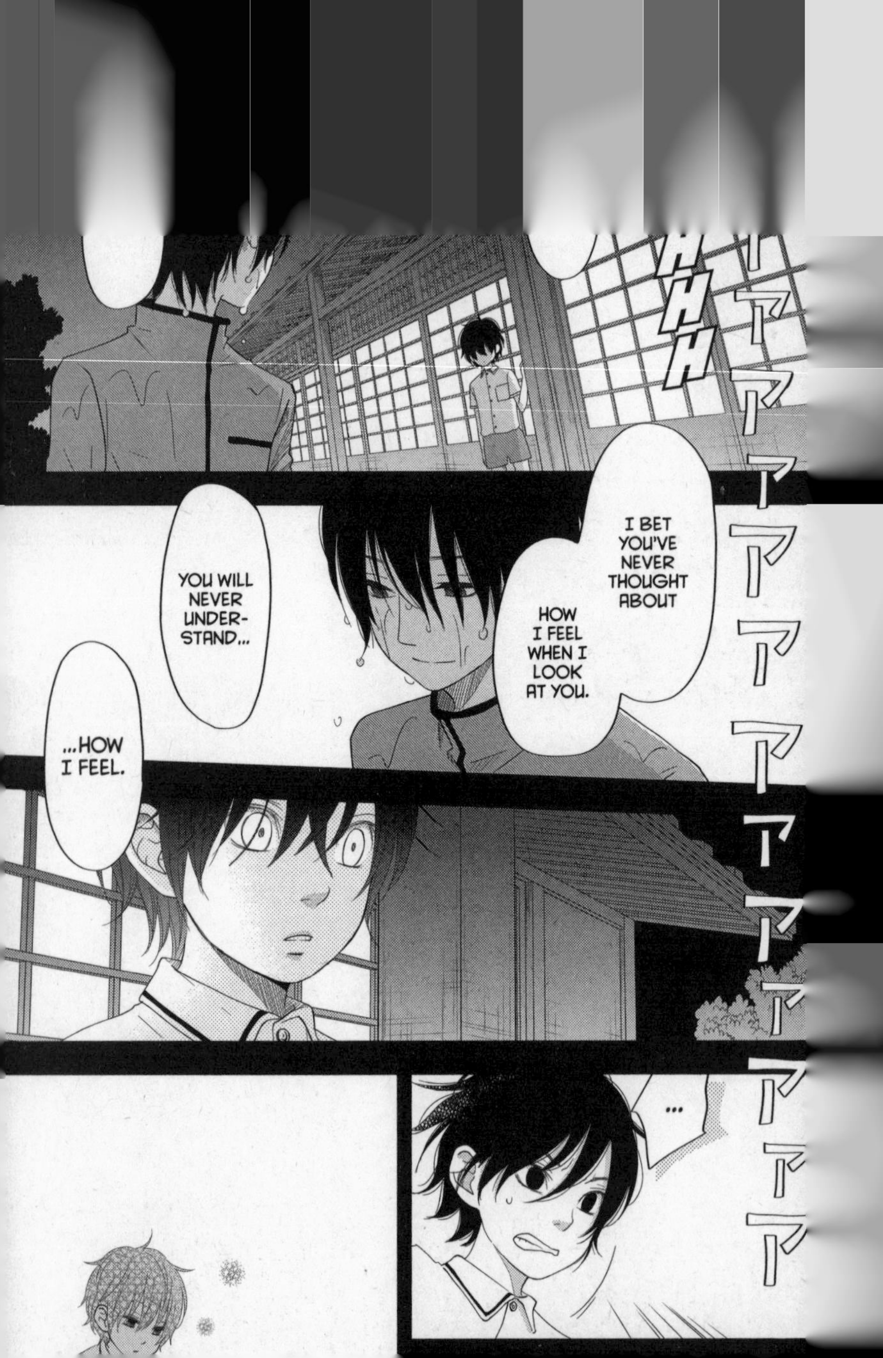
HHH
I BET YOU'VE NEVER THOUGHT ABOUT
HOW I FEEL WHEN I LOOK AT YOU.
YOU WILL NEVER UNDER-STAND...
...HOW I FEEL.
...

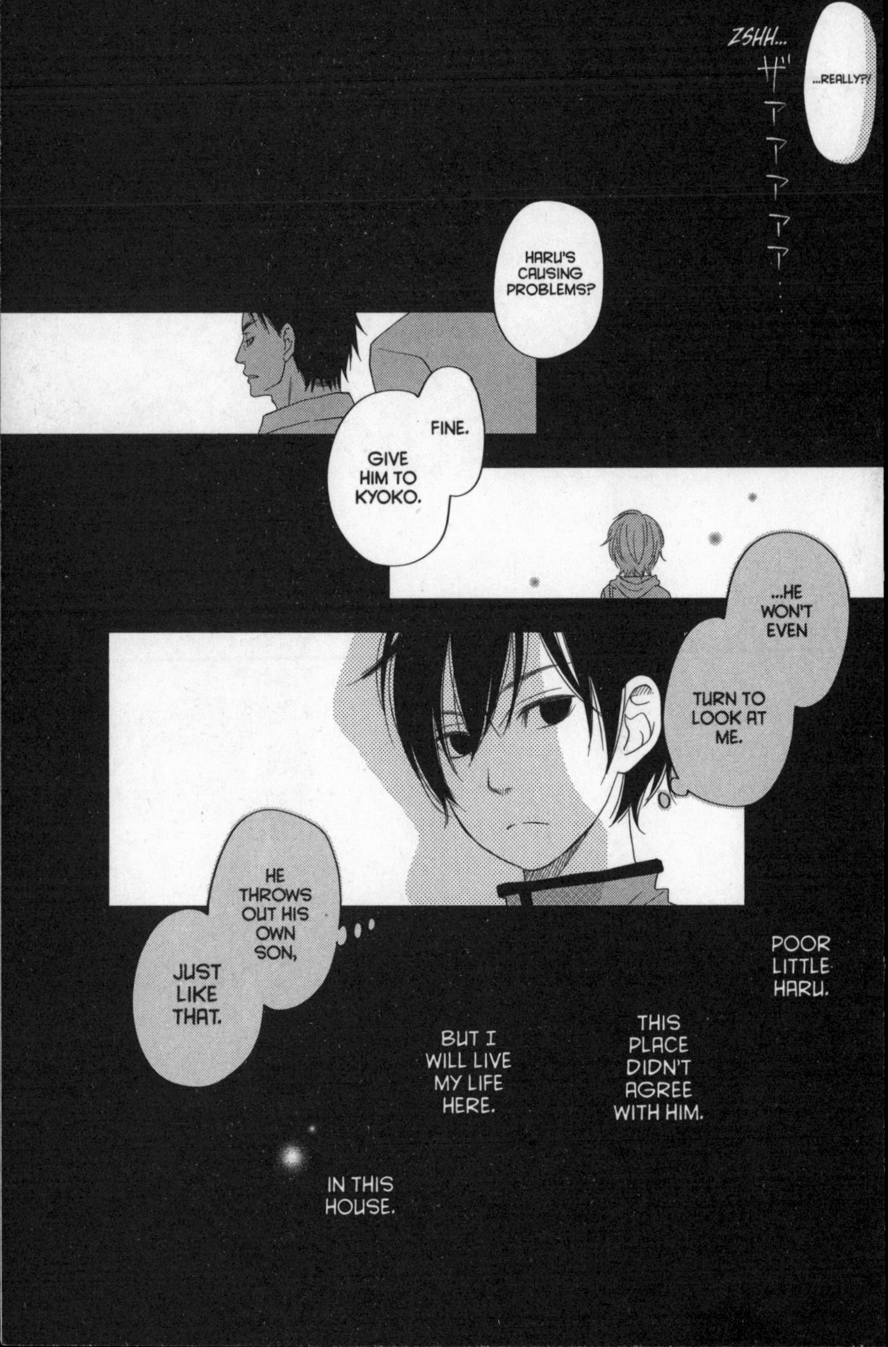
...REALLY?!
ZSHH...
ザァァァァァ…
HARU'S CAUSING PROBLEMS?
FINE.
GIVE HIM TO KYOKO.
...HE WON'T EVEN
TURN TO LOOK AT ME.
HE THROWS OUT HIS OWN SON,
JUST LIKE THAT.
POOR LITTLE HARU.
THIS PLACE DIDN'T AGREE WITH HIM.
BUT I WILL LIVE MY LIFE HERE.
IN THIS HOUSE.

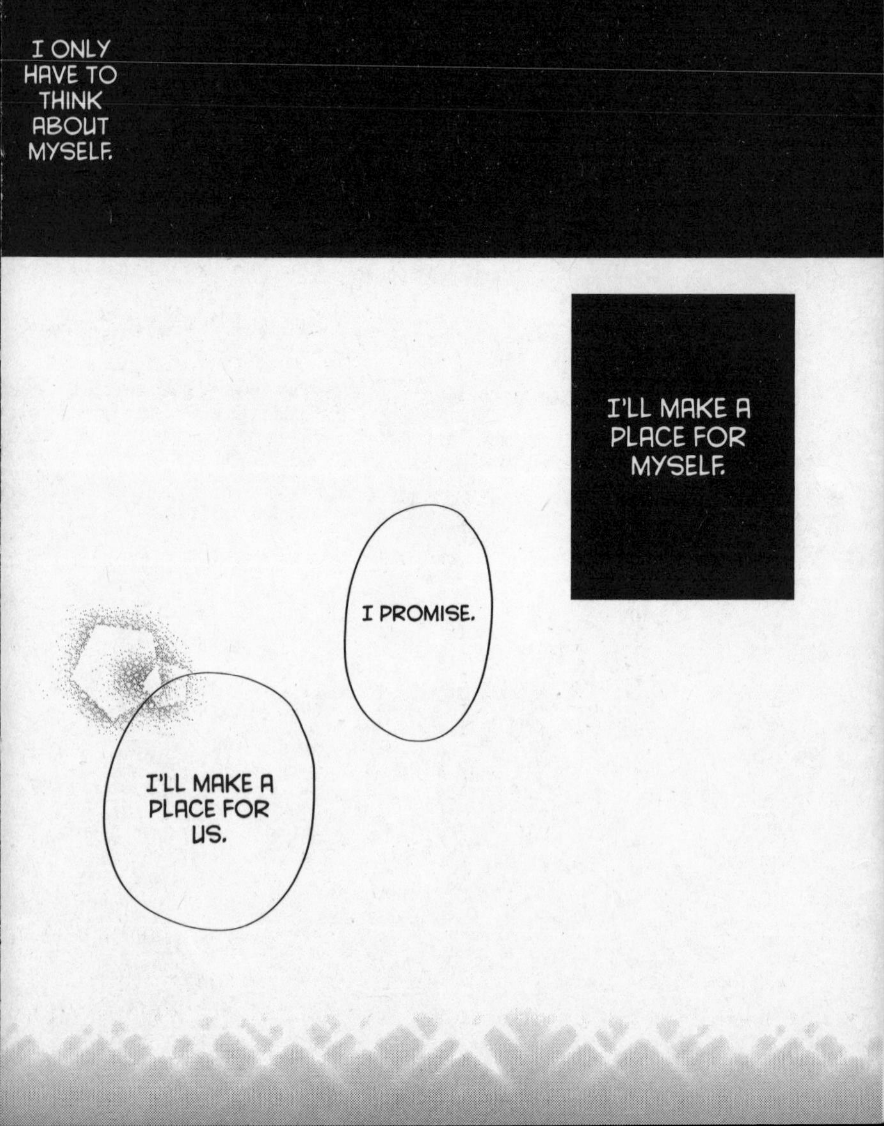
I ONLY HAVE TO THINK ABOUT MYSELF.
I'LL MAKE A PLACE FOR MYSELF.
I PROMISE.
I'LL MAKE A PLACE FOR US.

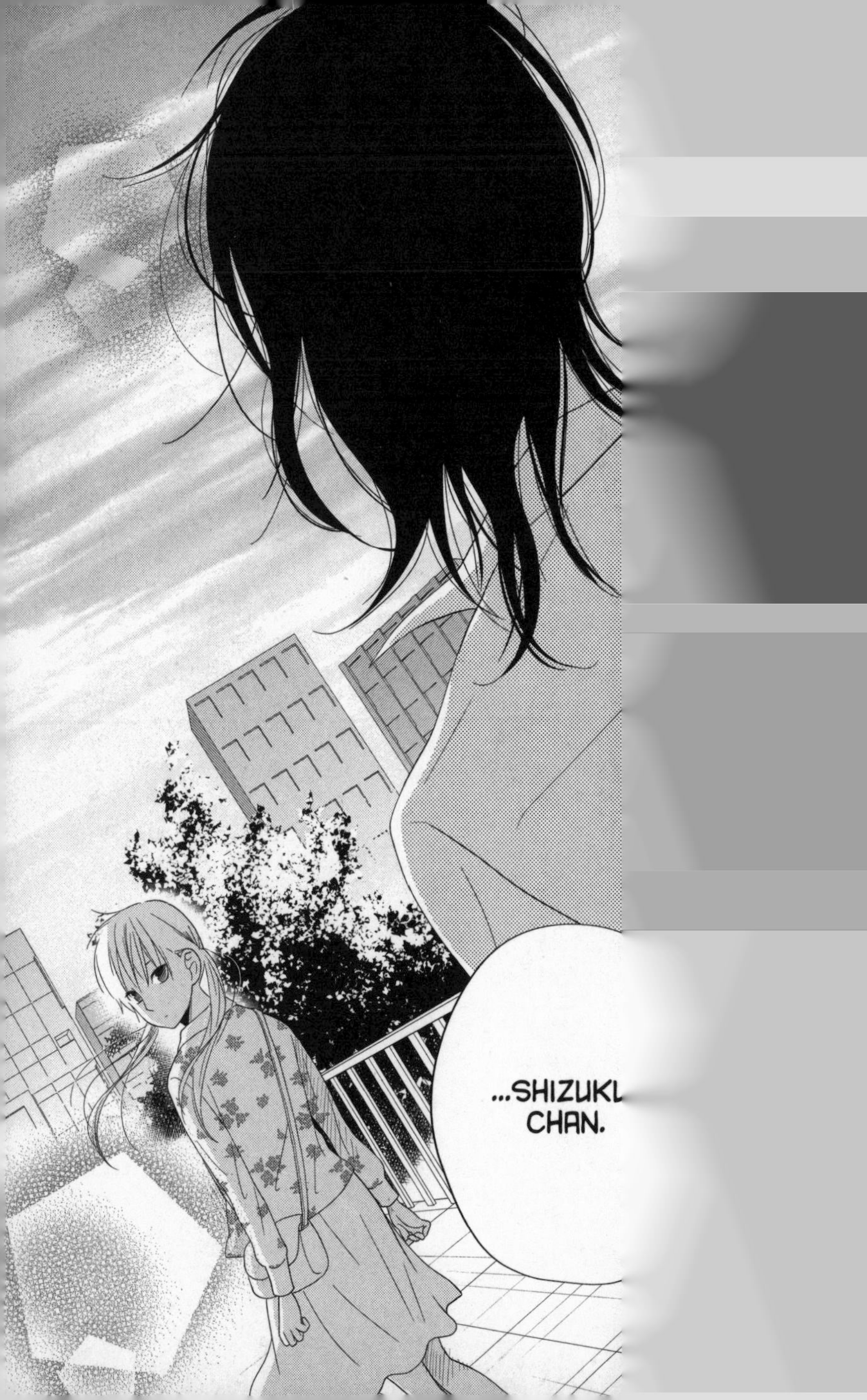
...SHIZUKU- CHAN.

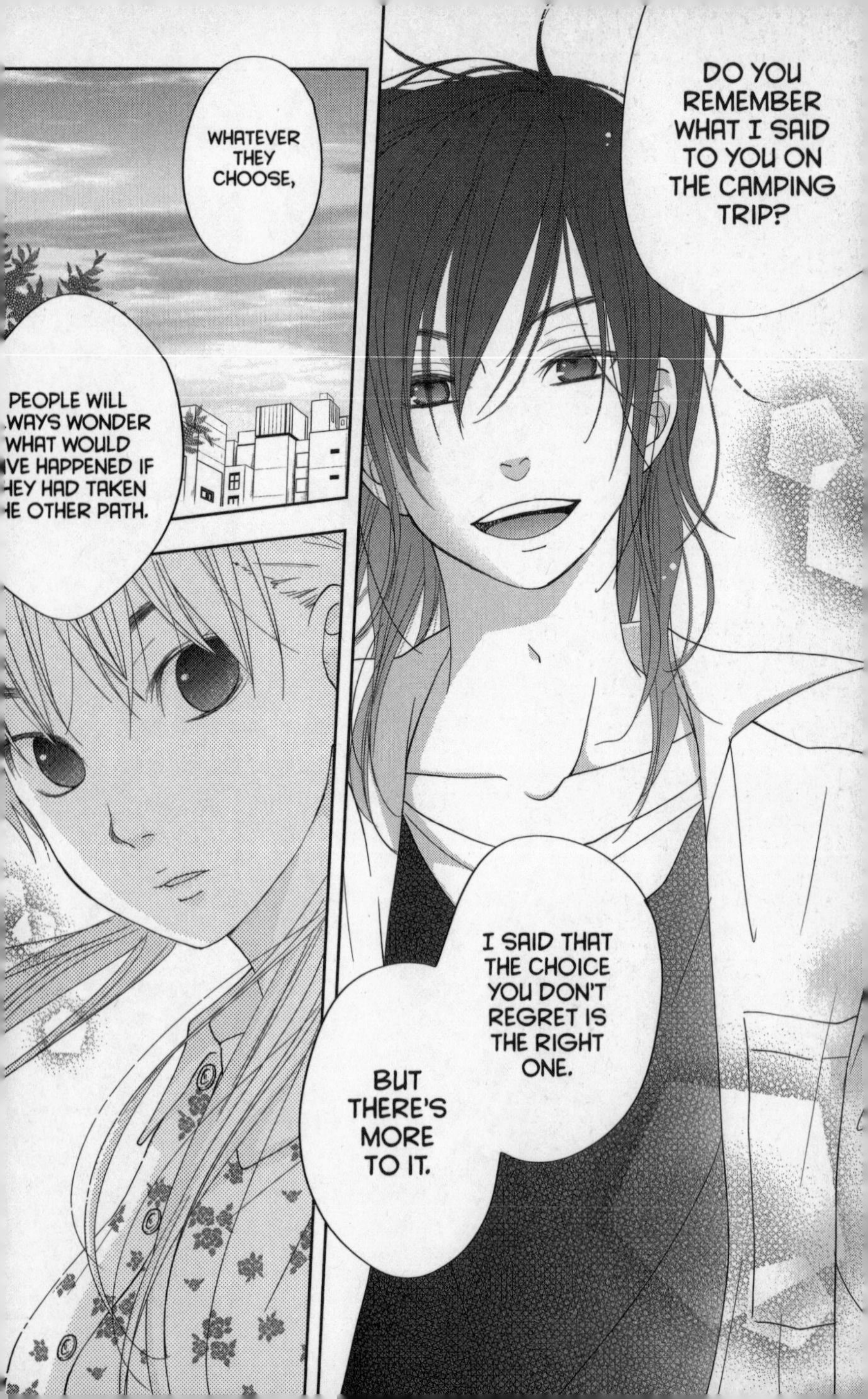
DO YOU REMEMBER WHAT I SAID TO YOU ON THE CAMPING TRIP?
I SAID THAT THE CHOICE YOU DON'T REGRET IS THE RIGHT ONE.
BUT THERE'S MORE TO IT.
WHATEVER THEY CHOOSE,
PEOPLE WILL WAYS WONDER WHAT WOULD VE HAPPENED IF HEY HAD TAKEN HE OTHER PATH.

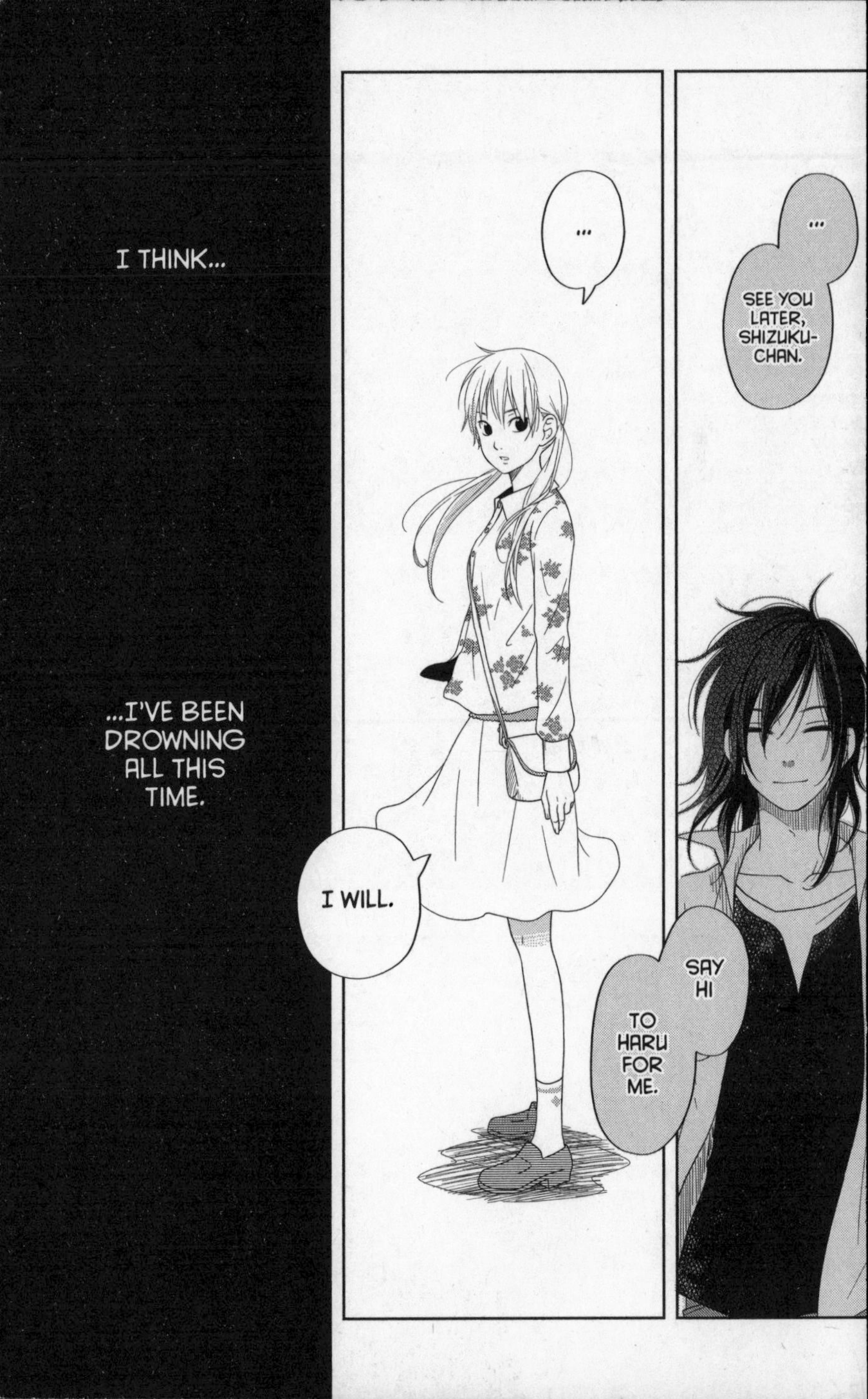
...
SEE YOU LATER, SHIZUKU-CHAN.
SAY HI TO HARU FOR ME.
...
I WILL.
I THINK...
...I'VE BEEN DROWNING ALL THIS TIME.

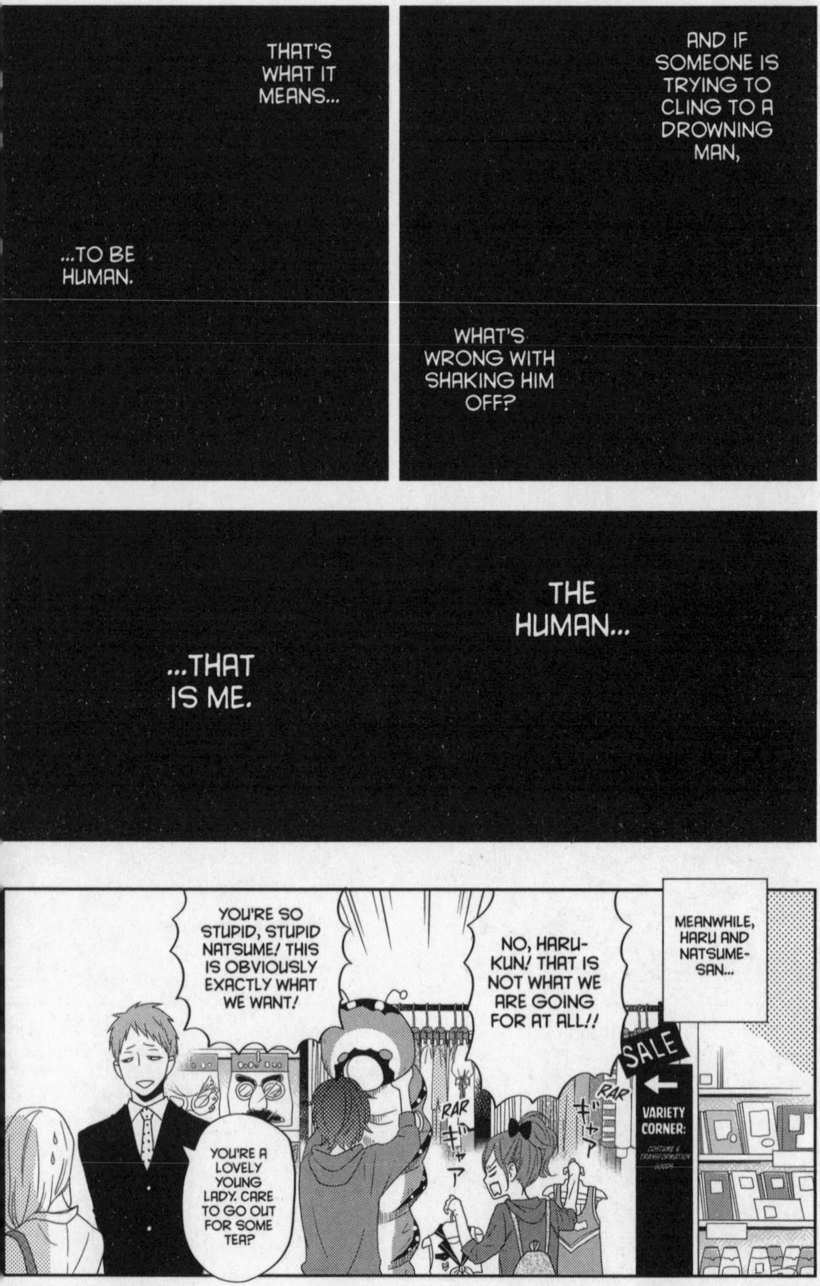
AND IF SOMEONE IS TRYING TO CLING TO A DROWNING MAN,
WHAT'S WRONG WITH SHAKING HIM OFF?
THAT'S WHAT IT MEANS...
...TO BE HUMAN.
THE HUMAN...
...THAT IS ME.
MEANWHILE, HARU AND NATSUME-SAN...
SALE
VARIETY CORNER: COSTUME & TRANSFORMATION GOODS
RAR ギャア
NO, HARU-KUN! THAT IS NOT WHAT WE ARE GOING FOR AT ALL!!
RAR ギャア
YOU'RE SO STUPID, STUPID NATSUME! THIS IS OBVIOUSLY EXACTLY WHAT WE WANT!
YOU'RE A LOVELY YOUNG LADY. CARE TO GO OUT FOR SOME TEA?

A JOKE BY THE HUMAN THAT IS ME, PART 1

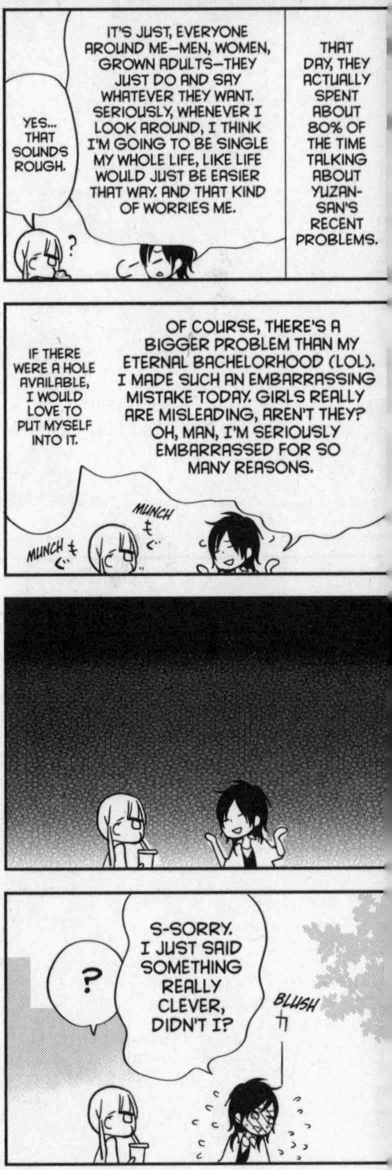
THAT DAY, THEY ACTUALLY SPENT ABOUT 80% OF THE TIME TALKING ABOUT YUZAN-SAN'S RECENT PROBLEMS.
IT'S JUST, EVERYONE AROUND ME—MEN, WOMEN, GROWN ADULTS—THEY JUST DO AND SAY WHATEVER THEY WANT. SERIOUSLY, WHENEVER I LOOK AROUND, I THINK I'M GOING TO BE SINGLE MY WHOLE LIFE, LIKE LIFE WOULD JUST BE EASIER THAT WAY. AND THAT KIND OF WORRIES ME.
YES... THAT SOUNDS ROUGH.
?
OF COURSE, THERE'S A BIGGER PROBLEM THAN MY ETERNAL BACHELORHOOD (LOL). I MADE SUCH AN EMBARRASSING MISTAKE TODAY. GIRLS REALLY ARE MISLEADING, AREN'T THEY? OH, MAN, I'M SERIOUSLY EMBARRASSED FOR SO MANY REASONS.
IF THERE WERE A HOLE AVAILABLE, I WOULD LOVE TO PUT MYSELF INTO IT.
MUNCH
MUNCH
S-SORRY. I JUST SAID SOMETHING REALLY CLEVER, DIDN'T I?
?
BLUSH

A JOKE BY THE HUMAN THAT IS ME, PART 2

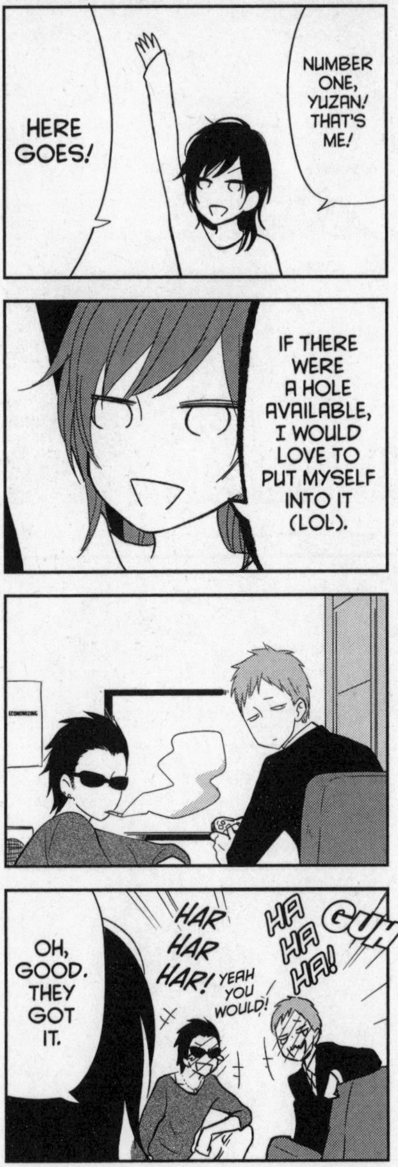
NUMBER ONE, YUZAN! THAT'S ME!
HERE GOES!
IF THERE WERE A HOLE AVAILABLE, I WOULD LOVE TO PUT MYSELF INTO IT (LOL).
ECONOMIZING
GUH
HA HA HA!
YEAH YOU WOULD!
HAR HAR HAR!
OH, GOOD. THEY GOT IT.

POST-CHAPTER-37 BONUS: MITCHAN'S DILEMMA

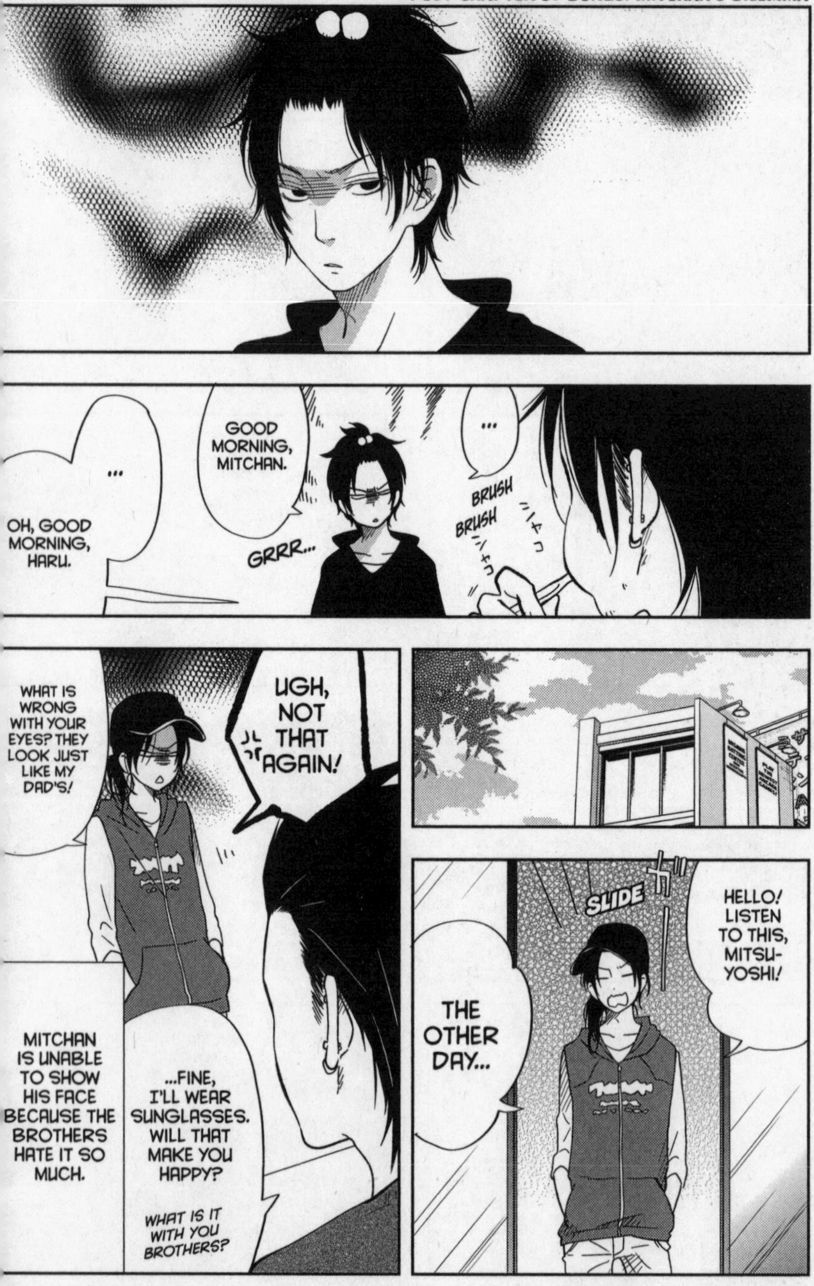
...
BRUSH BRUSH
GOOD MORNING, MITCHAN.
GRRR...
...
OH, GOOD MORNING, HARU.
HELLO! LISTEN TO THIS, MITSUYOSHI!
SLIDE
THE OTHER DAY...
WHAT IS WRONG WITH YOUR EYES? THEY LOOK JUST LIKE MY DAD'S!
UGH, NOT THAT AGAIN!
...FINE, I'LL WEAR SUNGLASSES. WILL THAT MAKE YOU HAPPY?
WHAT IS IT WITH YOU BROTHERS?
MITCHAN IS UNABLE TO SHOW HIS FACE BECAUSE THE BROTHERS HATE IT SO MUCH.

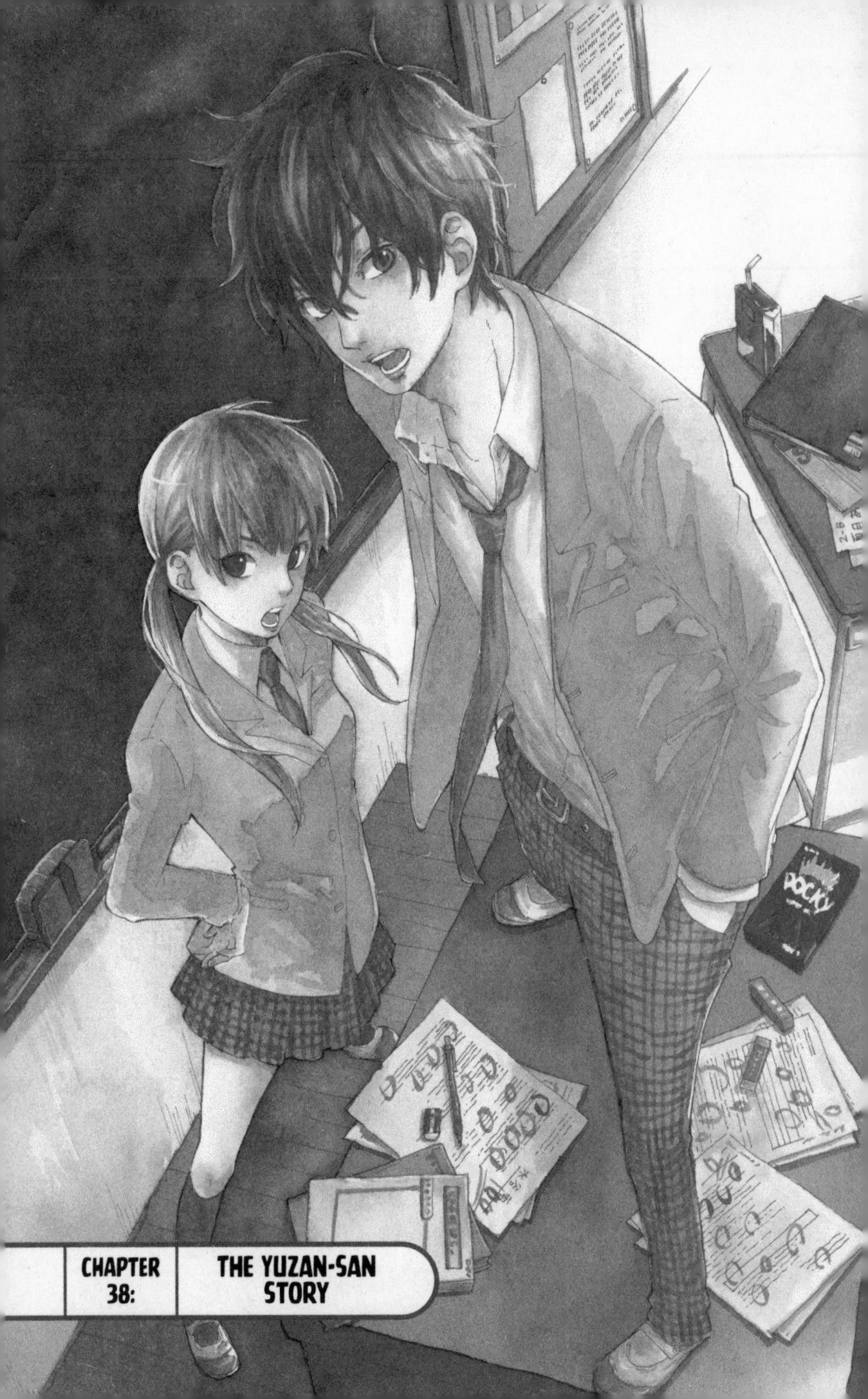
CHAPTER 38:
THE YUZAN-SAN STORY
POCKY

Wendy &
Tinker
Bell

HEE
HEE
HEE...

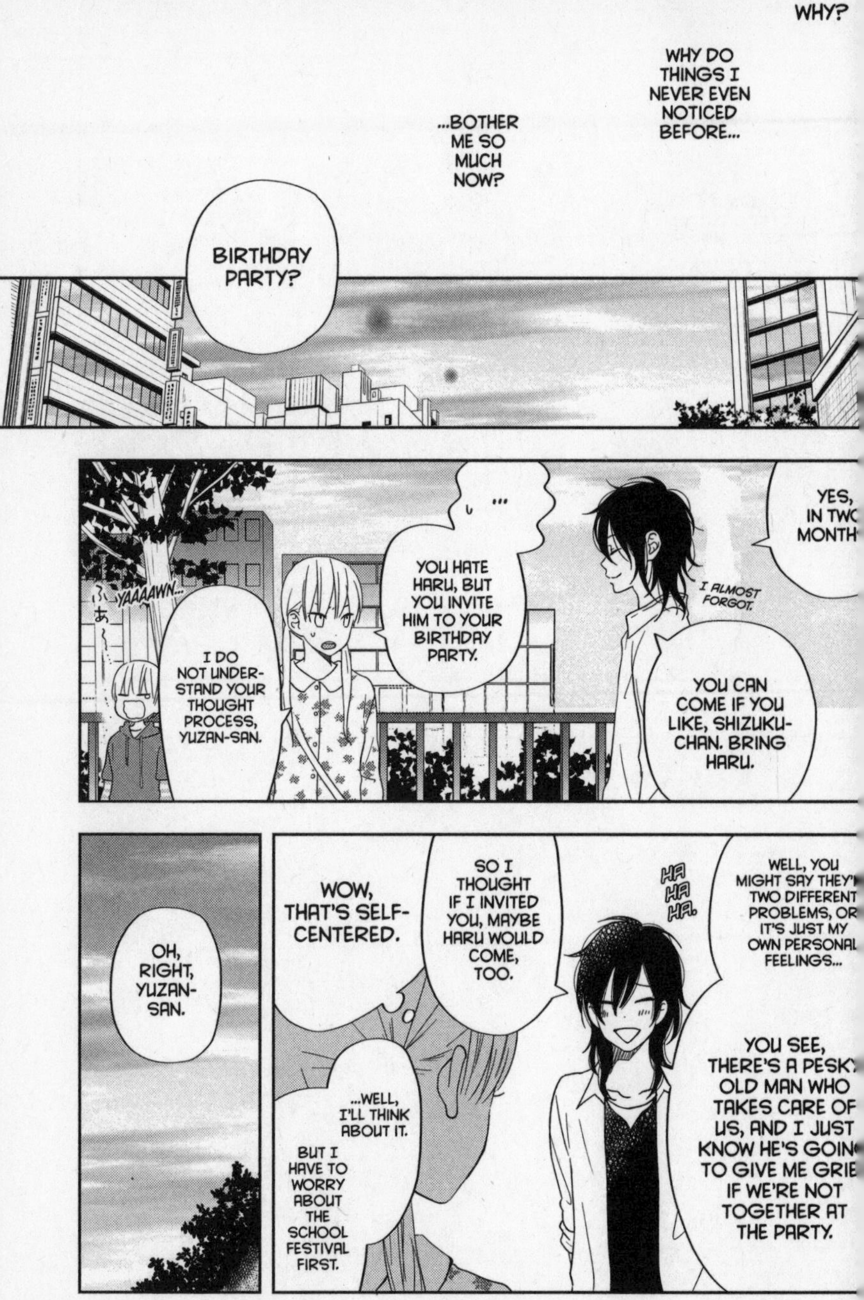
WHY?
WHY DO THINGS I NEVER EVEN NOTICED BEFORE...
...BOTHER ME SO MUCH NOW?
BIRTHDAY PARTY?
YES, IN TWO MONTH
I ALMOST FORGOT.
YOU CAN COME IF YOU LIKE, SHIZUKU-CHAN. BRING HARU.
...
YOU HATE HARU, BUT YOU INVITE HIM TO YOUR BIRTHDAY PARTY.
I DO NOT UNDERSTAND YOUR THOUGHT PROCESS, YUZAN-SAN.
ふあ~ YAAAAWN...
WELL, YOU MIGHT SAY THEY' TWO DIFFERENT PROBLEMS, OR IT'S JUST MY OWN PERSONAL FEELINGS...
YOU SEE, THERE'S A PESK OLD MAN WHO TAKES CARE OF US, AND I JUST KNOW HE'S GOIN TO GIVE ME GRIE IF WE'RE NOT TOGETHER AT THE PARTY.
HA HA HA.
SO I THOUGHT IF I INVITED YOU, MAYBE HARU WOULD COME, TOO.
WOW, THAT'S SELF-CENTERED.
...WELL, I'LL THINK ABOUT IT.
BUT I HAVE TO WORRY ABOUT THE SCHOOL FESTIVAL FIRST.
OH, RIGHT, YUZAN-SAN.

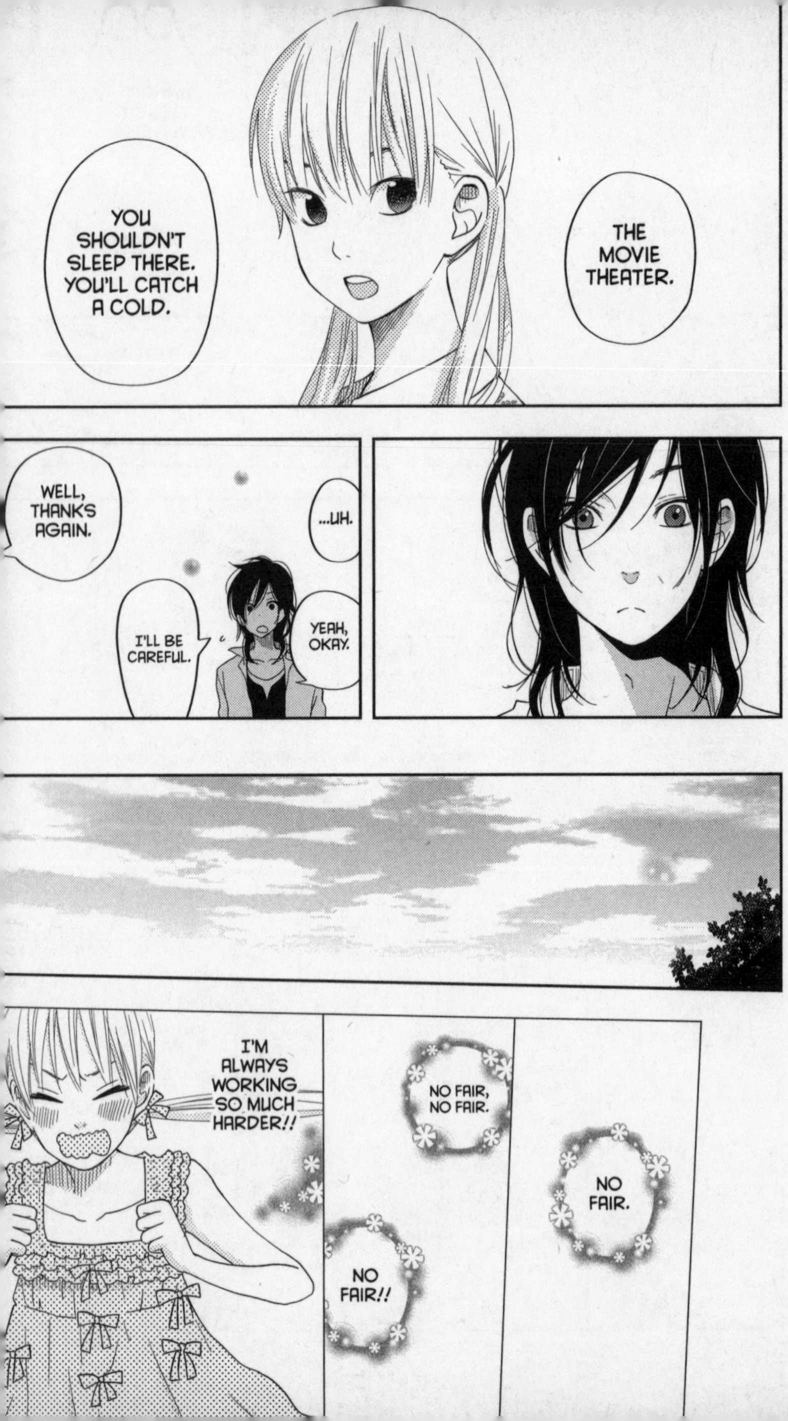
THE MOVIE THEATER.
YOU SHOULDN'T SLEEP THERE. YOU'LL CATCH A COLD.
...UH.
WELL, THANKS AGAIN.
YEAH, OKAY.
I'LL BE CAREFUL.
NO FAIR.
NO FAIR, NO FAIR.
NO FAIR!!
I'M ALWAYS WORKING SO MUCH HARDER!!

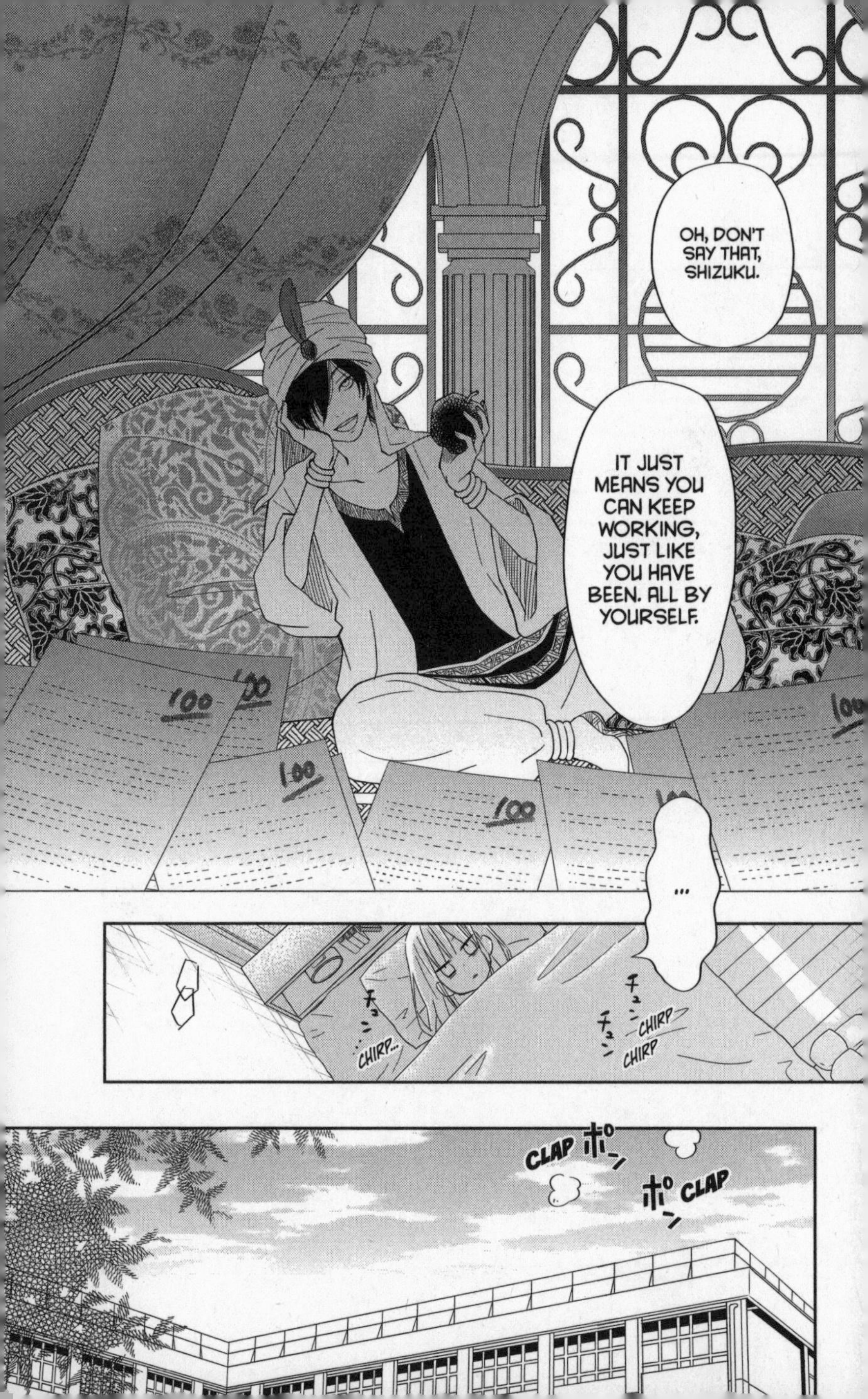
OH, DON'T SAY THAT, SHIZUKU.
IT JUST MEANS YOU CAN KEEP WORKING, JUST LIKE YOU HAVE BEEN. ALL BY YOURSELF.
100
100
100
100
100
...
チュン
チュン
CHIRP
CHIRP
チュン
CHIRP...
CLAP ポーン
ポーン CLAP

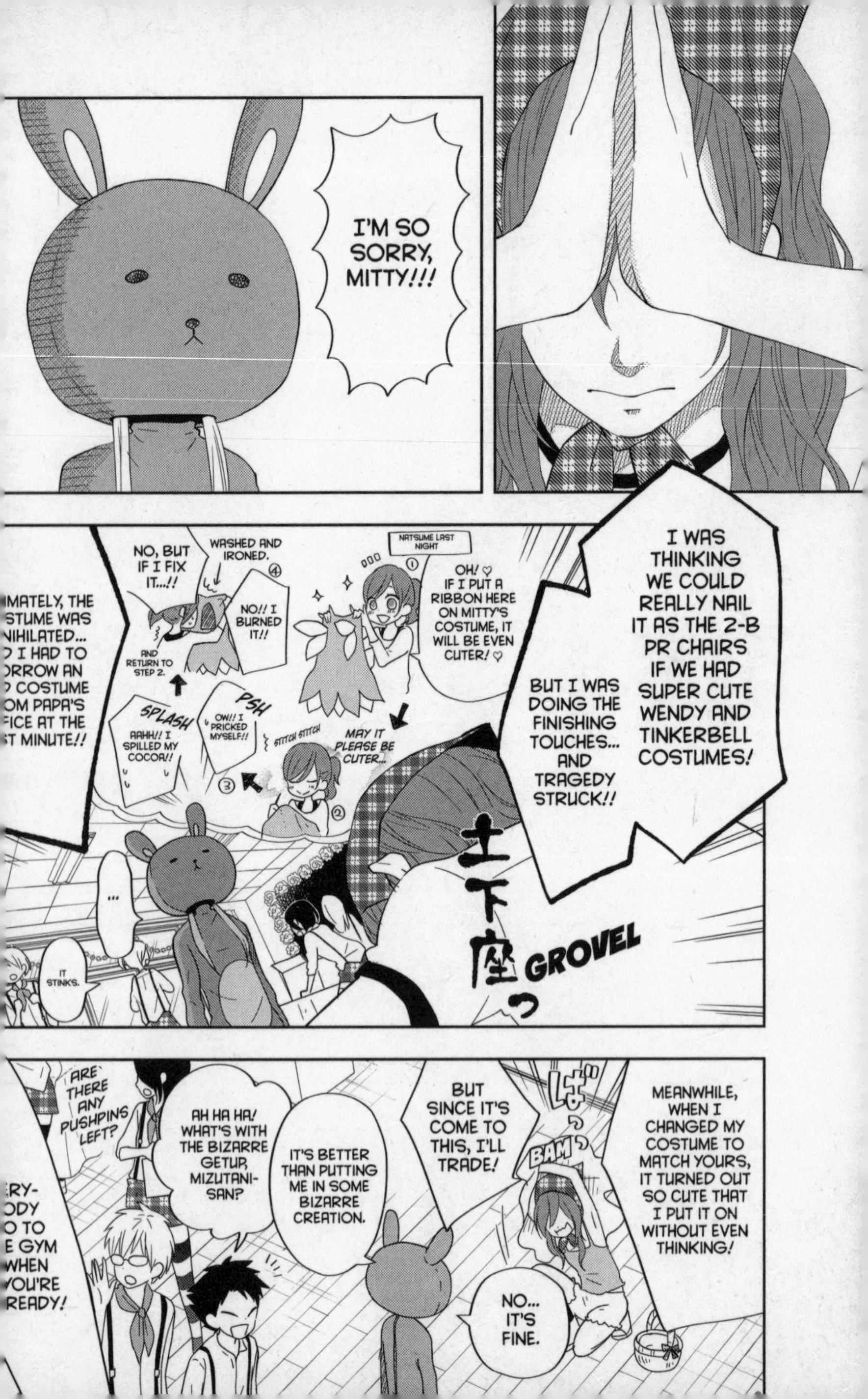
I'M SO SORRY, MITTY!!!
I WAS THINKING WE COULD REALLY NAIL IT AS THE 2-B PR CHAIRS IF WE HAD SUPER CUTE WENDY AND TINKERBELL COSTUMES!
BUT I WAS DOING THE FINISHING TOUCHES... AND TRAGEDY STRUCK!!
NATSUME LAST NIGHT
①
OH! ♡ IF I PUT A RIBBON HERE ON MITTY'S COSTUME, IT WILL BE EVEN CUTER! ♡
MAY IT PLEASE BE CUTER...
STITCH STITCH
②
PSH
OW!! I PRICKED MYSELF!!
③
SPLASH
AAHH!! I SPILLED MY COCOA!!
④
NO!! I BURNED IT!!
WASHED AND IRONED.
NO, BUT IF I FIX IT...!!
AND RETURN TO STEP 2.
IMATELY, THE STUME WAS NIHILATED... D I HAD TO ORROW AN D COSTUME OM PAPA'S FICE AT THE ST MINUTE!!
土下座っ
GROVEL
...
IT STINKS.
MEANWHILE, WHEN I CHANGED MY COSTUME TO MATCH YOURS, IT TURNED OUT SO CUTE THAT I PUT IT ON WITHOUT EVEN THINKING!
ばっ
BAM
BUT SINCE IT'S COME TO THIS, I'LL TRADE!
NO... IT'S FINE.
IT'S BETTER THAN PUTTING ME IN SOME BIZARRE CREATION.
AH HA HA! WHAT'S WITH THE BIZARRE GETUP, MIZUTANI-SAN?
ARE THERE ANY PUSHPINS LEFT?
ERY- ODY O TO E GYM WHEN YOU'RE READY!

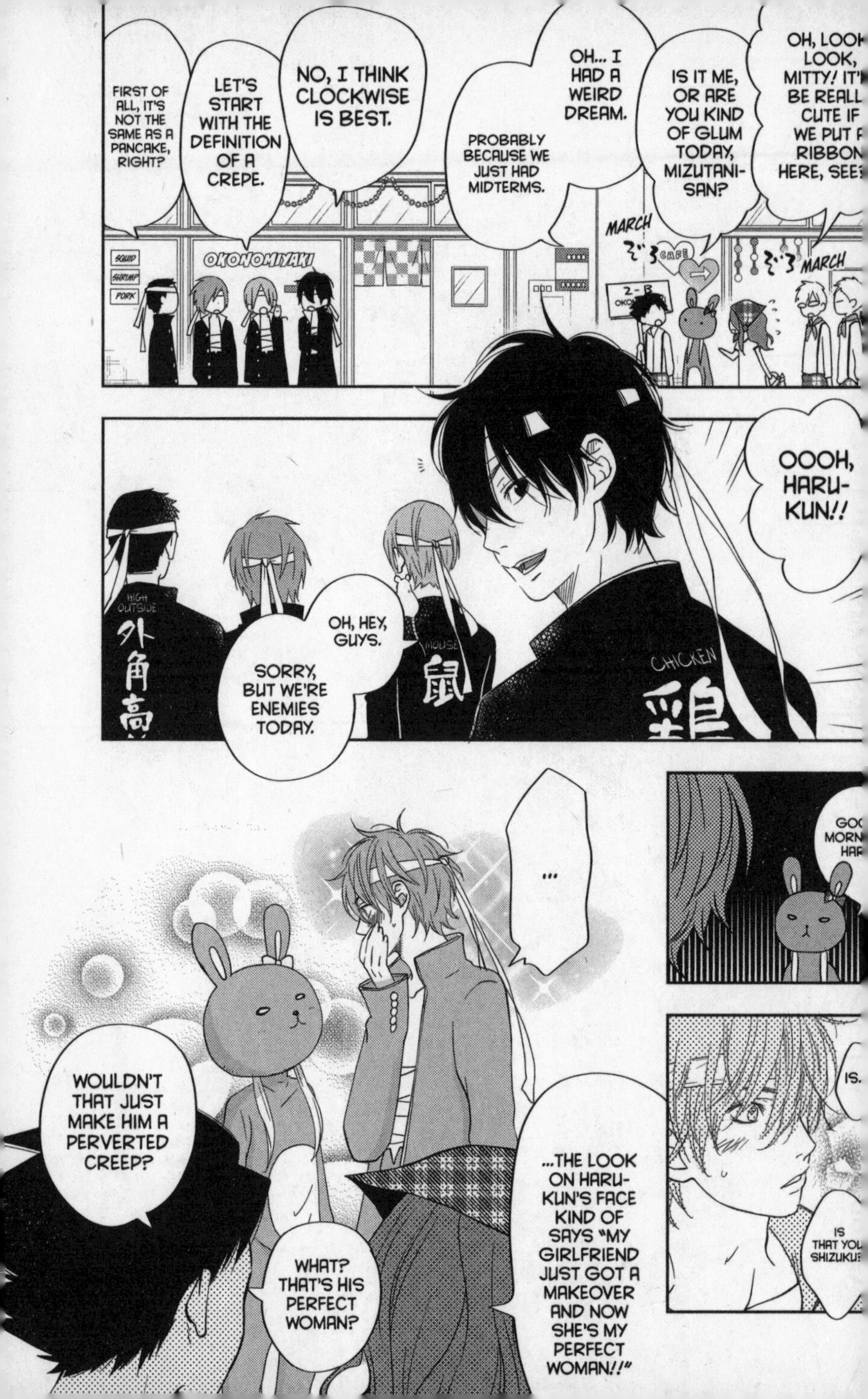
OH, LOOK LOOK, MITTY! IT' BE REALL CUTE IF WE PUT RIBBON HERE, SEE
MARCH
MARCH
IS IT ME, OR ARE YOU KIND OF GLUM TODAY, MIZUTANI-SAN?
CAFE
2-B
OH... I HAD A WEIRD DREAM.
PROBABLY BECAUSE WE JUST HAD MIDTERMS.
NO, I THINK CLOCKWISE IS BEST.
OKONOMIYAKI
LET'S START WITH THE DEFINITION OF A CREPE.
SQUID
SHRIMP
PORK
FIRST OF ALL, IT'S NOT THE SAME AS A PANCAKE, RIGHT?
OOOH, HARU-KUN!!
CHICKEN
MOUSE
鼠
OH, HEY, GUYS.
SORRY, BUT WE'RE ENEMIES TODAY.
HIGH OUTSIDE
IS.
IS THAT YOU SHIZUKU?
...
...THE LOOK ON HARU-KUN'S FACE KIND OF SAYS "MY GIRLFRIEND JUST GOT A MAKEOVER AND NOW SHE'S MY PERFECT WOMAN!!"
WHAT? THAT'S HIS PERFECT WOMAN?
WOULDN'T THAT JUST MAKE HIM A PERVERTED CREEP?

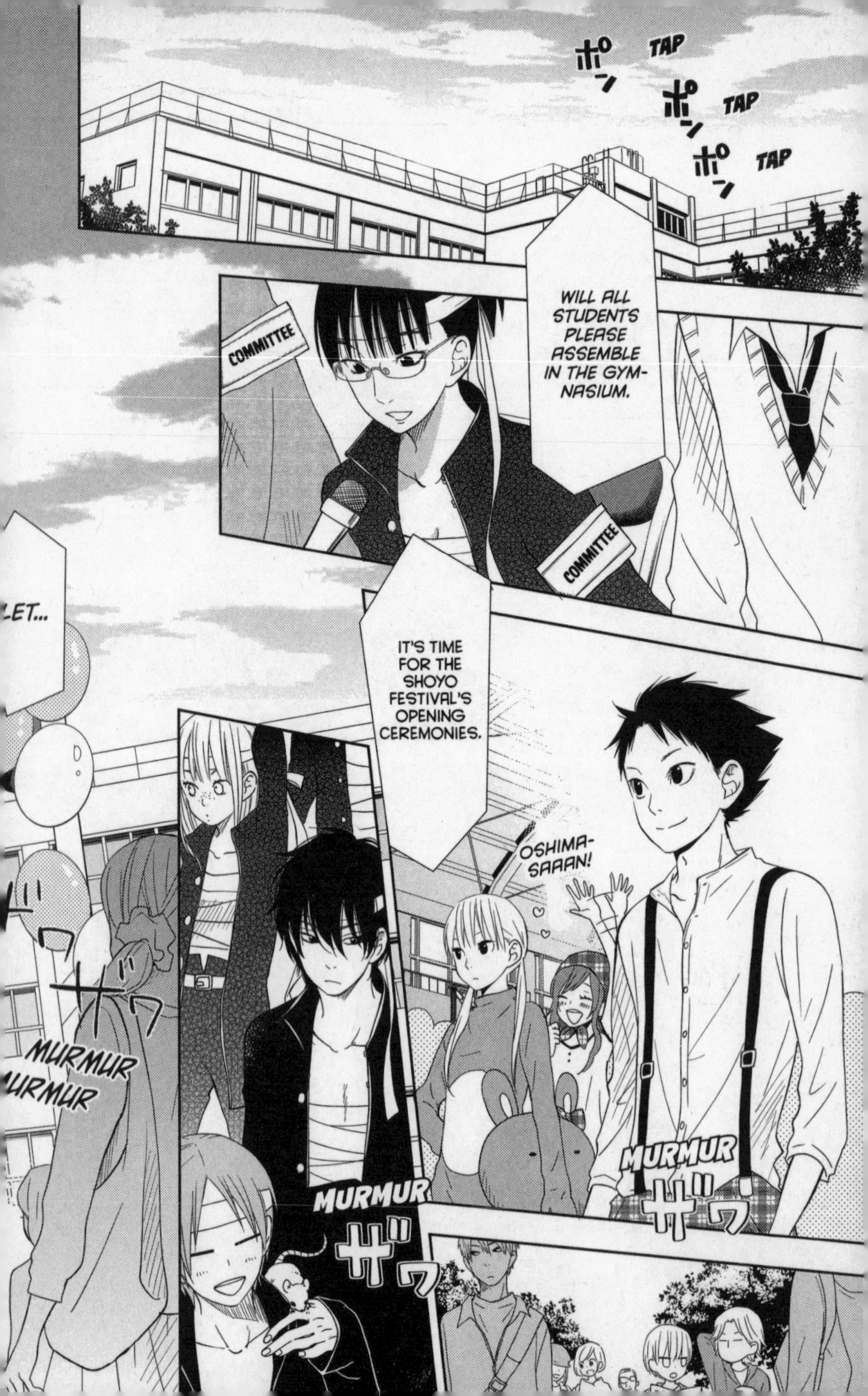
ポン TAP
ポン TAP
ポン TAP
COMMITTEE
WILL ALL STUDENTS PLEASE ASSEMBLE IN THE GYM-NASIUM.
COMMITTEE
IT'S TIME FOR THE SHOYO FESTIVAL'S OPENING CEREMONIES.
LET...
OSHIMA-SAAAN!
ザワ MURMUR
ザワ MURMUR
ザワ MURMUR
ザワ MURMUR

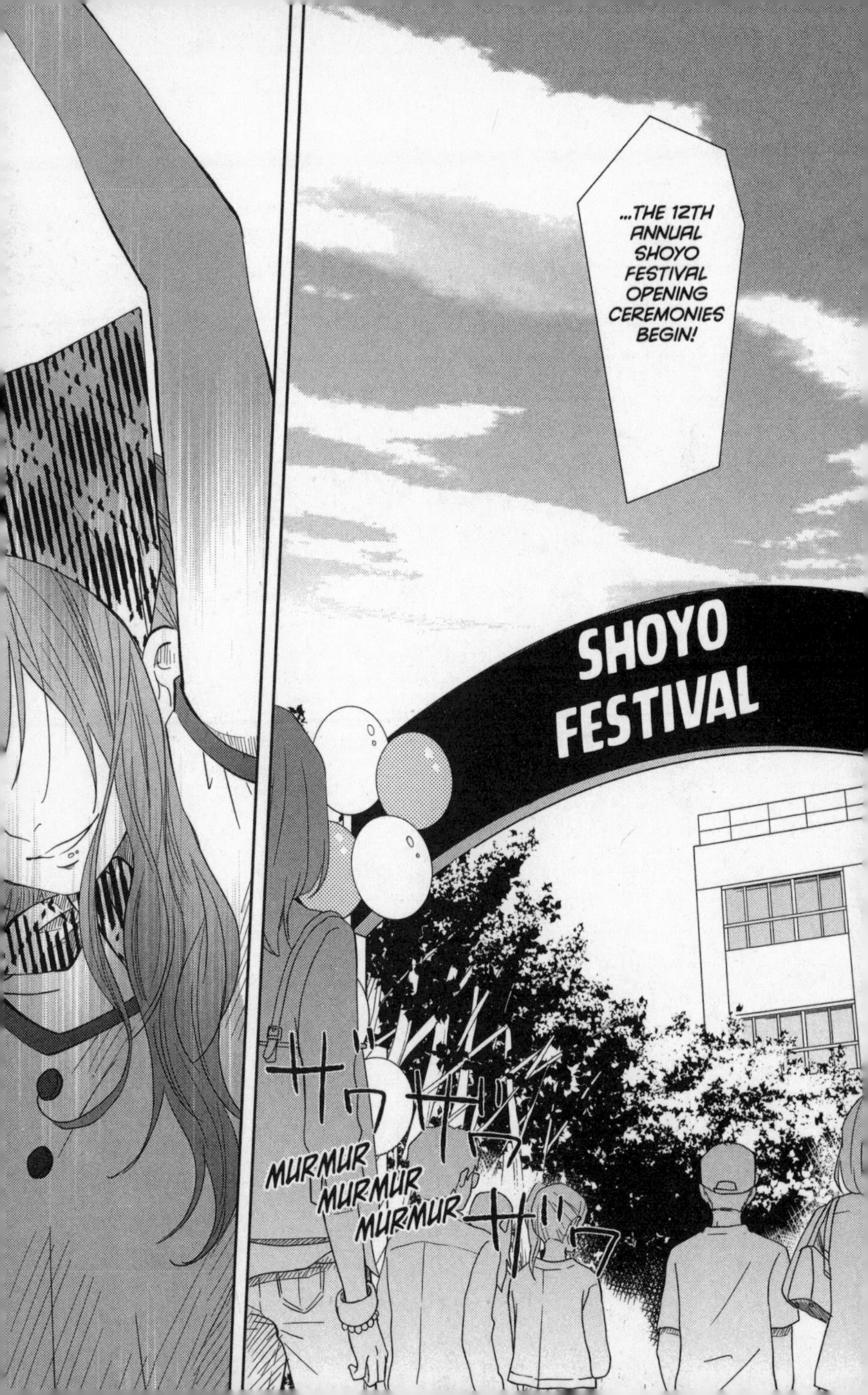
...THE 12TH ANNUAL SHOYO FESTIVAL OPENING CEREMONIES BEGIN!
SHOYO FESTIVAL
MURMUR MURMUR MURMUR

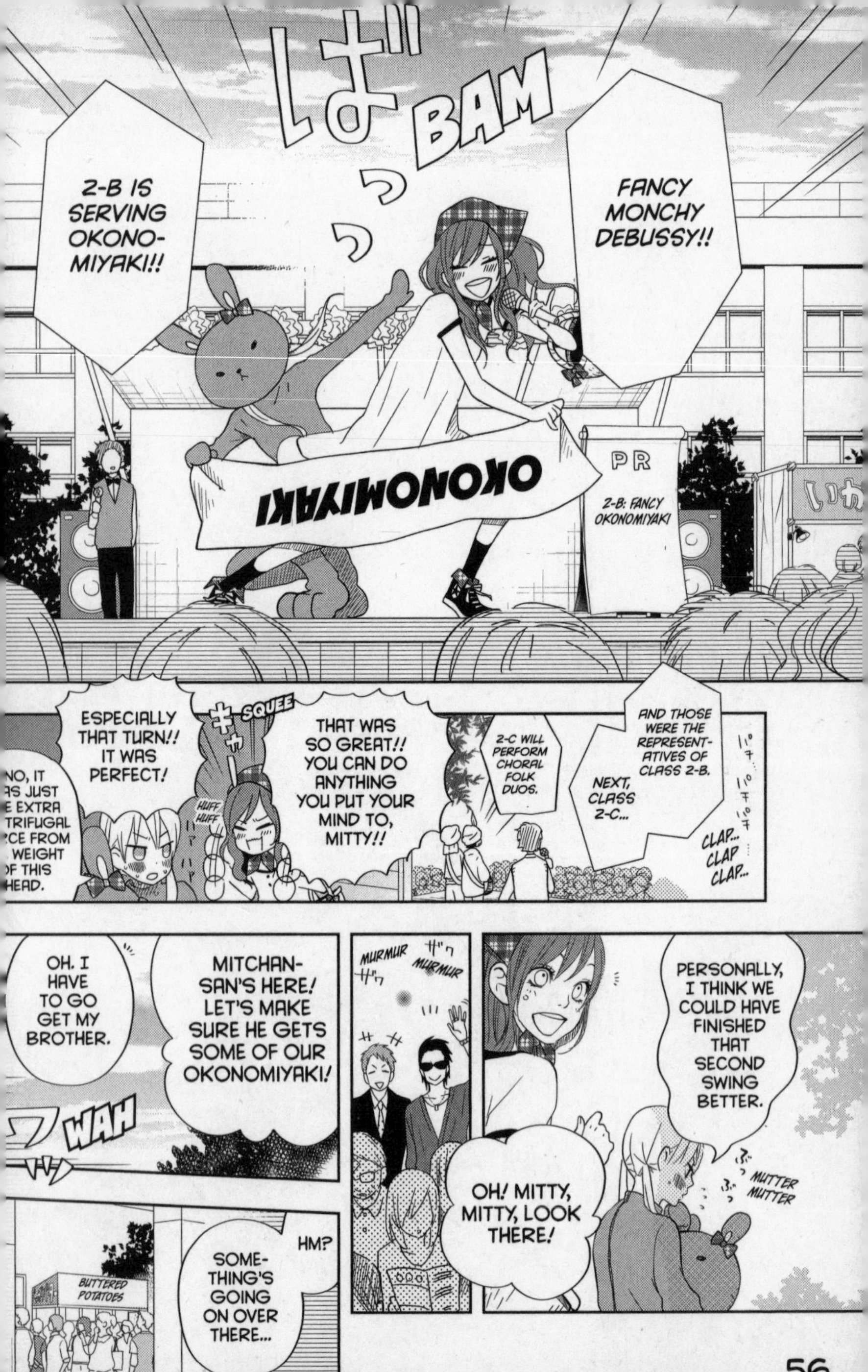
BAM
FANCY MONCHY DEBUSSY!!
2-B IS SERVING OKONOMIYAKI!!
OKONOMIYAKI
PR
2-B: FANCY OKONOMIYAKI
AND THOSE WERE THE REPRESENTATIVES OF CLASS 2-B.
NEXT, CLASS 2-C...
2-C WILL PERFORM CHORAL FOLK DUOS.
CLAP... CLAP CLAP...
THAT WAS SO GREAT!! YOU CAN DO ANYTHING YOU PUT YOUR MIND TO, MITTY!!
SQUEE
HUFF HUFF
ESPECIALLY THAT TURN!! IT WAS PERFECT!
NO, IT AS JUST E EXTRA TRIFUGAL RCE FROM WEIGHT OF THIS HEAD.
PERSONALLY, I THINK WE COULD HAVE FINISHED THAT SECOND SWING BETTER.
MUTTER MUTTER
OH! MITTY, MITTY, LOOK THERE!
MURMUR
MURMUR
MITCHAN-SAN'S HERE! LET'S MAKE SURE HE GETS SOME OF OUR OKONOMIYAKI!
OH. I HAVE TO GO GET MY BROTHER.
WAH
HM?
SOMETHING'S GOING ON OVER THERE...
BUTTERED POTATOES

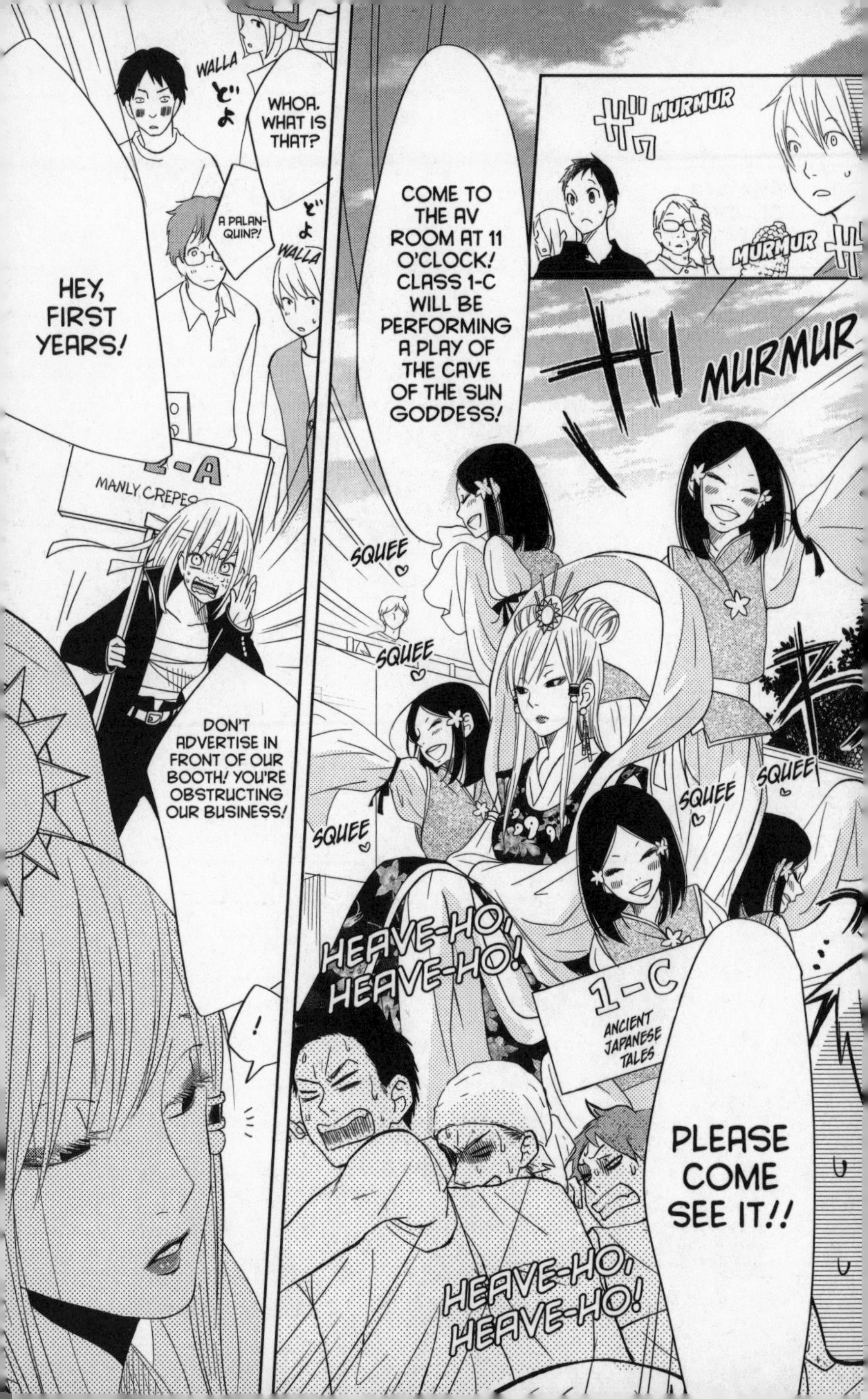

MURMUR
MURMUR
COME TO THE AV ROOM AT 11 O'CLOCK! CLASS 1-C WILL BE PERFORMING A PLAY OF THE CAVE OF THE SUN GODDESS!
MURMUR
SQUEE
SQUEE
SQUEE
SQUEE
SQUEE
HEAVE-HO! HEAVE-HO!
1-C
ANCIENT JAPANESE TALES
PLEASE COME SEE IT!!
HEAVE-HO! HEAVE-HO!
WALLA
どよ
WHOA. WHAT IS THAT?
A PALANQUIN?!
どよ
WALLA
HEY, FIRST YEARS!
MANLY CREPES
DON'T ADVERTISE IN FRONT OF OUR BOOTH! YOU'RE OBSTRUCTING OUR BUSINESS!
!

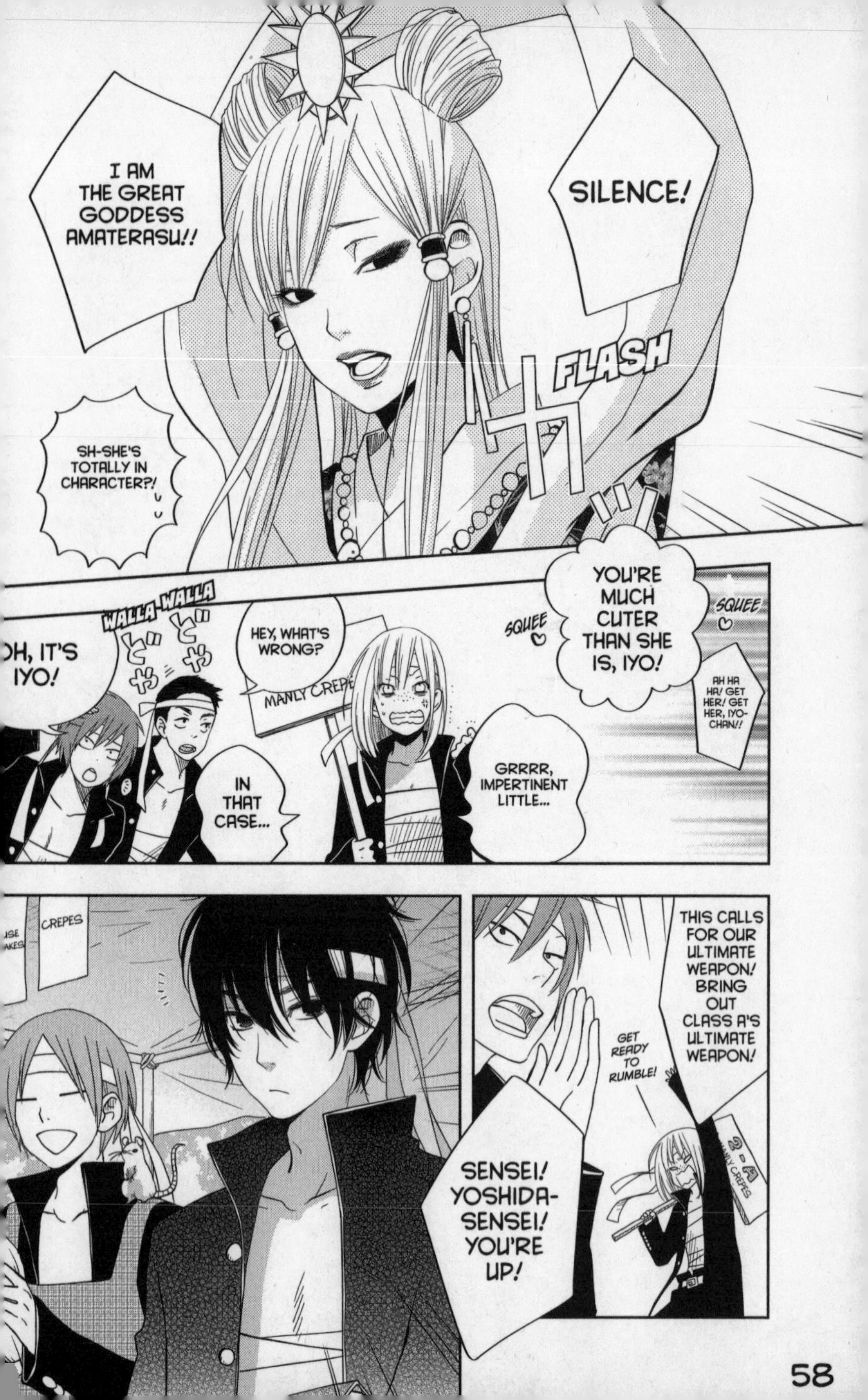
SILENCE!
I AM THE GREAT GODDESS AMATERASU!!
FLASH
SH-SHE'S TOTALLY IN CHARACTER?!
YOU'RE MUCH CUTER THAN SHE IS, IYO!
SQUEE
SQUEE
AH HA HA! GET HER! GET HER, IYO-CHAN!!
GRRRR, IMPERTINENT LITTLE...
MANLY CREPES
HEY, WHAT'S WRONG?
WALLA-WALLA
H, IT'S IYO!
IN THAT CASE...
THIS CALLS FOR OUR ULTIMATE WEAPON! BRING OUT CLASS A'S ULTIMATE WEAPON!
GET READY TO RUMBLE!
SENSEI! YOSHIDA-SENSEI! YOU'RE UP!
3-A MANLY CREPES
CREPES

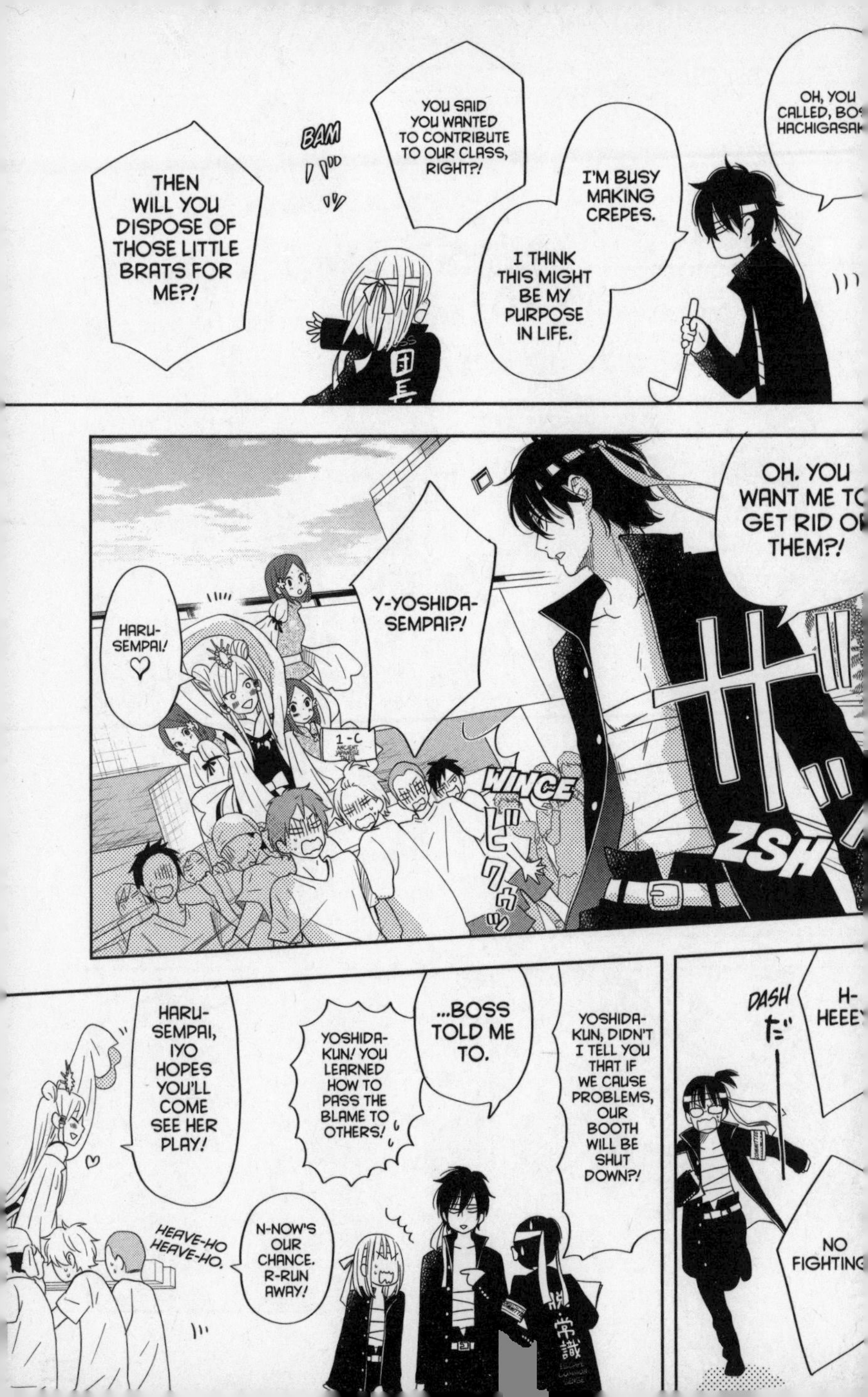
OH, YOU CALLED, BOS HACHIGASAK
I'M BUSY MAKING CREPES.
I THINK THIS MIGHT BE MY PURPOSE IN LIFE.
YOU SAID YOU WANTED TO CONTRIBUTE TO OUR CLASS, RIGHT?!
BAM
THEN WILL YOU DISPOSE OF THOSE LITTLE BRATS FOR ME?!
OH. YOU WANT ME TO GET RID OF THEM?!
ZSH
Y-YOSHIDA-SEMPAI?!
WINCE
1-C
HARU-SEMPAI! ♡
H-HEEEY
DASH
NO FIGHTING
YOSHIDA-KUN, DIDN'T I TELL YOU THAT IF WE CAUSE PROBLEMS, OUR BOOTH WILL BE SHUT DOWN?!
...BOSS TOLD ME TO.
YOSHIDA-KUN! YOU LEARNED HOW TO PASS THE BLAME TO OTHERS!
N-NOW'S OUR CHANCE. R-RUN AWAY!
HARU-SEMPAI, IYO HOPES YOU'LL COME SEE HER PLAY!
HEAVE-HO HEAVE-HO.

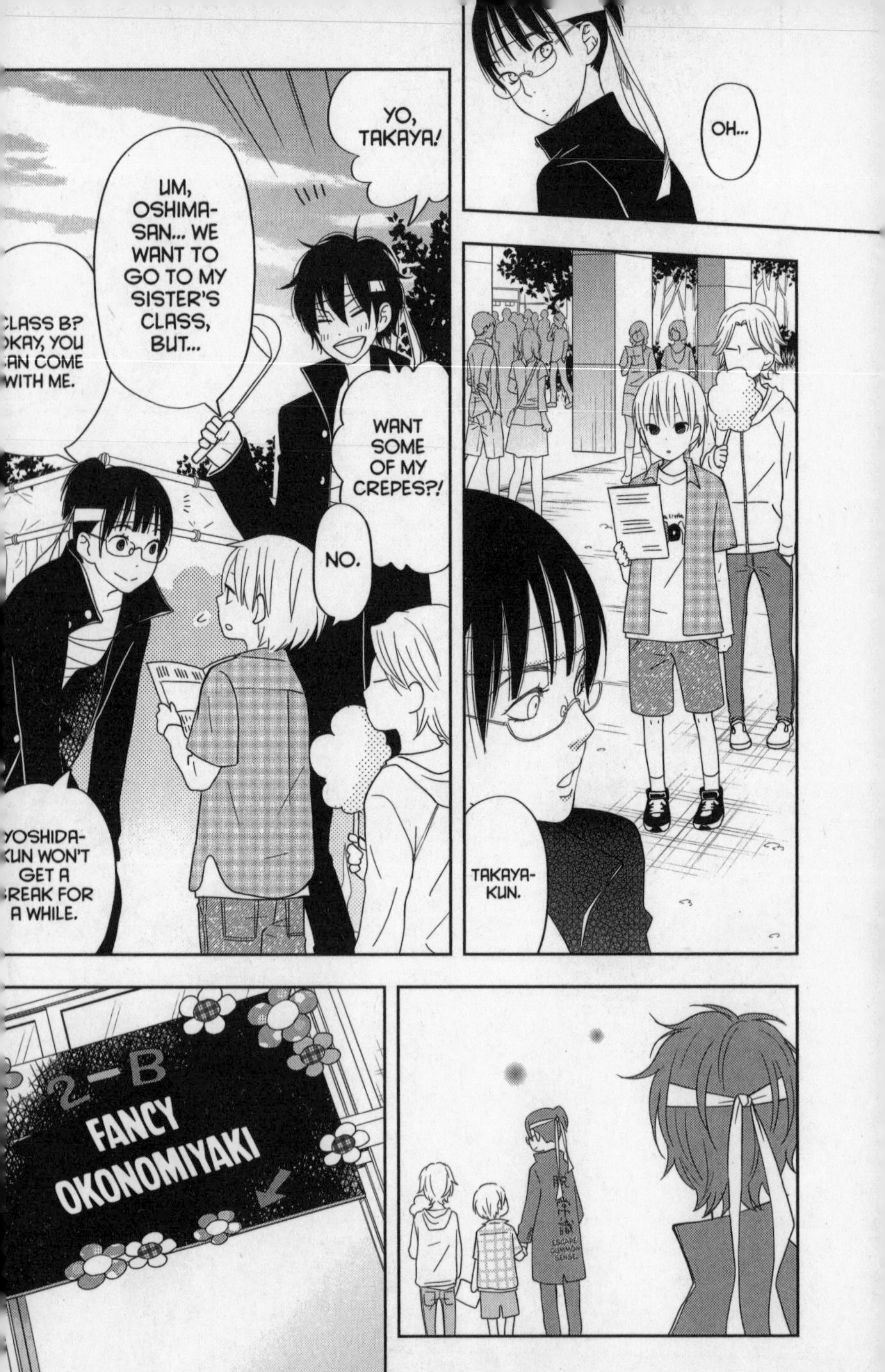
OH...
TAKAYA-KUN.
YO, TAKAYA!
UM, OSHIMA-SAN... WE WANT TO GO TO MY SISTER'S CLASS, BUT...
CLASS B? OKAY, YOU CAN COME WITH ME.
WANT SOME OF MY CREPES?!
NO.
YOSHIDA-KUN WON'T GET A BREAK FOR A WHILE.
ESCAPE COMMON SENSE
2-B
FANCY OKONOMIYAKI

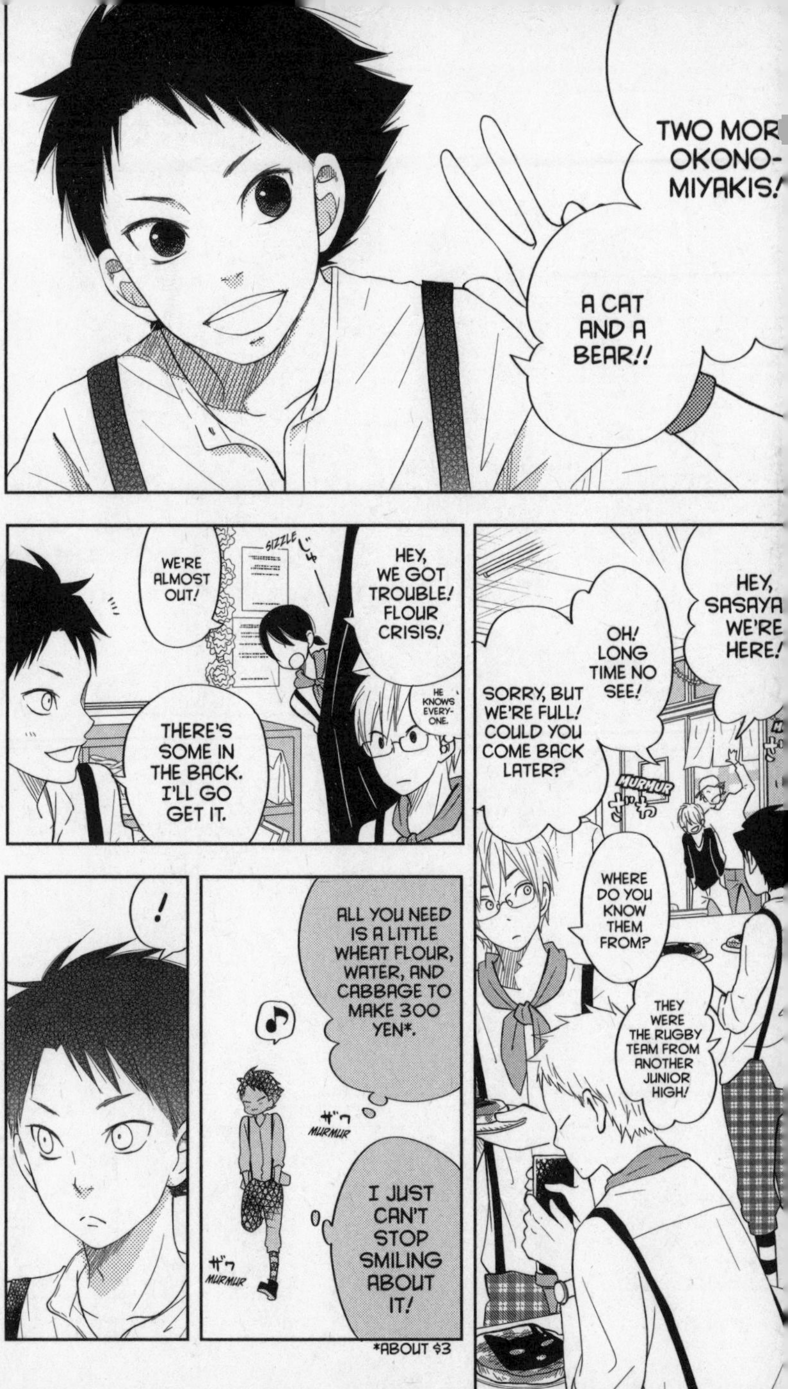
TWO MOR OKONO-MIYAKIS!
A CAT AND A BEAR!!
HEY, SASAYA WE'RE HERE!
OH! LONG TIME NO SEE!
SORRY, BUT WE'RE FULL! COULD YOU COME BACK LATER?
MURMUR
WHERE DO YOU KNOW THEM FROM?
THEY WERE THE RUGBY TEAM FROM ANOTHER JUNIOR HIGH!
SIZZLE
HEY, WE GOT TROUBLE! FLOUR CRISIS!
WE'RE ALMOST OUT!
HE KNOWS EVERYONE.
THERE'S SOME IN THE BACK. I'LL GO GET IT.
ALL YOU NEED IS A LITTLE WHEAT FLOUR, WATER, AND CABBAGE TO MAKE 300 YEN*.
MURMUR
I JUST CAN'T STOP SMILING ABOUT IT!
MURMUR
!

*ABOUT $3

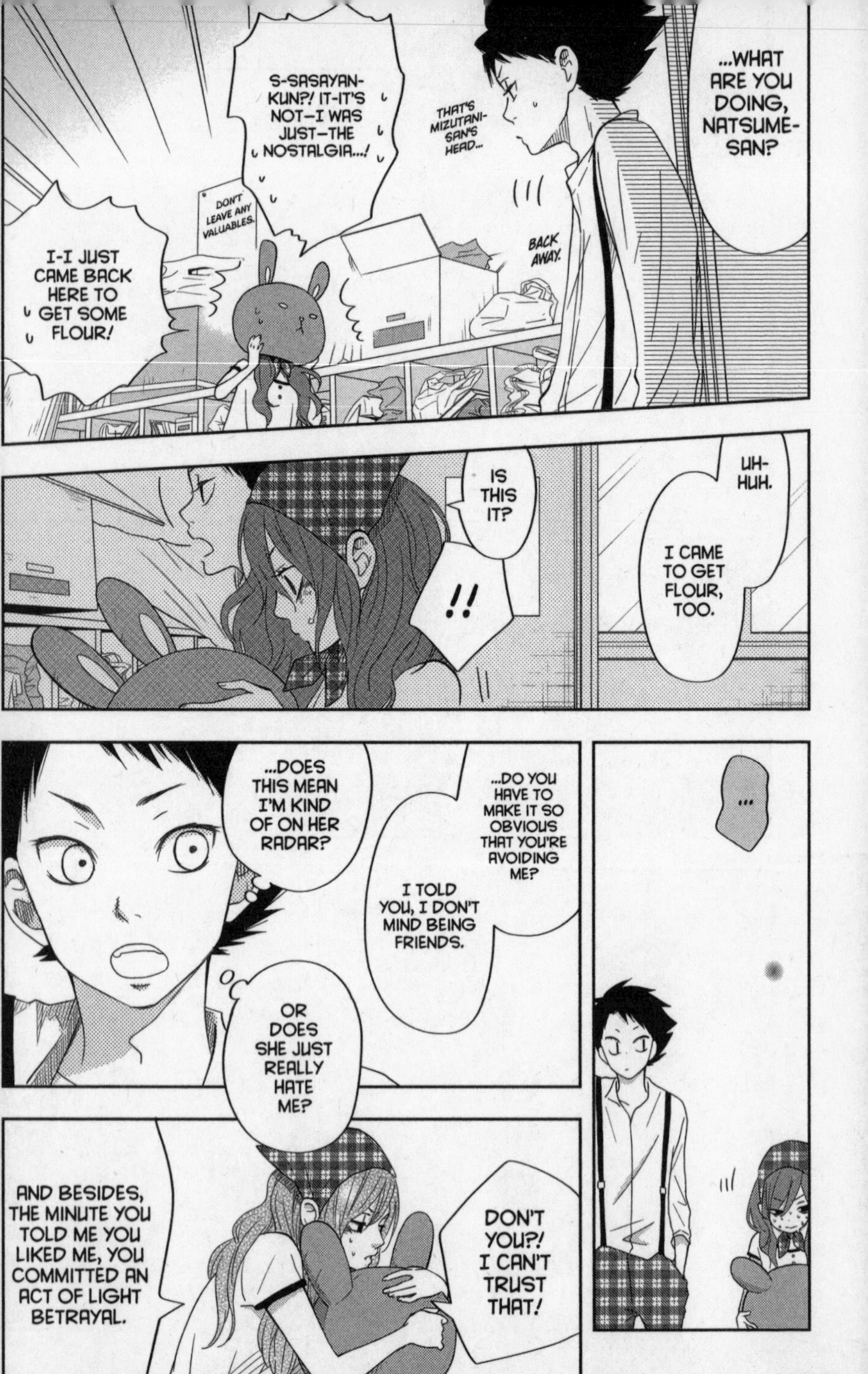
...WHAT ARE YOU DOING, NATSUME-SAN?
THAT'S MIZUTANI-SAN'S HEAD...
BACK AWAY.
S-SASAYAN-KUN?! IT-IT'S NOT—I WAS JUST—THE NOSTALGIA...!
DON'T LEAVE ANY VALUABLES.
I-I JUST CAME BACK HERE TO GET SOME FLOUR!
UH-HUH.
I CAME TO GET FLOUR, TOO.
IS THIS IT?
!!
...
...DO YOU HAVE TO MAKE IT SO OBVIOUS THAT YOU'RE AVOIDING ME?
I TOLD YOU, I DON'T MIND BEING FRIENDS.
...DOES THIS MEAN I'M KIND OF ON HER RADAR?
OR DOES SHE JUST REALLY HATE ME?
DON'T YOU?! I CAN'T TRUST THAT!
AND BESIDES, THE MINUTE YOU TOLD ME YOU LIKED ME, YOU COMMITTED AN ACT OF LIGHT BETRAYAL.

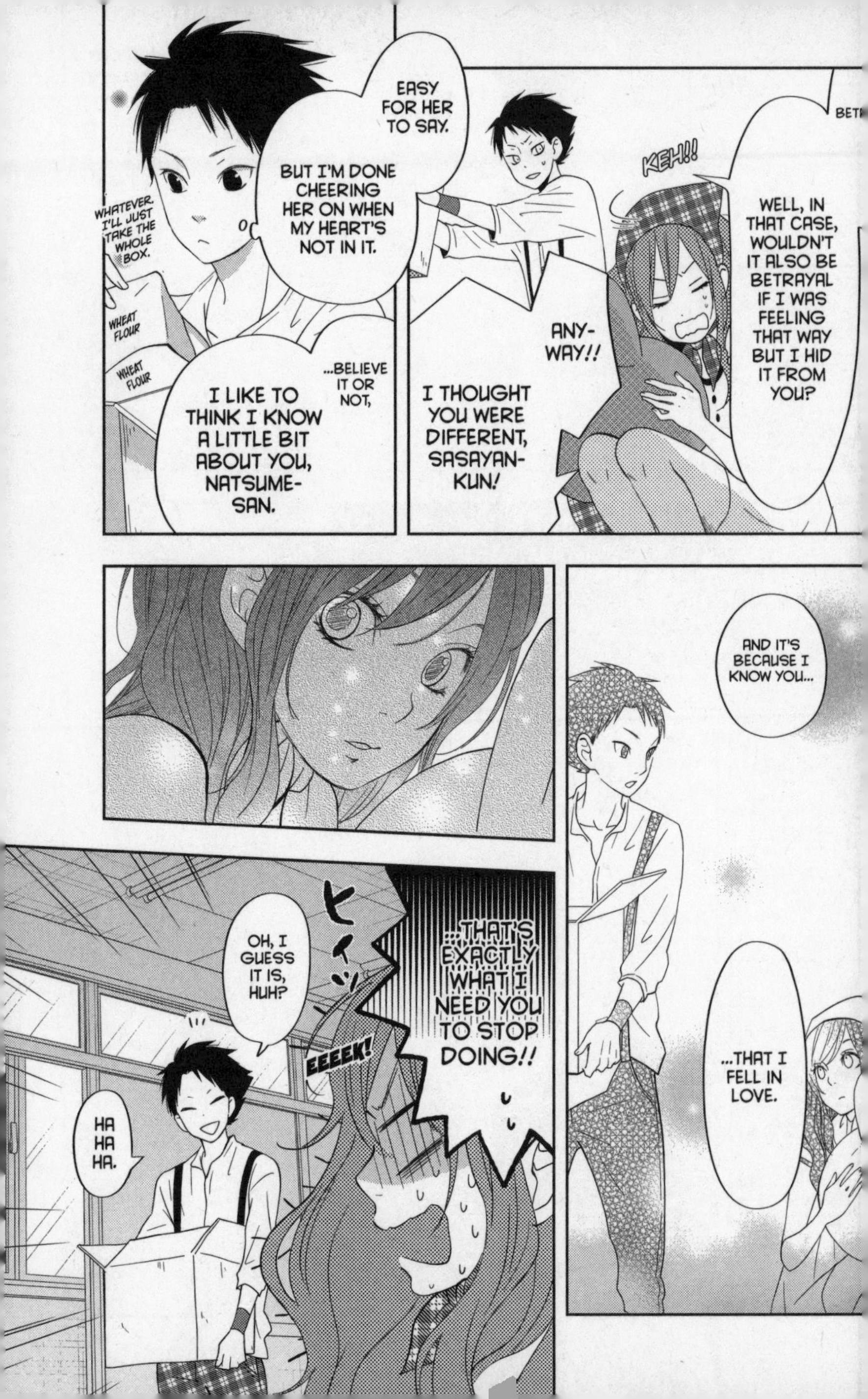
BETR
KEH!!
WELL, IN THAT CASE, WOULDN'T IT ALSO BE BETRAYAL IF I WAS FEELING THAT WAY BUT I HID IT FROM YOU?
ANY-WAY!!
I THOUGHT YOU WERE DIFFERENT, SASAYAN-KUN!
EASY FOR HER TO SAY.
BUT I'M DONE CHEERING HER ON WHEN MY HEART'S NOT IN IT.
WHATEVER. I'LL JUST TAKE THE WHOLE BOX.
WHEAT FLOUR
WHEAT FLOUR
...BELIEVE IT OR NOT,
I LIKE TO THINK I KNOW A LITTLE BIT ABOUT YOU, NATSUME-SAN.
AND IT'S BECAUSE I KNOW YOU...
...THAT I FELL IN LOVE.
...THAT'S EXACTLY WHAT I NEED YOU TO STOP DOING!!
ヒィッ
EEEEK!
OH, I GUESS IT IS, HUH?
HA HA HA.

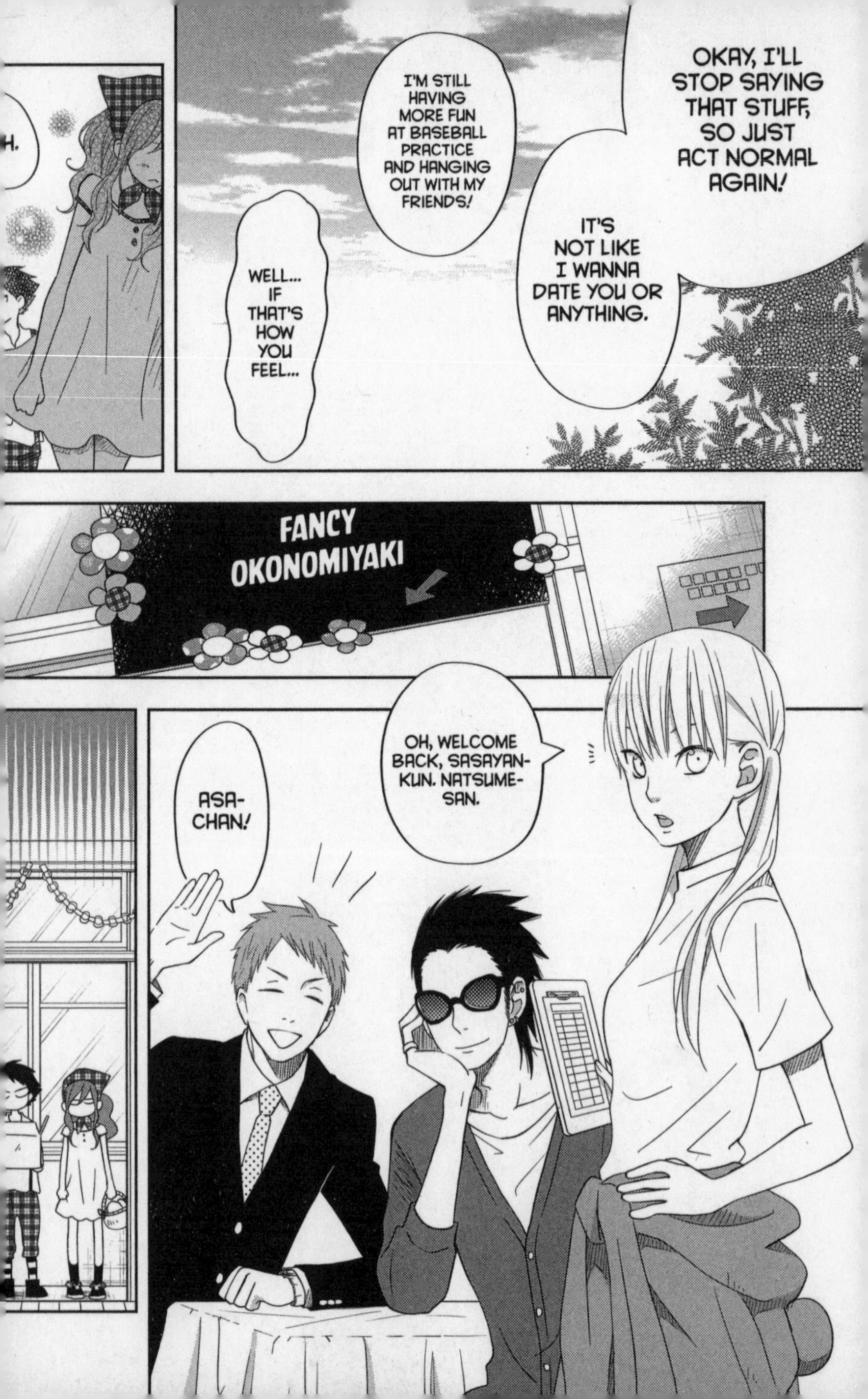
OKAY, I'LL STOP SAYING THAT STUFF, SO JUST ACT NORMAL AGAIN!
IT'S NOT LIKE I WANNA DATE YOU OR ANYTHING.
I'M STILL HAVING MORE FUN AT BASEBALL PRACTICE AND HANGING OUT WITH MY FRIENDS!
WELL... IF THAT'S HOW YOU FEEL...
FANCY OKONOMIYAKI
OH, WELCOME BACK, SASAYAN-KUN. NATSUME-SAN.
ASA-CHAN!

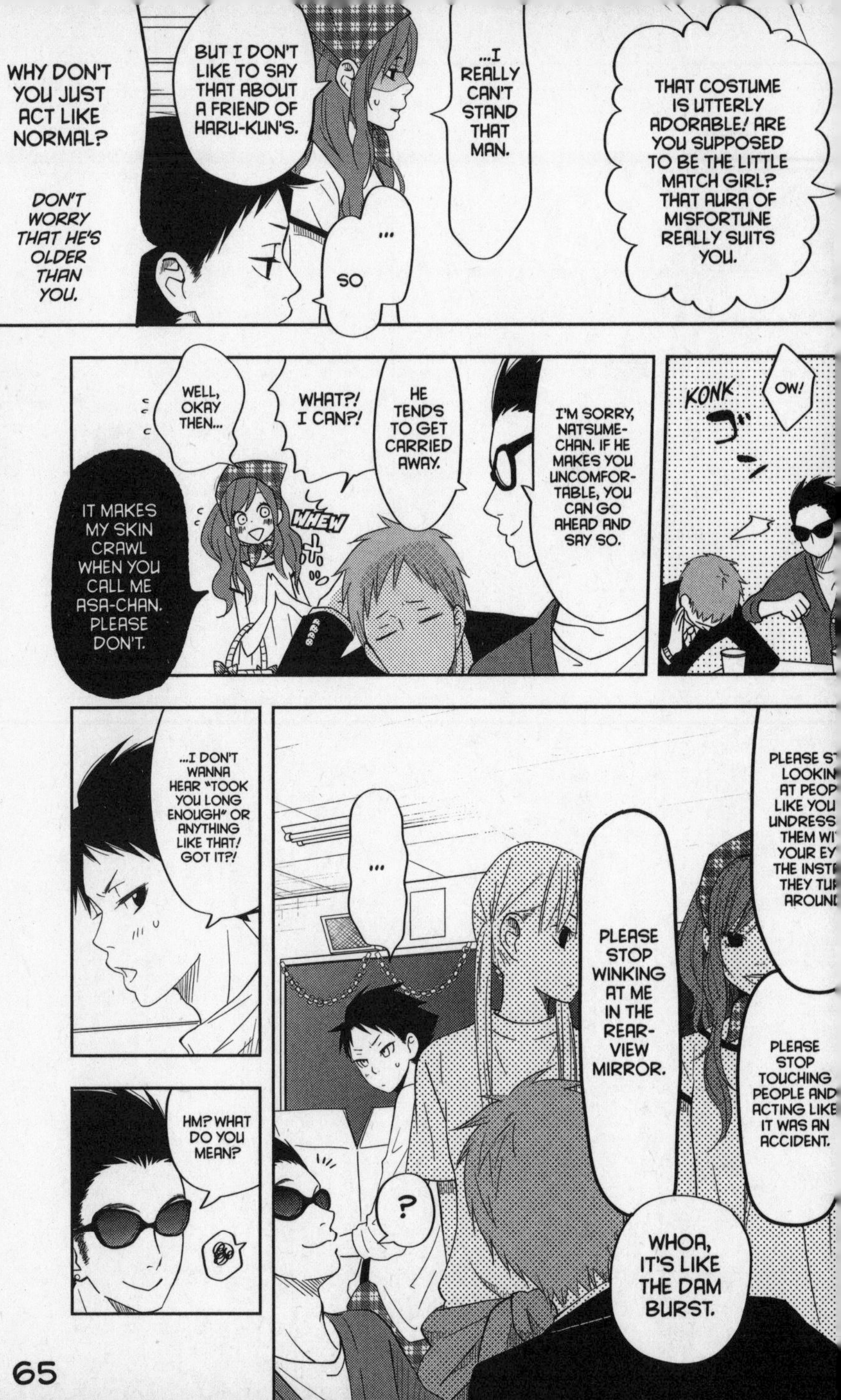

THAT COSTUME IS UTTERLY ADORABLE! ARE YOU SUPPOSED TO BE THE LITTLE MATCH GIRL? THAT AURA OF MISFORTUNE REALLY SUITS YOU.
...I REALLY CAN'T STAND THAT MAN.
BUT I DON'T LIKE TO SAY THAT ABOUT A FRIEND OF HARU-KUN'S.
... SO
WHY DON'T YOU JUST ACT LIKE NORMAL?
DON'T WORRY THAT HE'S OLDER THAN YOU.
KONK
OW!
I'M SORRY, NATSUME-CHAN. IF HE MAKES YOU UNCOMFOR-TABLE, YOU CAN GO AHEAD AND SAY SO.
HE TENDS TO GET CARRIED AWAY.
WHAT?! I CAN?!
WHEW
WELL, OKAY THEN...
IT MAKES MY SKIN CRAWL WHEN YOU CALL ME ASA-CHAN. PLEASE DON'T.
PLEASE ST LOOKIN AT PEOP LIKE YOU UNDRESS THEM WI YOUR EY THE INST THEY TU AROUND
PLEASE STOP TOUCHING PEOPLE AND ACTING LIKE IT WAS AN ACCIDENT.
PLEASE STOP WINKING AT ME IN THE REAR-VIEW MIRROR.
...
?
WHOA, IT'S LIKE THE DAM BURST.
...I DON'T WANNA HEAR "TOOK YOU LONG ENOUGH" OR ANYTHING LIKE THAT! GOT IT?!
HM? WHAT DO YOU MEAN?

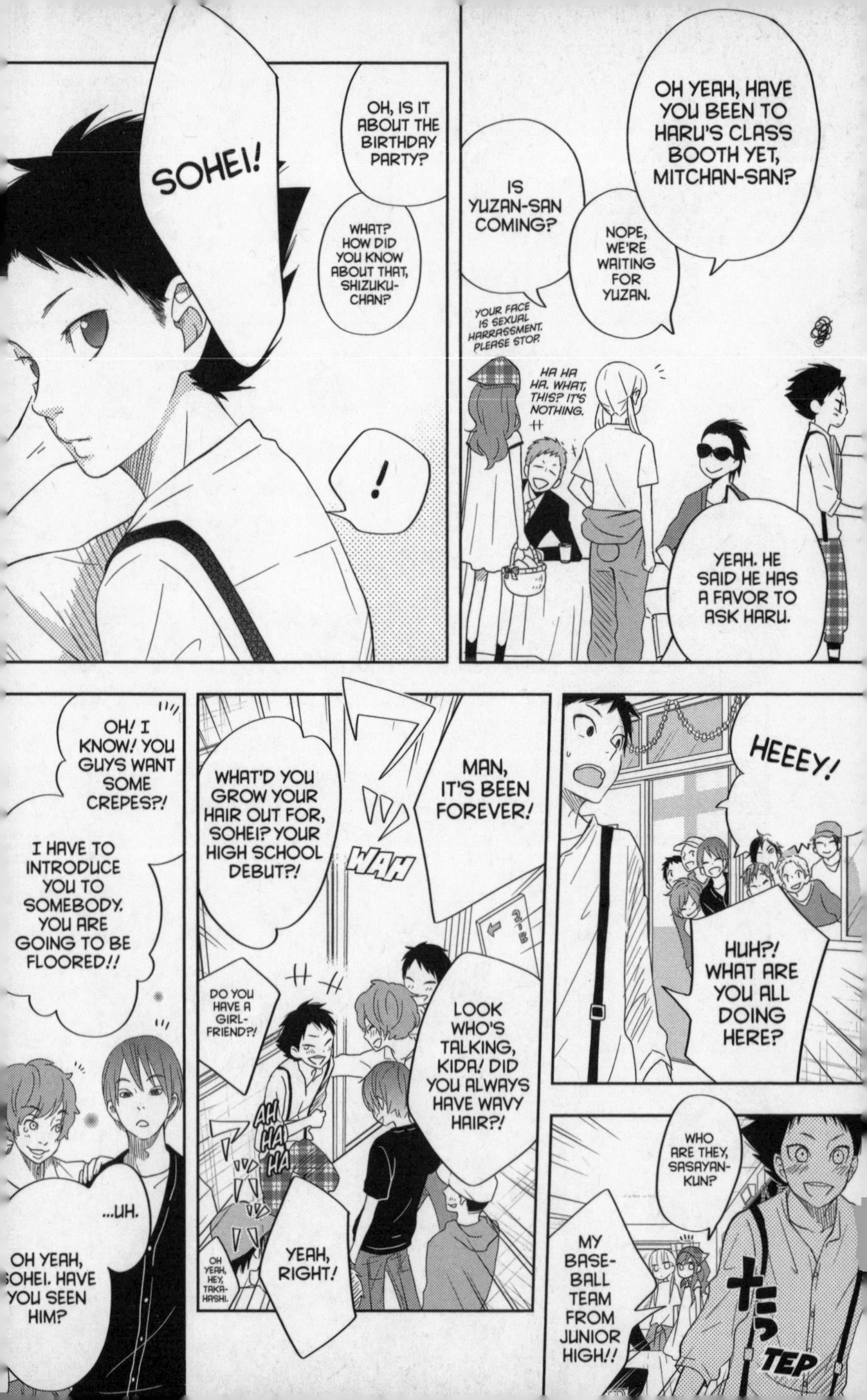
OH YEAH, HAVE YOU BEEN TO HARU'S CLASS BOOTH YET, MITCHAN-SAN?
NOPE, WE'RE WAITING FOR YUZAN.
IS YUZAN-SAN COMING?
YOUR FACE IS SEXUAL HARRASSMENT. PLEASE STOP.
HA HA HA. WHAT, THIS? IT'S NOTHING.
YEAH. HE SAID HE HAS A FAVOR TO ASK HARU.
OH, IS IT ABOUT THE BIRTHDAY PARTY?
WHAT? HOW DID YOU KNOW ABOUT THAT, SHIZUKU-CHAN?
!
SOHEI!
HEEEY!
HUH?! WHAT ARE YOU ALL DOING HERE?
WHO ARE THEY, SASAYAN-KUN?
MY BASEBALL TEAM FROM JUNIOR HIGH!!
TEP
MAN, IT'S BEEN FOREVER!
WHAT'D YOU GROW YOUR HAIR OUT FOR, SOHEI? YOUR HIGH SCHOOL DEBUT?!
WAH
LOOK WHO'S TALKING, KIDA! DID YOU ALWAYS HAVE WAVY HAIR?!
DO YOU HAVE A GIRLFRIEND?!
AH HA HA
YEAH, RIGHT!
OH YEAH, HEY, TAKAHASHI.
OH! I KNOW! YOU GUYS WANT SOME CREPES?!
I HAVE TO INTRODUCE YOU TO SOMEBODY. YOU ARE GOING TO BE FLOORED!!
...UH.
OH YEAH, SOHEI. HAVE YOU SEEN HIM?

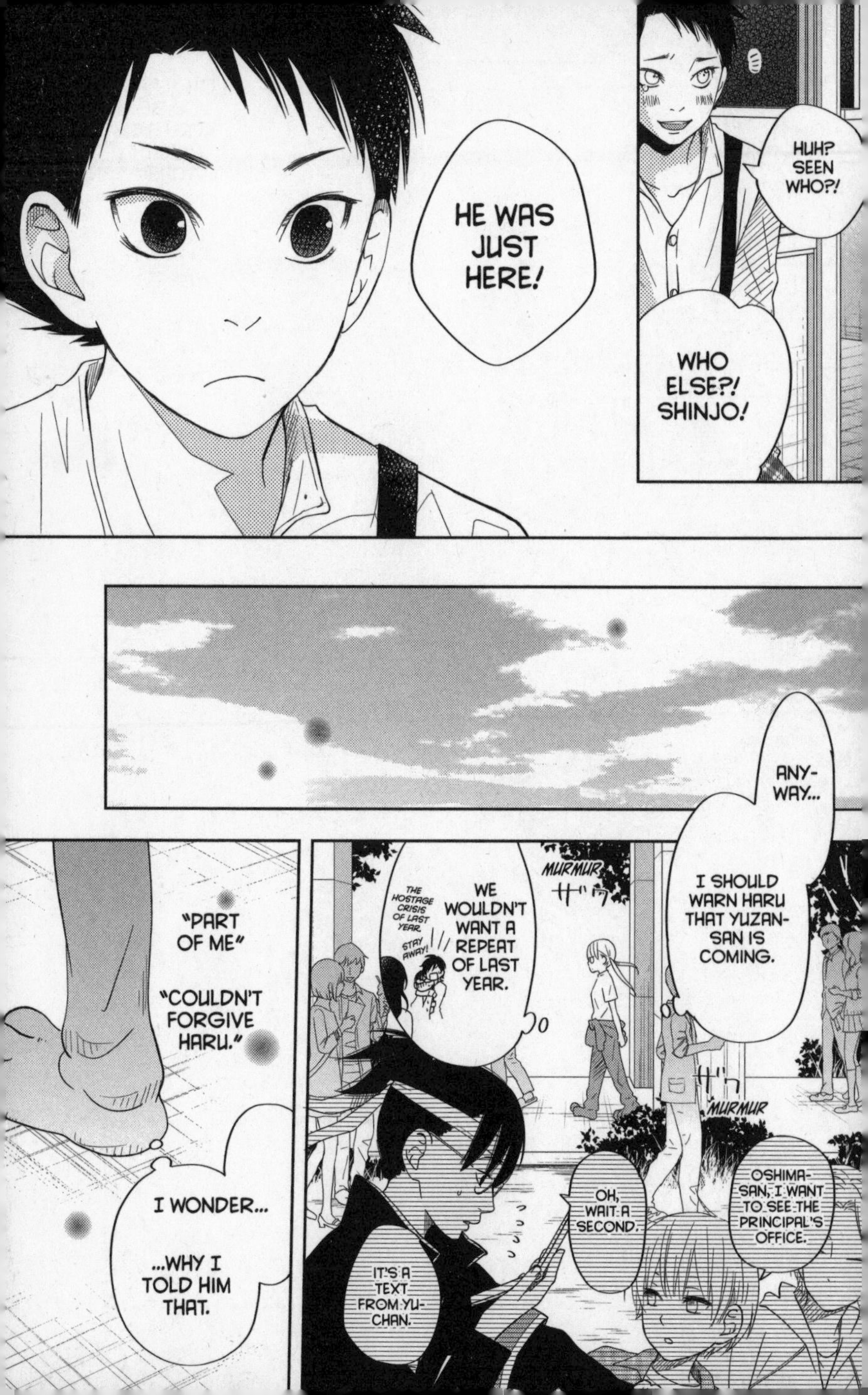
HUH? SEEN WHO?!
WHO ELSE?! SHINJO!
HE WAS JUST HERE!
ANY-WAY...
I SHOULD WARN HARU THAT YUZAN-SAN IS COMING.
MURMUR
ザワ
WE WOULDN'T WANT A REPEAT OF LAST YEAR.
THE HOSTAGE CRISIS OF LAST YEAR.
STAY AWAY!
ザワ
MURMUR
OSHIMA-SAN, I WANT TO SEE THE PRINCIPAL'S OFFICE.
OH, WAIT A SECOND.
IT'S A TEXT FROM YU-CHAN.
"PART OF ME"
"COULDN'T FORGIVE HARU."
I WONDER...
...WHY I TOLD HIM THAT.

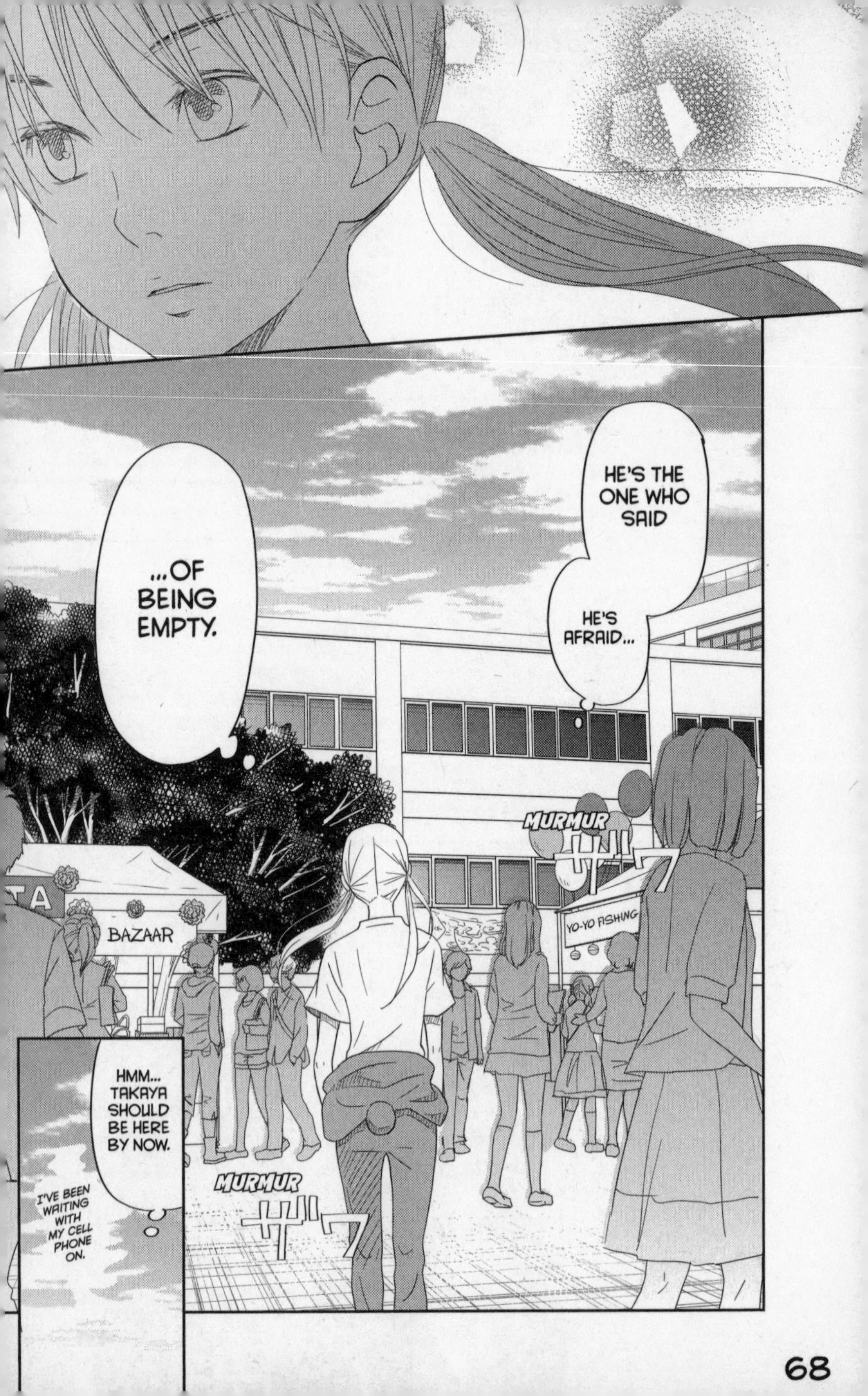
HE'S THE ONE WHO SAID
HE'S AFRAID...
...OF BEING EMPTY.
MURMUR ザワ
YO-YO FISHING
BAZAAR
MURMUR ザワ
HMM... TAKAYA SHOULD BE HERE BY NOW.
I'VE BEEN WAITING WITH MY CELL PHONE ON.

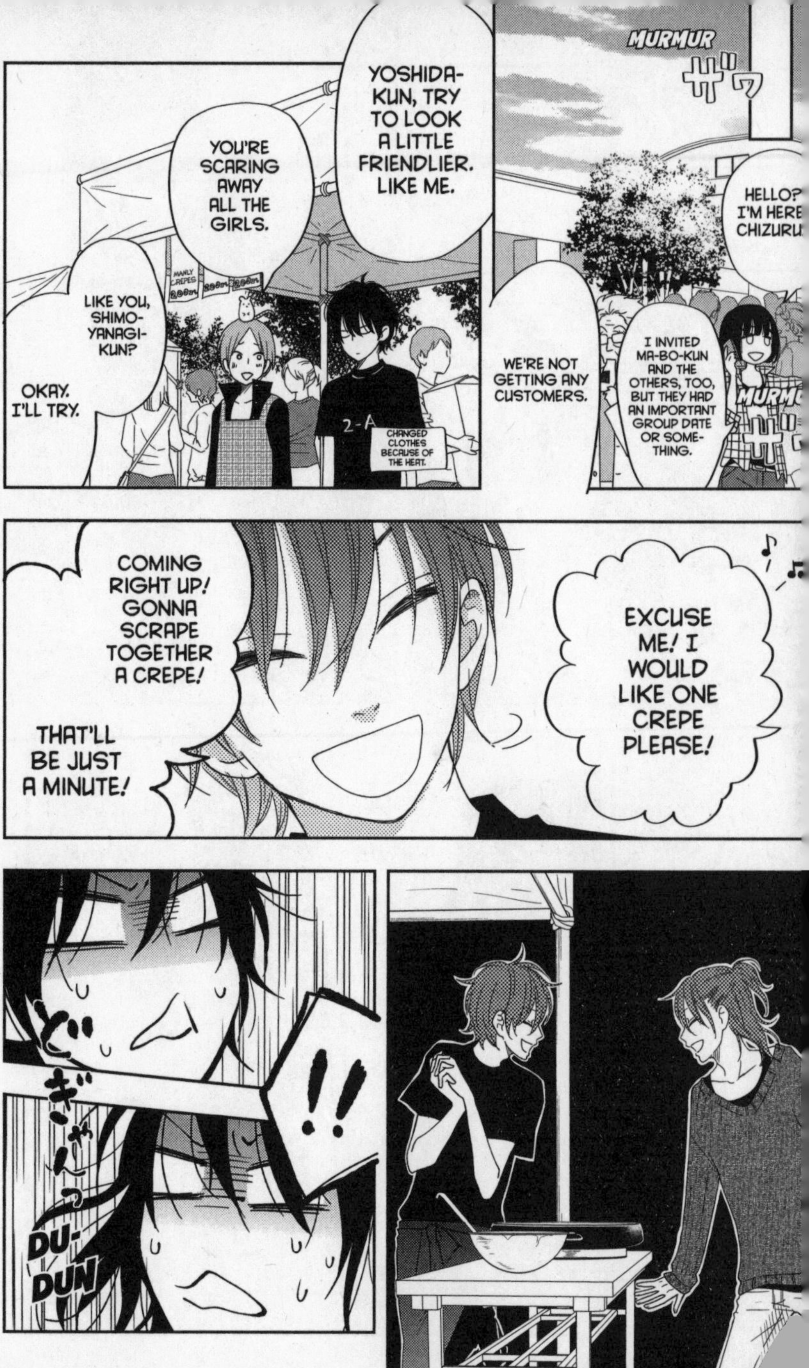
MURMUR
ザワ
HELLO? I'M HERE CHIZURU
I INVITED MA-BO-KUN AND THE OTHERS, TOO, BUT THEY HAD AN IMPORTANT GROUP DATE OR SOME-THING.
MURMUR
WE'RE NOT GETTING ANY CUSTOMERS.
YOSHIDA-KUN, TRY TO LOOK A LITTLE FRIENDLIER. LIKE ME.
YOU'RE SCARING AWAY ALL THE GIRLS.
LIKE YOU, SHIMO-YANAGI-KUN?
OKAY. I'LL TRY.
MANLY CREPES
2-A
CHANGED CLOTHES BECAUSE OF THE HEAT.
EXCUSE ME! I WOULD LIKE ONE CREPE PLEASE!
COMING RIGHT UP! GONNA SCRAPE TOGETHER A CREPE!
THAT'LL BE JUST A MINUTE!
!!
DU-DUN

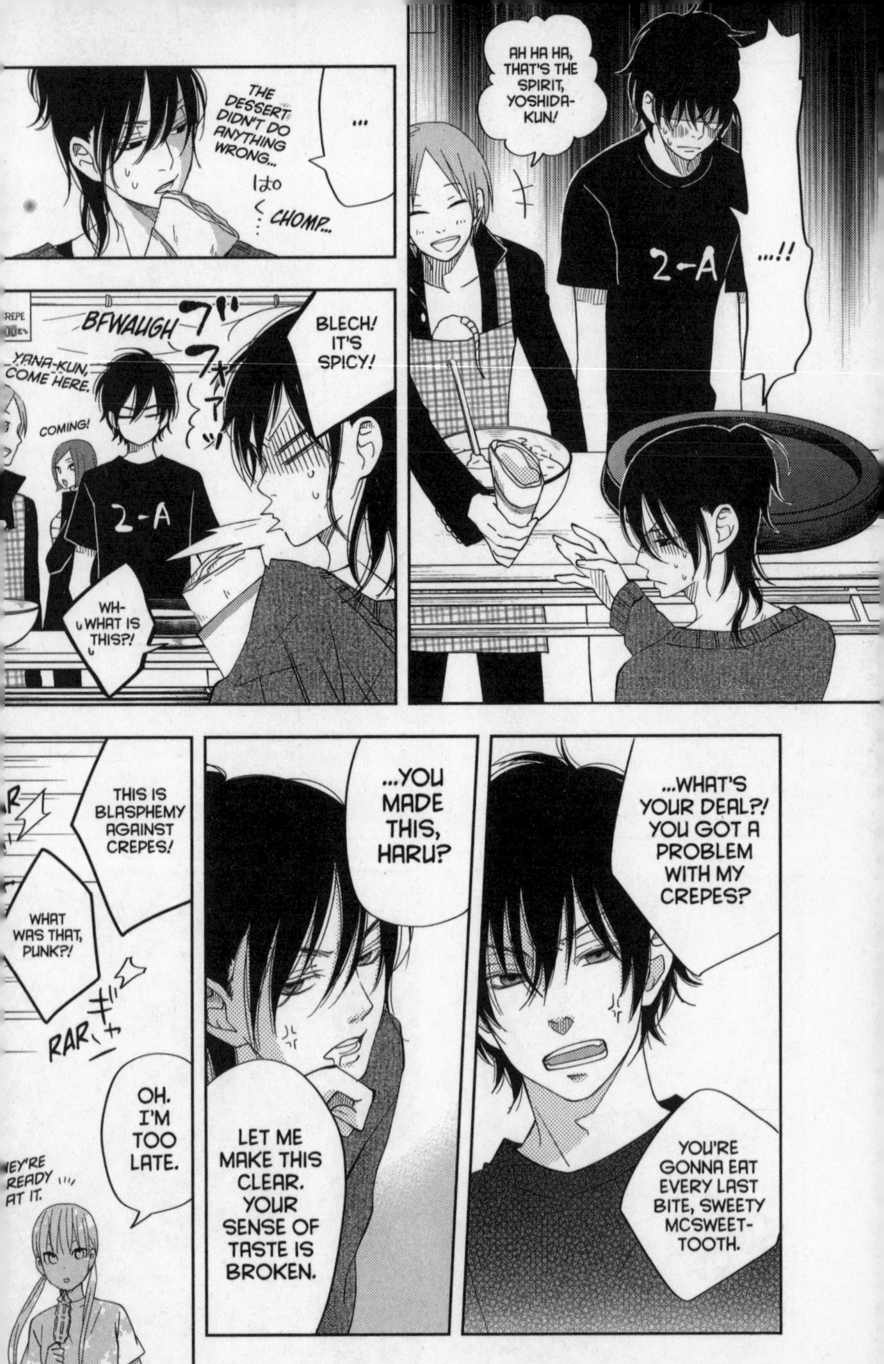
AH HA HA, THAT'S THE SPIRIT, YOSHIDA-KUN!
...!!
...
THE DESSERT DIDN'T DO ANYTHING WRONG...
CHOMP...
BLECH! IT'S SPICY!
BFWAUGH
YANA-KUN, COME HERE.
COMING!
WH-WHAT IS THIS?!
...WHAT'S YOUR DEAL?! YOU GOT A PROBLEM WITH MY CREPES?
YOU'RE GONNA EAT EVERY LAST BITE, SWEETY MCSWEET-TOOTH.
...YOU MADE THIS, HARU?
LET ME MAKE THIS CLEAR. YOUR SENSE OF TASTE IS BROKEN.
THIS IS BLASPHEMY AGAINST CREPES!
WHAT WAS THAT, PUNK?!
RAR
OH. I'M TOO LATE.

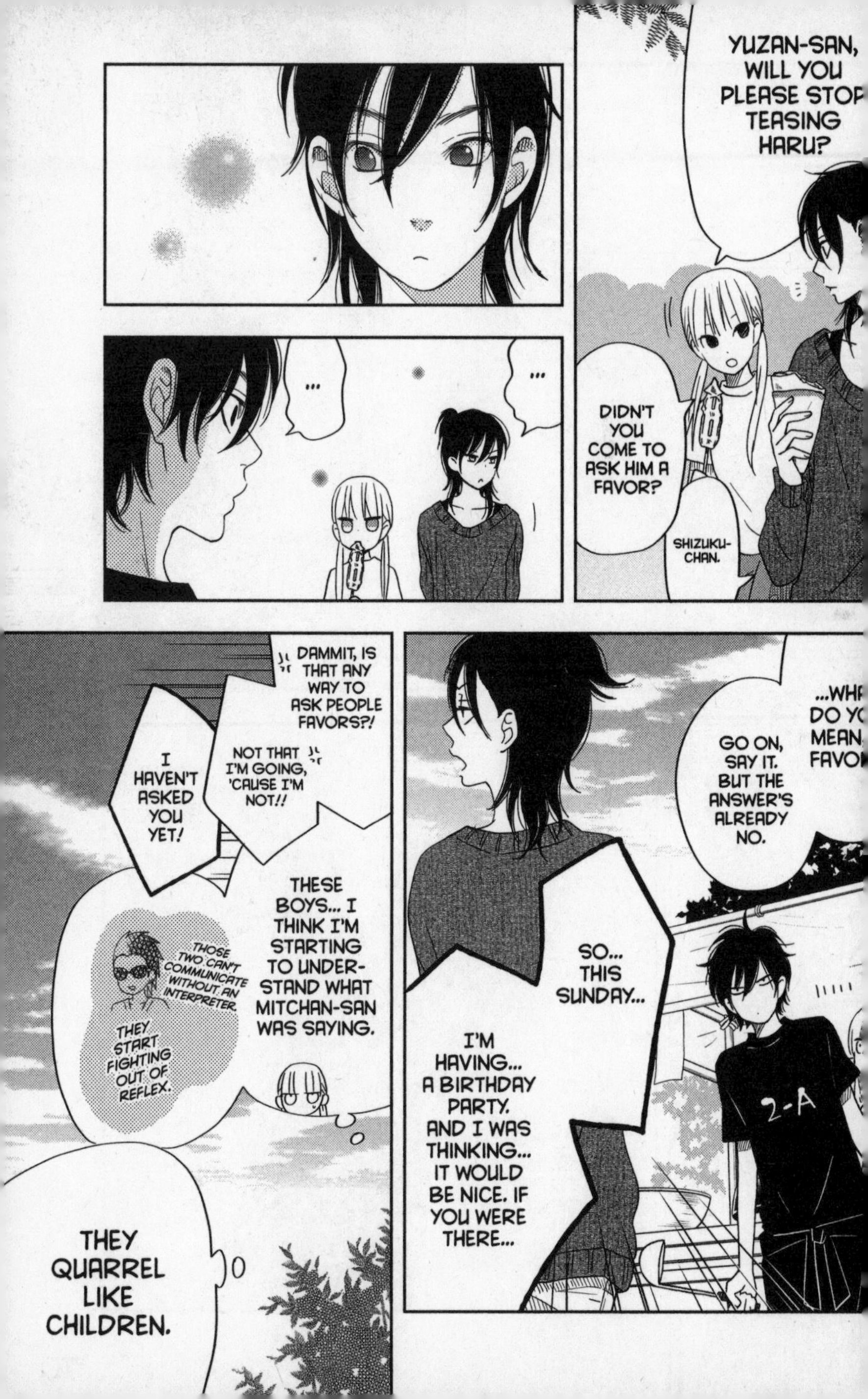
YUZAN-SAN, WILL YOU PLEASE STOP TEASING HARU?
DIDN'T YOU COME TO ASK HIM A FAVOR?
SHIZUKU-CHAN.
...
...
...WHA DO YO MEAN, FAVO
GO ON, SAY IT. BUT THE ANSWER'S ALREADY NO.
SO... THIS SUNDAY...
I'M HAVING... A BIRTHDAY PARTY. AND I WAS THINKING... IT WOULD BE NICE. IF YOU WERE THERE...
DAMMIT, IS THAT ANY WAY TO ASK PEOPLE FAVORS?!
NOT THAT I'M GOING, 'CAUSE I'M NOT!!
I HAVEN'T ASKED YOU YET!
THESE BOYS... I THINK I'M STARTING TO UNDERSTAND WHAT MITCHAN-SAN WAS SAYING.
THOSE TWO CAN'T COMMUNICATE WITHOUT AN INTERPRETER.
THEY START FIGHTING OUT OF REFLEX.
THEY QUARREL LIKE CHILDREN.

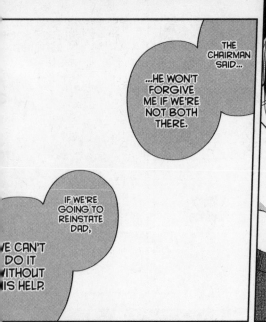

THE CHAIRMAN SAID...

...HE WON'T FORGIVE ME IF WE'RE NOT BOTH THERE.

IF WE'RE GOING TO REINSTATE DAD,

WE CAN'T DO IT WITHOUT HIS HELP.

I KNOW IT'S SELFISH OF ME.

AND I PROMISE I WILL NEVER BOTHER YOU AGAIN AFTER THIS.

SO PLEASE, COME TO THE PARTY.

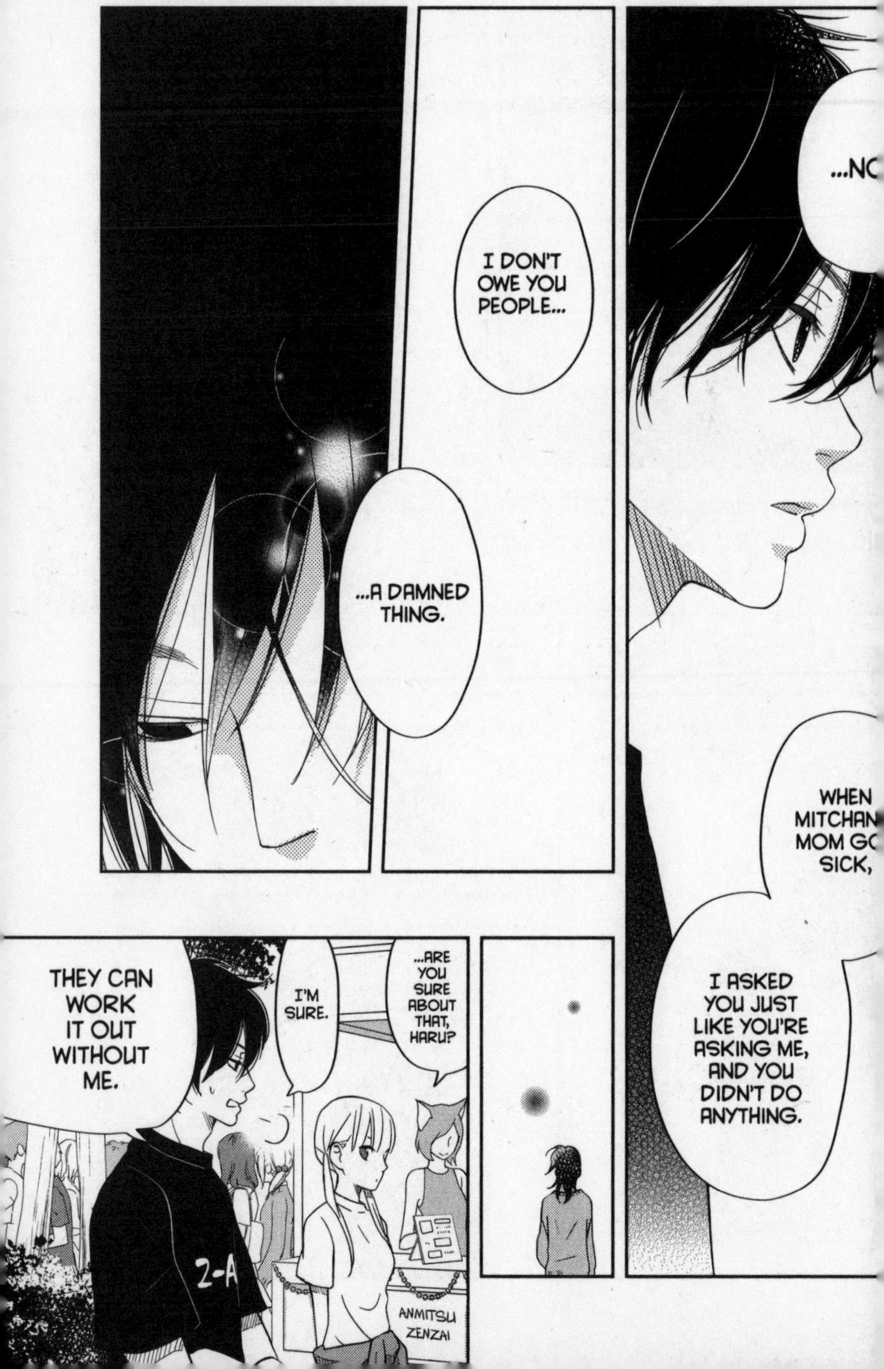
...NC
WHEN MITCHAN MOM GC SICK,
I ASKED YOU JUST LIKE YOU'RE ASKING ME, AND YOU DIDN'T DO ANYTHING.
I DON'T OWE YOU PEOPLE...
...A DAMNED THING.
...ARE YOU SURE ABOUT THAT, HARU?
I'M SURE.
THEY CAN WORK IT OUT WITHOUT ME.
2-A
ANMITSU ZENZAI

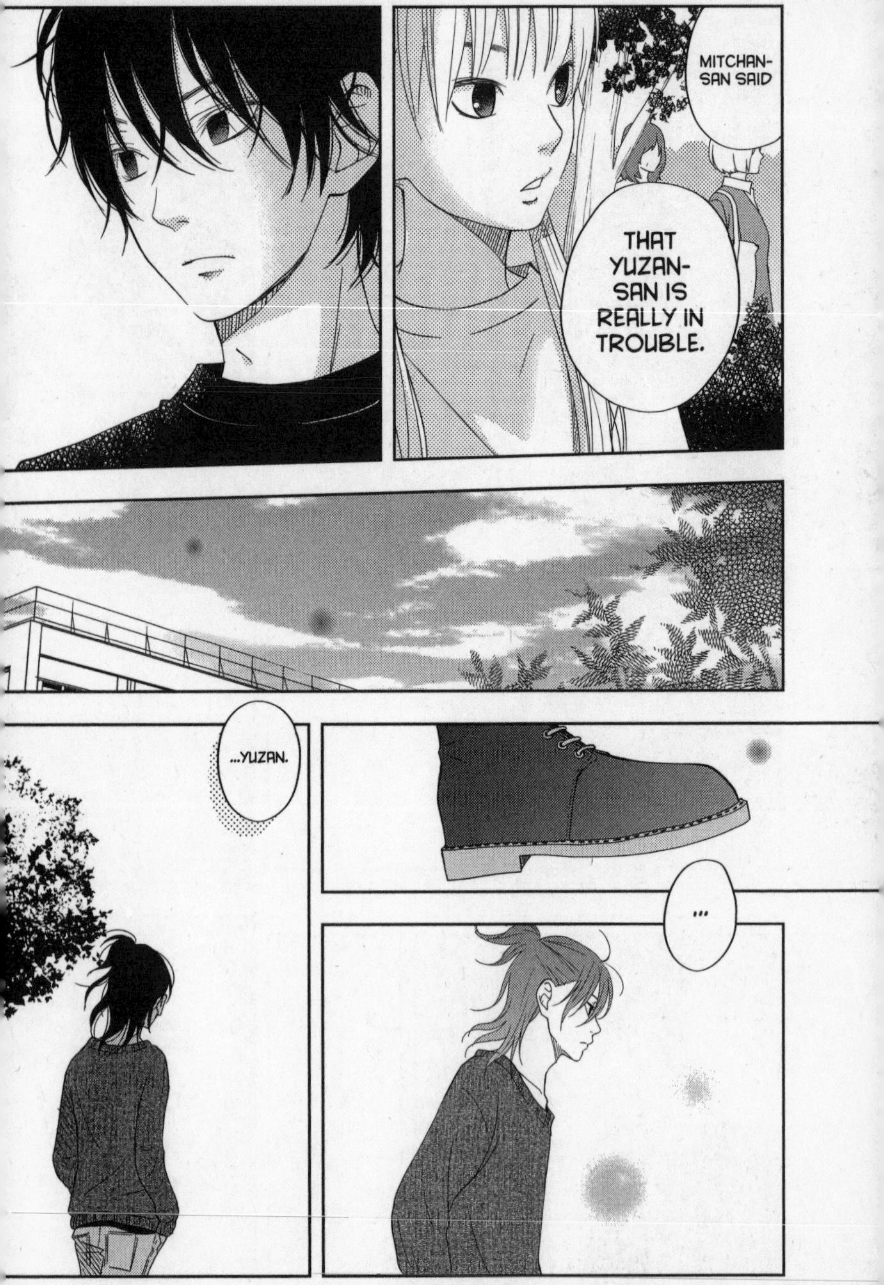
MITCHAN-SAN SAID
THAT YUZAN-SAN IS REALLY IN TROUBLE.
...
...YUZAN.

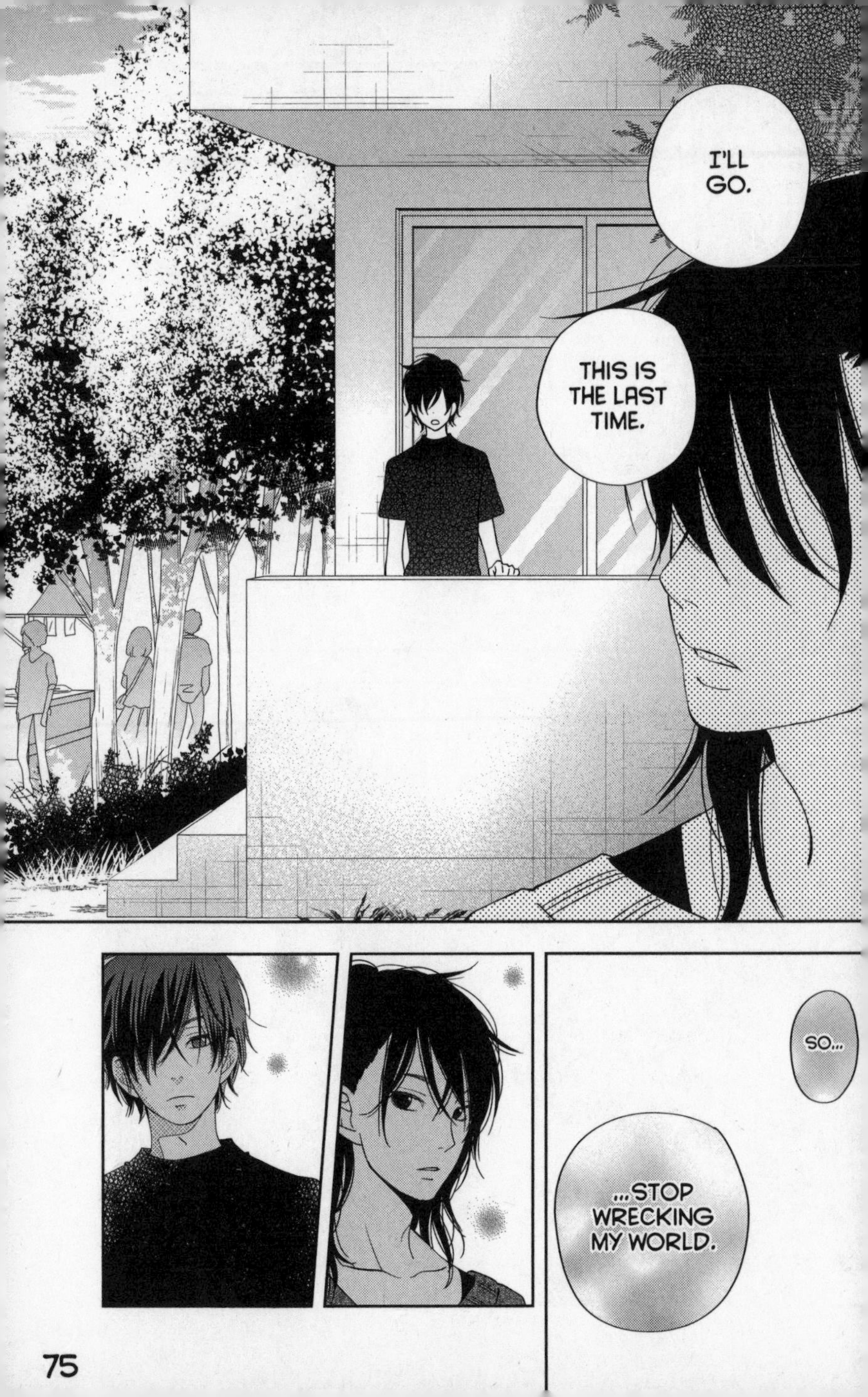
I'LL GO.
THIS IS THE LAST TIME.
SO...
...STOP WRECKING MY WORLD.

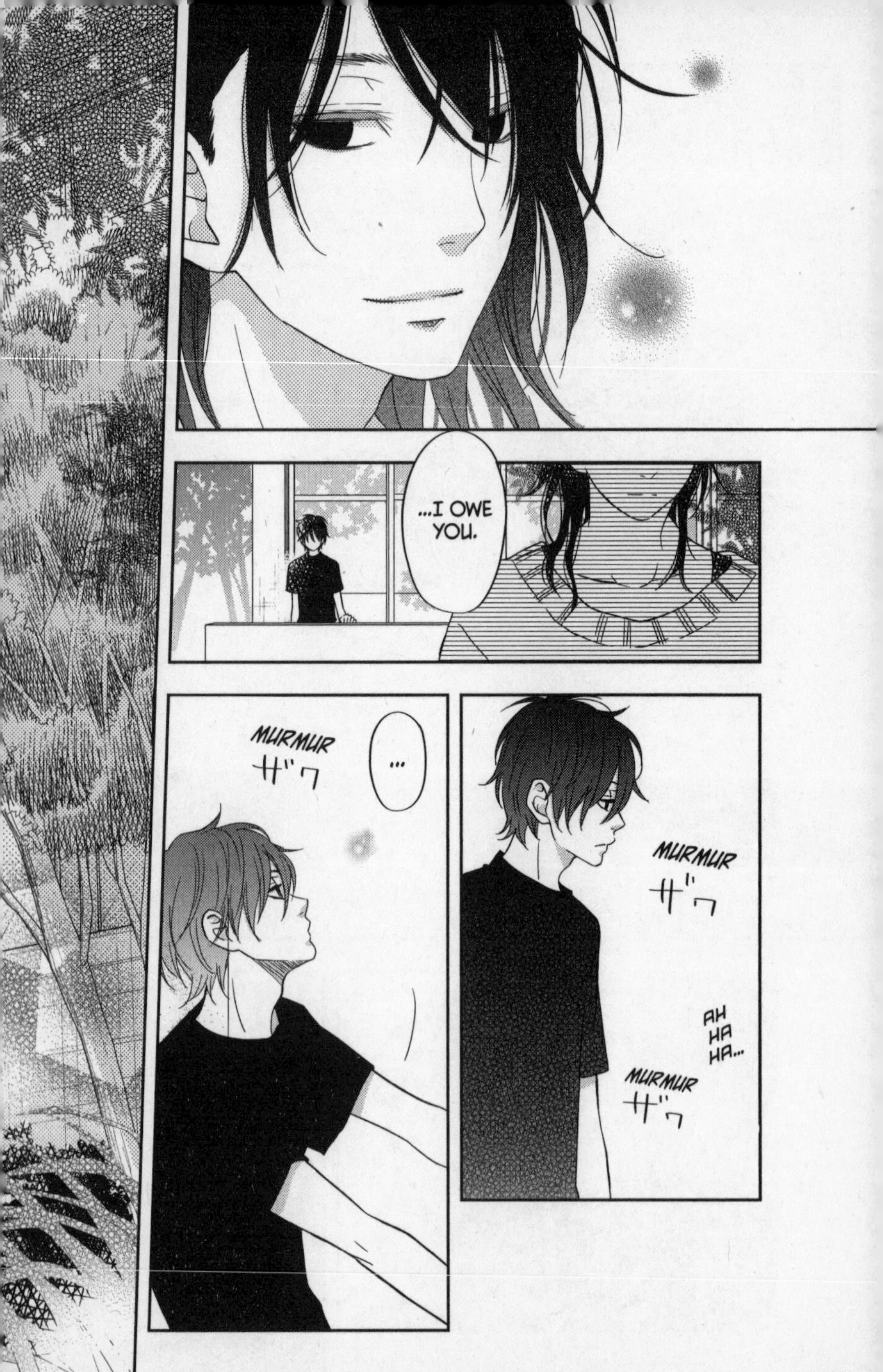
...I OWE YOU.
MURMUR ザワ
AH HA HA...
MURMUR ザワ
...
MURMUR ザワ

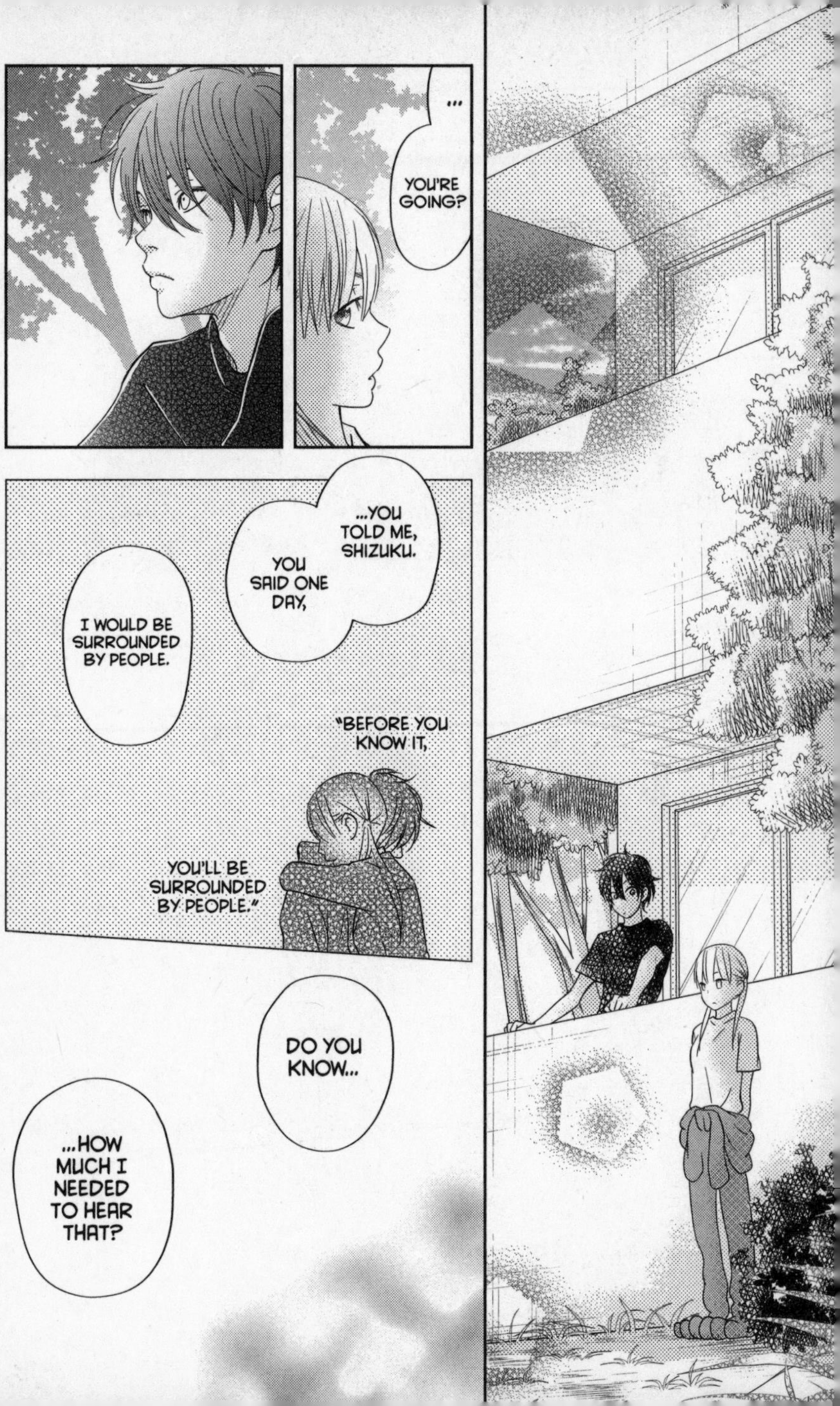
...
YOU'RE GOING?
...YOU TOLD ME, SHIZUKU.
YOU SAID ONE DAY,
I WOULD BE SURROUNDED BY PEOPLE.
"BEFORE YOU KNOW IT,
YOU'LL BE SURROUNDED BY PEOPLE."
DO YOU KNOW...
...HOW MUCH I NEEDED TO HEAR THAT?

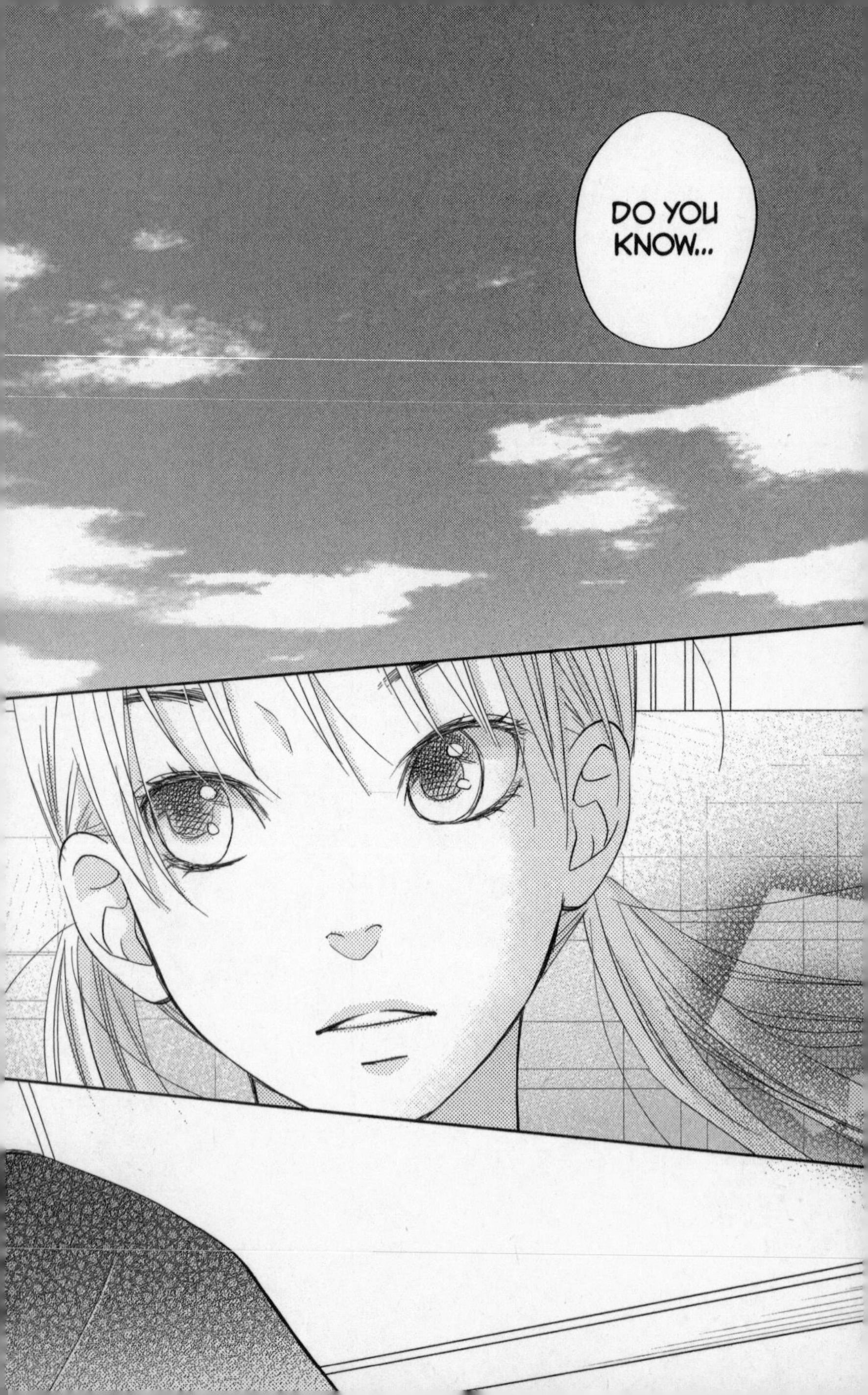
DO YOU KNOW...

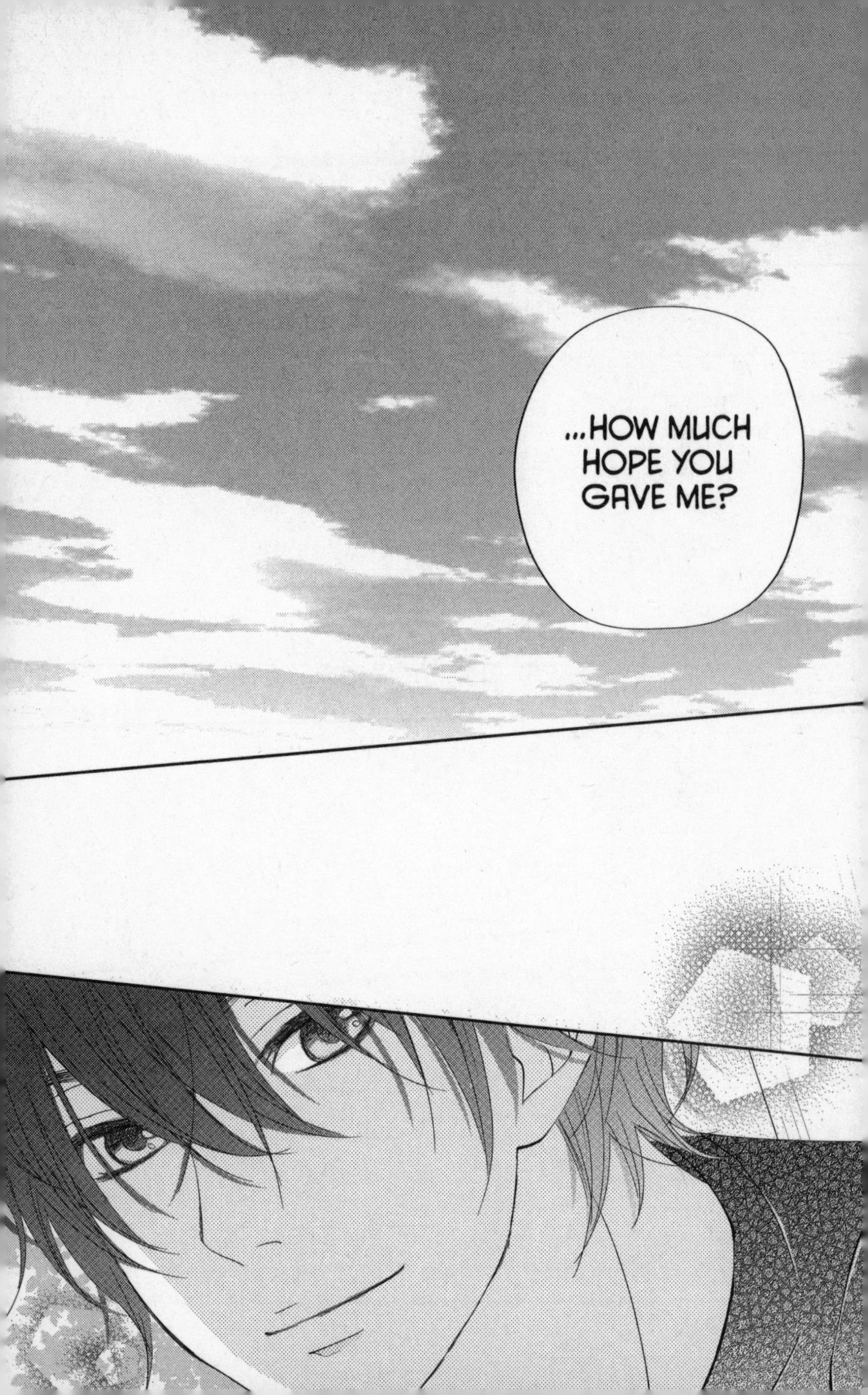
...HOW MUCH HOPE YOU GAVE ME?

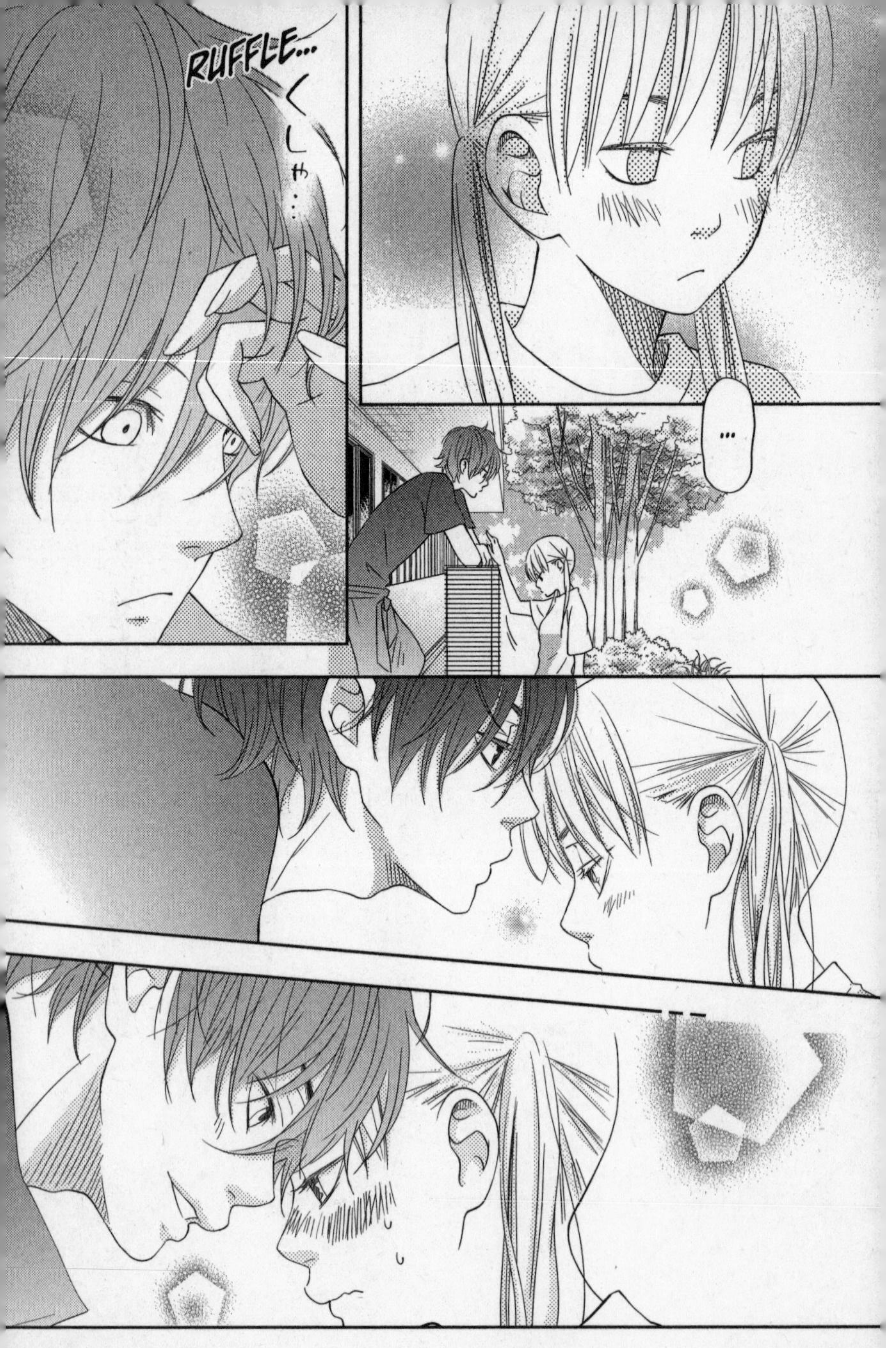

...
RUFFLE...
くしゃ…

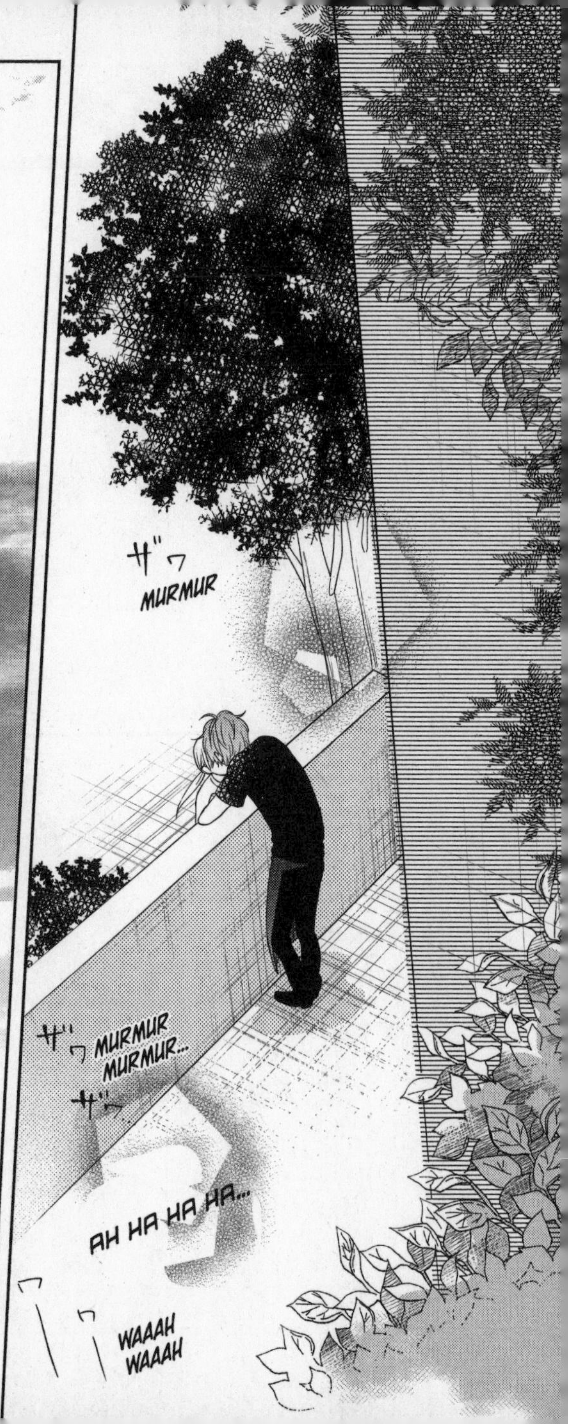
ザワ
MURMUR
ザワ
MURMUR
MURMUR...
ザワ
AH HA HA HA...
ワー
ワー
WAAAH
WAAAH
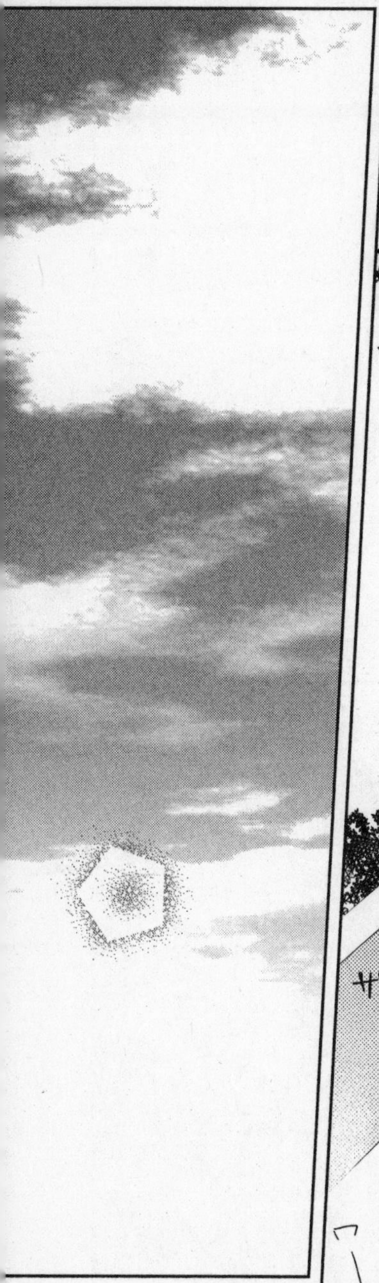

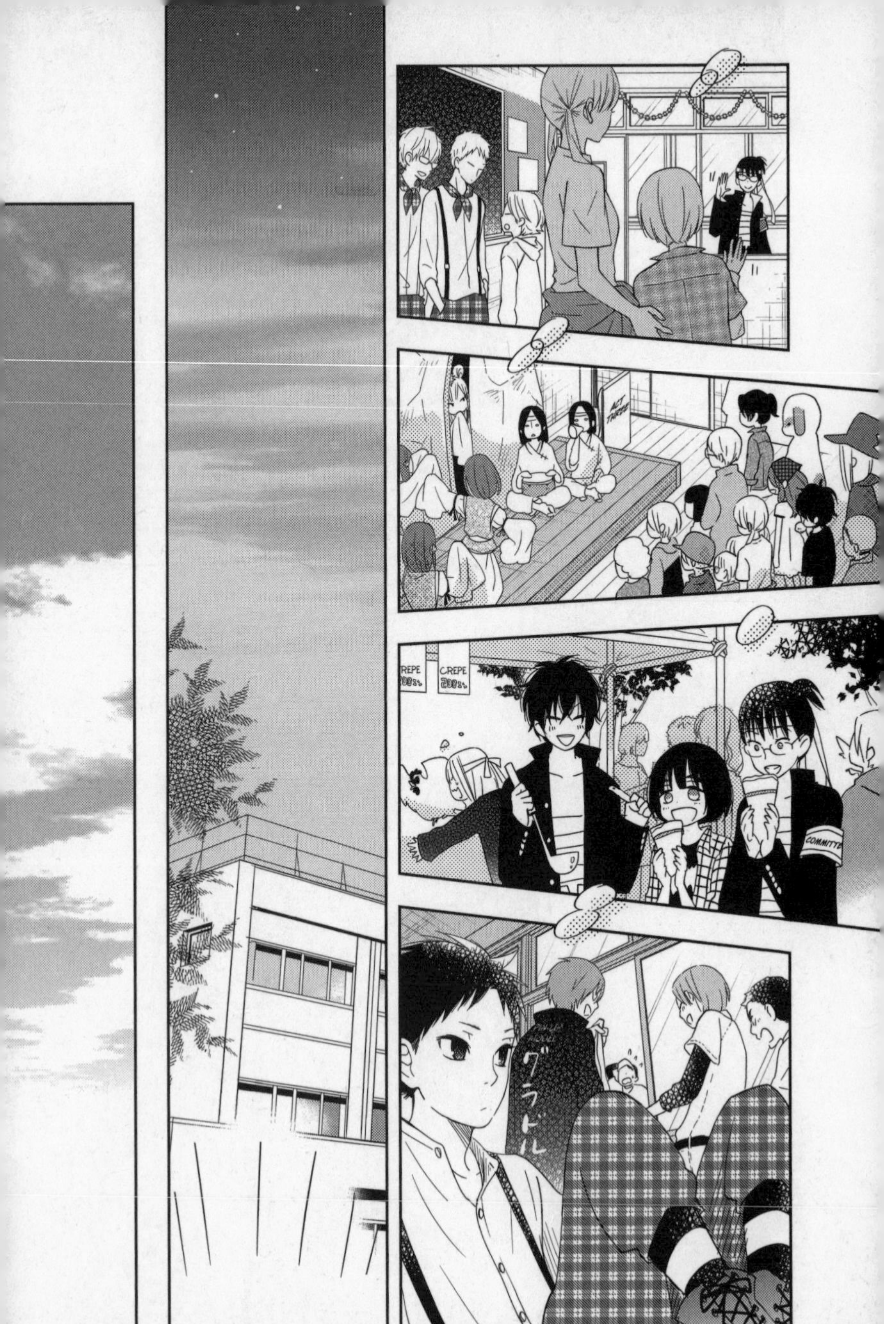
ACT THREE
CREPE 200円
REPE 200円
COMMITTE
グラドル

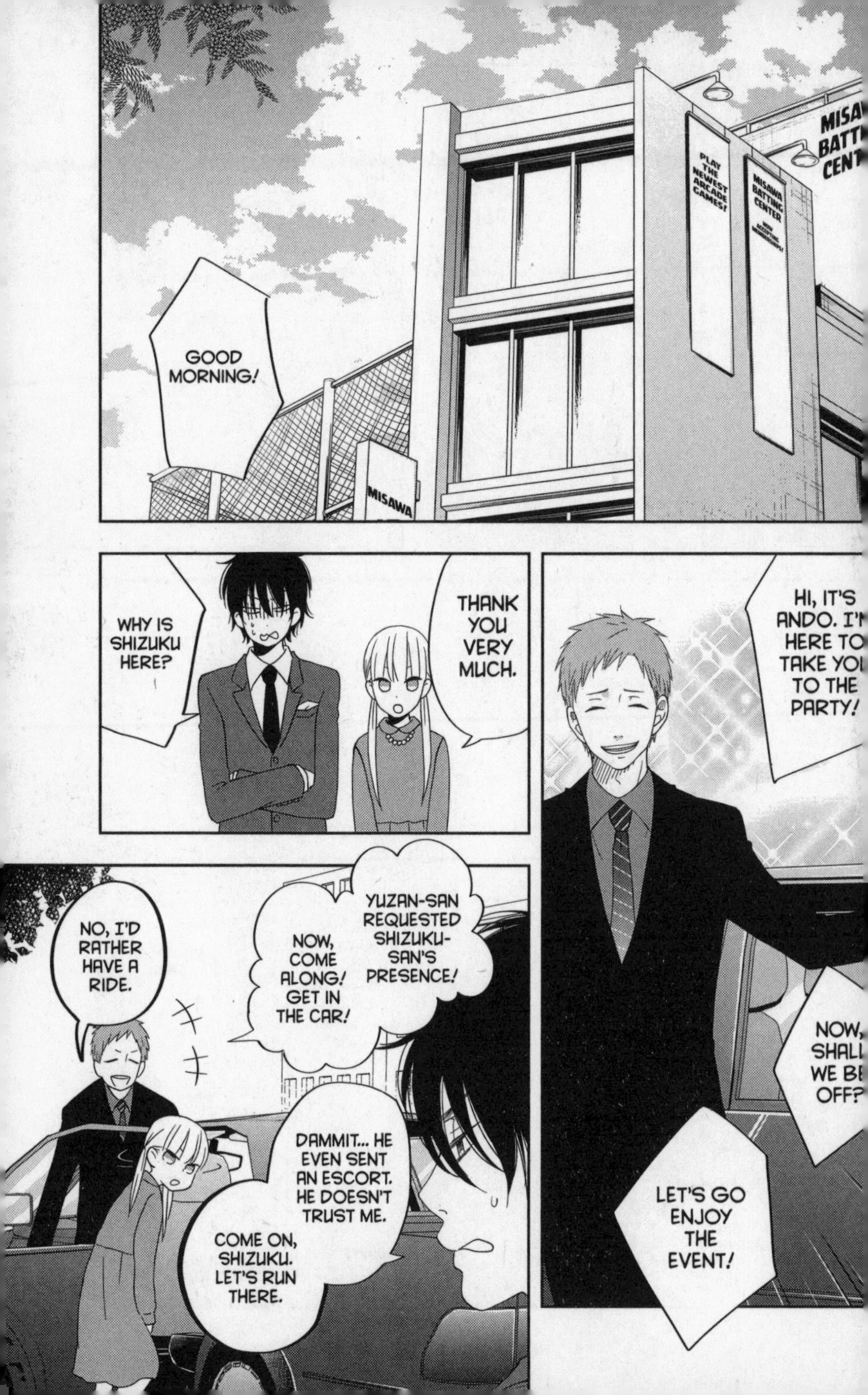
MISAW
BATT
CENT
PLAY THE NEWEST ARCADE GAMES!
MISAWA BATTING CENTER
MISAWA
GOOD MORNING!
HI, IT'S ANDO. I' HERE TO TAKE YO TO THE PARTY!
NOW, SHAL WE B OFF?
LET'S GO ENJOY THE EVENT!
THANK YOU VERY MUCH.
WHY IS SHIZUKU HERE?
YUZAN-SAN REQUESTED SHIZUKU-SAN'S PRESENCE!
NOW, COME ALONG! GET IN THE CAR!
DAMMIT... HE EVEN SENT AN ESCORT. HE DOESN'T TRUST ME.
COME ON, SHIZUKU. LET'S RUN THERE.
NO, I'D RATHER HAVE A RIDE.

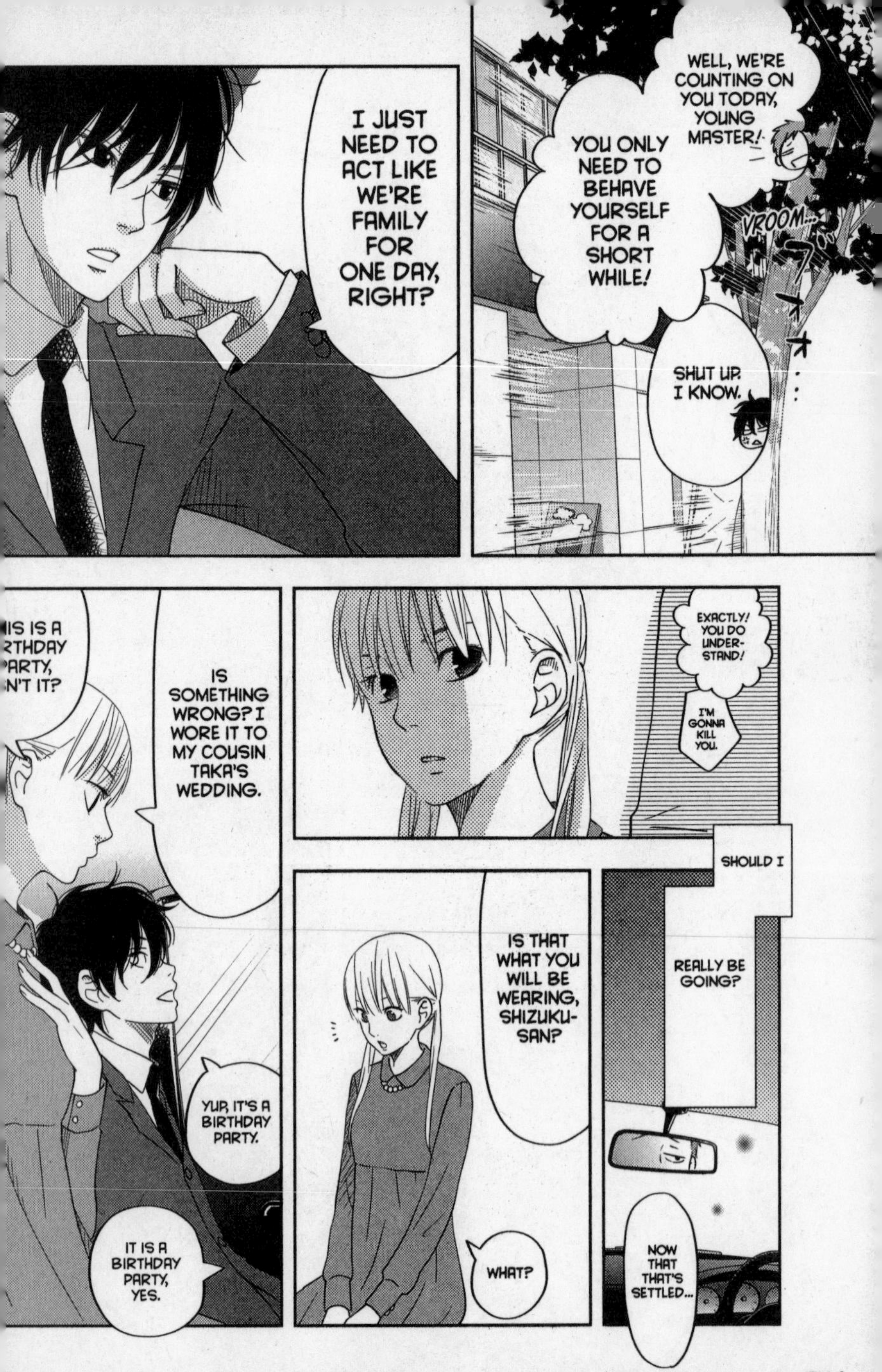
WELL, WE'RE COUNTING ON YOU TODAY, YOUNG MASTER!
YOU ONLY NEED TO BEHAVE YOURSELF FOR A SHORT WHILE!
VROOM...
SHUT UP. I KNOW.
I JUST NEED TO ACT LIKE WE'RE FAMILY FOR ONE DAY, RIGHT?
EXACTLY! YOU DO UNDER-STAND!
I'M GONNA KILL YOU.
SHOULD I
REALLY BE GOING?
NOW THAT THAT'S SETTLED...
IS THAT WHAT YOU WILL BE WEARING, SHIZUKU-SAN?
WHAT?
IS SOMETHING WRONG? I WORE IT TO MY COUSIN TAKA'S WEDDING.
IS IS A RTHDAY ARTY, N'T IT?
YUP, IT'S A BIRTHDAY PARTY.
IT IS A BIRTHDAY PARTY, YES.

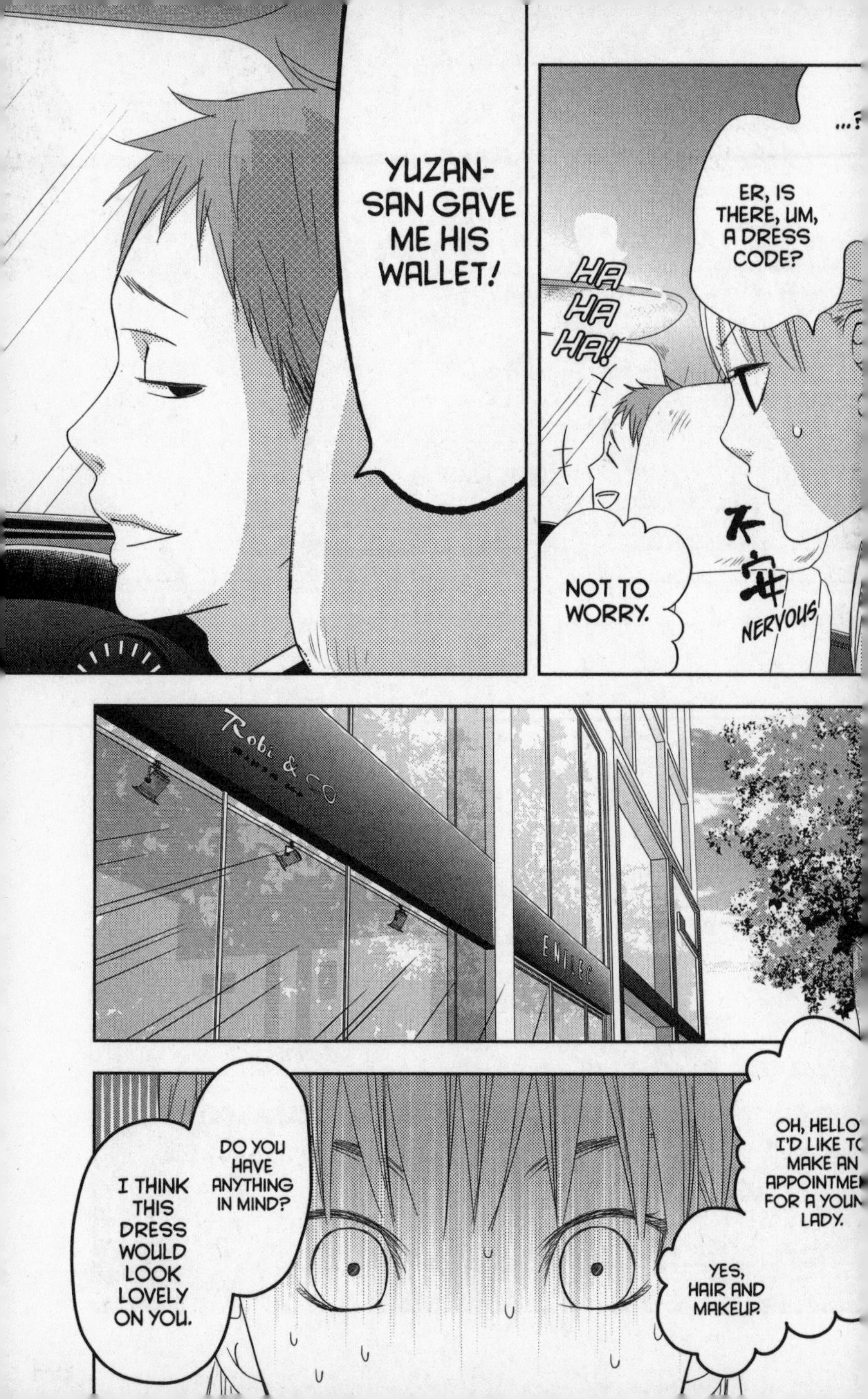
...!?
ER, IS THERE, UM, A DRESS CODE?
不安
NERVOUS
HA HA HA!
NOT TO WORRY.
YUZAN-SAN GAVE ME HIS WALLET!
OH, HELLO I'D LIKE TO MAKE AN APPOINTME FOR A YOUN LADY.
YES, HAIR AND MAKEUP.
DO YOU HAVE ANYTHING IN MIND?
I THINK THIS DRESS WOULD LOOK LOVELY ON YOU.

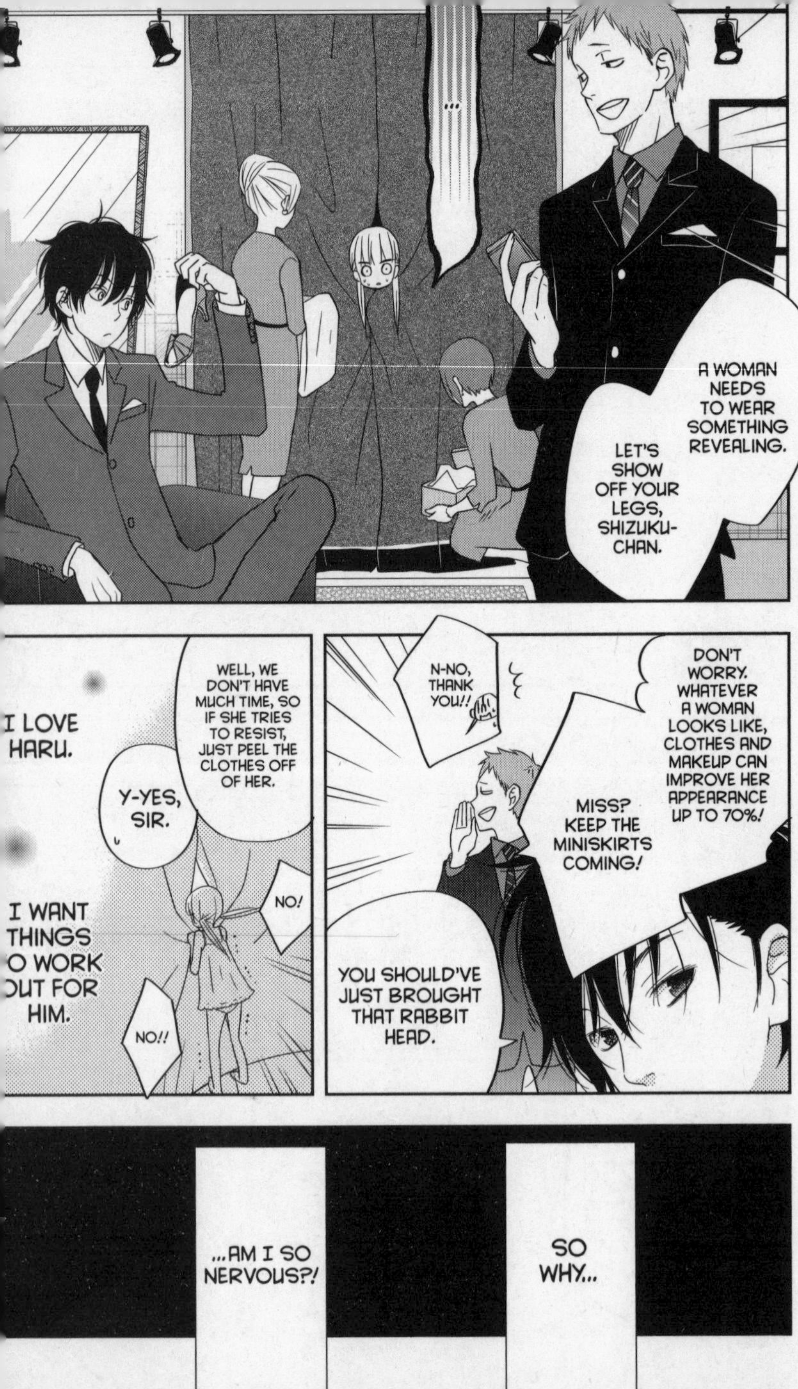
A WOMAN NEEDS TO WEAR SOMETHING REVEALING.
LET'S SHOW OFF YOUR LEGS, SHIZUKU-CHAN.
DON'T WORRY. WHATEVER A WOMAN LOOKS LIKE, CLOTHES AND MAKEUP CAN IMPROVE HER APPEARANCE UP TO 70%!
MISS? KEEP THE MINISKIRTS COMING!
N-NO, THANK YOU!!
YOU SHOULD'VE JUST BROUGHT THAT RABBIT HEAD.
WELL, WE DON'T HAVE MUCH TIME, SO IF SHE TRIES TO RESIST, JUST PEEL THE CLOTHES OFF OF HER.
Y-YES, SIR.
I LOVE HARU.
NO!
I WANT THINGS O WORK UT FOR HIM.
NO!!
SO WHY...
...AM I SO NERVOUS?!

SIR, YES SIR!! CLASS A SCHOOL OF MANLINESS!!

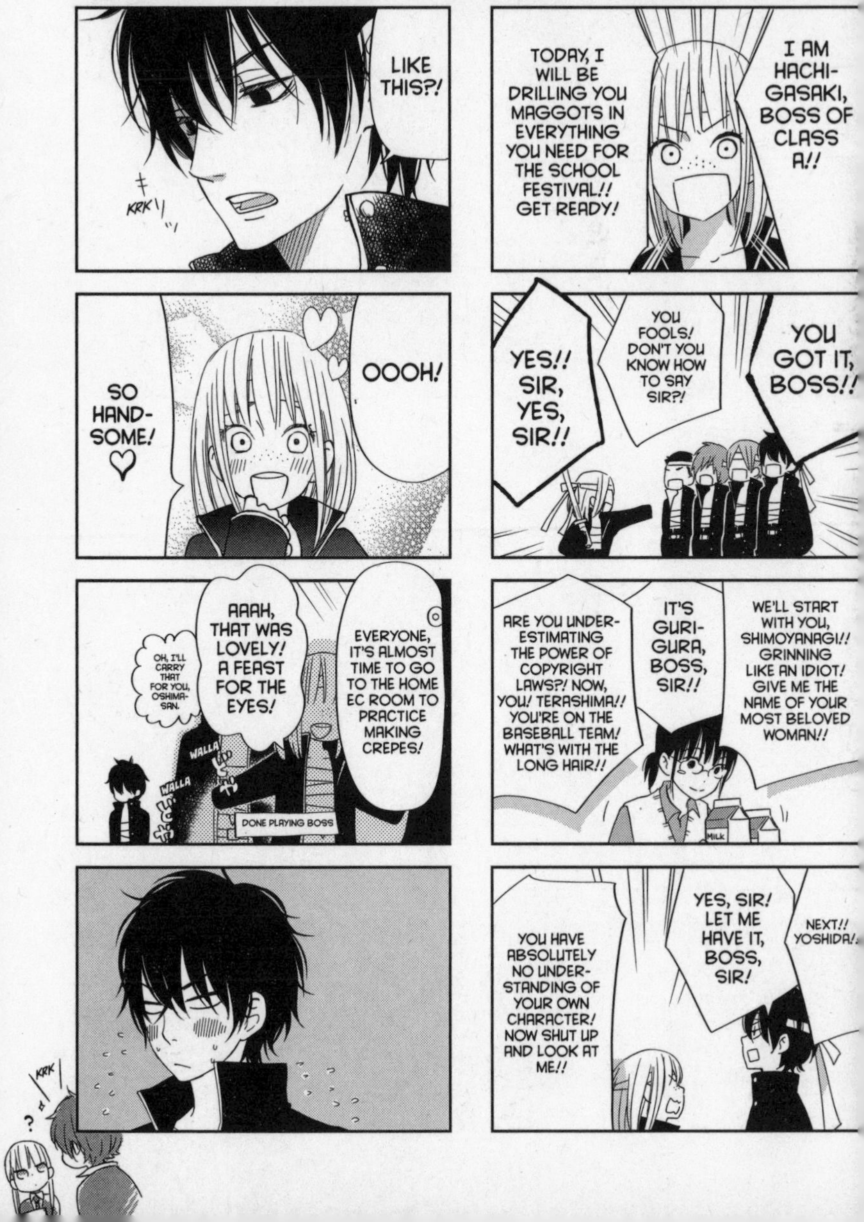
I AM HACHI-GASAKI, BOSS OF CLASS A!!
TODAY, I WILL BE DRILLING YOU MAGGOTS IN EVERYTHING YOU NEED FOR THE SCHOOL FESTIVAL!! GET READY!
YOU GOT IT, BOSS!!
YOU FOOLS! DON'T YOU KNOW HOW TO SAY SIR?!
YES!! SIR, YES, SIR!!
WE'LL START WITH YOU, SHIMOYANAGI!! GRINNING LIKE AN IDIOT! GIVE ME THE NAME OF YOUR MOST BELOVED WOMAN!!
IT'S GURI-GURA, BOSS, SIR!!
ARE YOU UNDER-ESTIMATING THE POWER OF COPYRIGHT LAWS?! NOW, YOU! TERASHIMA!! YOU'RE ON THE BASEBALL TEAM! WHAT'S WITH THE LONG HAIR!!
MILK
NEXT!! YOSHIDA!!
YES, SIR! LET ME HAVE IT, BOSS, SIR!
YOU HAVE ABSOLUTELY NO UNDER-STANDING OF YOUR OWN CHARACTER! NOW SHUT UP AND LOOK AT ME!!
LIKE THIS?!
KRK
OOOH!
SO HAND-SOME!
EVERYONE, IT'S ALMOST TIME TO GO TO THE HOME EC ROOM TO PRACTICE MAKING CREPES!
AAAH, THAT WAS LOVELY! A FEAST FOR THE EYES!
OH, I'LL CARRY THAT FOR YOU, OSHIMA-SAN.
WALLA
WALLA
DONE PLAYING BOSS
KRK
?

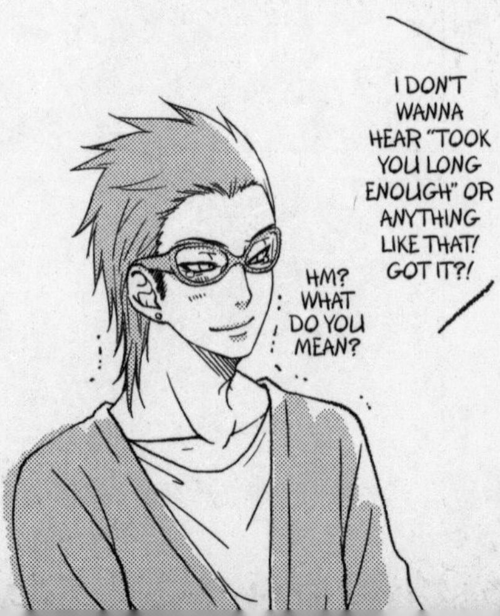
I DON'T WANNA HEAR "TOOK YOU LONG ENOUGH" OR ANYTHING LIKE THAT! GOT IT?!
HM? WHAT DO YOU MEAN?

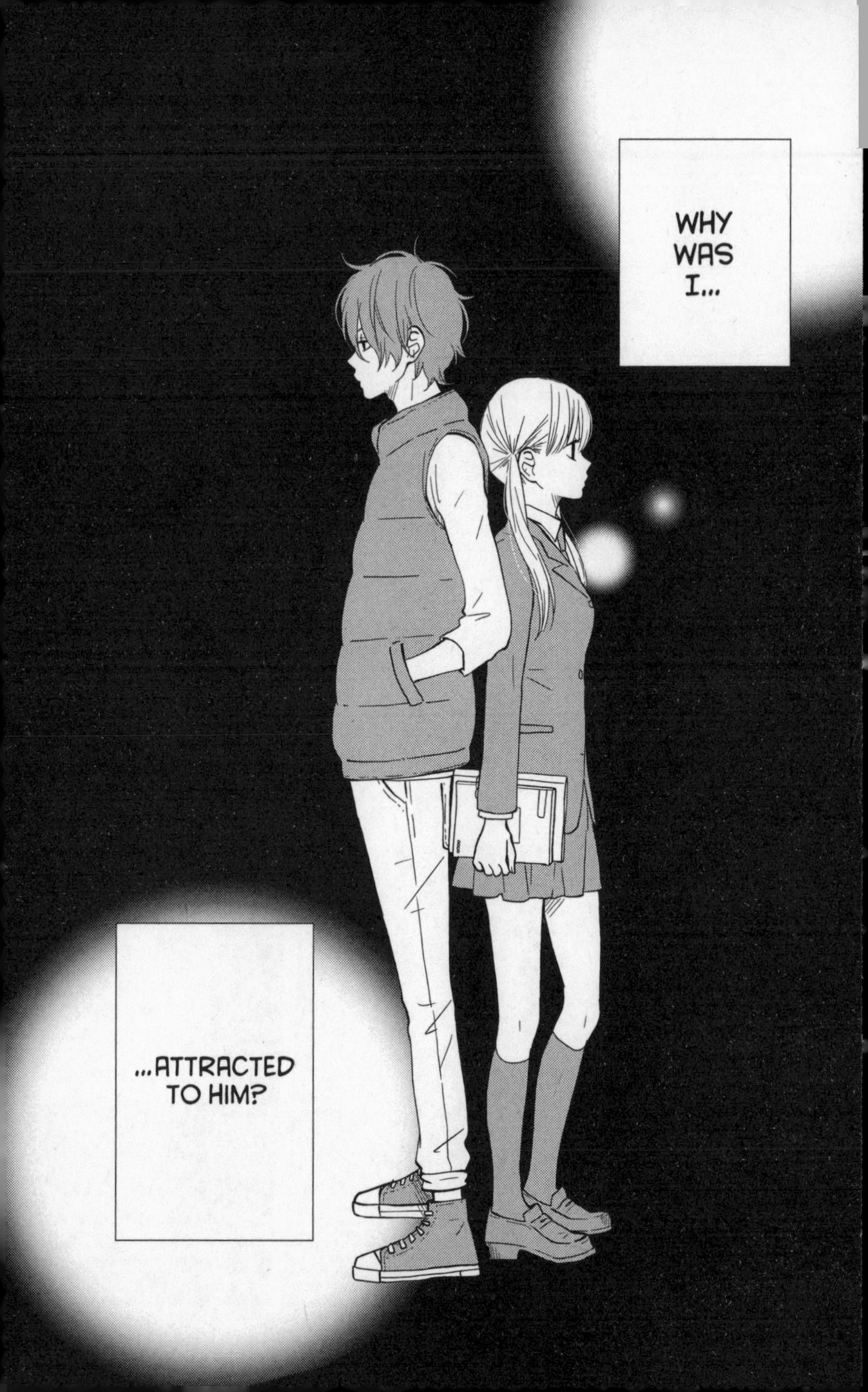
WHY WAS I...
...ATTRACTED TO HIM?

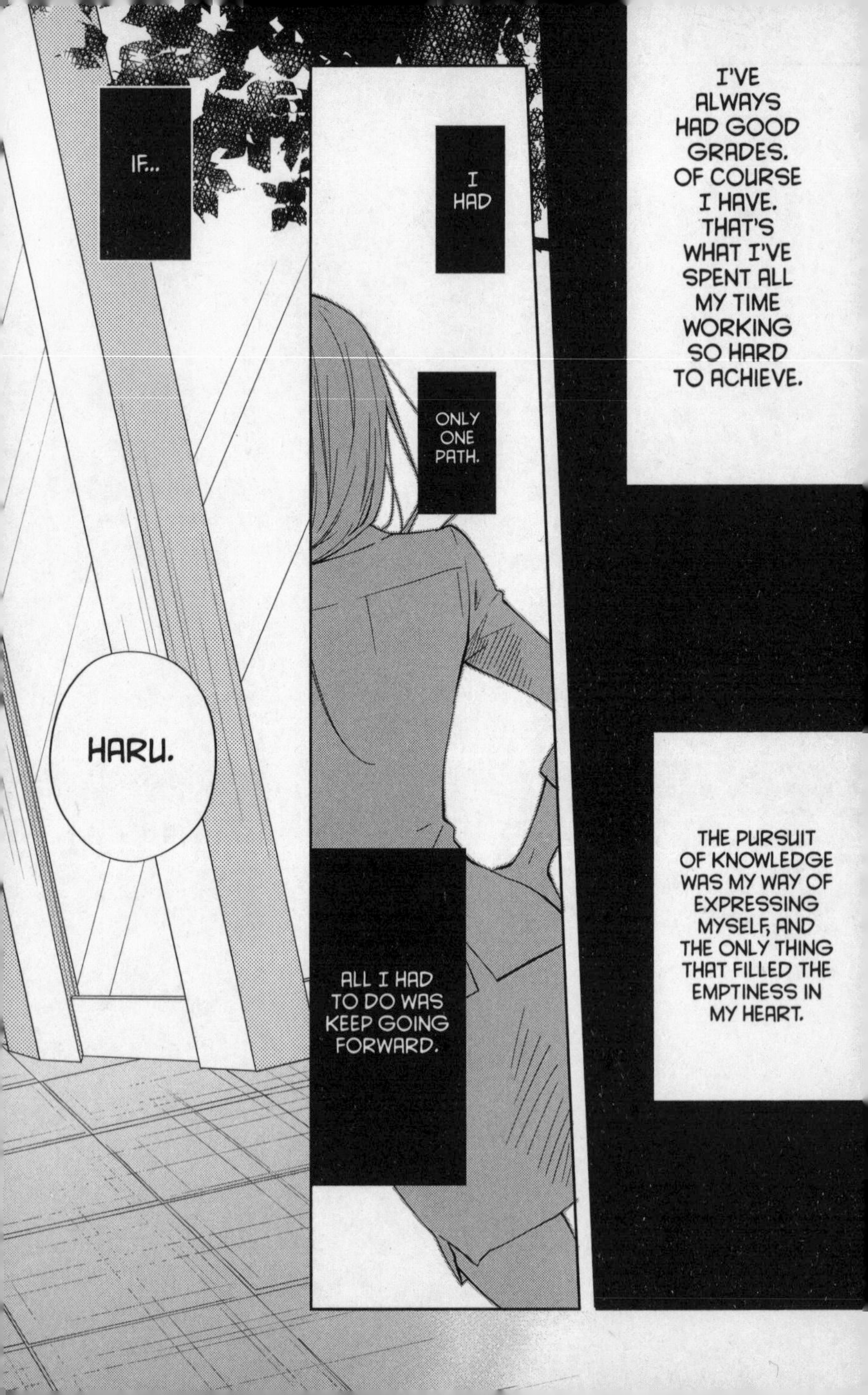
I'VE ALWAYS HAD GOOD GRADES. OF COURSE I HAVE. THAT'S WHAT I'VE SPENT ALL MY TIME WORKING SO HARD TO ACHIEVE.
THE PURSUIT OF KNOWLEDGE WAS MY WAY OF EXPRESSING MYSELF, AND THE ONLY THING THAT FILLED THE EMPTINESS IN MY HEART.
I HAD
ONLY ONE PATH.
ALL I HAD TO DO WAS KEEP GOING FORWARD.
IF...
HARU.

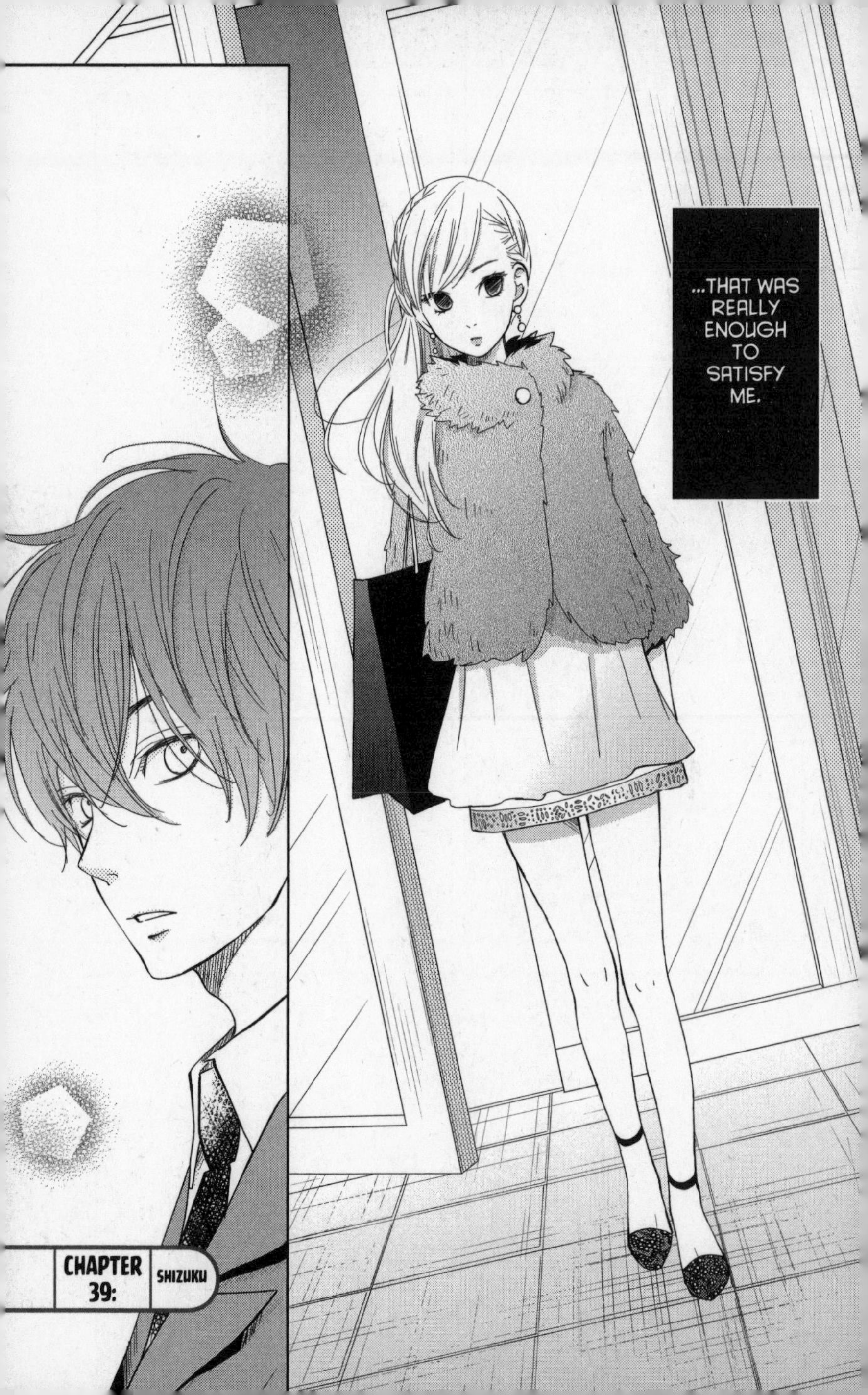
...THAT WAS REALLY ENOUGH TO SATISFY ME.
CHAPTER 39:
SHIZUKU

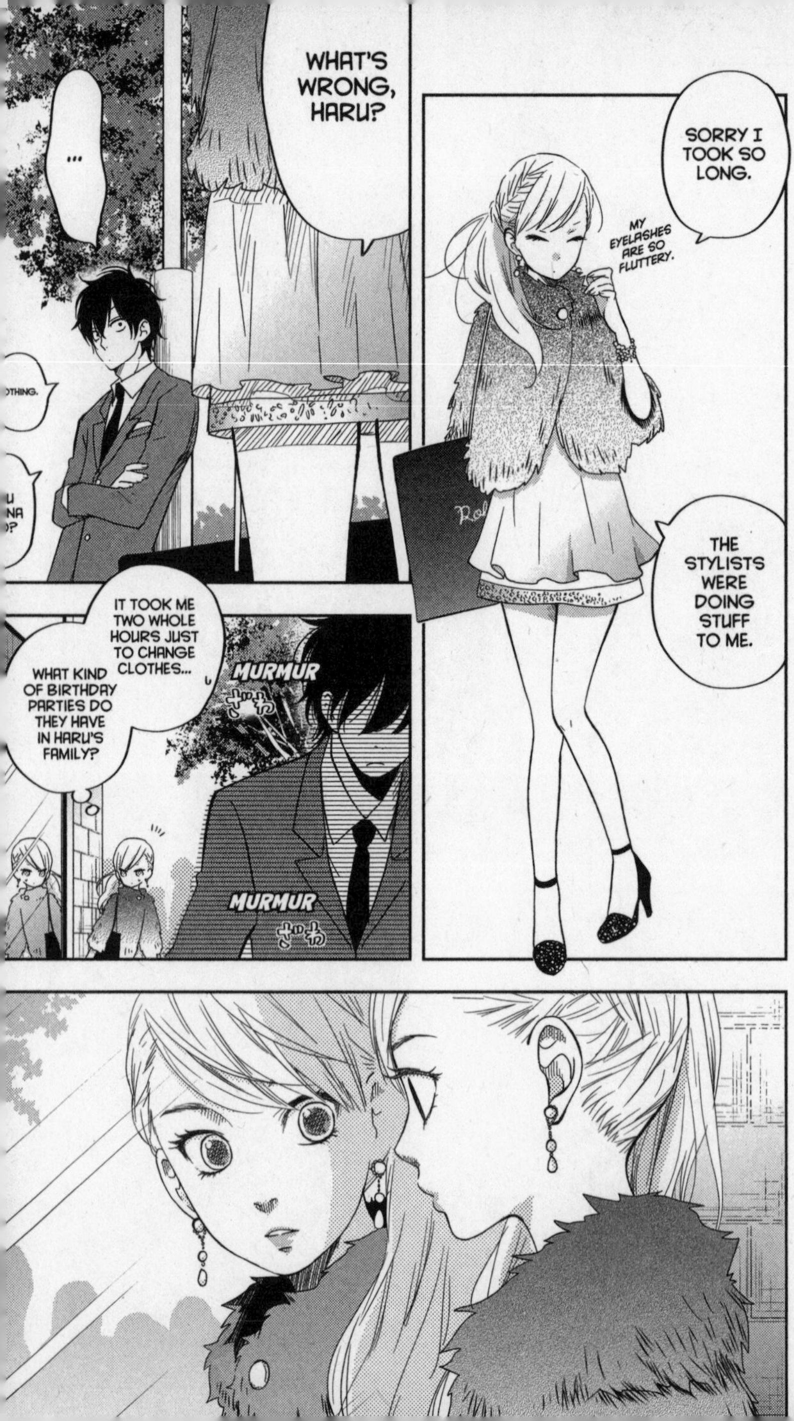
SORRY I TOOK SO LONG.
MY EYELASHES ARE SO FLUTTERY.
THE STYLISTS WERE DOING STUFF TO ME.
WHAT'S WRONG, HARU?
...
IT TOOK ME TWO WHOLE HOURS JUST TO CHANGE CLOTHES...
WHAT KIND OF BIRTHDAY PARTIES DO THEY HAVE IN HARU'S FAMILY?
MURMUR
MURMUR

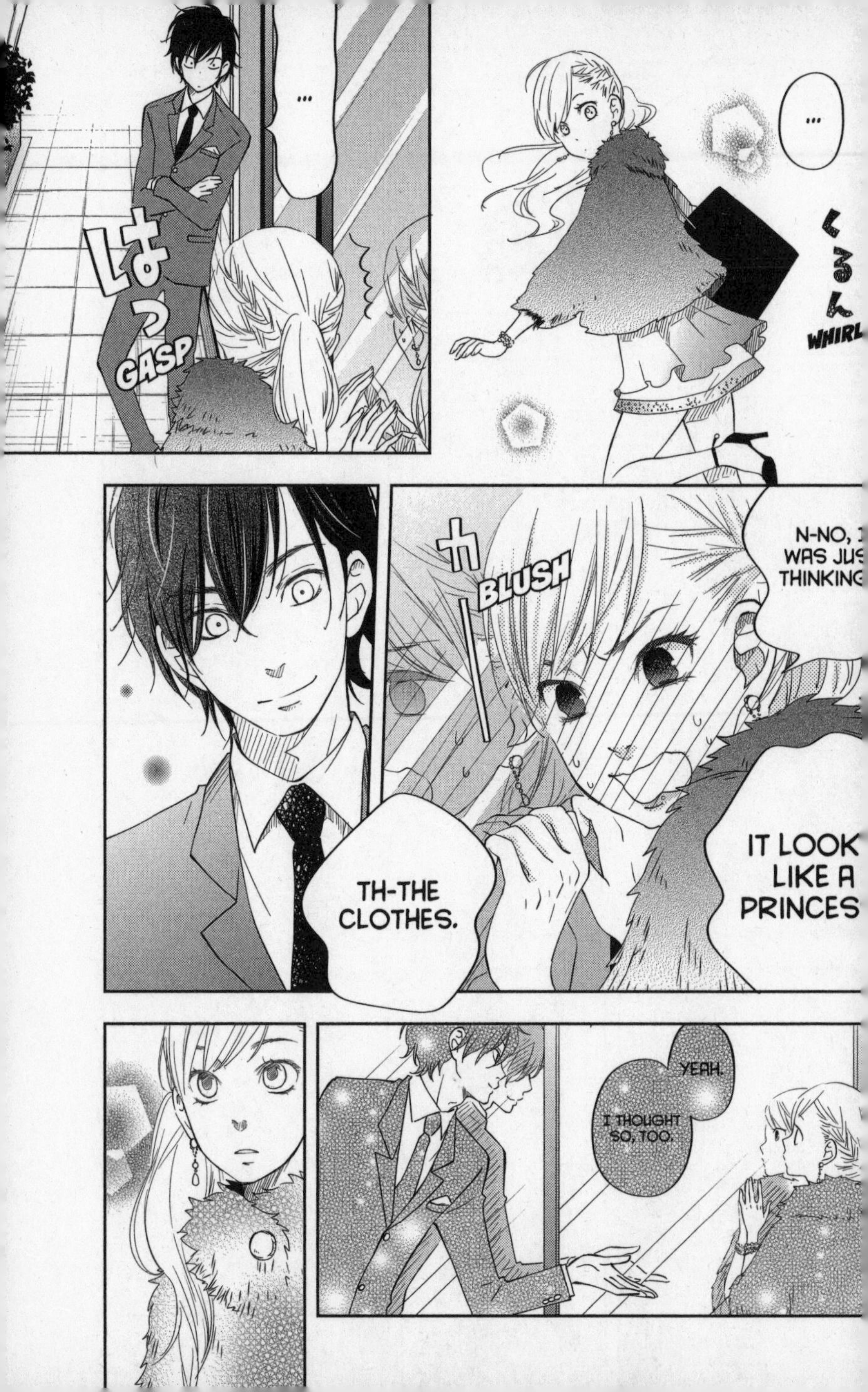
...
くるん
WHIRL
...
はっ
GASP
N-NO, I
WAS JUS
THINKING
IT LOOK
LIKE A
PRINCES
カ
BLUSH
TH-THE
CLOTHES.
YEAH.
I THOUGHT
SO, TOO.

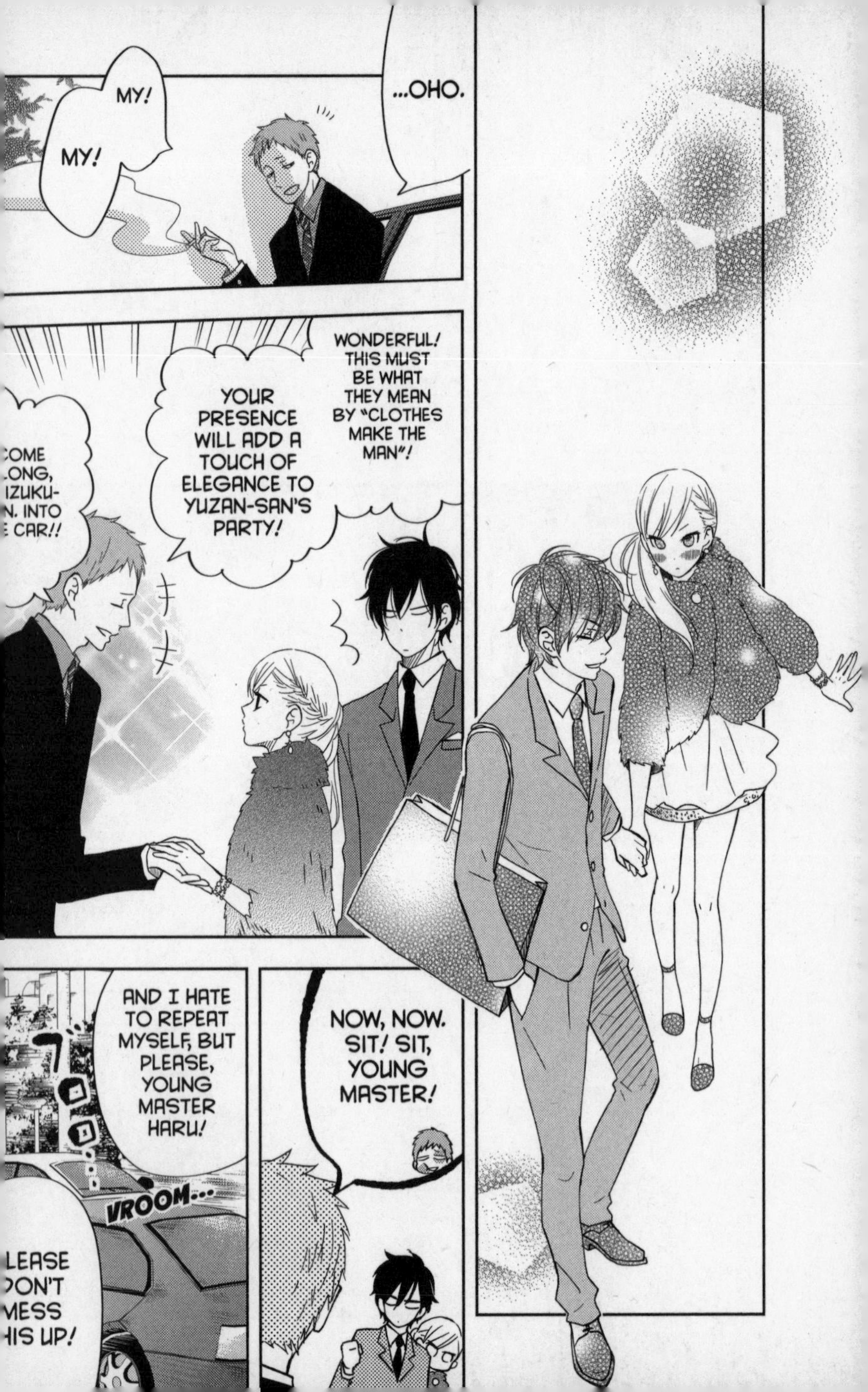
...OHO.
MY! MY!
WONDERFUL! THIS MUST BE WHAT THEY MEAN BY "CLOTHES MAKE THE MAN"!
YOUR PRESENCE WILL ADD A TOUCH OF ELEGANCE TO YUZAN-SAN'S PARTY!
COME LONG, IZUKU- N. INTO E CAR!!
NOW, NOW. SIT! SIT, YOUNG MASTER!
AND I HATE TO REPEAT MYSELF, BUT PLEASE, YOUNG MASTER HARU!
VROOM...
LEASE DON'T MESS HIS UP!

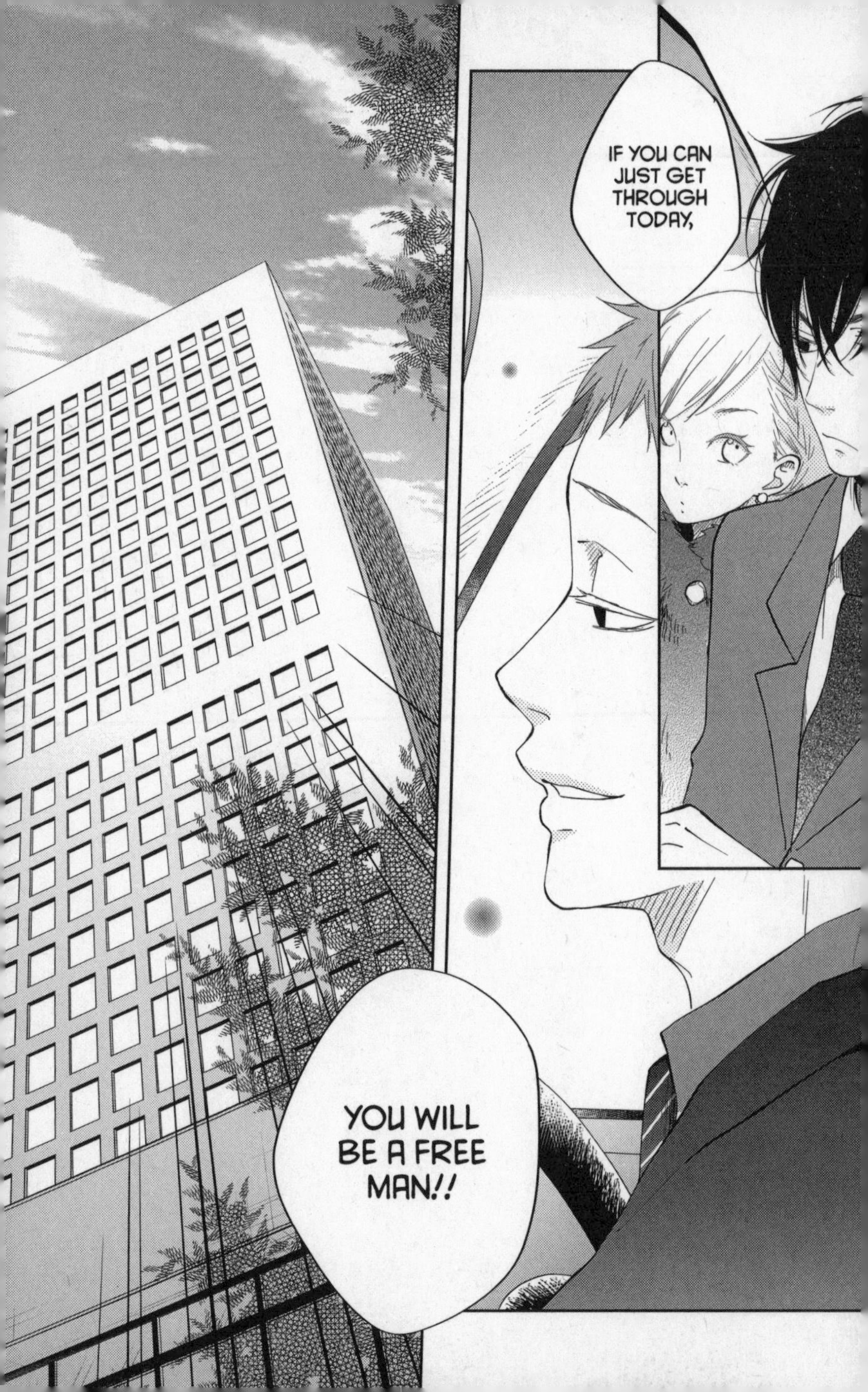
IF YOU CAN JUST GET THROUGH TODAY,
YOU WILL BE A FREE MAN!!

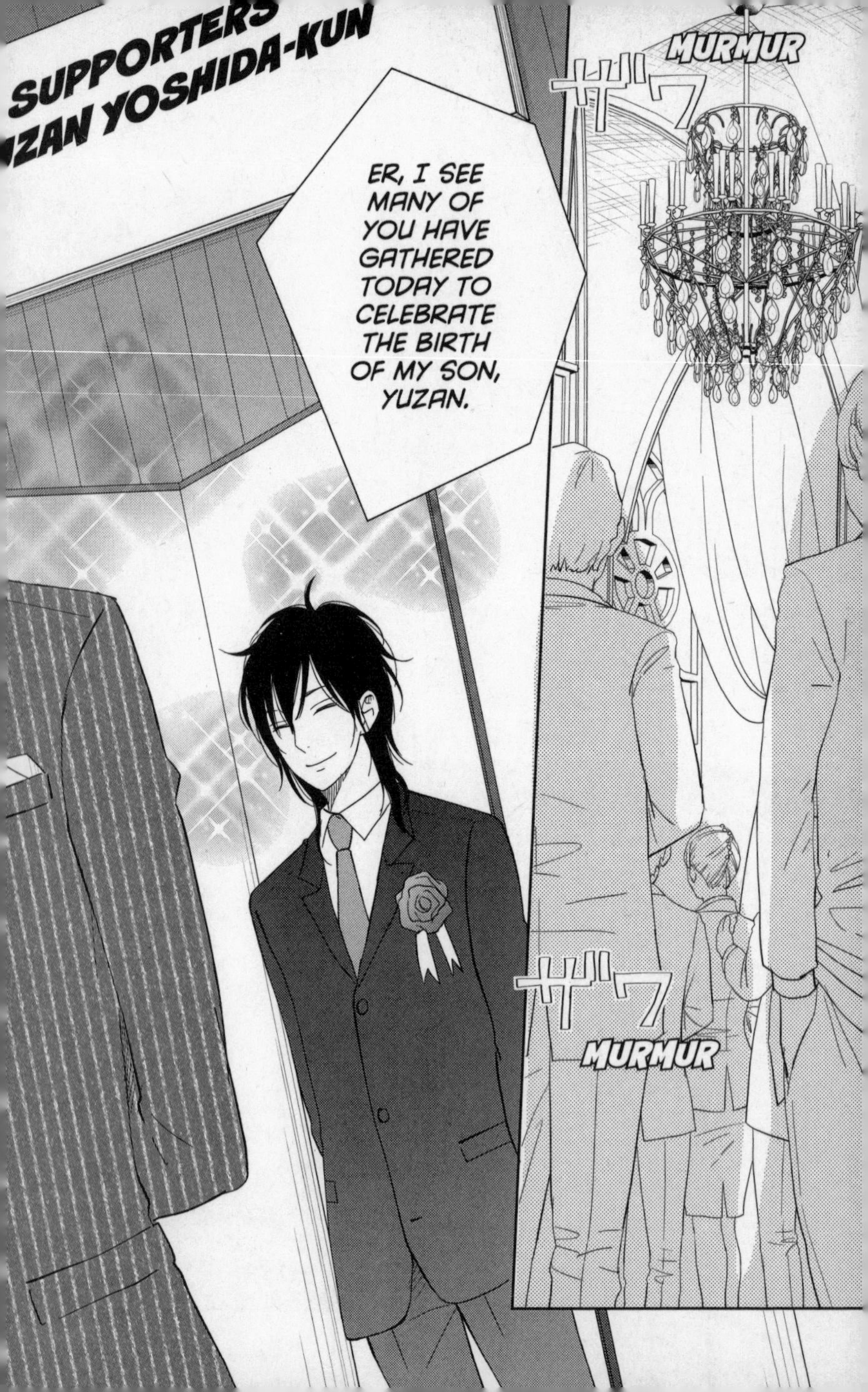
MURMUR
ザワ
ザワ
MURMUR
SUPPORTERS
ZAN YOSHIDA-KUN
ER, I SEE MANY OF YOU HAVE GATHERED TODAY TO CELEBRATE THE BIRTH OF MY SON, YUZAN.

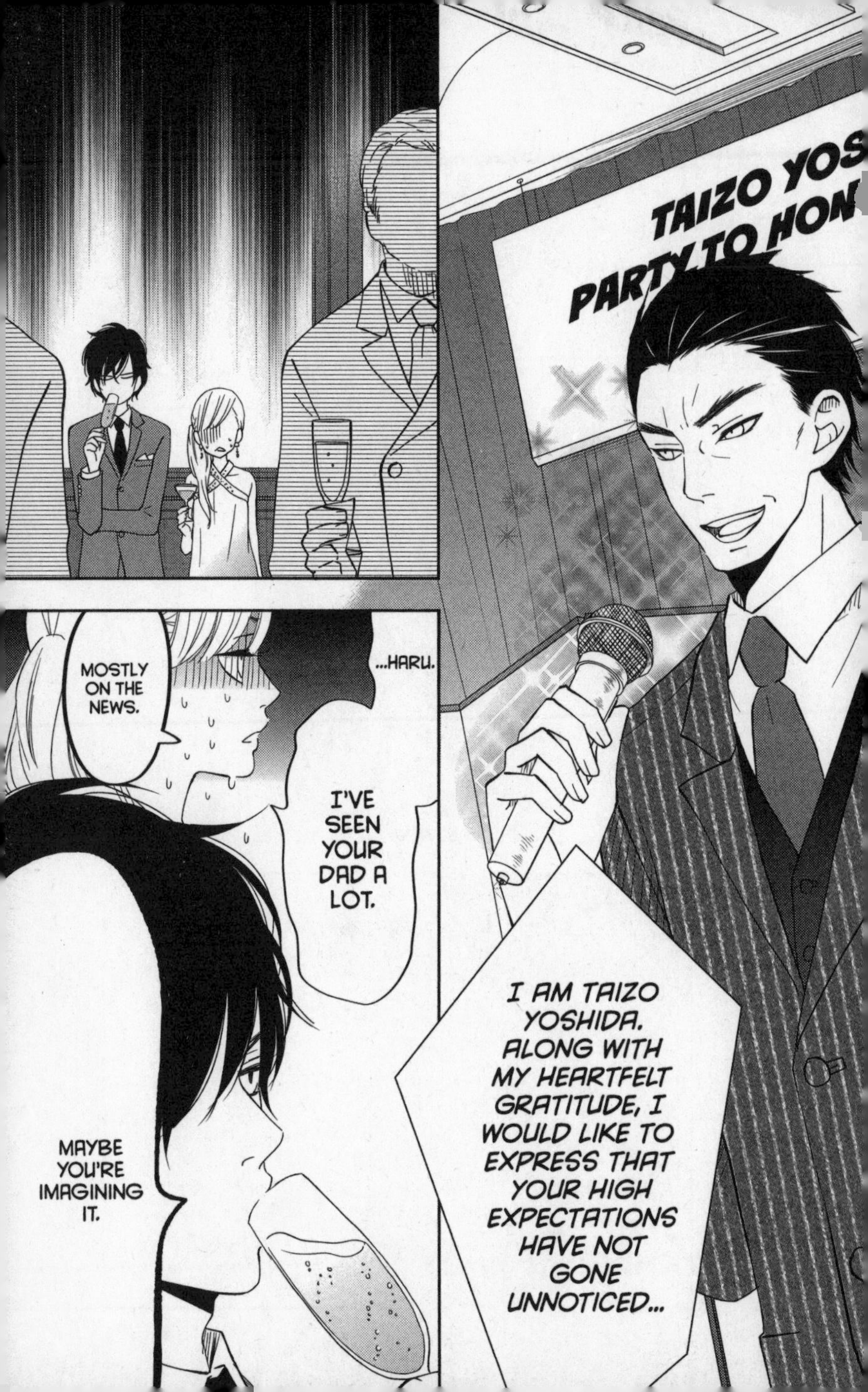
TAIZO YOS
PARTY TO HON
I AM TAIZO YOSHIDA. ALONG WITH MY HEARTFELT GRATITUDE, I WOULD LIKE TO EXPRESS THAT YOUR HIGH EXPECTATIONS HAVE NOT GONE UNNOTICED...
...HARU.
I'VE SEEN YOUR DAD A LOT.
MOSTLY ON THE NEWS.
MAYBE YOU'RE IMAGINING IT.

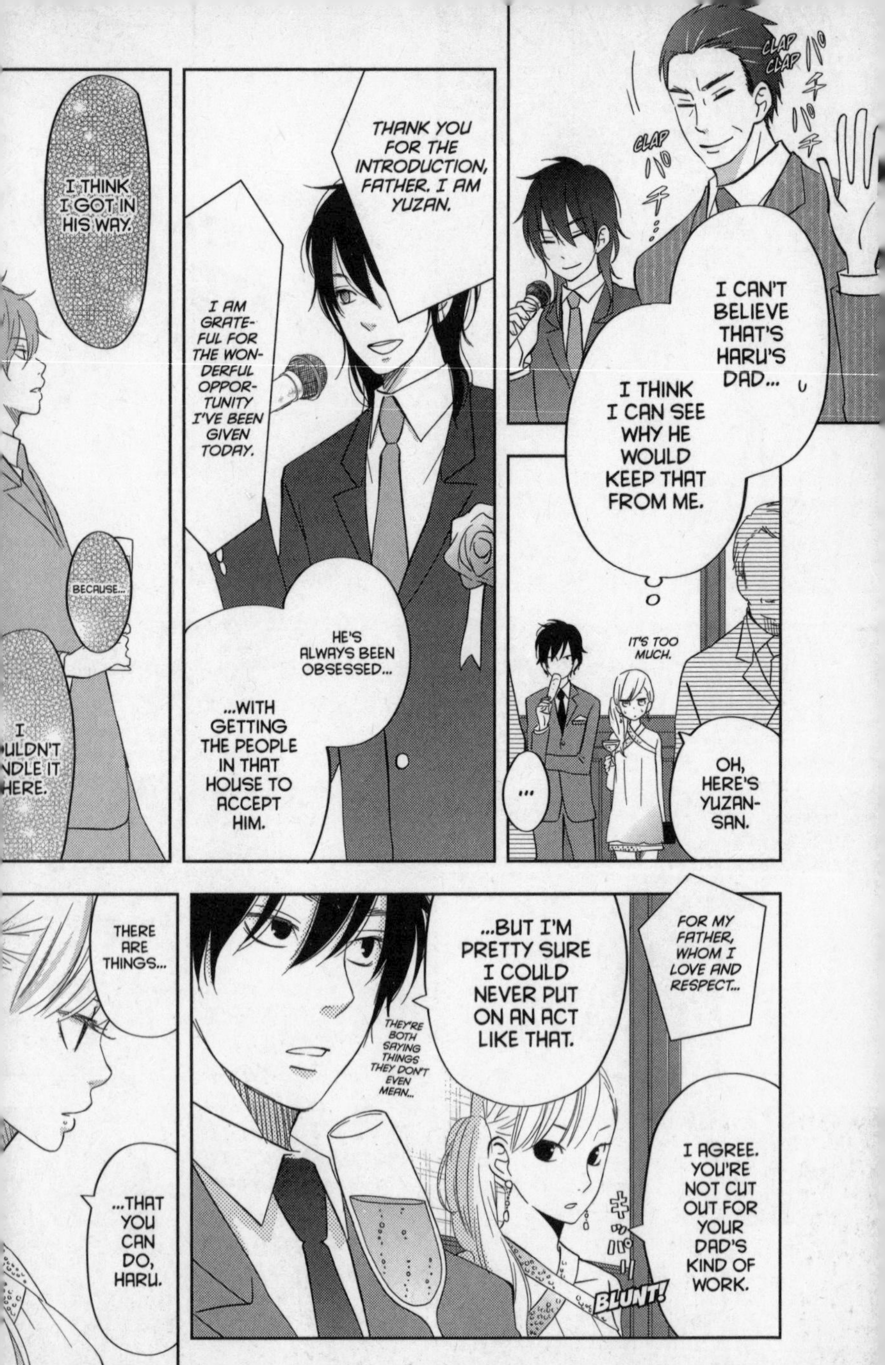
CLAP CLAP
パチパチ
CLAP
パチ…
I CAN'T BELIEVE THAT'S HARU'S DAD...
I THINK I CAN SEE WHY HE WOULD KEEP THAT FROM ME.
IT'S TOO MUCH.
OH, HERE'S YUZAN-SAN.
...
THANK YOU FOR THE INTRODUCTION, FATHER. I AM YUZAN.
I AM GRATEFUL FOR THE WONDERFUL OPPORTUNITY I'VE BEEN GIVEN TODAY.
HE'S ALWAYS BEEN OBSESSED...
...WITH GETTING THE PEOPLE IN THAT HOUSE TO ACCEPT HIM.
I THINK I GOT IN HIS WAY.
BECAUSE...
I ULDN'T NDLE IT HERE.
FOR MY FATHER, WHOM I LOVE AND RESPECT...
...BUT I'M PRETTY SURE I COULD NEVER PUT ON AN ACT LIKE THAT.
THEY'RE BOTH SAYING THINGS THEY DON'T EVEN MEAN...
I AGREE. YOU'RE NOT CUT OUT FOR YOUR DAD'S KIND OF WORK.
キッパリ
BLUNT!
THERE ARE THINGS...
...THAT YOU CAN DO, HARU.

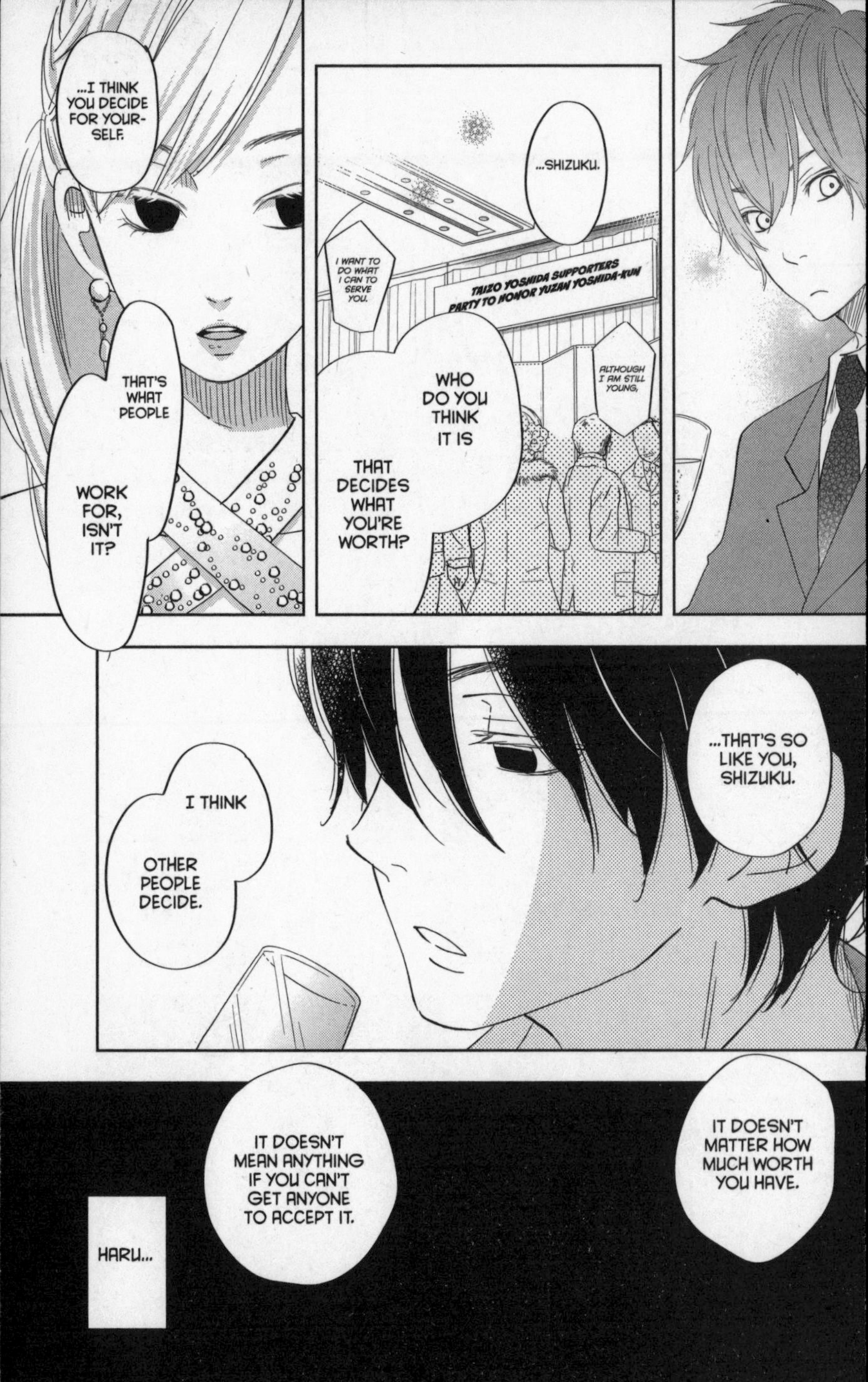
...SHIZUKU.
ALTHOUGH I AM STILL YOUNG,
I WANT TO DO WHAT I CAN TO SERVE YOU.
TAIZO YOSHIDA SUPPORTERS PARTY TO HONOR YUZAN YOSHIDA-KUN
WHO DO YOU THINK IT IS THAT DECIDES WHAT YOU'RE WORTH?
...I THINK YOU DECIDE FOR YOUR-SELF.
THAT'S WHAT PEOPLE WORK FOR, ISN'T IT?
...THAT'S SO LIKE YOU, SHIZUKU.
I THINK OTHER PEOPLE DECIDE.
IT DOESN'T MATTER HOW MUCH WORTH YOU HAVE.
IT DOESN'T MEAN ANYTHING IF YOU CAN'T GET ANYONE TO ACCEPT IT.
HARU...

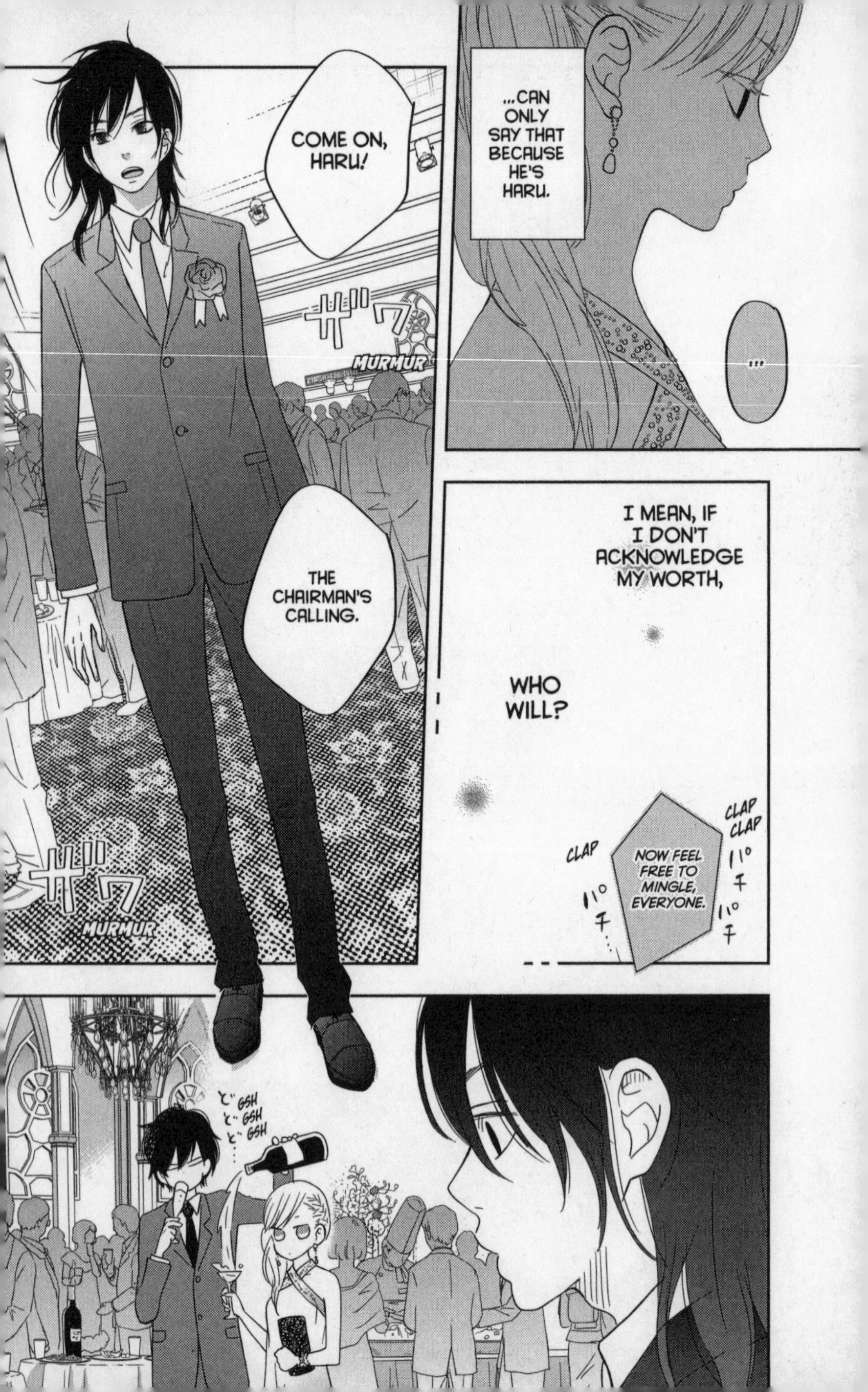
...CAN ONLY SAY THAT BECAUSE HE'S HARU.
...
I MEAN, IF I DON'T ACKNOWLEDGE MY WORTH,
WHO WILL?
CLAP CLAP
パチ
パチ
NOW FEEL FREE TO MINGLE, EVERYONE.
CLAP
パチ...
COME ON, HARU!
ザワ
MURMUR
THE CHAIRMAN'S CALLING.
ザワ
MURMUR
ど GSH
ど GSH
ど GSH

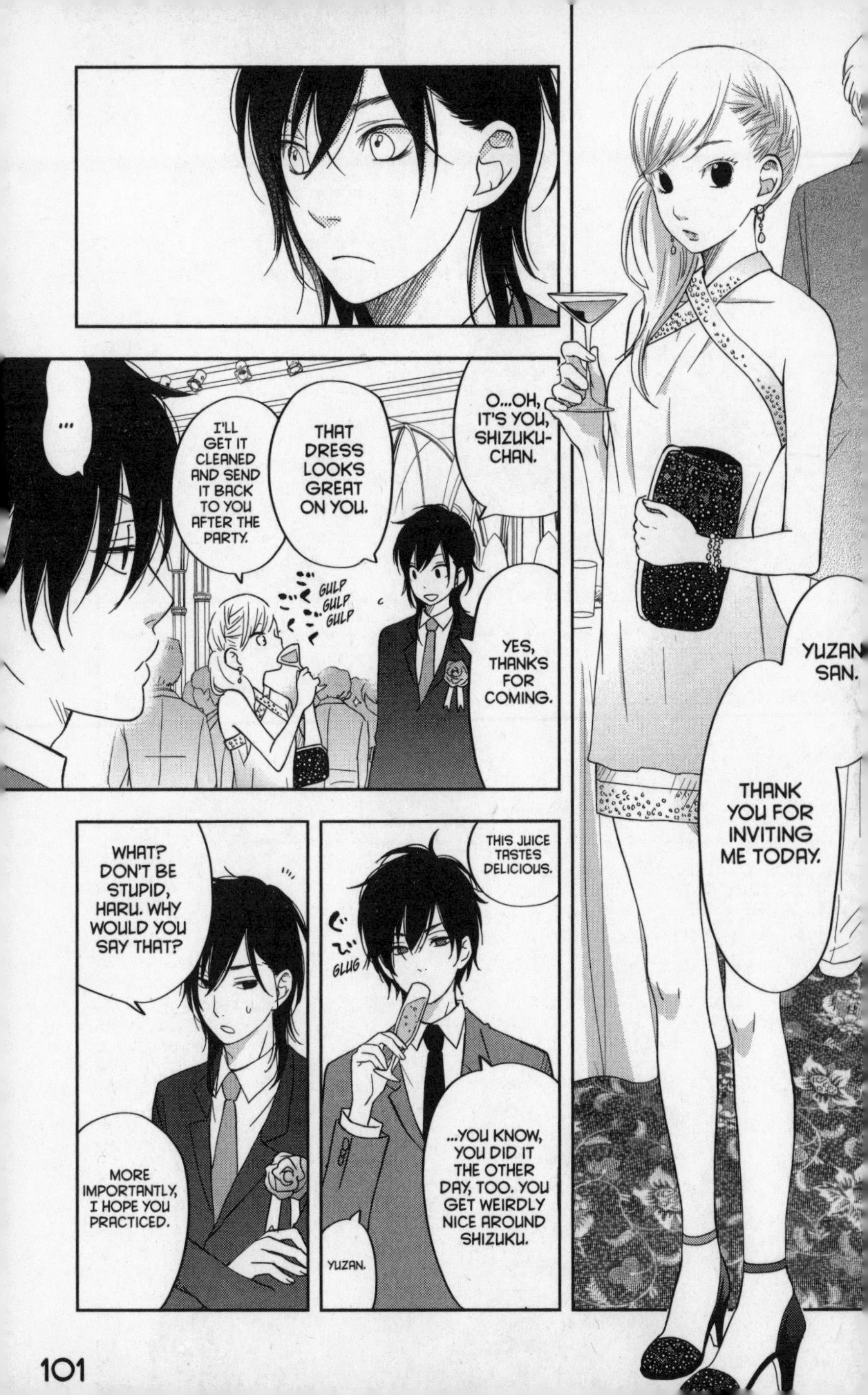

YUZAN SAN.
THANK YOU FOR INVITING ME TODAY.
O...OH, IT'S YOU, SHIZUKU-CHAN.
YES, THANKS FOR COMING.
THAT DRESS LOOKS GREAT ON YOU.
I'LL GET IT CLEANED AND SEND IT BACK TO YOU AFTER THE PARTY.
GULP GULP GULP
...
THIS JUICE TASTES DELICIOUS.
GLUG
...YOU KNOW, YOU DID IT THE OTHER DAY, TOO. YOU GET WEIRDLY NICE AROUND SHIZUKU.
YUZAN.
WHAT? DON'T BE STUPID, HARU. WHY WOULD YOU SAY THAT?
MORE IMPORTANTLY, I HOPE YOU PRACTICED.

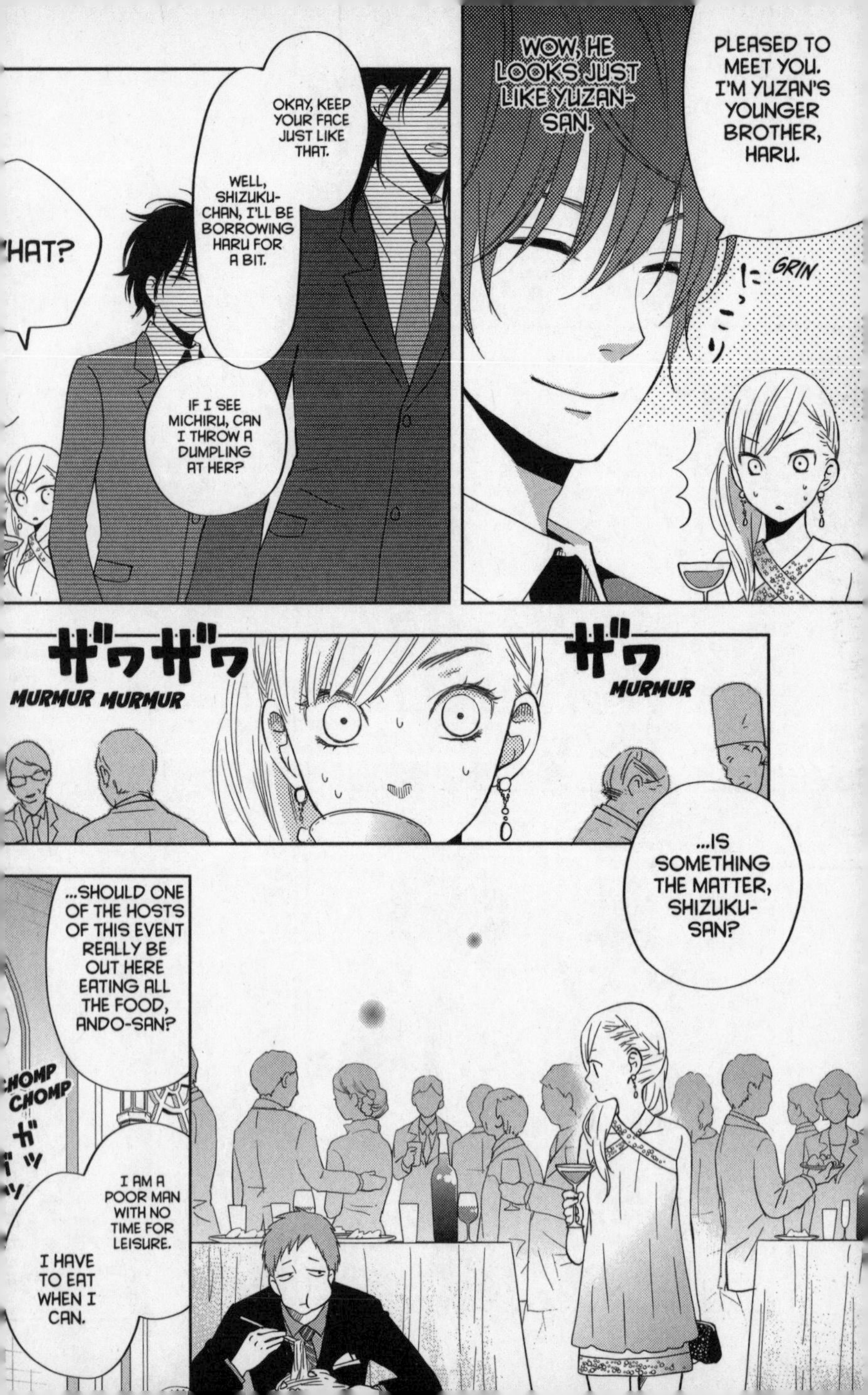
PLEASED TO MEET YOU. I'M YUZAN'S YOUNGER BROTHER, HARU.
WOW, HE LOOKS JUST LIKE YUZAN-SAN.
GRIN
OKAY, KEEP YOUR FACE JUST LIKE THAT.
WELL, SHIZUKU-CHAN, I'LL BE BORROWING HARU FOR A BIT.
IF I SEE MICHIRU, CAN I THROW A DUMPLING AT HER?
HAT?
ザワ
MURMUR
ザワザワ
MURMUR MURMUR
...IS SOMETHING THE MATTER, SHIZUKU-SAN?
...SHOULD ONE OF THE HOSTS OF THIS EVENT REALLY BE OUT HERE EATING ALL THE FOOD, ANDO-SAN?
CHOMP CHOMP
I AM A POOR MAN WITH NO TIME FOR LEISURE.
I HAVE TO EAT WHEN I CAN.

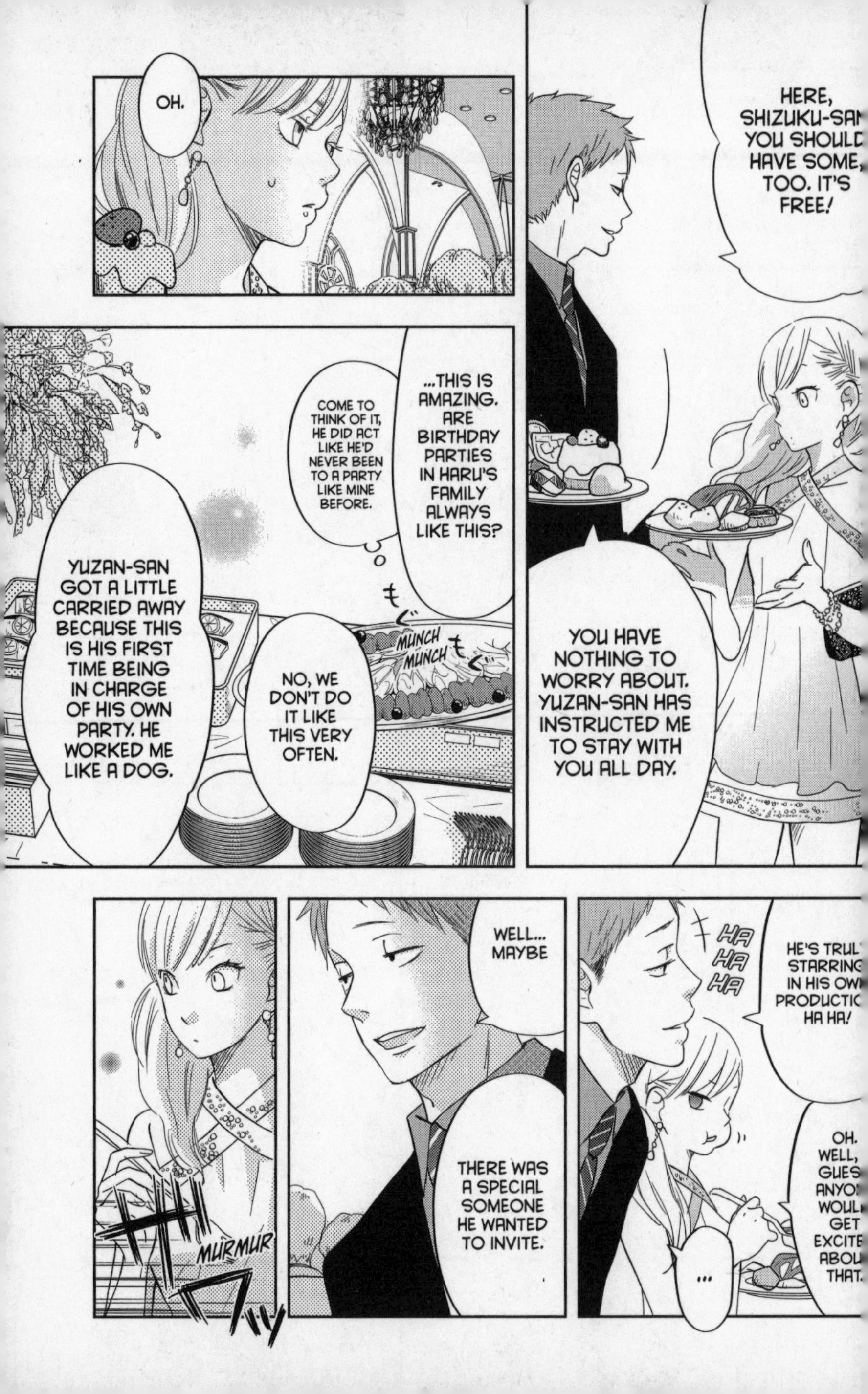
HERE, SHIZUKU-SAN YOU SHOULD HAVE SOME, TOO. IT'S FREE!
YOU HAVE NOTHING TO WORRY ABOUT. YUZAN-SAN HAS INSTRUCTED ME TO STAY WITH YOU ALL DAY.
OH.
...THIS IS AMAZING. ARE BIRTHDAY PARTIES IN HARU'S FAMILY ALWAYS LIKE THIS?
COME TO THINK OF IT, HE DID ACT LIKE HE'D NEVER BEEN TO A PARTY LIKE MINE BEFORE.
MUNCH MUNCH
NO, WE DON'T DO IT LIKE THIS VERY OFTEN.
YUZAN-SAN GOT A LITTLE CARRIED AWAY BECAUSE THIS IS HIS FIRST TIME BEING IN CHARGE OF HIS OWN PARTY. HE WORKED ME LIKE A DOG.
HA HA HA
HE'S TRUL STARRING IN HIS OW PRODUCTIO HA HA!
OH. WELL, GUES ANYO WOUL GET EXCITE ABOU THAT.
...
WELL... MAYBE
THERE WAS A SPECIAL SOMEONE HE WANTED TO INVITE.
MURMUR

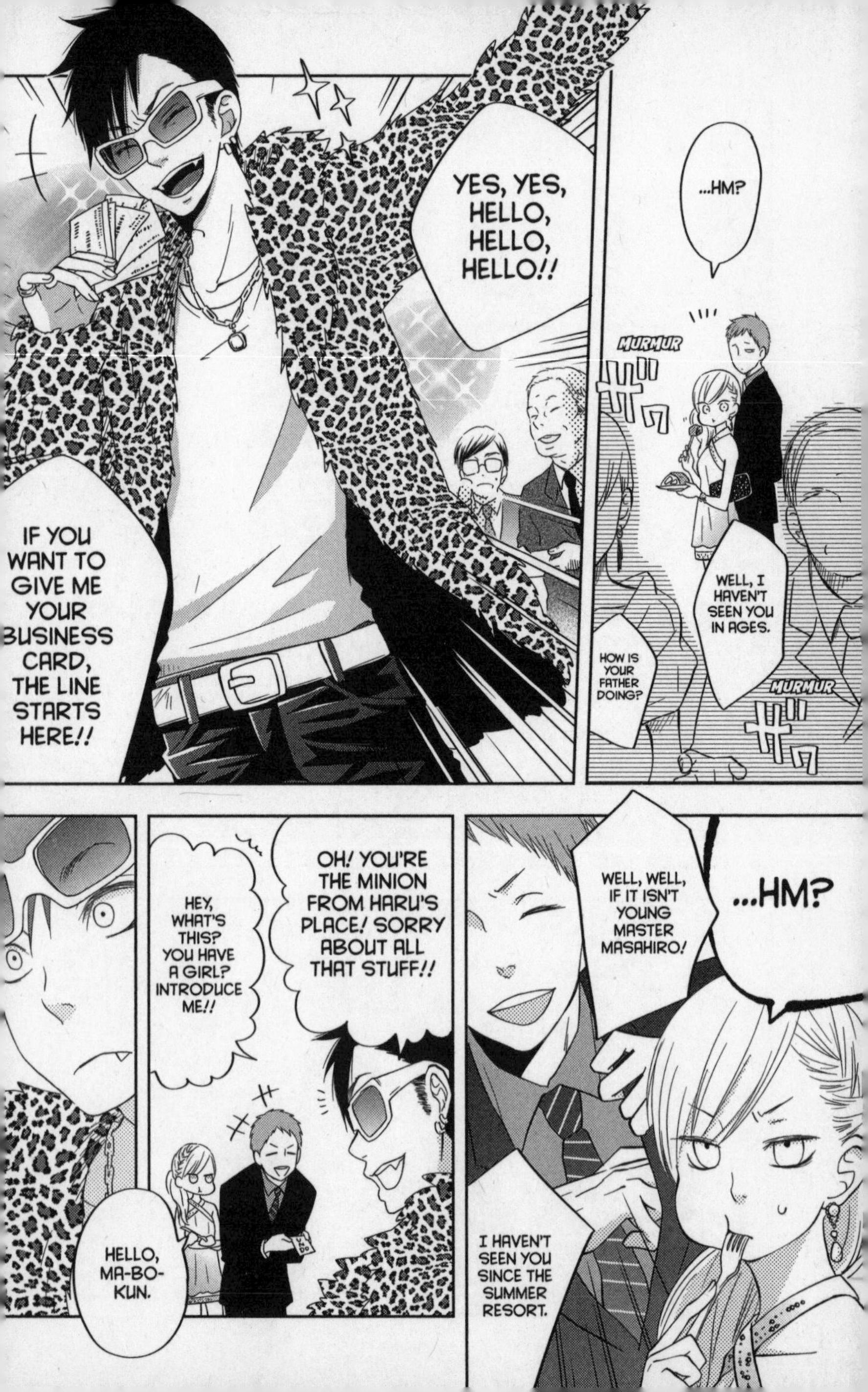
...HM?
MURMUR
ザワ
WELL, I HAVEN'T SEEN YOU IN AGES.
HOW IS YOUR FATHER DOING?
MURMUR
ザワ
YES, YES, HELLO, HELLO, HELLO!!
IF YOU WANT TO GIVE ME YOUR BUSINESS CARD, THE LINE STARTS HERE!!
...HM?
WELL, WELL, IF IT ISN'T YOUNG MASTER MASAHIRO!
I HAVEN'T SEEN YOU SINCE THE SUMMER RESORT.
OH! YOU'RE THE MINION FROM HARU'S PLACE! SORRY ABOUT ALL THAT STUFF!!
HEY, WHAT'S THIS? YOU HAVE A GIRL? INTRODUCE ME!!
HELLO, MA-BO-KUN.

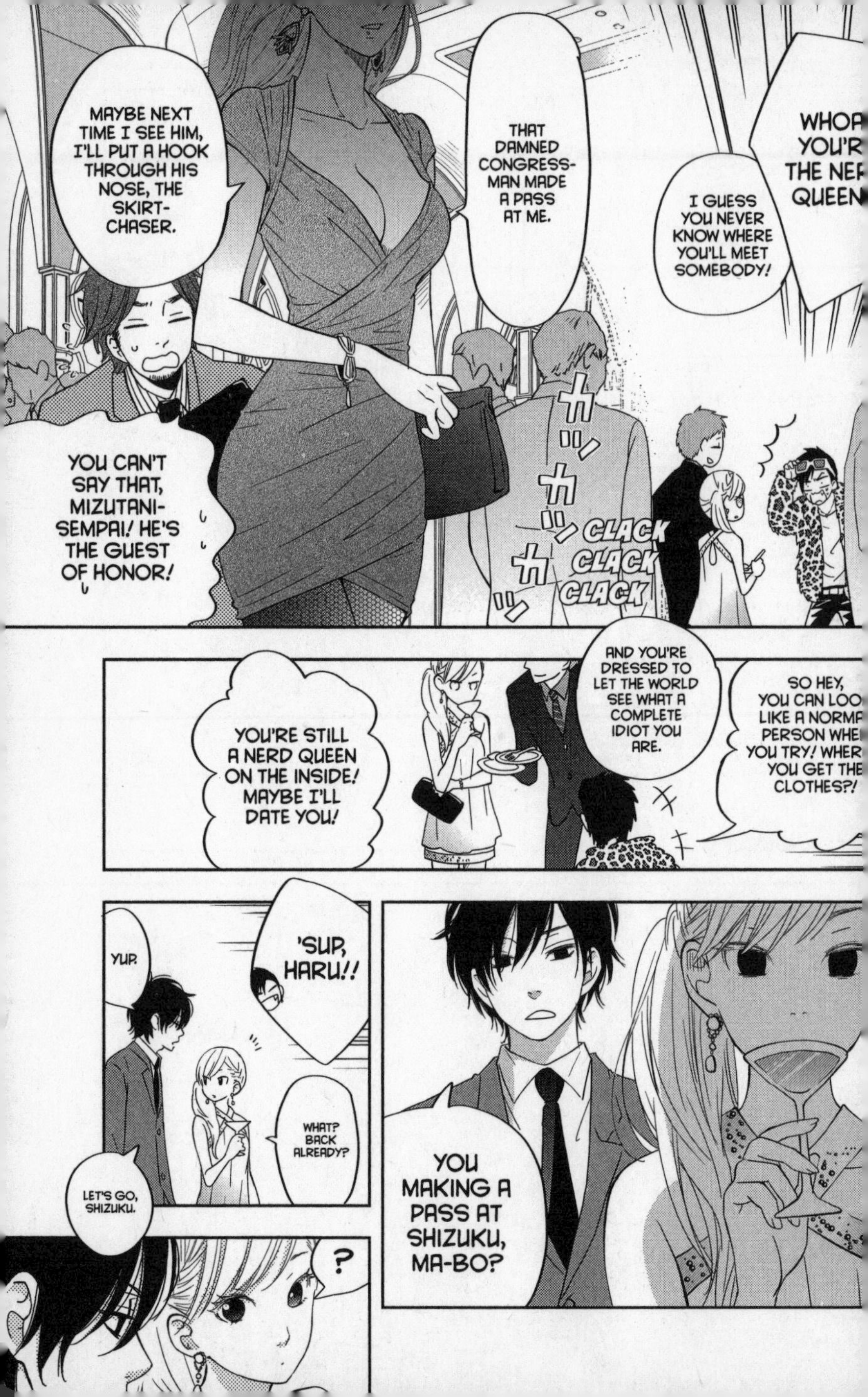
WHOA YOU'R THE NER QUEEN
I GUESS YOU NEVER KNOW WHERE YOU'LL MEET SOMEBODY!
THAT DAMNED CONGRESS-MAN MADE A PASS AT ME.
MAYBE NEXT TIME I SEE HIM, I'LL PUT A HOOK THROUGH HIS NOSE, THE SKIRT-CHASER.
CLACK CLACK CLACK
YOU CAN'T SAY THAT, MIZUTANI-SEMPAI! HE'S THE GUEST OF HONOR!
SO HEY, YOU CAN LOO LIKE A NORMA PERSON WHE YOU TRY! WHER YOU GET THE CLOTHES?!
AND YOU'RE DRESSED TO LET THE WORLD SEE WHAT A COMPLETE IDIOT YOU ARE.
YOU'RE STILL A NERD QUEEN ON THE INSIDE! MAYBE I'LL DATE YOU!
YOU MAKING A PASS AT SHIZUKU, MA-BO?
'SUP, HARU!!
YUP.
WHAT? BACK ALREADY?
LET'S GO, SHIZUKU.
?

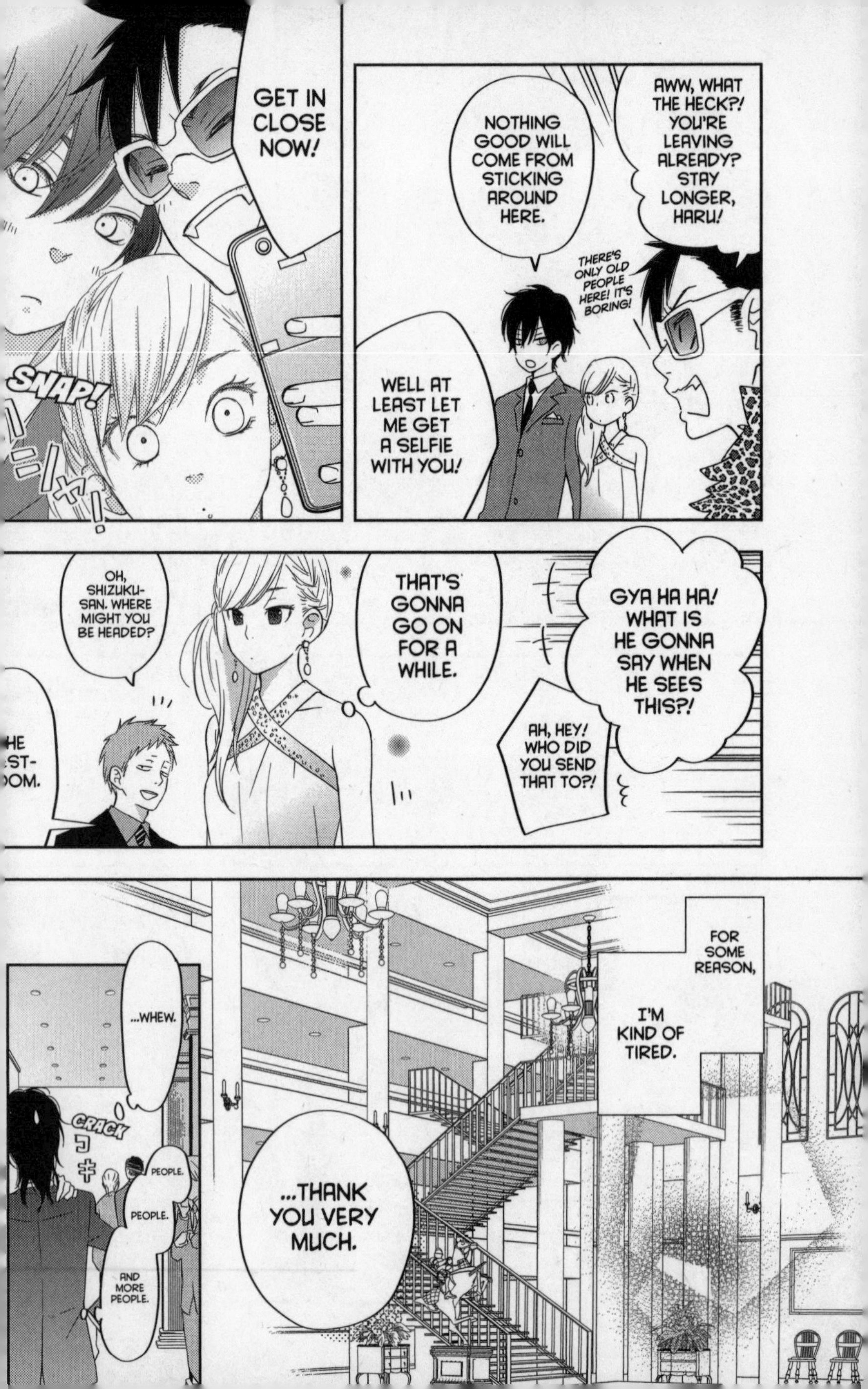
AWW, WHAT THE HECK?! YOU'RE LEAVING ALREADY? STAY LONGER, HARU!
NOTHING GOOD WILL COME FROM STICKING AROUND HERE.
THERE'S ONLY OLD PEOPLE HERE! IT'S BORING!
WELL AT LEAST LET ME GET A SELFIE WITH YOU!
GET IN CLOSE NOW!
SNAP!
GYA HA HA! WHAT IS HE GONNA SAY WHEN HE SEES THIS?!
AH, HEY! WHO DID YOU SEND THAT TO?!
THAT'S GONNA GO ON FOR A WHILE.
OH, SHIZUKU-SAN. WHERE MIGHT YOU BE HEADED?
FOR SOME REASON,
I'M KIND OF TIRED.
...THANK YOU VERY MUCH.
...WHEW.
CRACK
PEOPLE.
PEOPLE.
AND MORE PEOPLE.

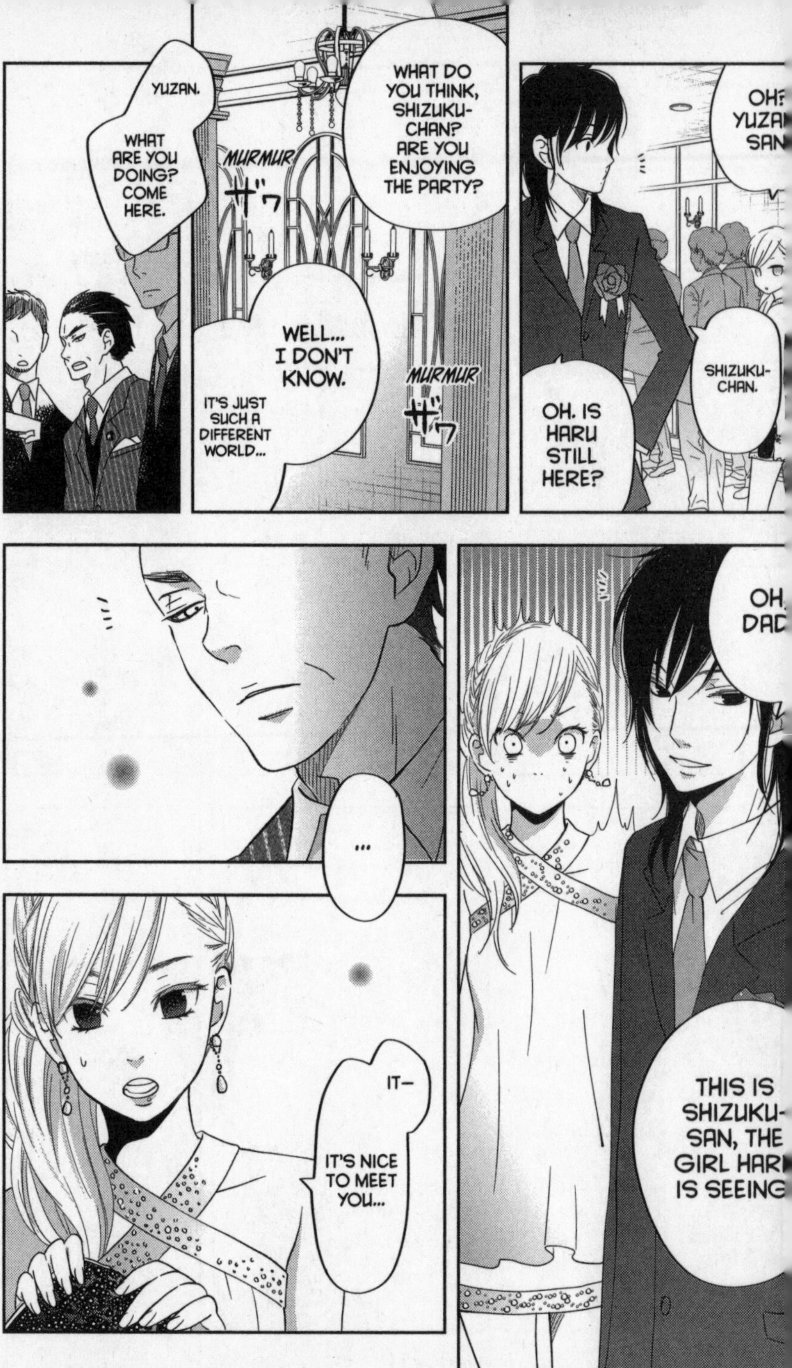
OH? YUZAN SAN
SHIZUKU-CHAN.
OH. IS HARU STILL HERE?
WHAT DO YOU THINK, SHIZUKU-CHAN? ARE YOU ENJOYING THE PARTY?
MURMUR
ザワ
WELL... I DON'T KNOW.
IT'S JUST SUCH A DIFFERENT WORLD...
MURMUR
ザワ
YUZAN.
WHAT ARE YOU DOING? COME HERE.
OH, DAD
THIS IS SHIZUKU-SAN, THE GIRL HAR IS SEEING
...
IT—
IT'S NICE TO MEET YOU...

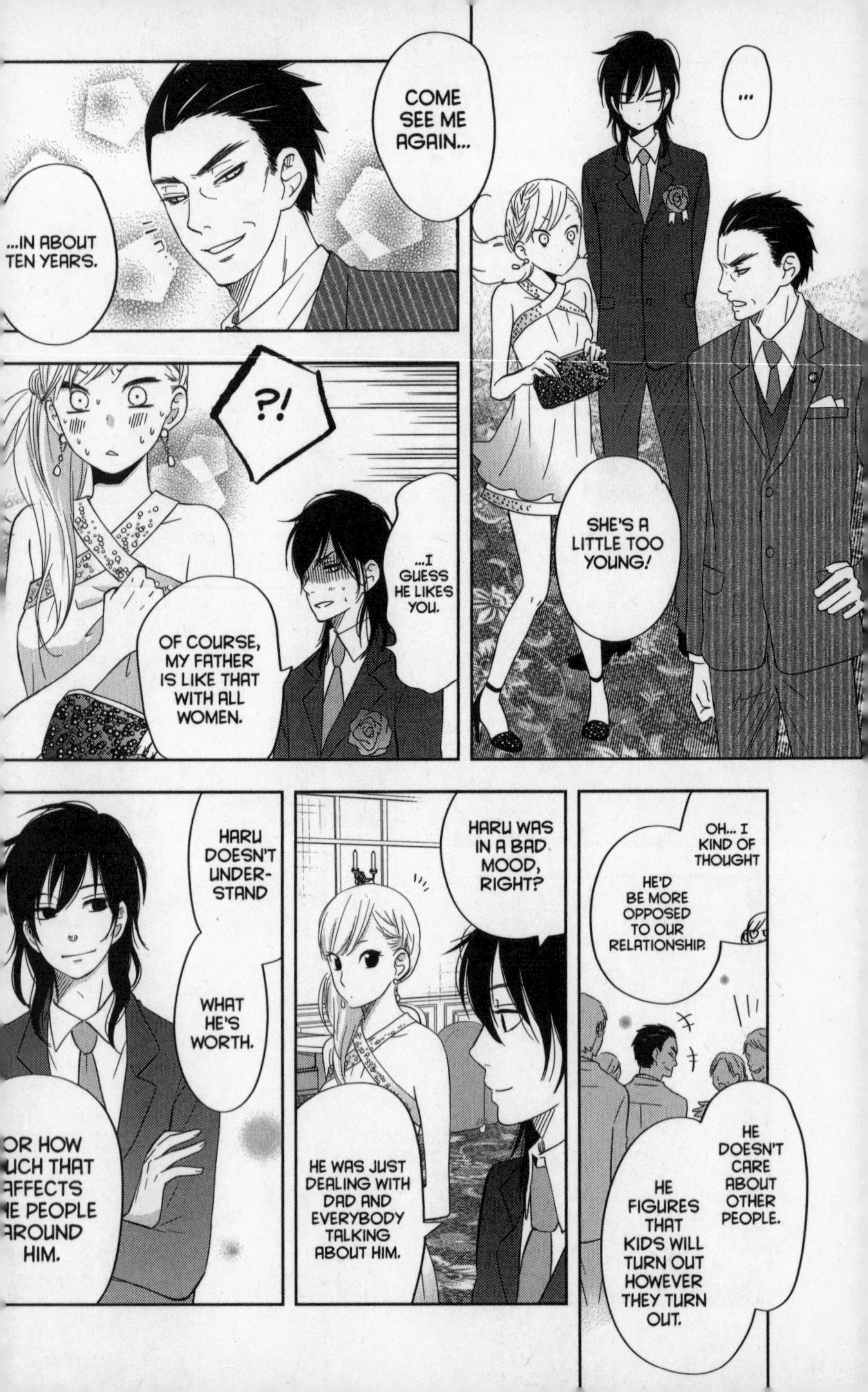
...
SHE'S A LITTLE TOO YOUNG!
COME SEE ME AGAIN...
...IN ABOUT TEN YEARS.
?!
...I GUESS HE LIKES YOU.
OF COURSE, MY FATHER IS LIKE THAT WITH ALL WOMEN.
OH... I KIND OF THOUGHT
HE'D BE MORE OPPOSED TO OUR RELATIONSHIP.
HE DOESN'T CARE ABOUT OTHER PEOPLE.
HE FIGURES THAT KIDS WILL TURN OUT HOWEVER THEY TURN OUT.
HARU WAS IN A BAD MOOD, RIGHT?
HE WAS JUST DEALING WITH DAD AND EVERYBODY TALKING ABOUT HIM.
HARU DOESN'T UNDER-STAND
WHAT HE'S WORTH.
OR HOW UCH THAT AFFECTS E PEOPLE AROUND HIM.

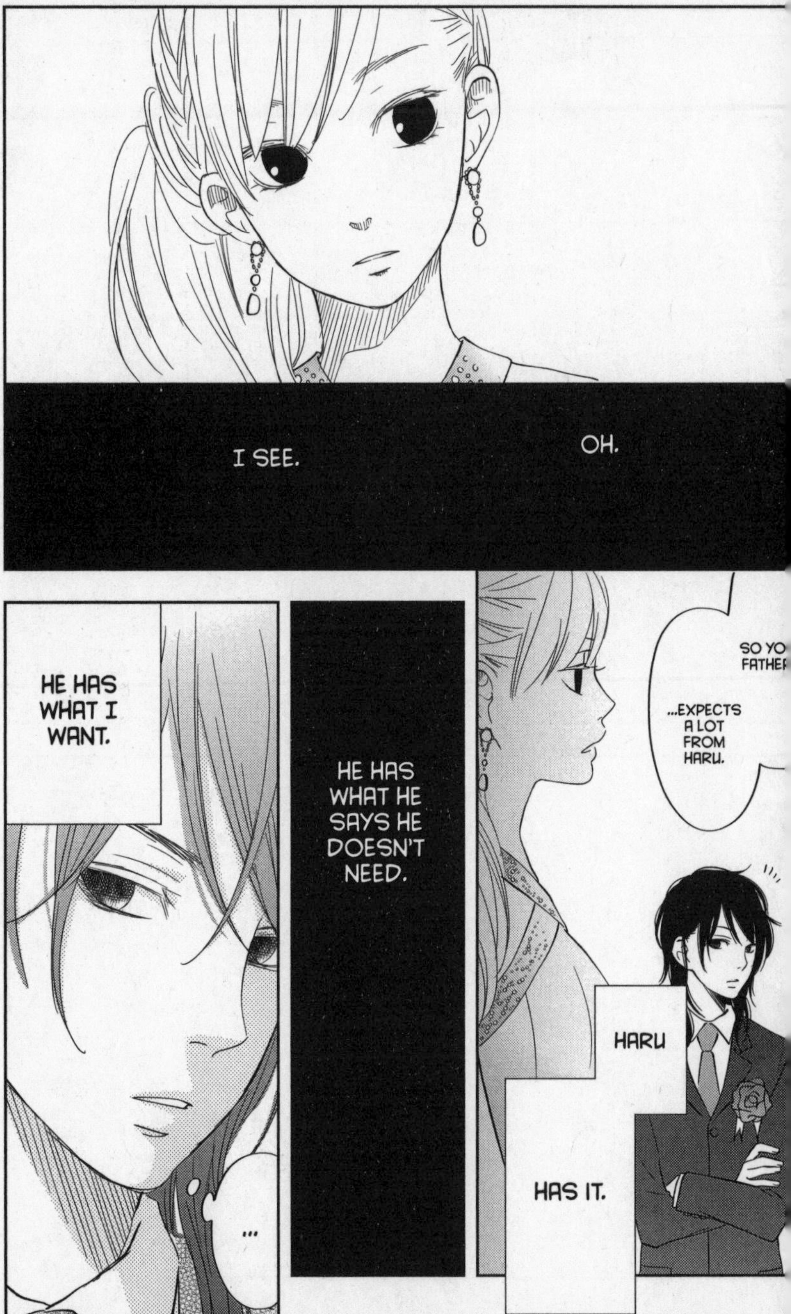

OH.
I SEE.
SO YO FATHE
...EXPECTS A LOT FROM HARU.
HARU
HAS IT.
HE HAS WHAT HE SAYS HE DOESN'T NEED.
HE HAS WHAT I WANT.
...

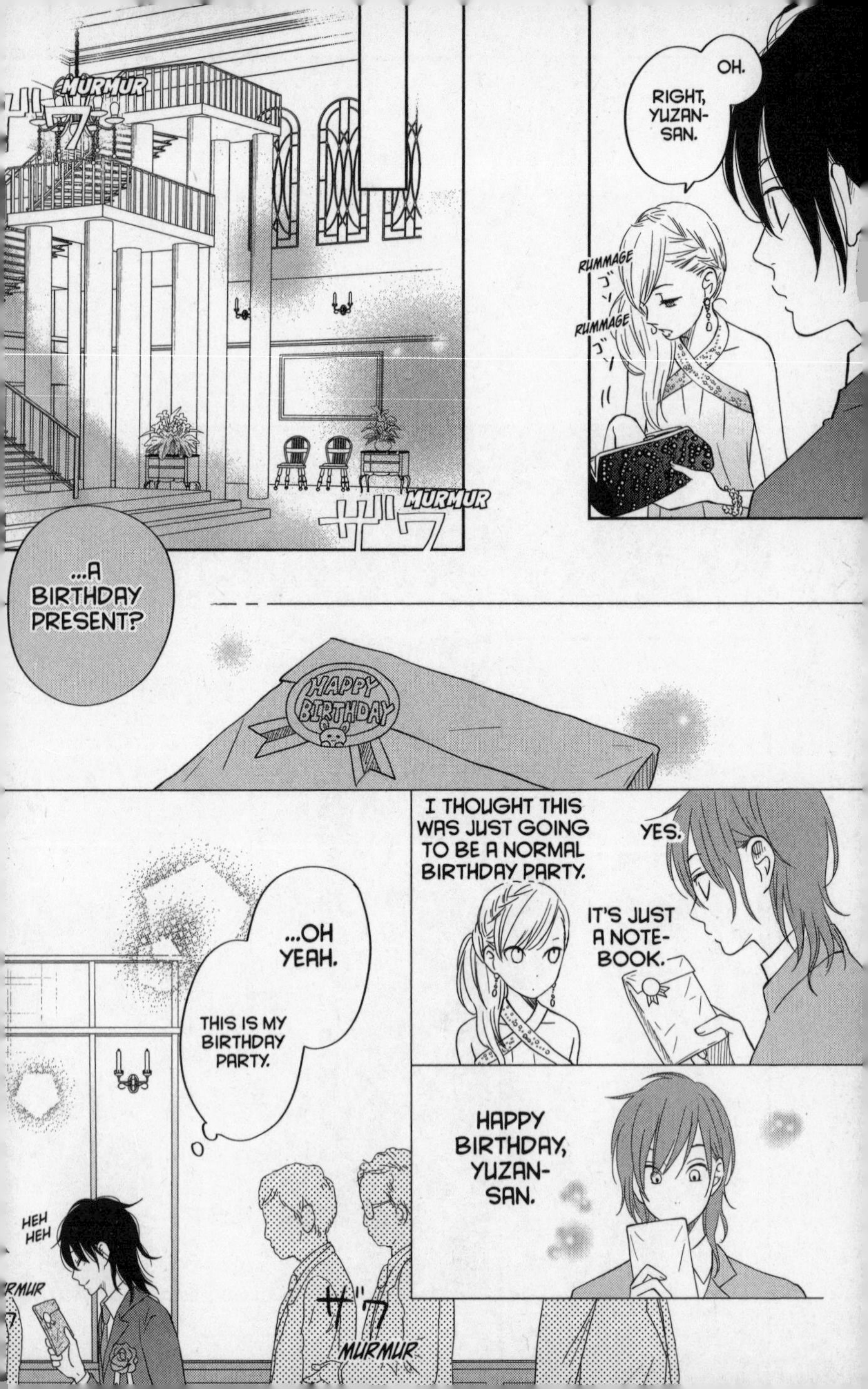
OH.
RIGHT, YUZAN-SAN.
RUMMAGE
RUMMAGE
MURMUR
MURMUR
...A BIRTHDAY PRESENT?
HAPPY BIRTHDAY
YES.
I THOUGHT THIS WAS JUST GOING TO BE A NORMAL BIRTHDAY PARTY.
IT'S JUST A NOTE-BOOK.
HAPPY BIRTHDAY, YUZAN-SAN.
...OH YEAH.
THIS IS MY BIRTHDAY PARTY.
HEH HEH
MURMUR
MURMUR

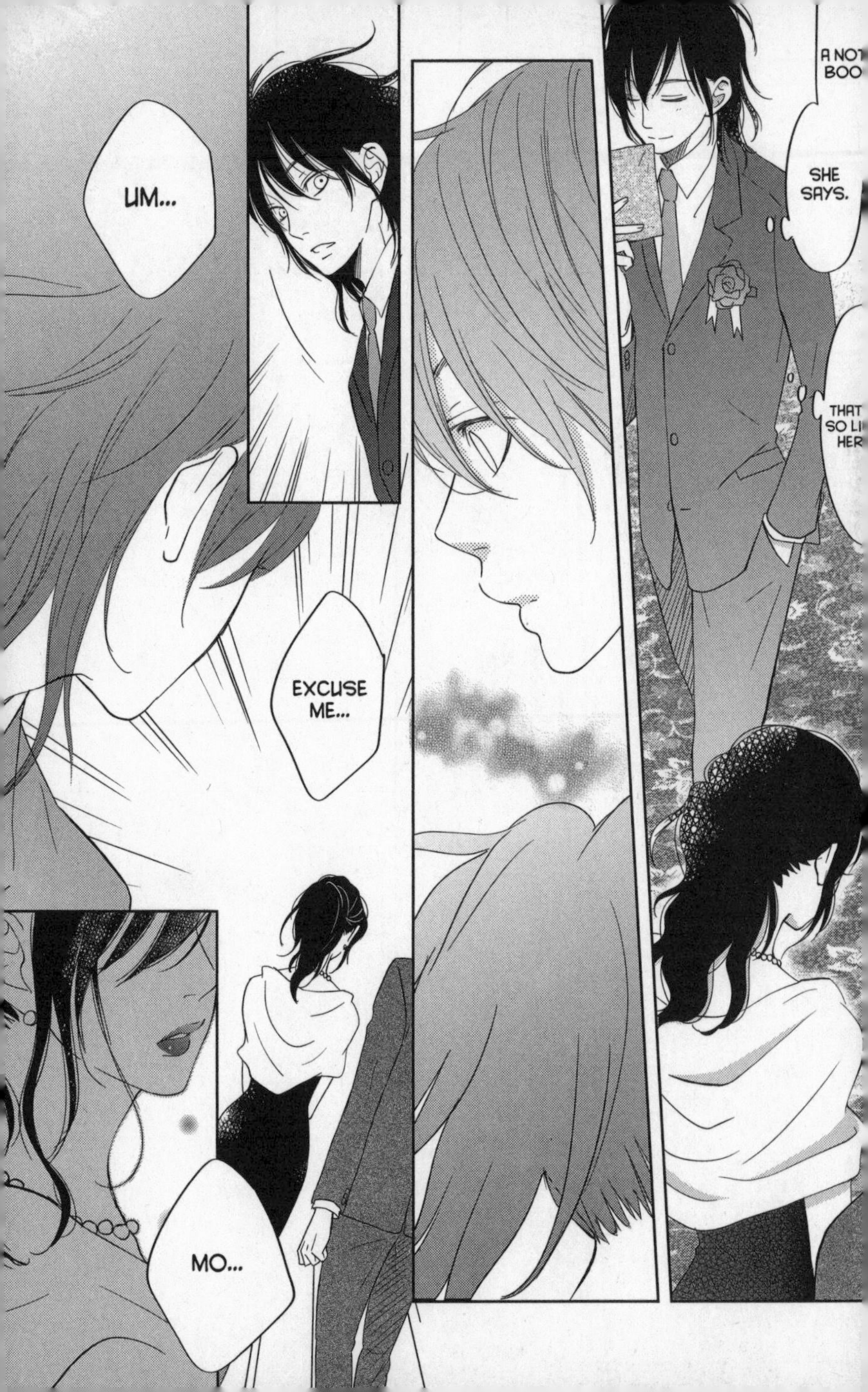
A NOT BOO
SHE SAYS.
THAT SO LI HER
UM...
EXCUSE ME...
MO...

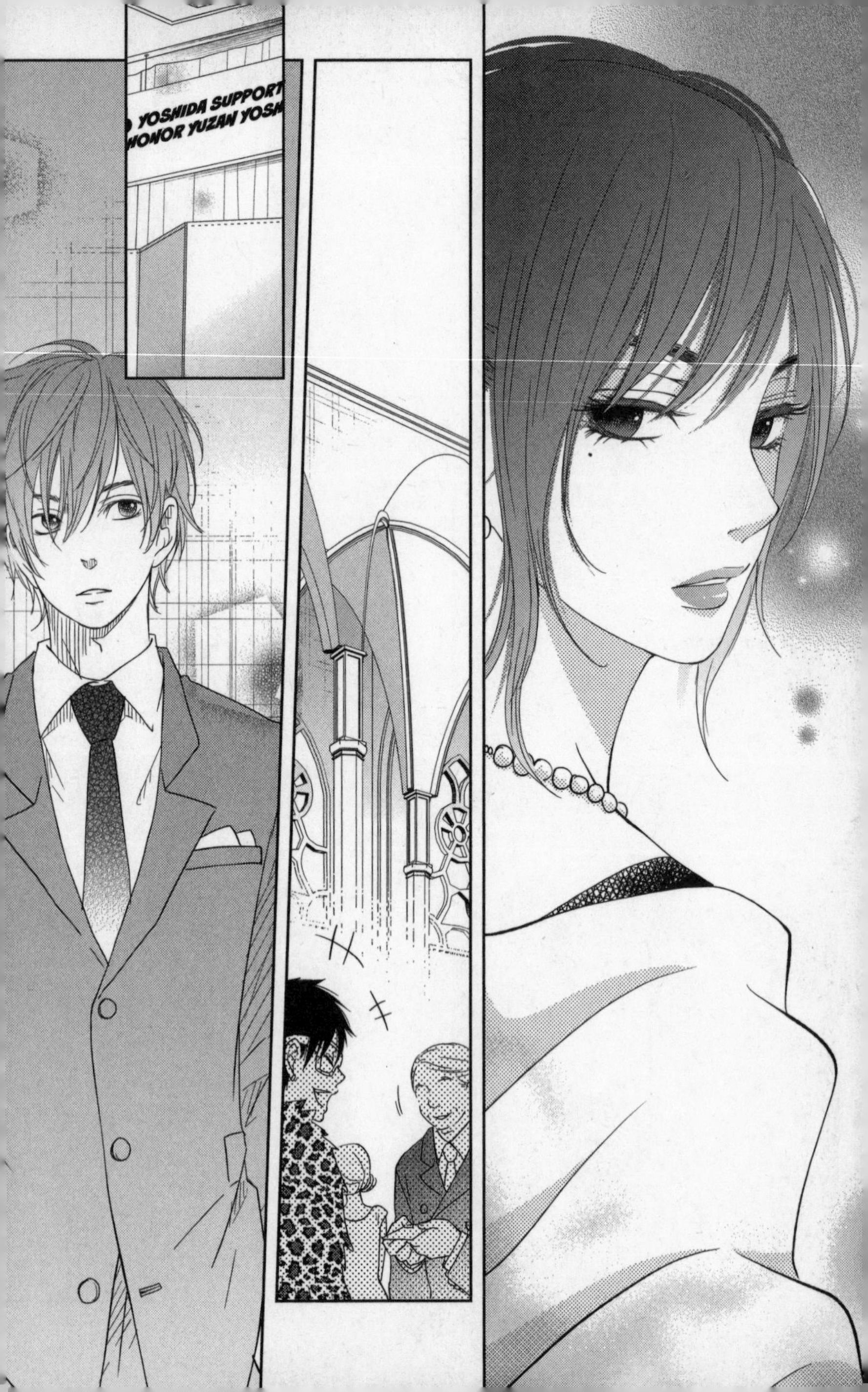
YOSHIDA SUPPORT
HONOR YUZAN YOSH

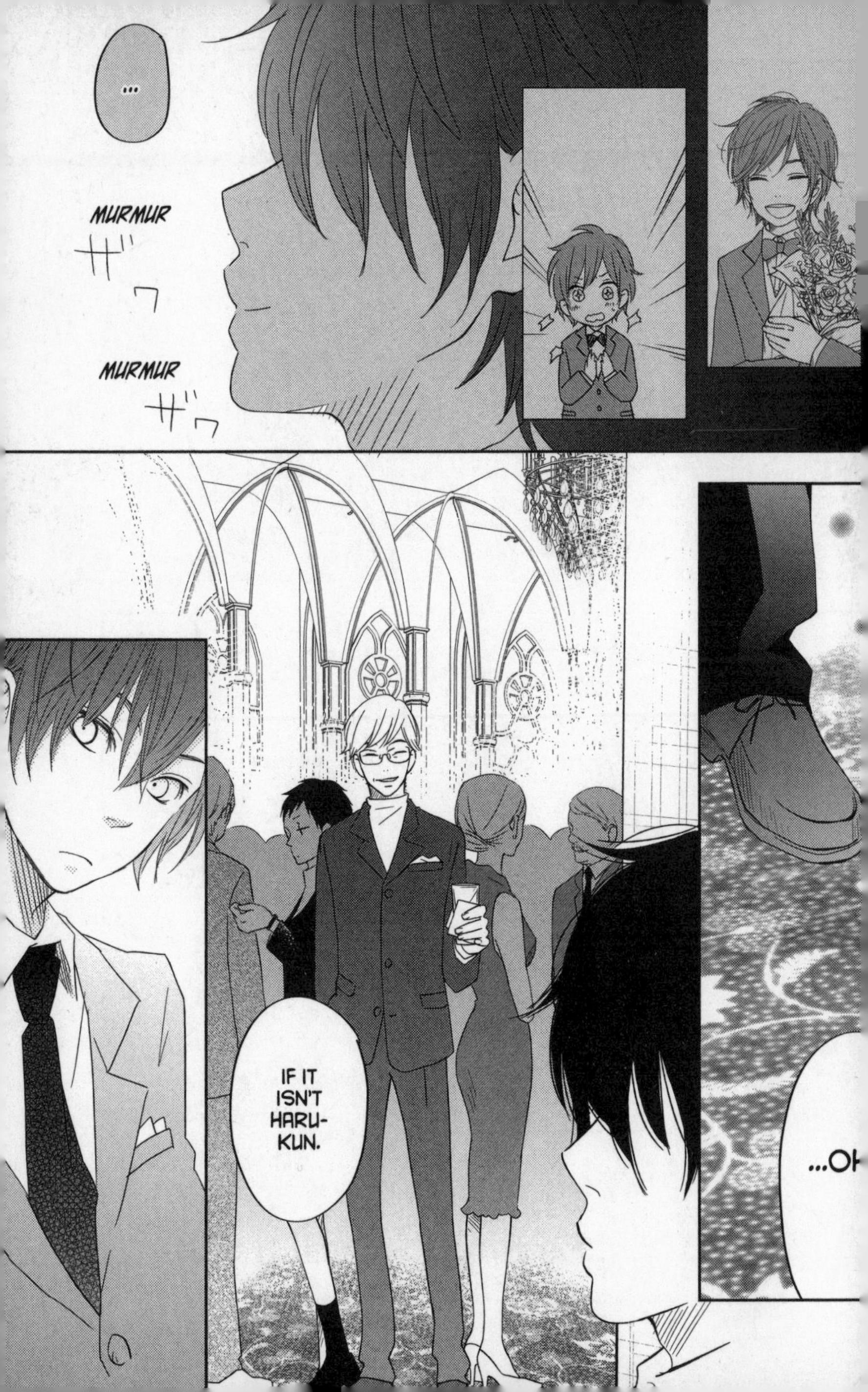
...
MURMUR
ザワ
MURMUR
ザワ
...OH
IF IT ISN'T HARU-KUN.

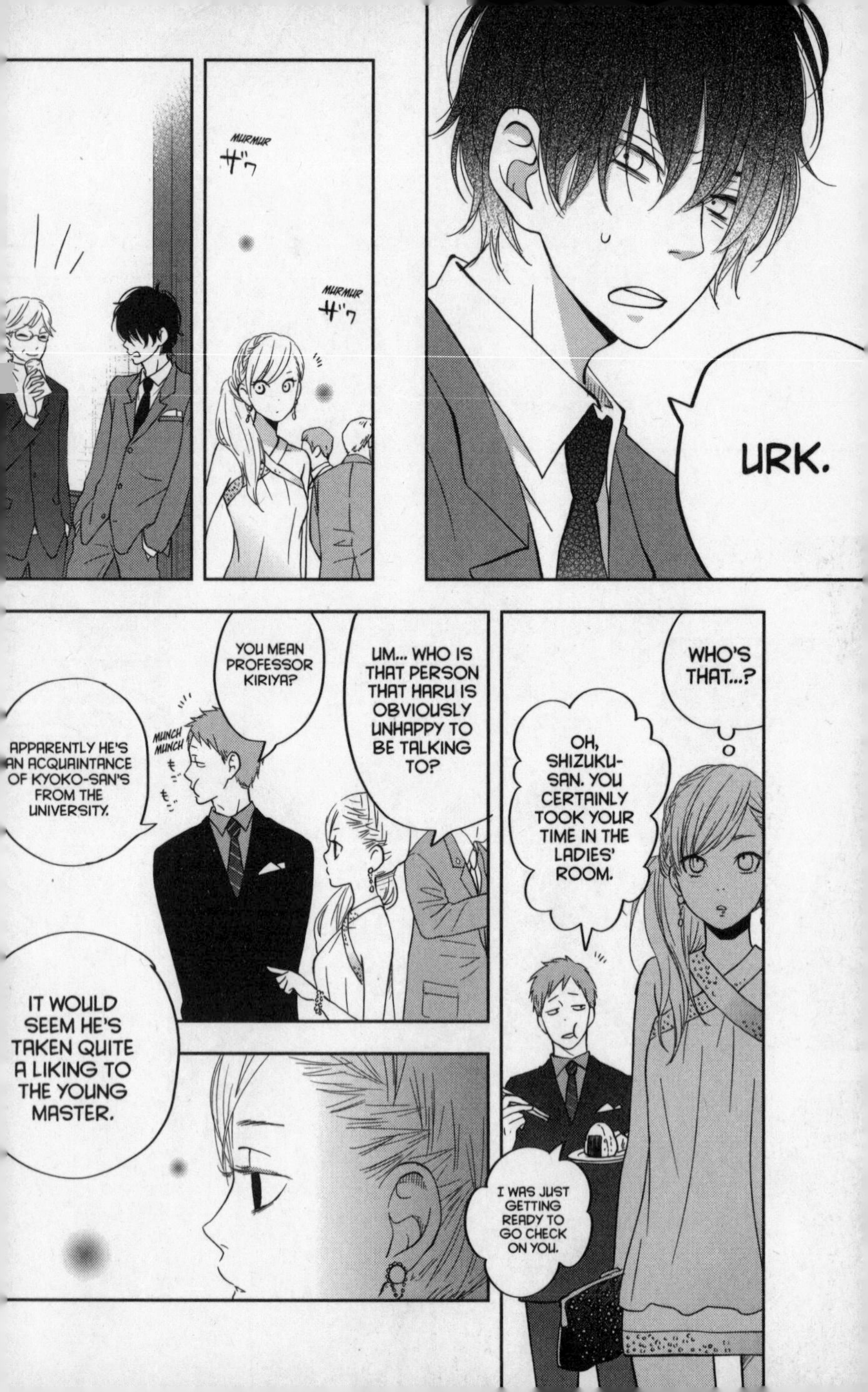
URK.
MURMUR
ザワ
MURMUR
ザワ
WHO'S THAT...?
OH, SHIZUKU-SAN. YOU CERTAINLY TOOK YOUR TIME IN THE LADIES' ROOM.
I WAS JUST GETTING READY TO GO CHECK ON YOU.
UM... WHO IS THAT PERSON THAT HARU IS OBVIOUSLY UNHAPPY TO BE TALKING TO?
YOU MEAN PROFESSOR KIRIYA?
MUNCH MUNCH
APPARENTLY HE'S AN ACQUAINTANCE OF KYOKO-SAN'S FROM THE UNIVERSITY.
IT WOULD SEEM HE'S TAKEN QUITE A LIKING TO THE YOUNG MASTER.

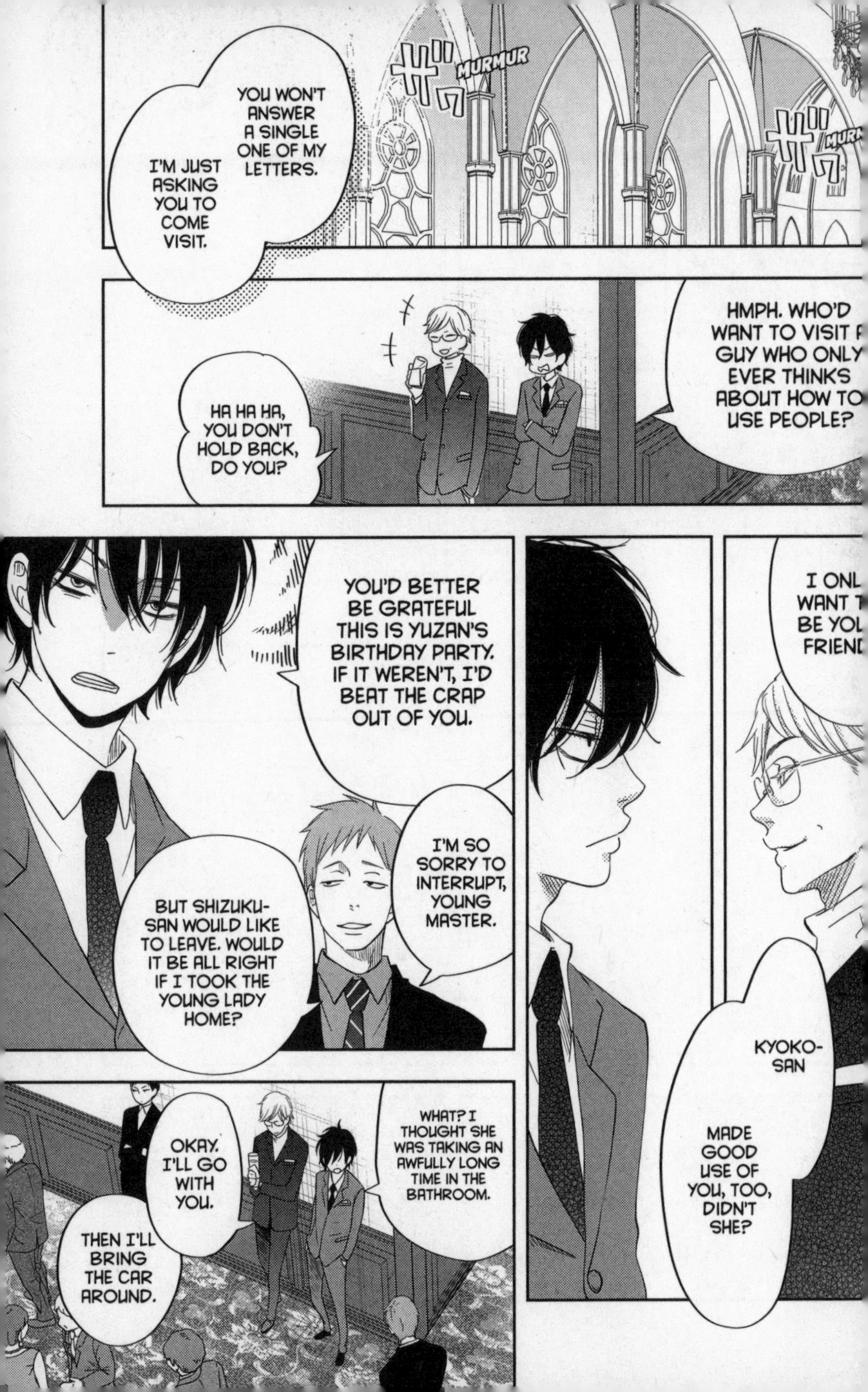
ザワ MURMUR
ザワ MURM
YOU WON'T ANSWER A SINGLE ONE OF MY LETTERS.
I'M JUST ASKING YOU TO COME VISIT.
HMPH. WHO'D WANT TO VISIT GUY WHO ONLY EVER THINKS ABOUT HOW TO USE PEOPLE?
HA HA HA, YOU DON'T HOLD BACK, DO YOU?
I ONL WANT T BE YO FRIEN
KYOKO-SAN
MADE GOOD USE OF YOU, TOO, DIDN'T SHE?
YOU'D BETTER BE GRATEFUL THIS IS YUZAN'S BIRTHDAY PARTY. IF IT WEREN'T, I'D BEAT THE CRAP OUT OF YOU.
I'M SO SORRY TO INTERRUPT, YOUNG MASTER.
BUT SHIZUKU-SAN WOULD LIKE TO LEAVE. WOULD IT BE ALL RIGHT IF I TOOK THE YOUNG LADY HOME?
WHAT? I THOUGHT SHE WAS TAKING AN AWFULLY LONG TIME IN THE BATHROOM.
OKAY. I'LL GO WITH YOU.
THEN I'LL BRING THE CAR AROUND.

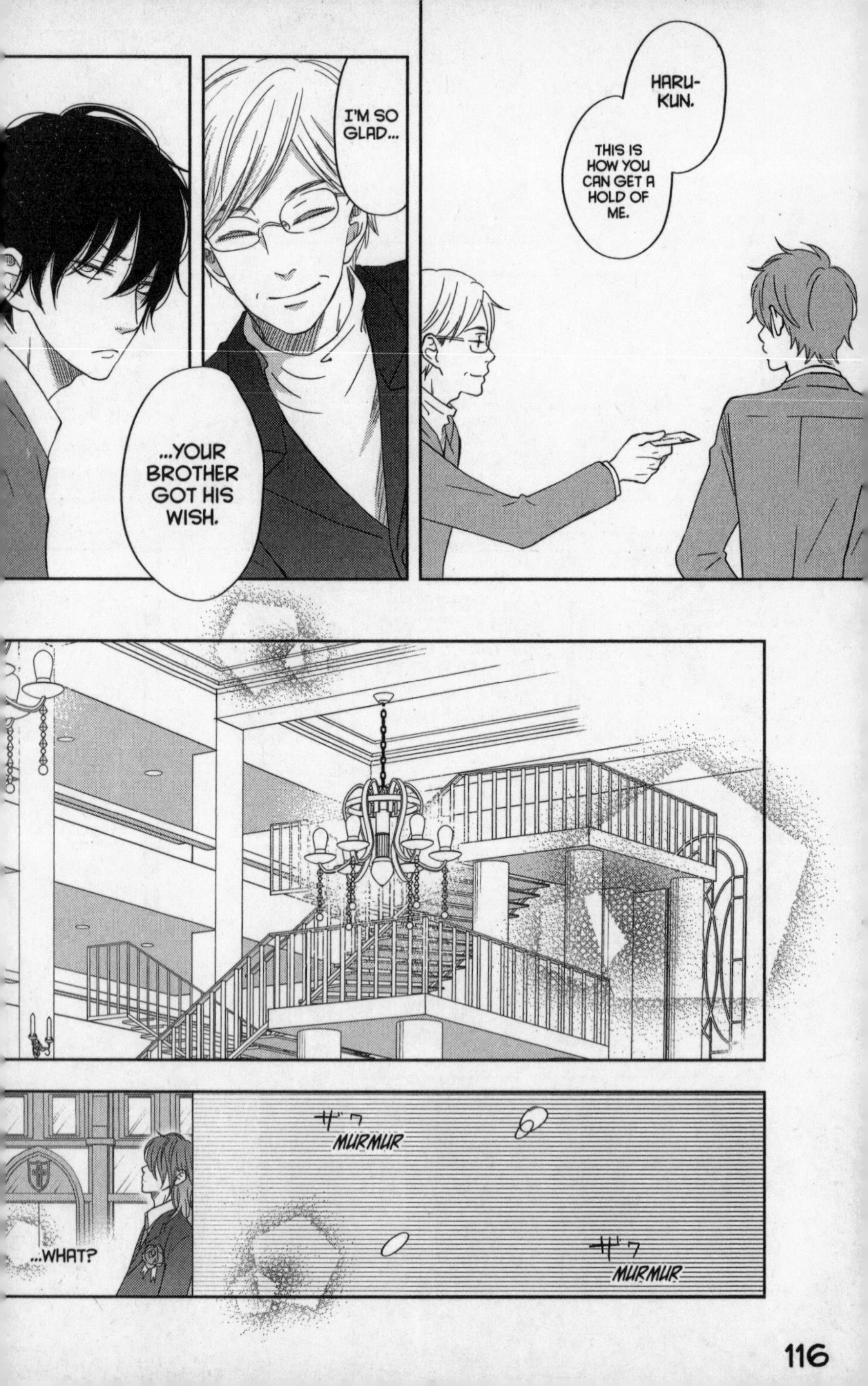
HARU-KUN.
THIS IS HOW YOU CAN GET A HOLD OF ME.
I'M SO GLAD...
...YOUR BROTHER GOT HIS WISH.
ザワ
MURMUR
ザワ
MURMUR
...WHAT?

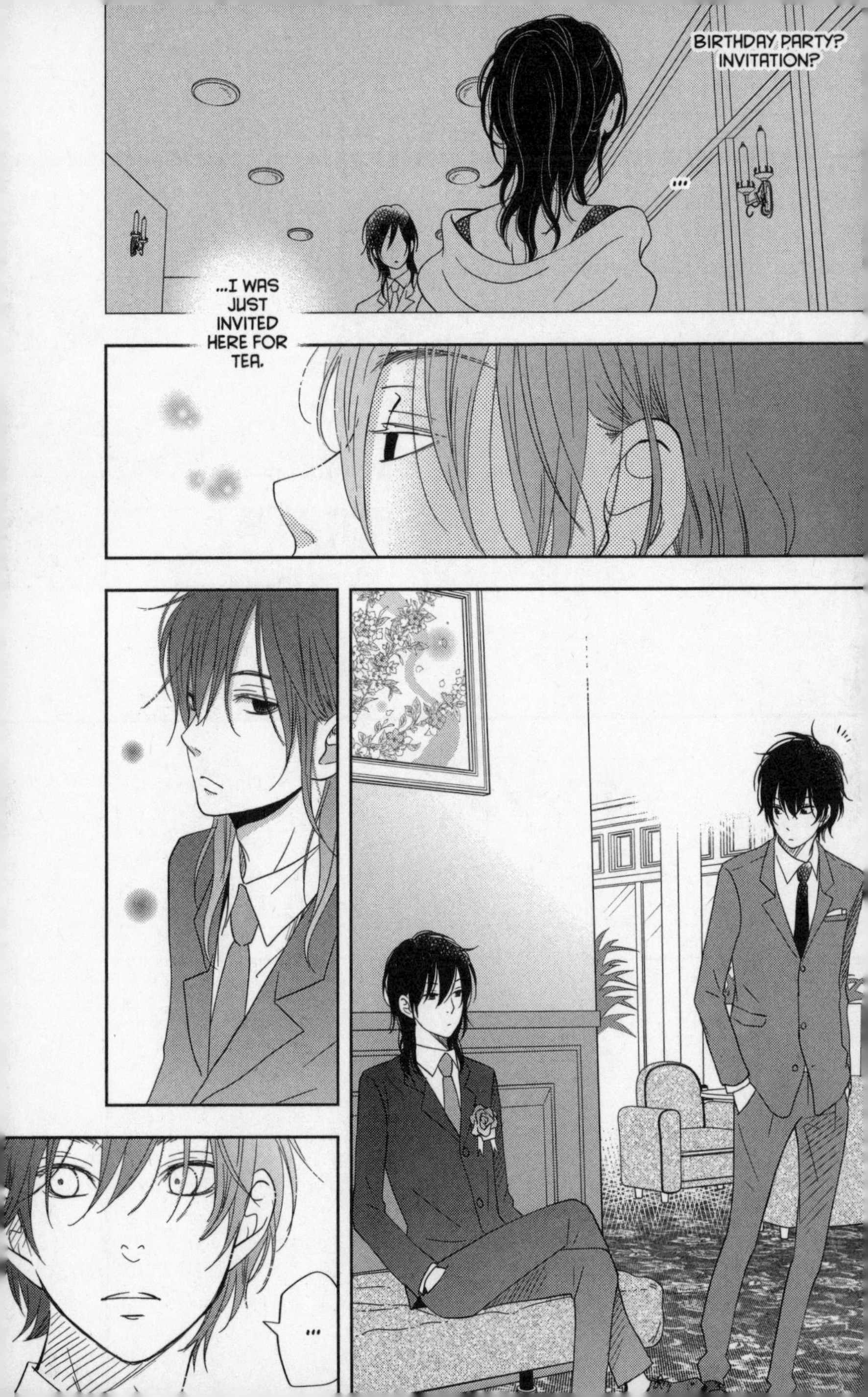
BIRTHDAY PARTY? INVITATION?
...
...I WAS JUST INVITED HERE FOR TEA.
...

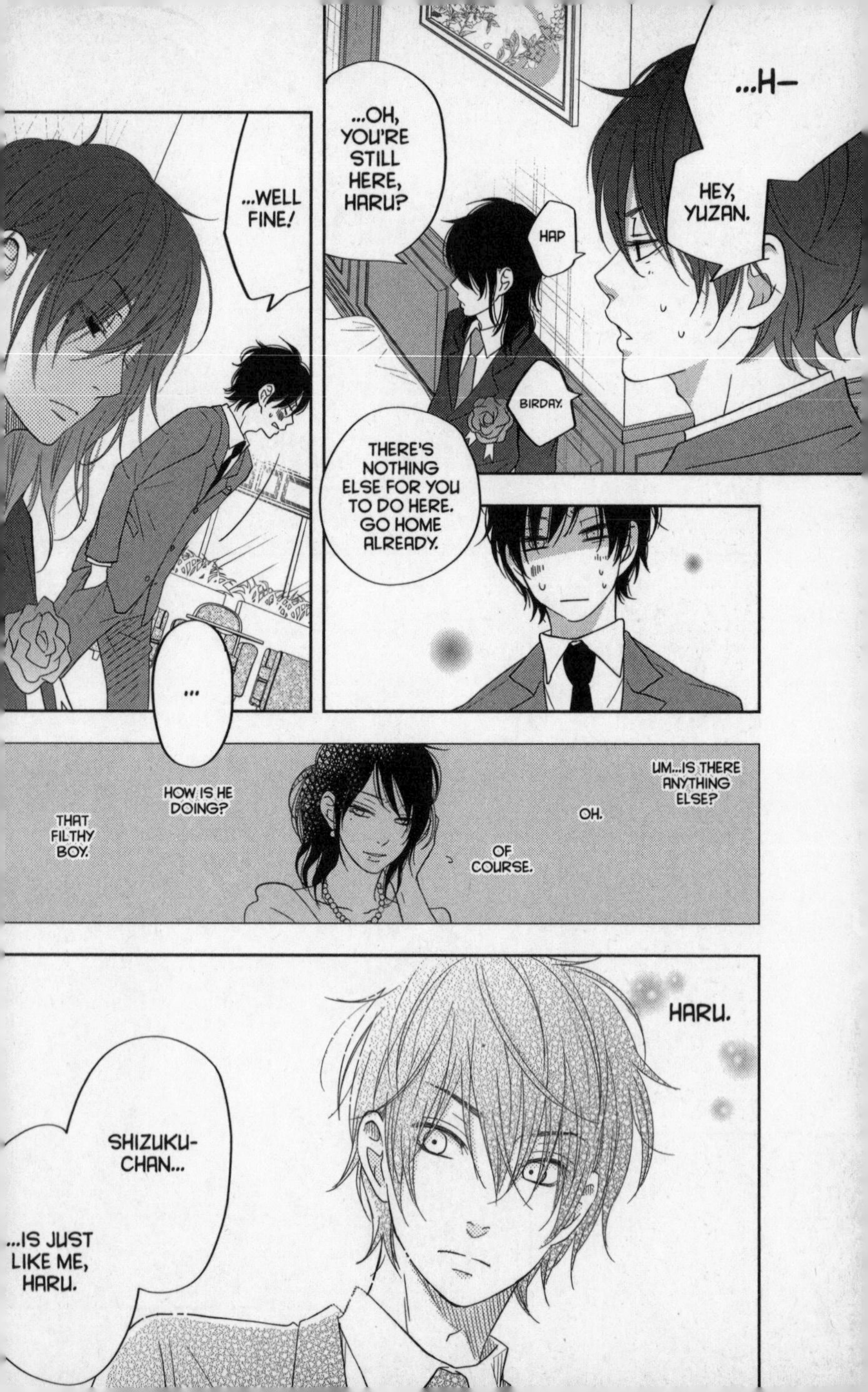
...H—
HEY, YUZAN.
...OH, YOU'RE STILL HERE, HARU?
HAP
BIRDAY.
THERE'S NOTHING ELSE FOR YOU TO DO HERE. GO HOME ALREADY.
...WELL FINE!
...
UM...IS THERE ANYTHING ELSE?
OH.
OF COURSE.
HOW IS HE DOING?
THAT FILTHY BOY.
HARU.
SHIZUKU-CHAN...
...IS JUST LIKE ME, HARU.

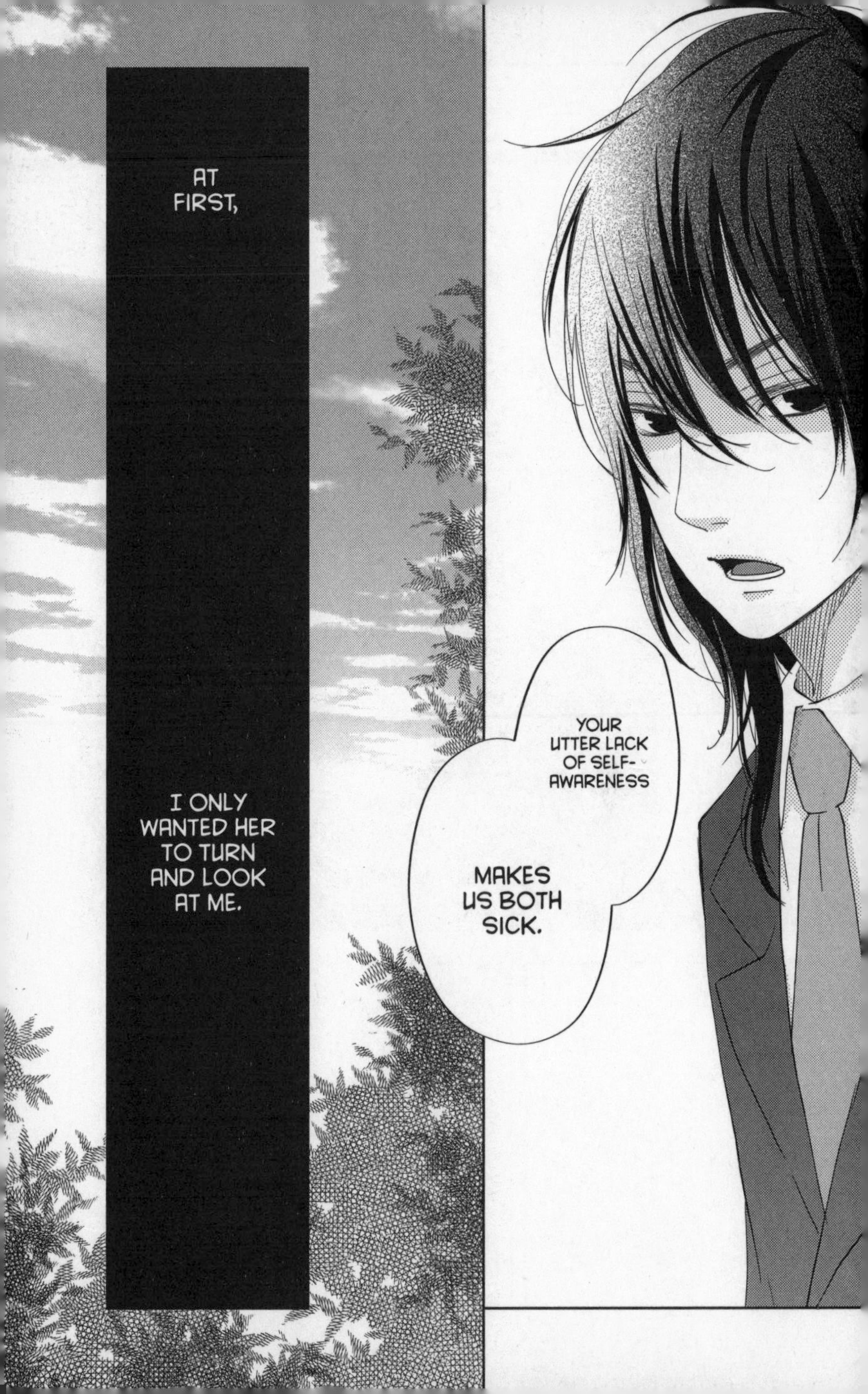
YOUR UTTER LACK OF SELF-AWARENESS
MAKES US BOTH SICK.
AT FIRST,
I ONLY WANTED HER TO TURN AND LOOK AT ME.

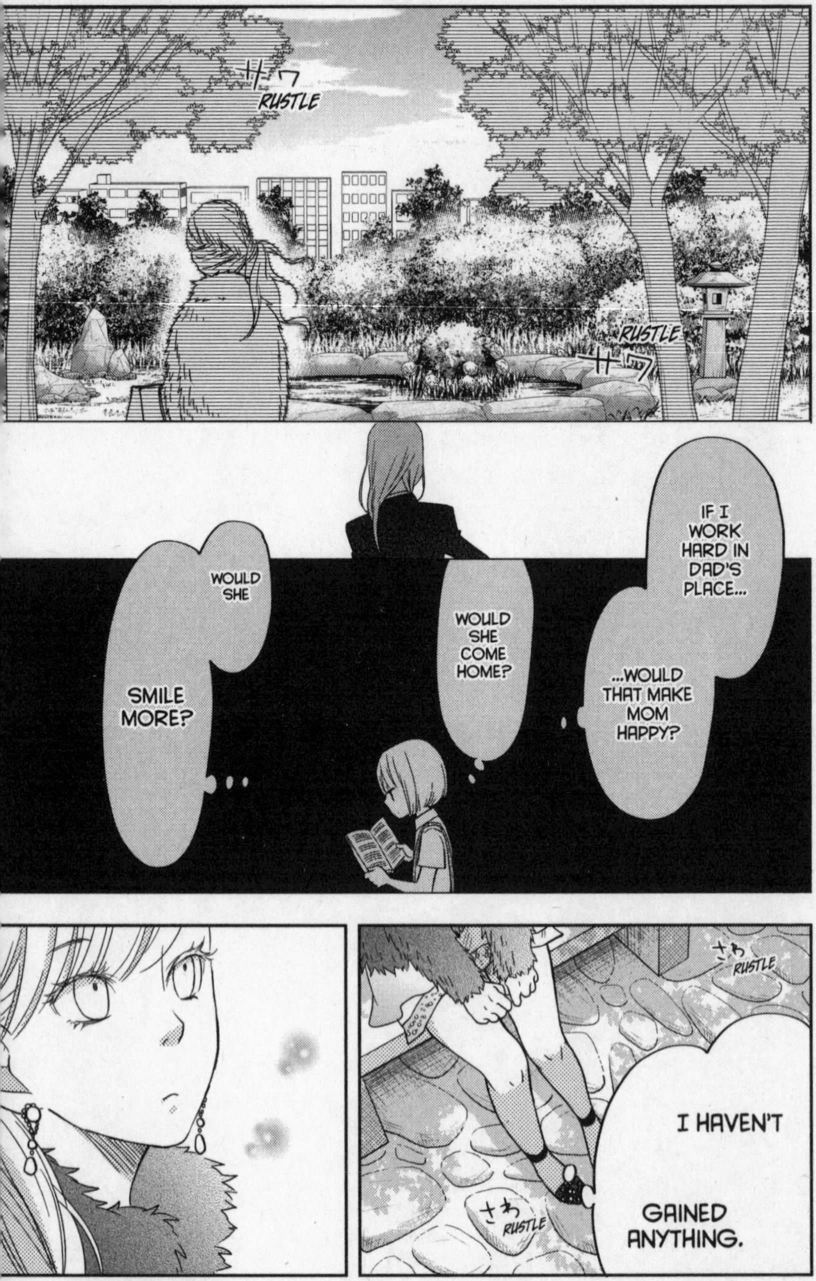
RUSTLE
サワ
サワ
RUSTLE
IF I WORK HARD IN DAD'S PLACE...
...WOULD THAT MAKE MOM HAPPY?
WOULD SHE COME HOME?
WOULD SHE
SMILE MORE?
さわ
RUSTLE
I HAVEN'T
GAINED ANYTHING.
さわ
RUSTLE

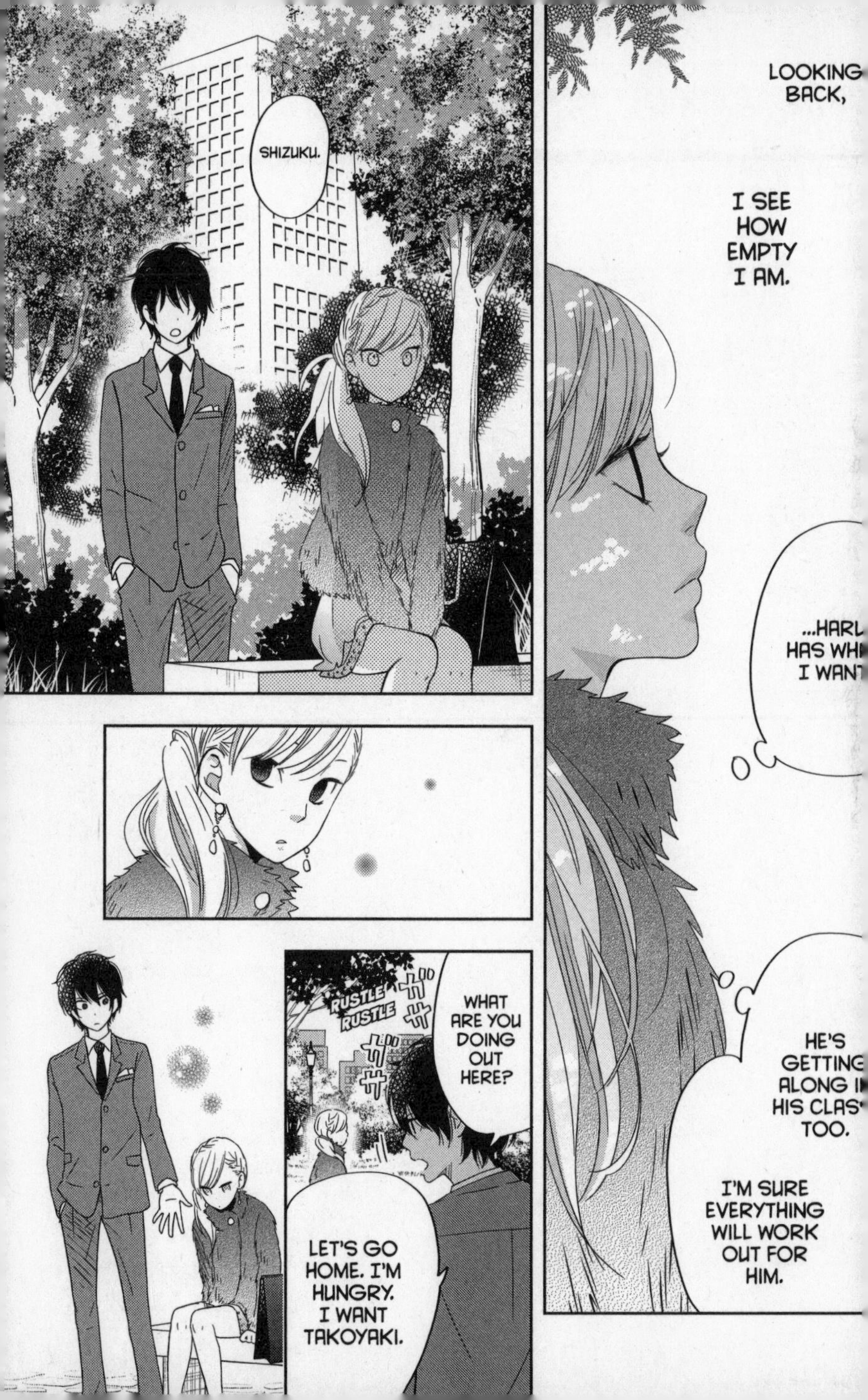
LOOKING BACK,
I SEE HOW EMPTY I AM.
...HAR HAS WH I WAN
HE'S GETTIN ALONG I HIS CLAS TOO.
I'M SURE EVERYTHING WILL WORK OUT FOR HIM.
SHIZUKU.
RUSTLE RUSTLE
WHAT ARE YOU DOING OUT HERE?
LET'S GO HOME. I'M HUNGRY. I WANT TAKOYAKI.

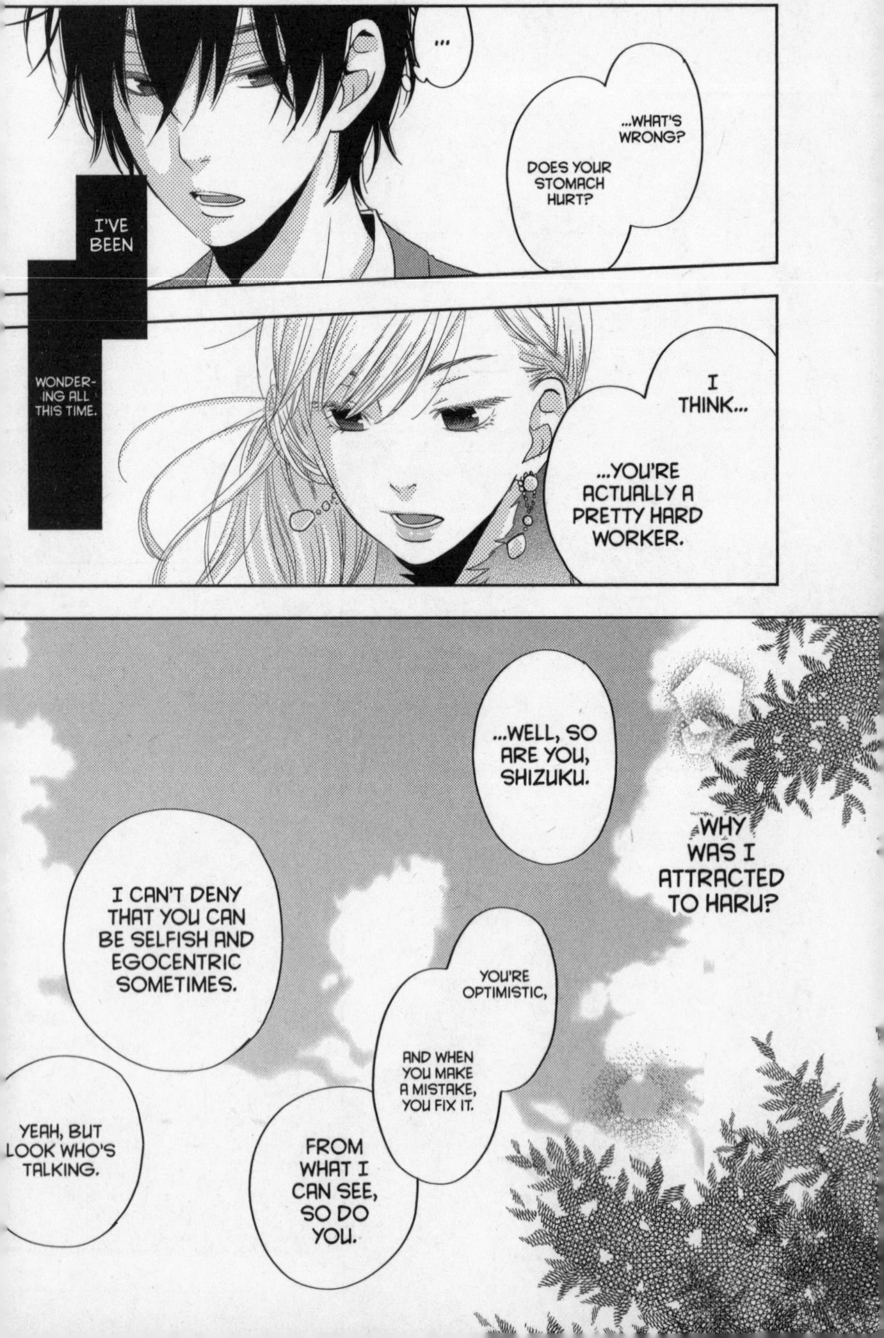
...
...WHAT'S WRONG?
DOES YOUR STOMACH HURT?
I'VE BEEN
WONDERING ALL THIS TIME.
I THINK...
...YOU'RE ACTUALLY A PRETTY HARD WORKER.
...WELL, SO ARE YOU, SHIZUKU.
WHY WAS I ATTRACTED TO HARU?
YOU'RE OPTIMISTIC,
AND WHEN YOU MAKE A MISTAKE, YOU FIX IT.
I CAN'T DENY THAT YOU CAN BE SELFISH AND EGOCENTRIC SOMETIMES.
FROM WHAT I CAN SEE, SO DO YOU.
YEAH, BUT LOOK WHO'S TALKING.

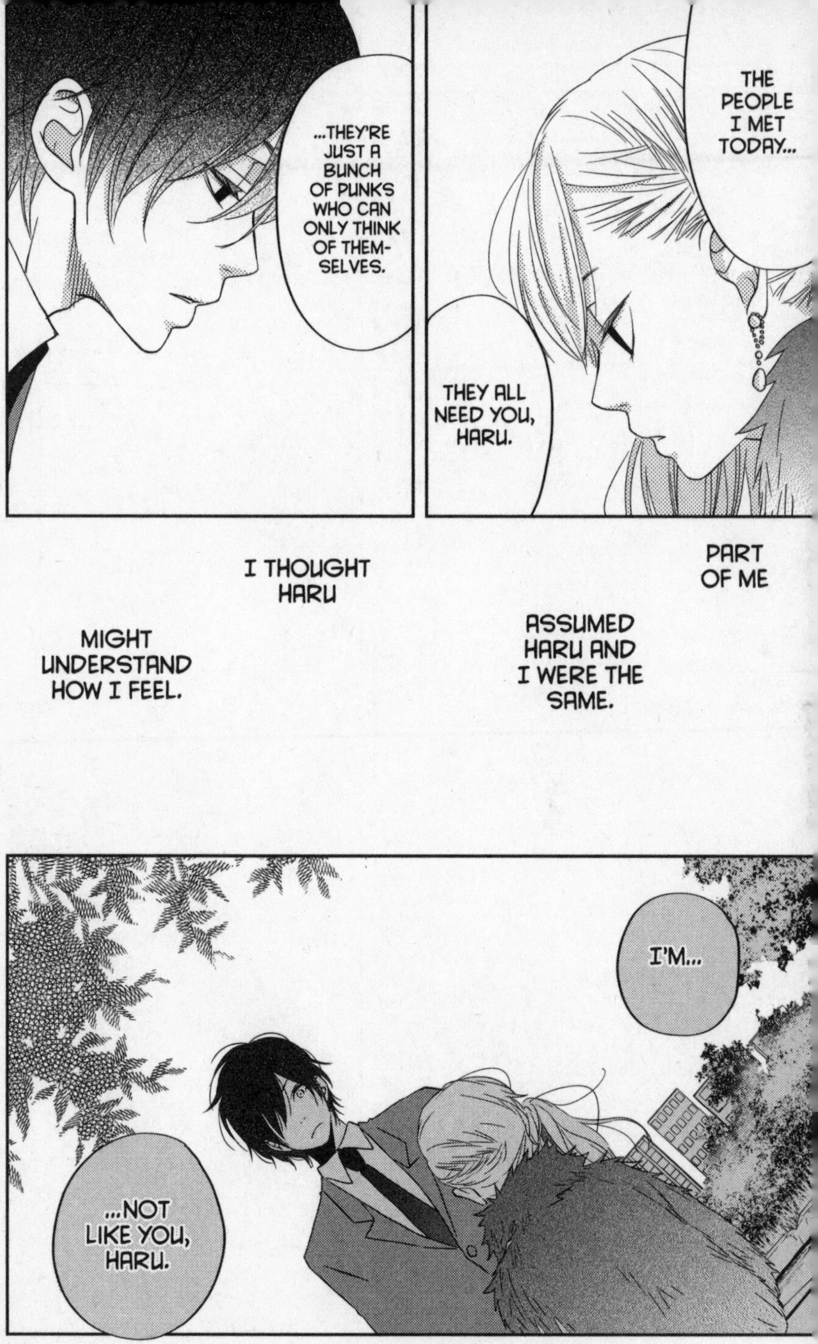
THE PEOPLE I MET TODAY...
THEY ALL NEED YOU, HARU.
...THEY'RE JUST A BUNCH OF PUNKS WHO CAN ONLY THINK OF THEM-SELVES.
PART OF ME
ASSUMED HARU AND I WERE THE SAME.
I THOUGHT HARU
MIGHT UNDERSTAND HOW I FEEL.
I'M...
...NOT LIKE YOU, HARU.

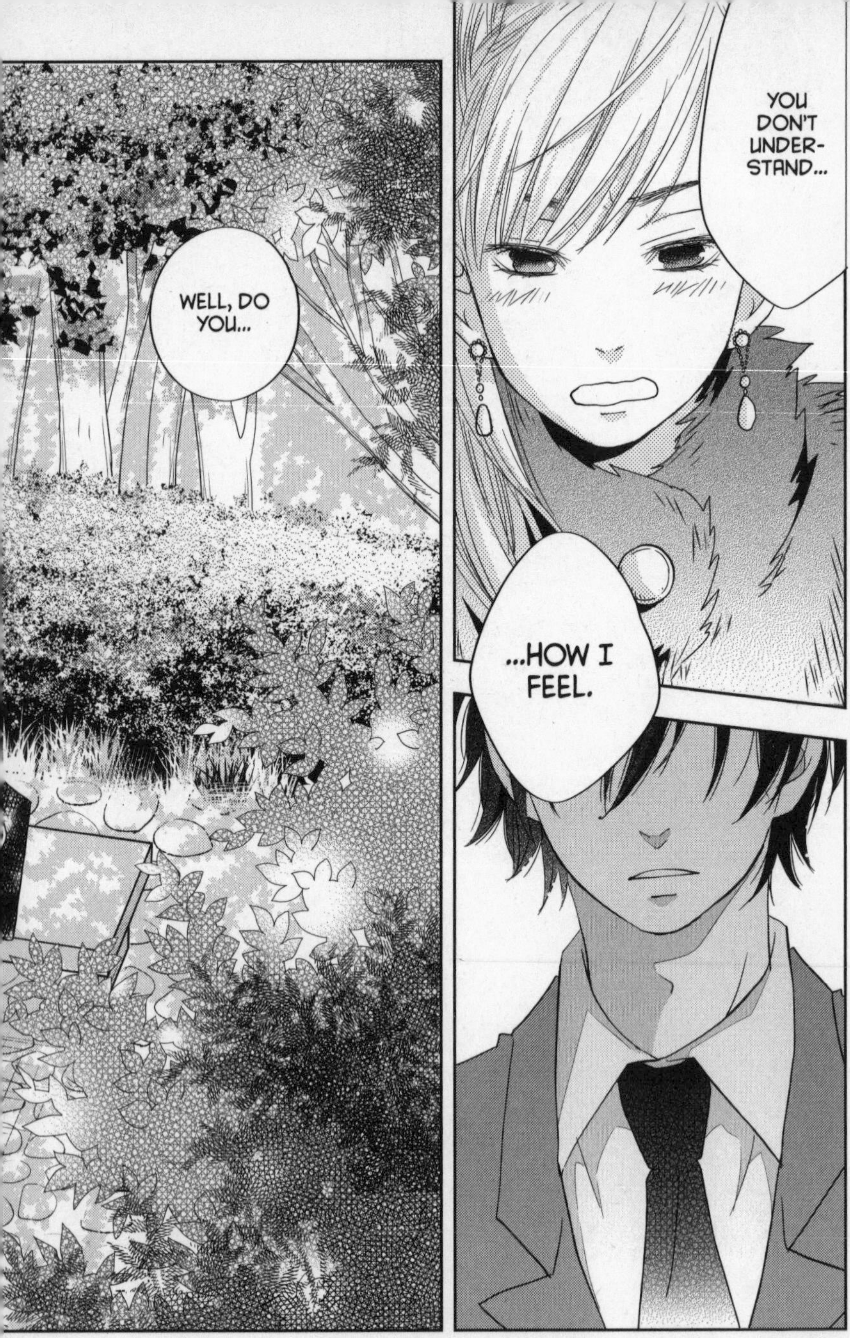
YOU DON'T UNDER-STAND...
...HOW I FEEL.
WELL, DO YOU...

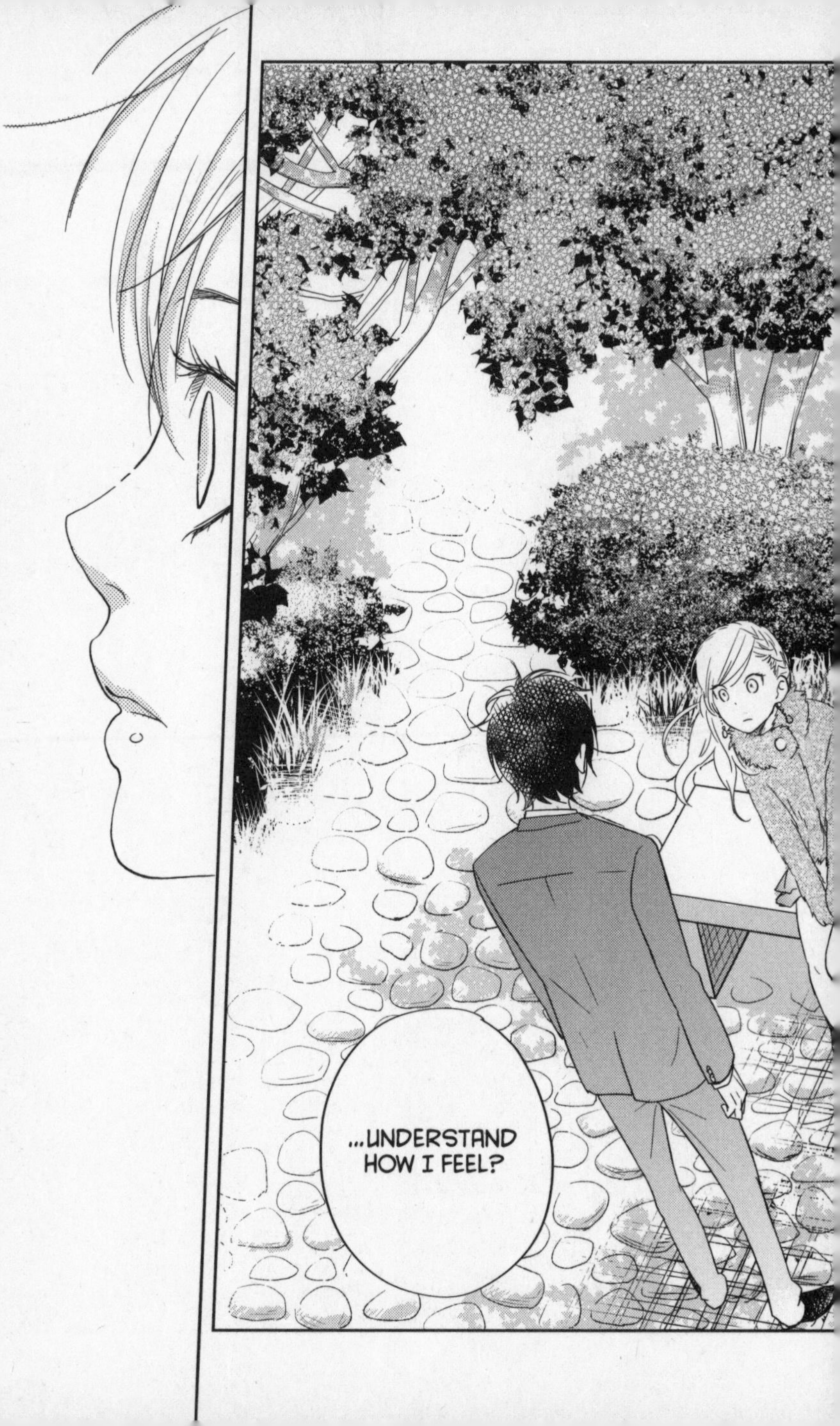
...UNDERSTAND HOW I FEEL?

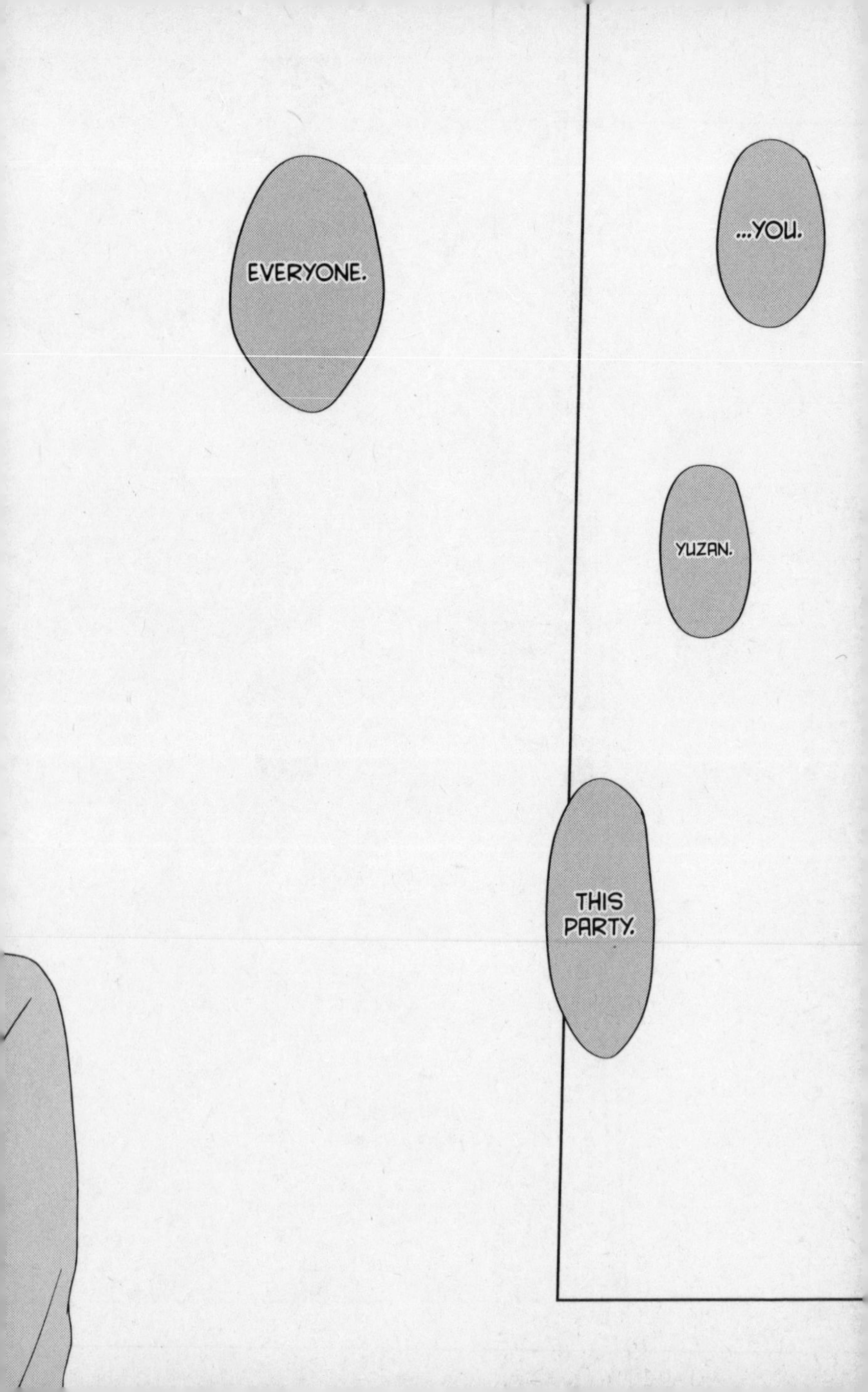

EVERYONE.

...YOU.

YUZAN.

THIS PARTY.

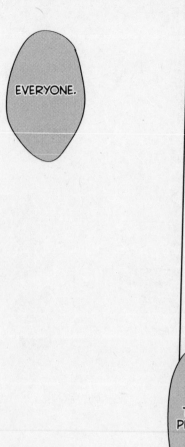

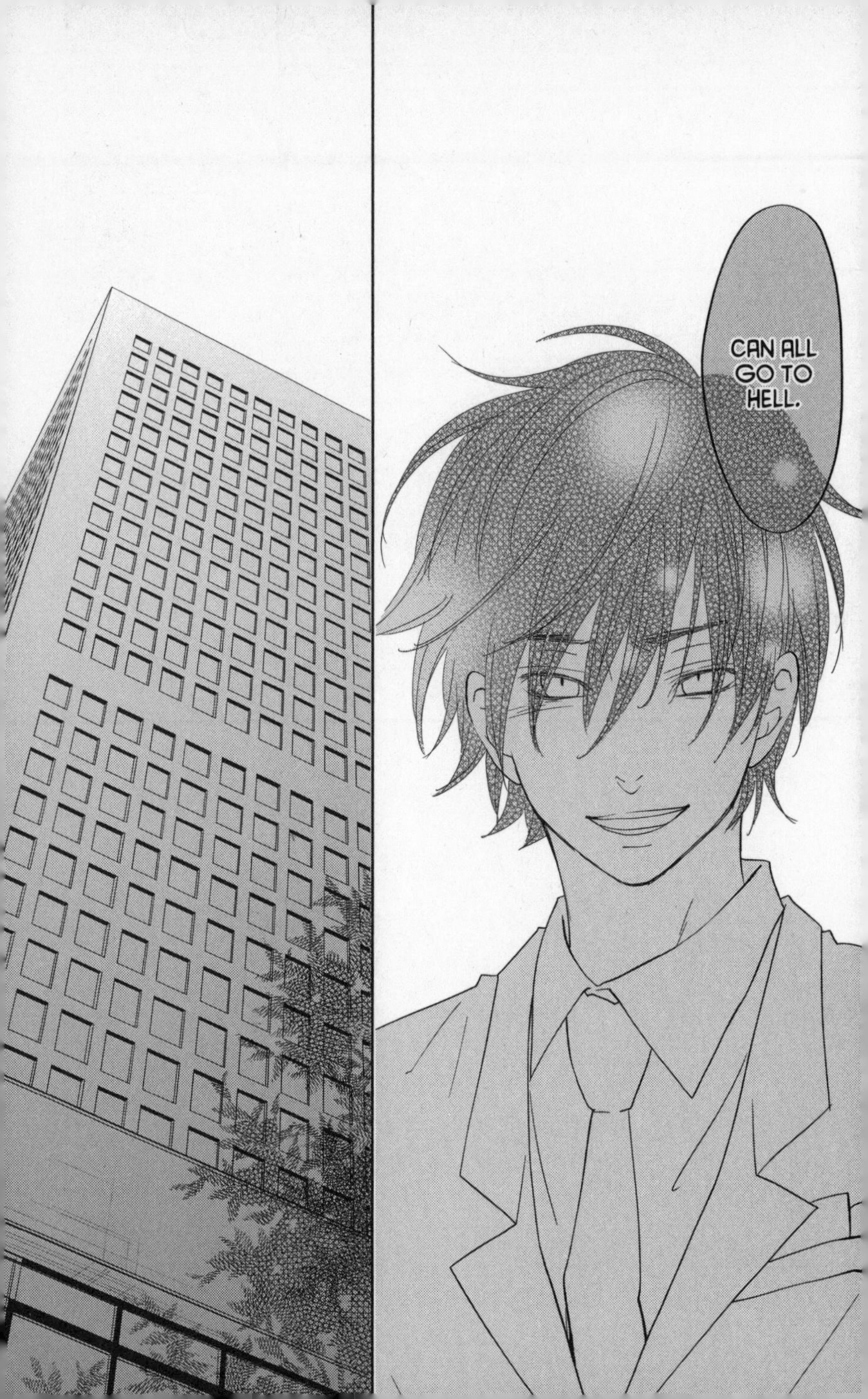
CAN ALL GO TO HELL.

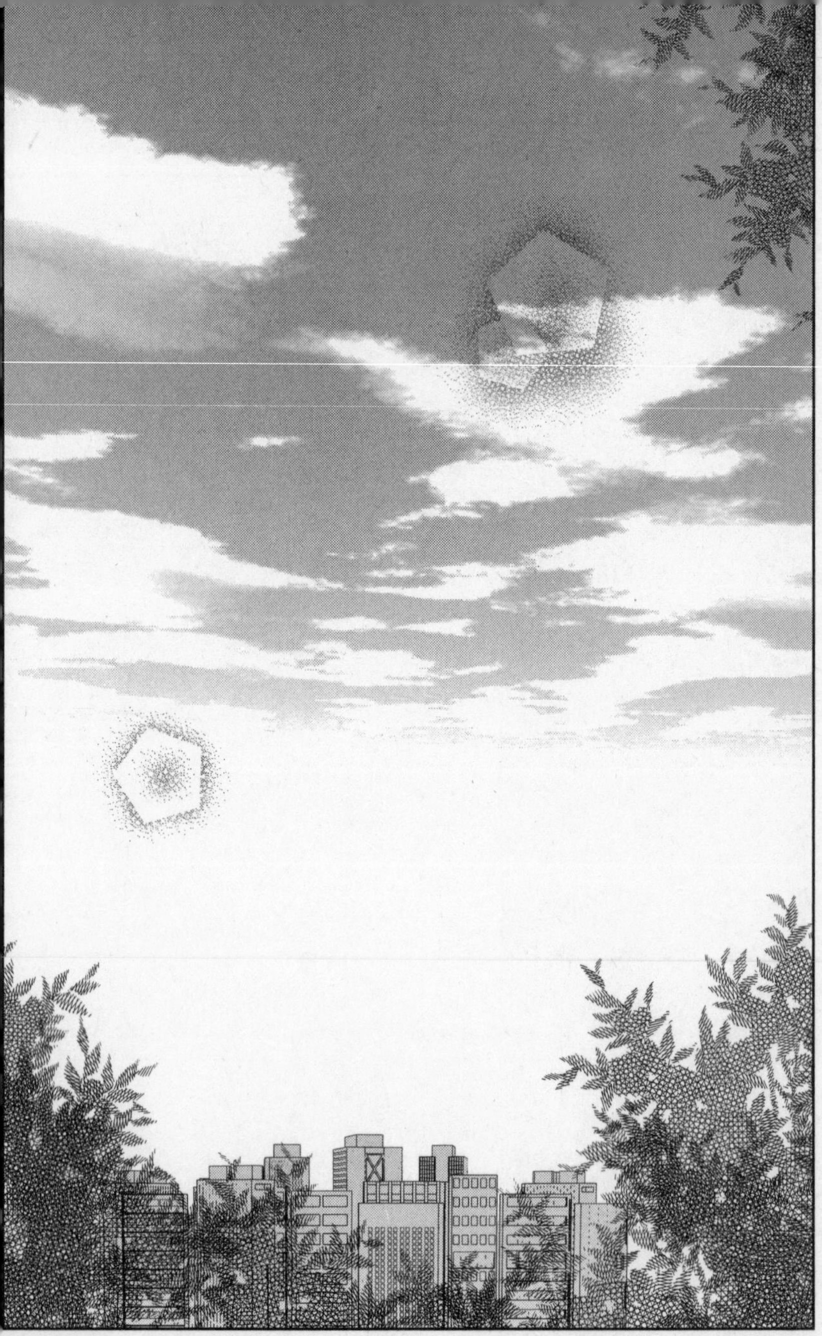

BOOTY

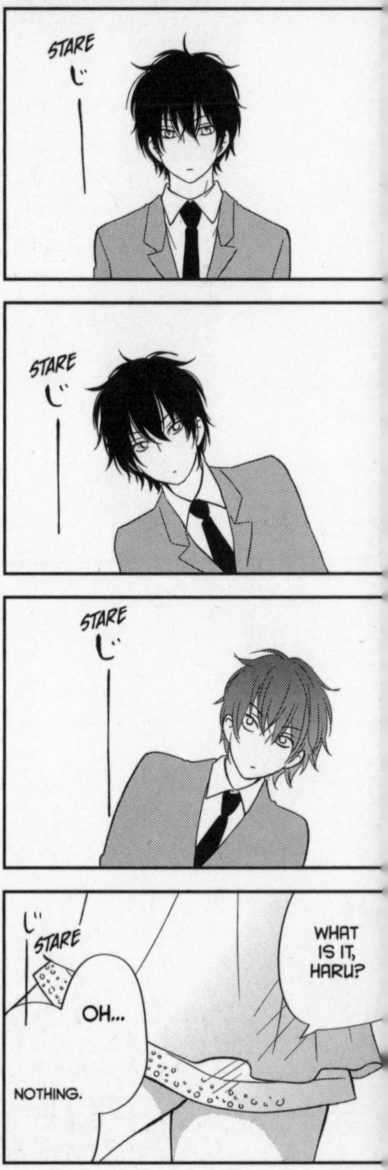
STARE
じー
STARE
じー
STARE
じー
WHAT IS IT, HARU?
STARE
じ
OH...
NOTHING.

AFTER THE PARTY

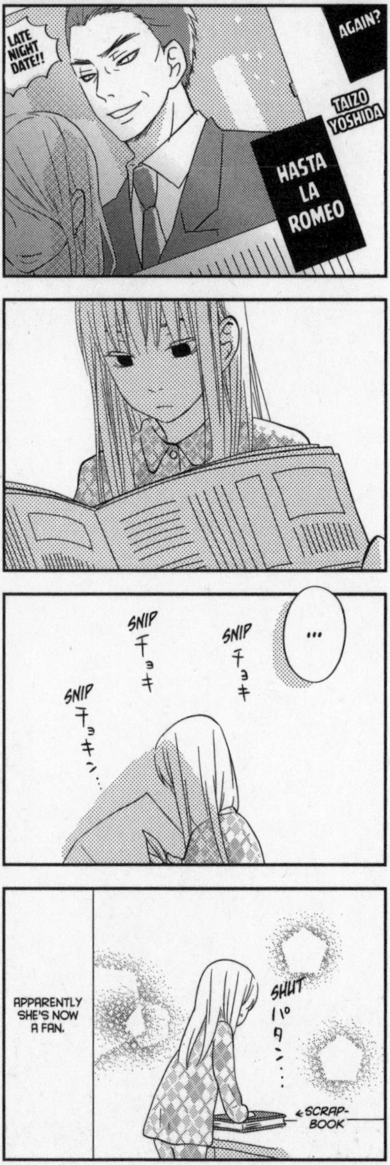
AGAIN?
TAIZO YOSHIDA
HASTA LA ROMEO
LATE NIGHT DATE!!
...
SNIP
チョキ
SNIP
チョキ
SNIP
チョキン…
SHUT
パタン…
SCRAP-BOOK
APPARENTLY SHE'S NOW A FAN.

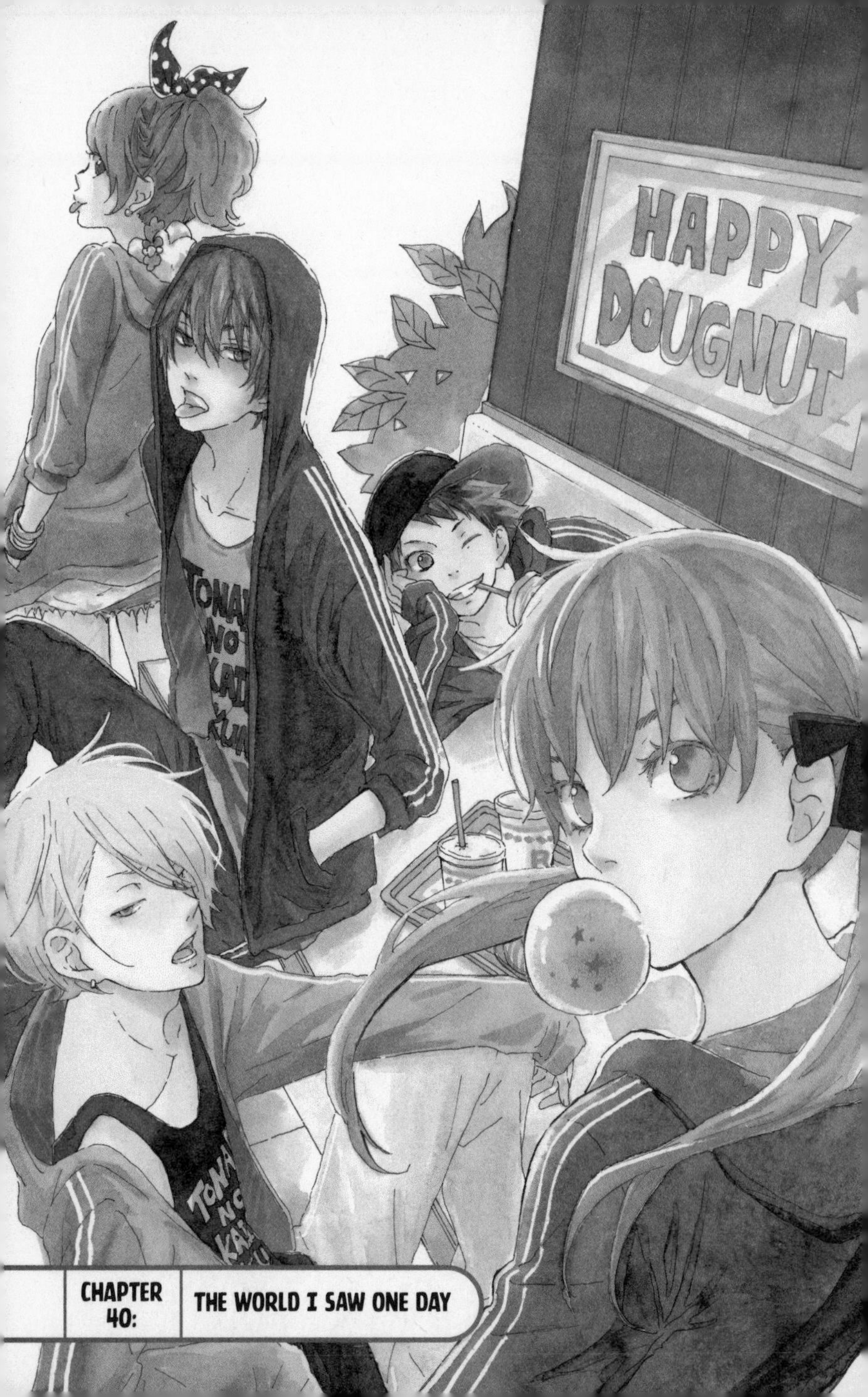
HAPPY DOUGNUT

CHAPTER 40: THE WORLD I SAW ONE DAY

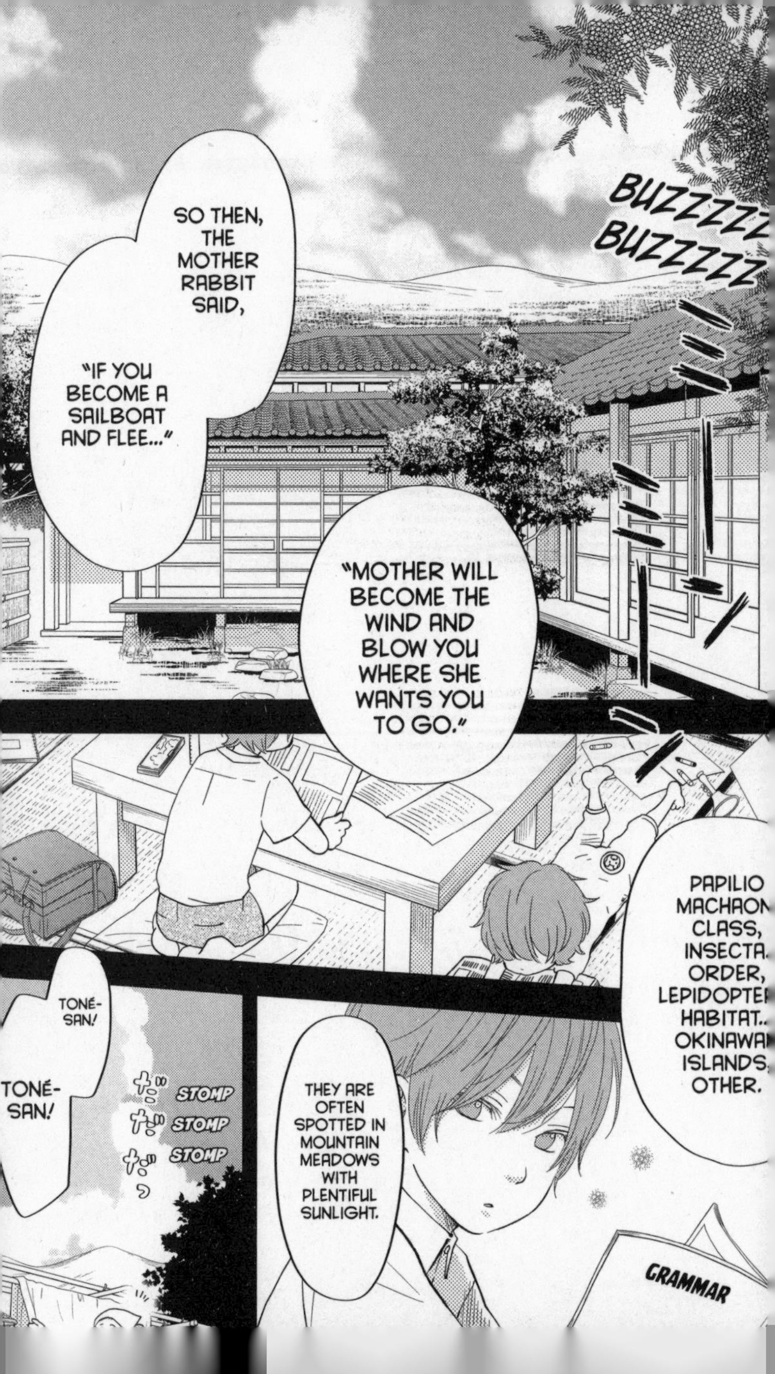
BUZZZZZZ
BUZZZZZZ
SO THEN, THE MOTHER RABBIT SAID,
"IF YOU BECOME A SAILBOAT AND FLEE..."
"MOTHER WILL BECOME THE WIND AND BLOW YOU WHERE SHE WANTS YOU TO GO."
PAPILIO MACHAON CLASS, INSECTA ORDER, LEPIDOPTE HABITAT... OKINAWA ISLANDS, OTHER.
THEY ARE OFTEN SPOTTED IN MOUNTAIN MEADOWS WITH PLENTIFUL SUNLIGHT.
GRAMMAR
TONÉ-SAN!
TONÉ-SAN!
STOMP
STOMP
STOMP

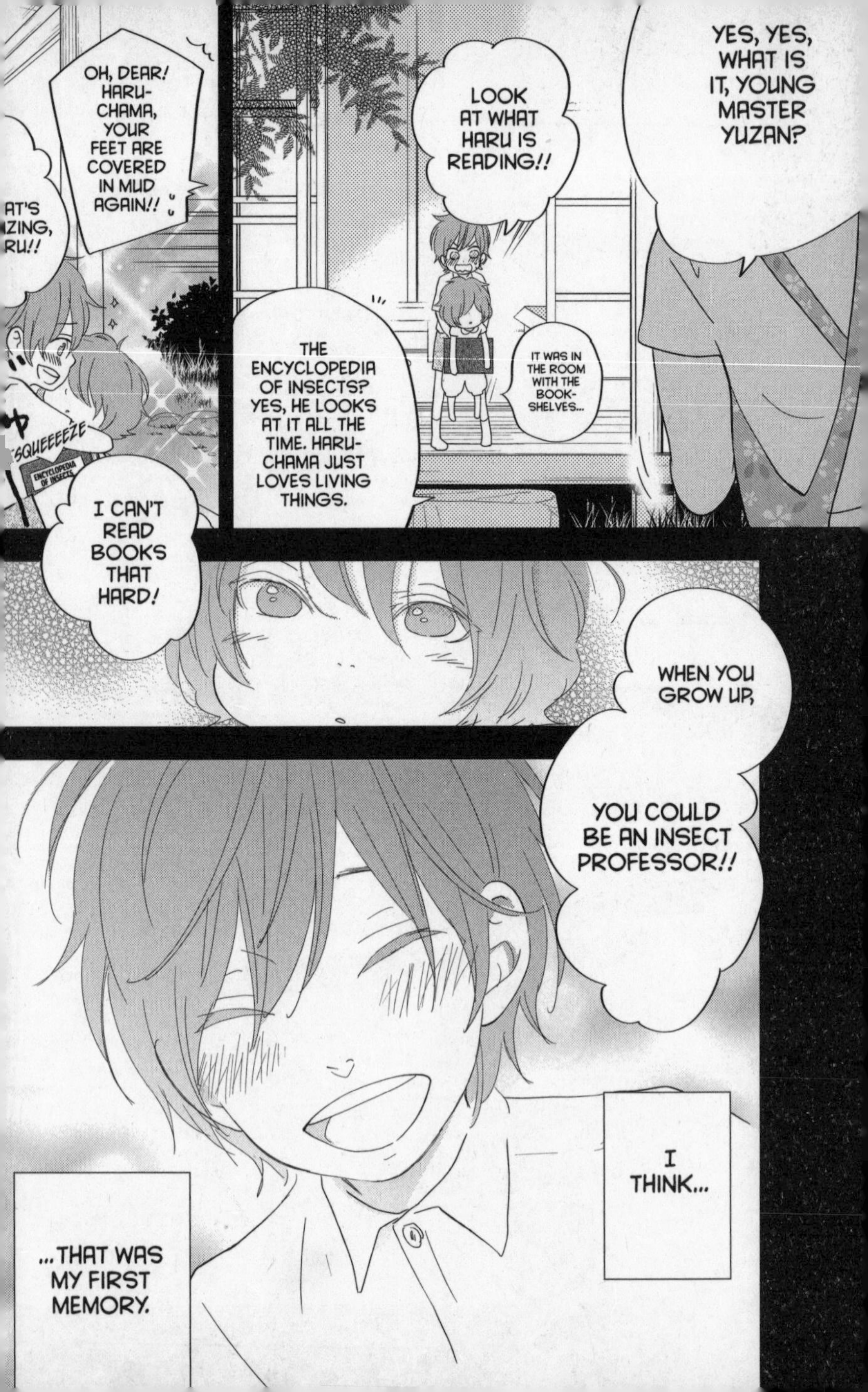
YES, YES, WHAT IS IT, YOUNG MASTER YUZAN?
LOOK AT WHAT HARU IS READING!!
IT WAS IN THE ROOM WITH THE BOOK-SHELVES...
THE ENCYCLOPEDIA OF INSECTS? YES, HE LOOKS AT IT ALL THE TIME. HARU-CHAMA JUST LOVES LIVING THINGS.
OH, DEAR! HARU-CHAMA, YOUR FEET ARE COVERED IN MUD AGAIN!!
SQUEEEEEZE
ENCYCLOPEDIA OF INSECTS
I CAN'T READ BOOKS THAT HARD!
WHEN YOU GROW UP,
YOU COULD BE AN INSECT PROFESSOR!!
I THINK...
...THAT WAS MY FIRST MEMORY.

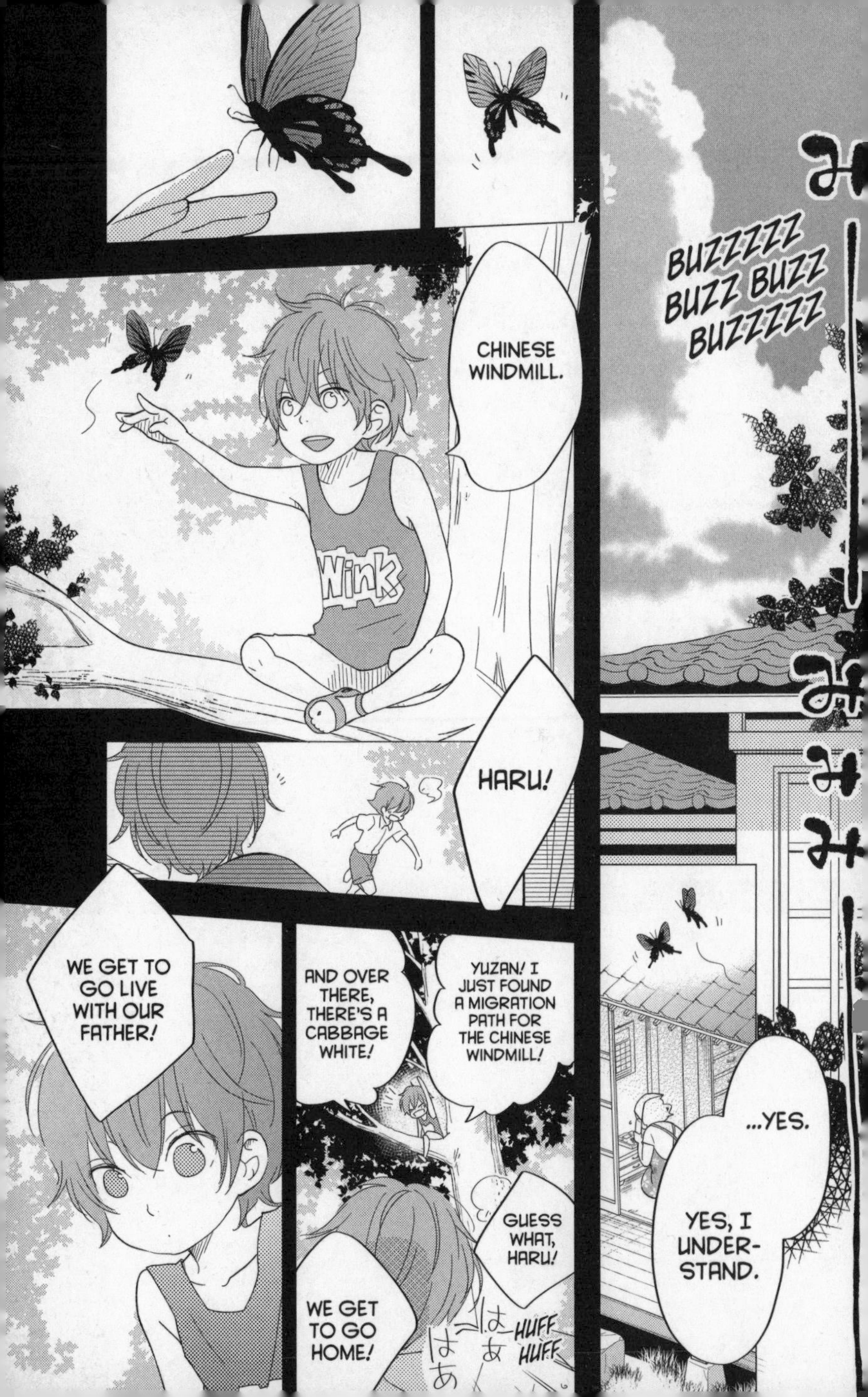
BUZZZZZZ BUZZ BUZZ BUZZZZZ
...YES.
YES, I UNDER-STAND.
CHINESE WINDMILL.
HARU!
YUZAN! I JUST FOUND A MIGRATION PATH FOR THE CHINESE WINDMILL!
AND OVER THERE, THERE'S A CABBAGE WHITE!
GUESS WHAT, HARU!
WE GET TO GO HOME!
HUFF HUFF
WE GET TO GO LIVE WITH OUR FATHER!

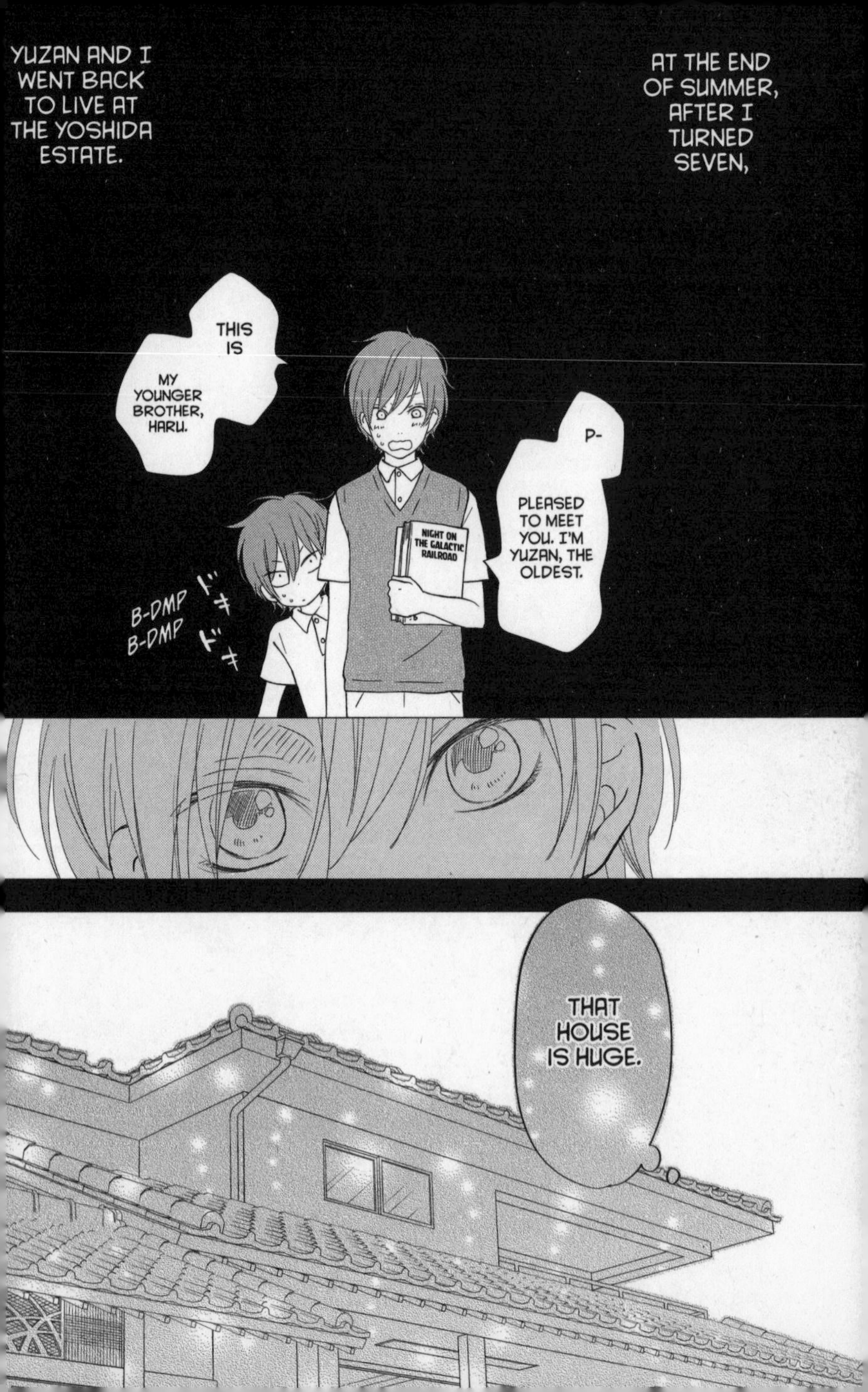
AT THE END OF SUMMER, AFTER I TURNED SEVEN,
YUZAN AND I WENT BACK TO LIVE AT THE YOSHIDA ESTATE.
P-
PLEASED TO MEET YOU. I'M YUZAN, THE OLDEST.
NIGHT ON THE GALACTIC RAILROAD
THIS IS
MY YOUNGER BROTHER, HARU.
ドキドキ
B-DMP B-DMP
THAT HOUSE IS HUGE.

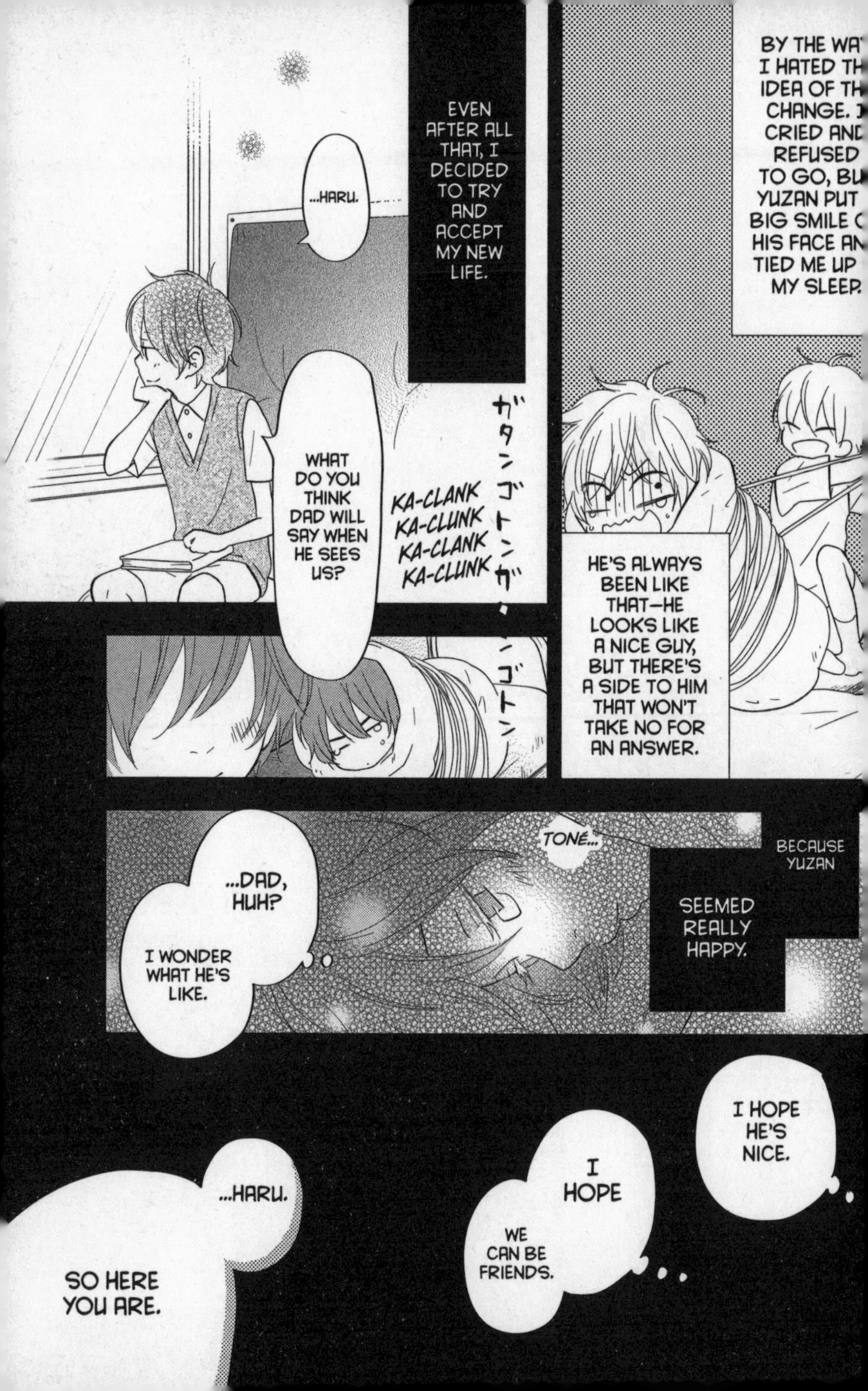
BY THE WA
I HATED TH
IDEA OF TH
CHANGE. I
CRIED AND
REFUSED
TO GO, BU
YUZAN PUT
BIG SMILE C
HIS FACE AN
TIED ME UP
MY SLEEP.
HE'S ALWAYS BEEN LIKE THAT—HE LOOKS LIKE A NICE GUY, BUT THERE'S A SIDE TO HIM THAT WON'T TAKE NO FOR AN ANSWER.
EVEN AFTER ALL THAT, I DECIDED TO TRY AND ACCEPT MY NEW LIFE.
...HARU.
WHAT DO YOU THINK DAD WILL SAY WHEN HE SEES US?
ガタンゴトンガタンゴトン
KA-CLANK KA-CLUNK KA-CLANK KA-CLUNK
BECAUSE YUZAN
SEEMED REALLY HAPPY.
TONÉ...
...DAD, HUH?
I WONDER WHAT HE'S LIKE.
I HOPE HE'S NICE.
I HOPE
WE CAN BE FRIENDS.
...HARU.
SO HERE YOU ARE.

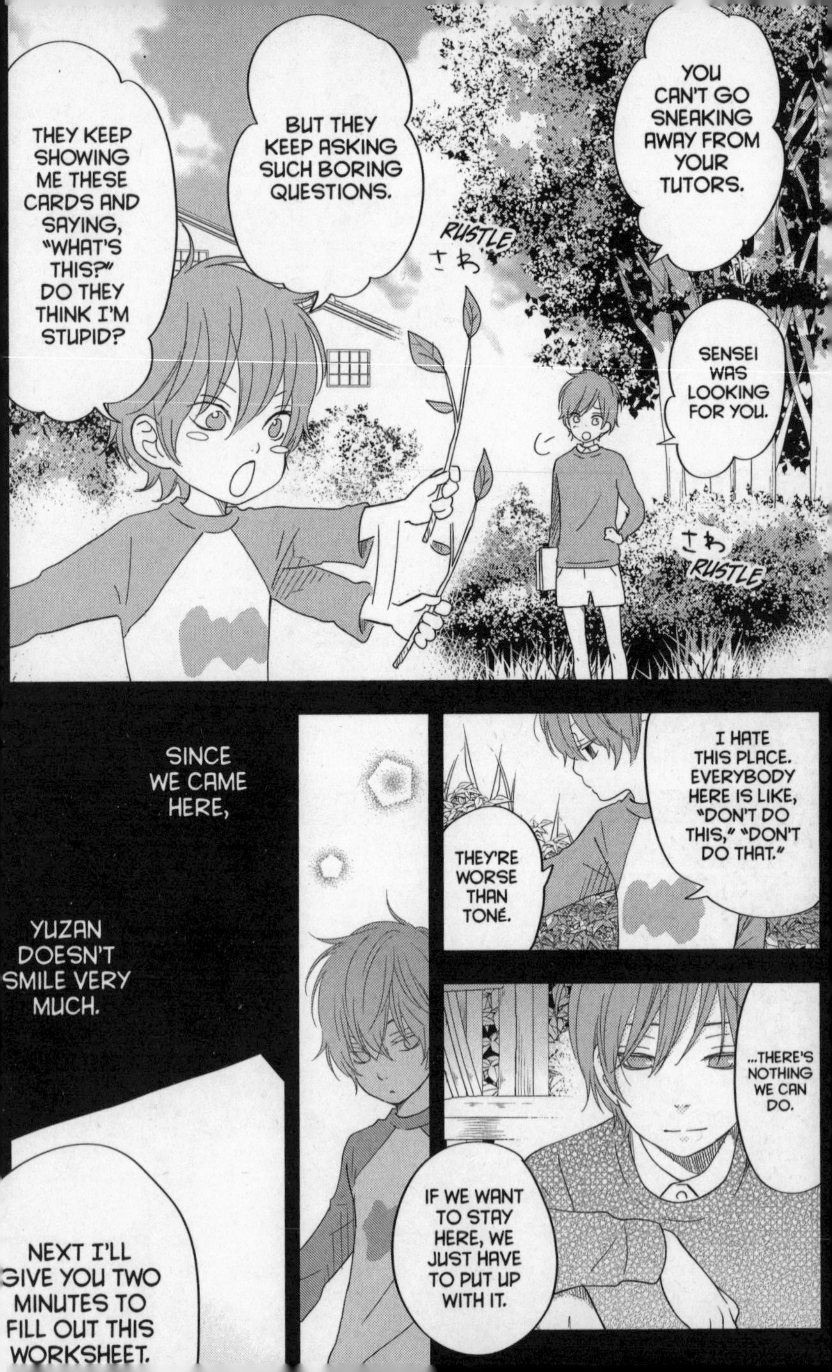
YOU CAN'T GO SNEAKING AWAY FROM YOUR TUTORS.
SENSEI WAS LOOKING FOR YOU.
さわ RUSTLE
さわ RUSTLE
BUT THEY KEEP ASKING SUCH BORING QUESTIONS.
THEY KEEP SHOWING ME THESE CARDS AND SAYING, "WHAT'S THIS?" DO THEY THINK I'M STUPID?
I HATE THIS PLACE. EVERYBODY HERE IS LIKE, "DON'T DO THIS," "DON'T DO THAT."
THEY'RE WORSE THAN TONÉ.
...THERE'S NOTHING WE CAN DO.
IF WE WANT TO STAY HERE, WE JUST HAVE TO PUT UP WITH IT.
SINCE WE CAME HERE,
YUZAN DOESN'T SMILE VERY MUCH.
NEXT I'LL GIVE YOU TWO MINUTES TO FILL OUT THIS WORKSHEET.

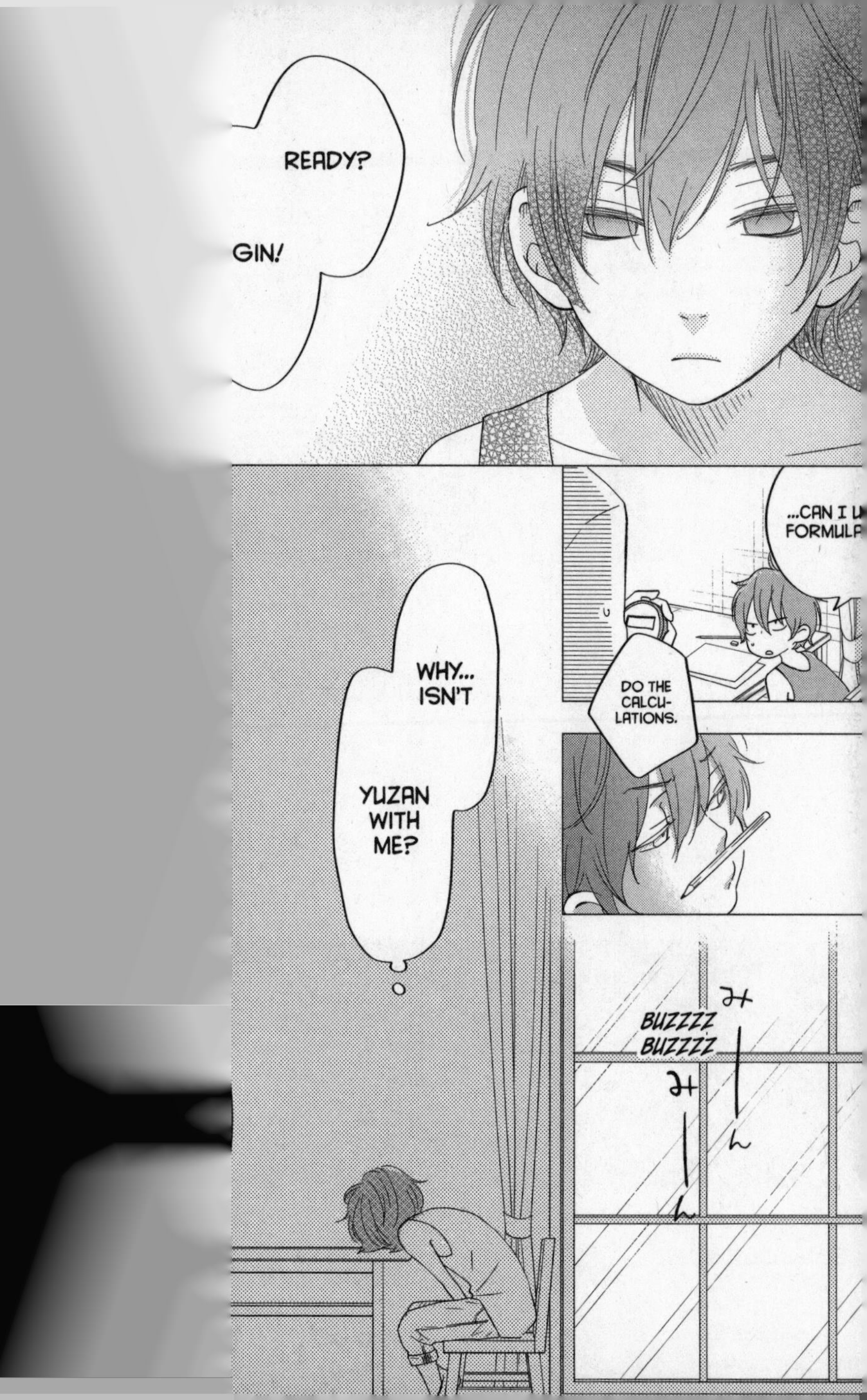
READY?
GIN!
...CAN I U FORMULA
DO THE CALCULATIONS.
WHY... ISN'T YUZAN WITH ME?
BUZZZZ BUZZZZ
みーん
みーん

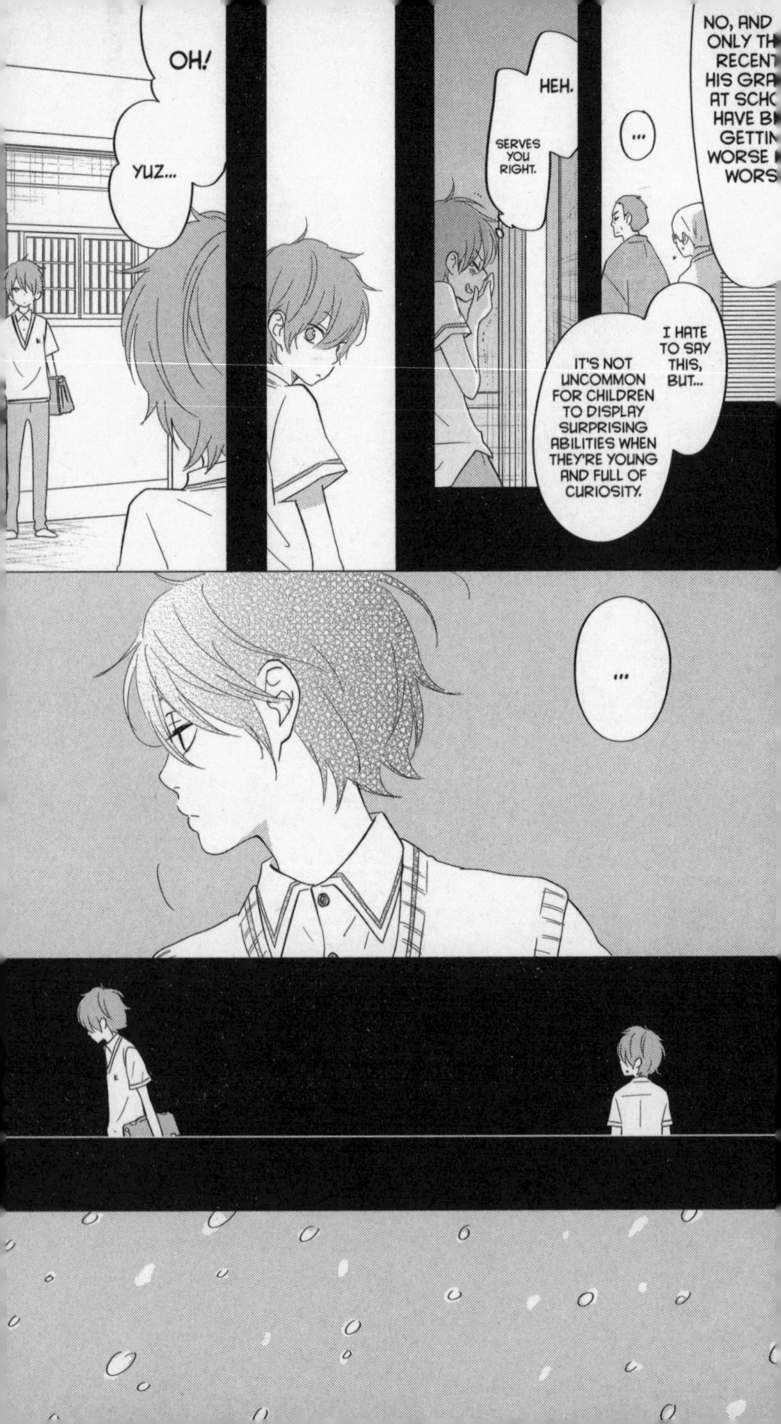
NO, AND ONLY TH RECENT HIS GRA AT SCHO HAVE B GETTIN WORSE WORS
I HATE TO SAY THIS, BUT...
IT'S NOT UNCOMMON FOR CHILDREN TO DISPLAY SURPRISING ABILITIES WHEN THEY'RE YOUNG AND FULL OF CURIOSITY.
...
HEH.
SERVES YOU RIGHT.
OH!
YUZ...
...

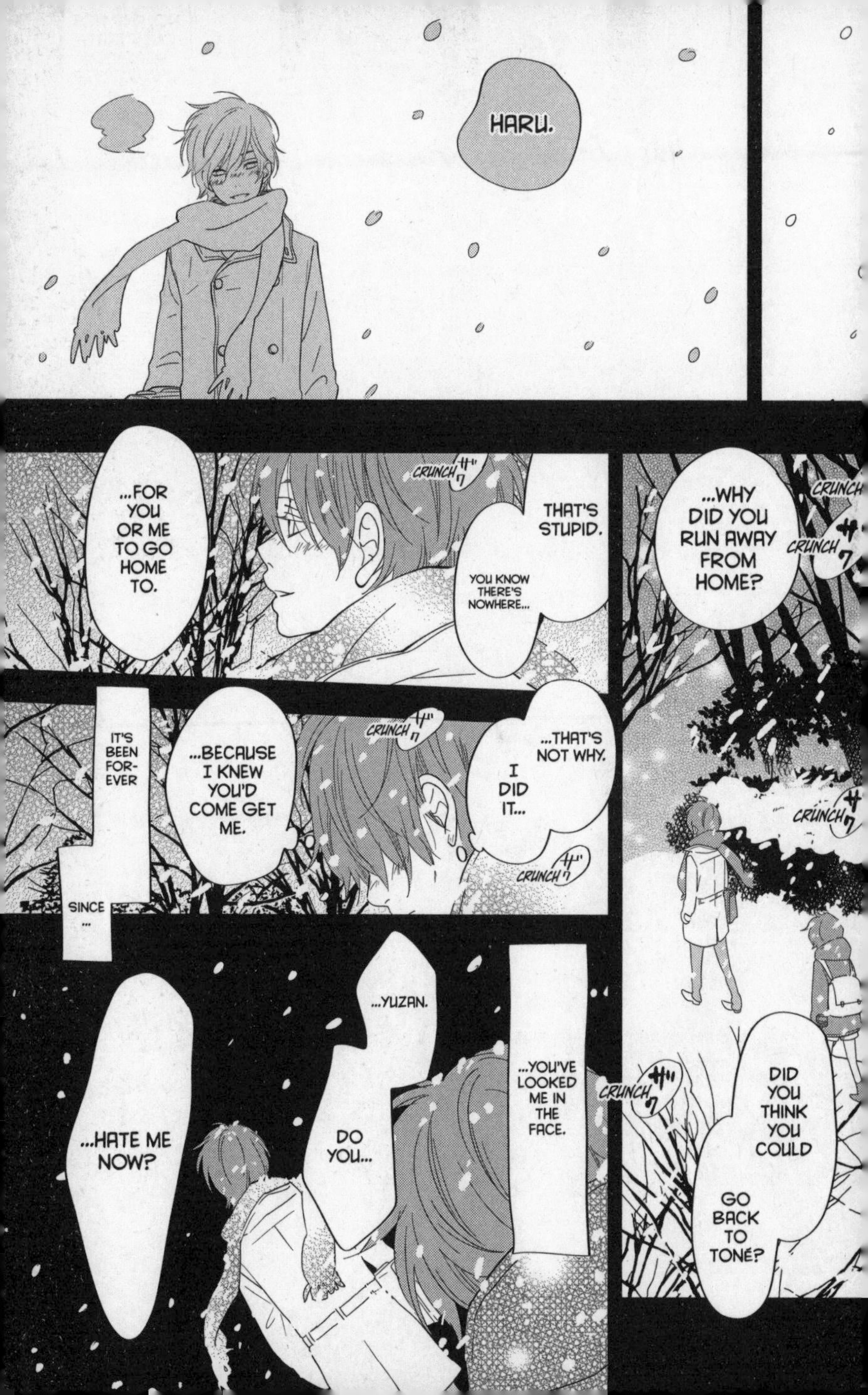
HARU.
...WHY DID YOU RUN AWAY FROM HOME?
CRUNCH
CRUNCH
CRUNCH
CRUNCH
DID YOU THINK YOU COULD
GO BACK TO TONÉ?
CRUNCH
THAT'S STUPID.
YOU KNOW THERE'S NOWHERE...
...FOR YOU OR ME TO GO HOME TO.
CRUNCH
CRUNCH
...THAT'S NOT WHY.
I DID IT...
...BECAUSE I KNEW YOU'D COME GET ME.
IT'S BEEN FOR-EVER
SINCE ...
...YOU'VE LOOKED ME IN THE FACE.
...YUZAN.
DO YOU...
...HATE ME NOW?

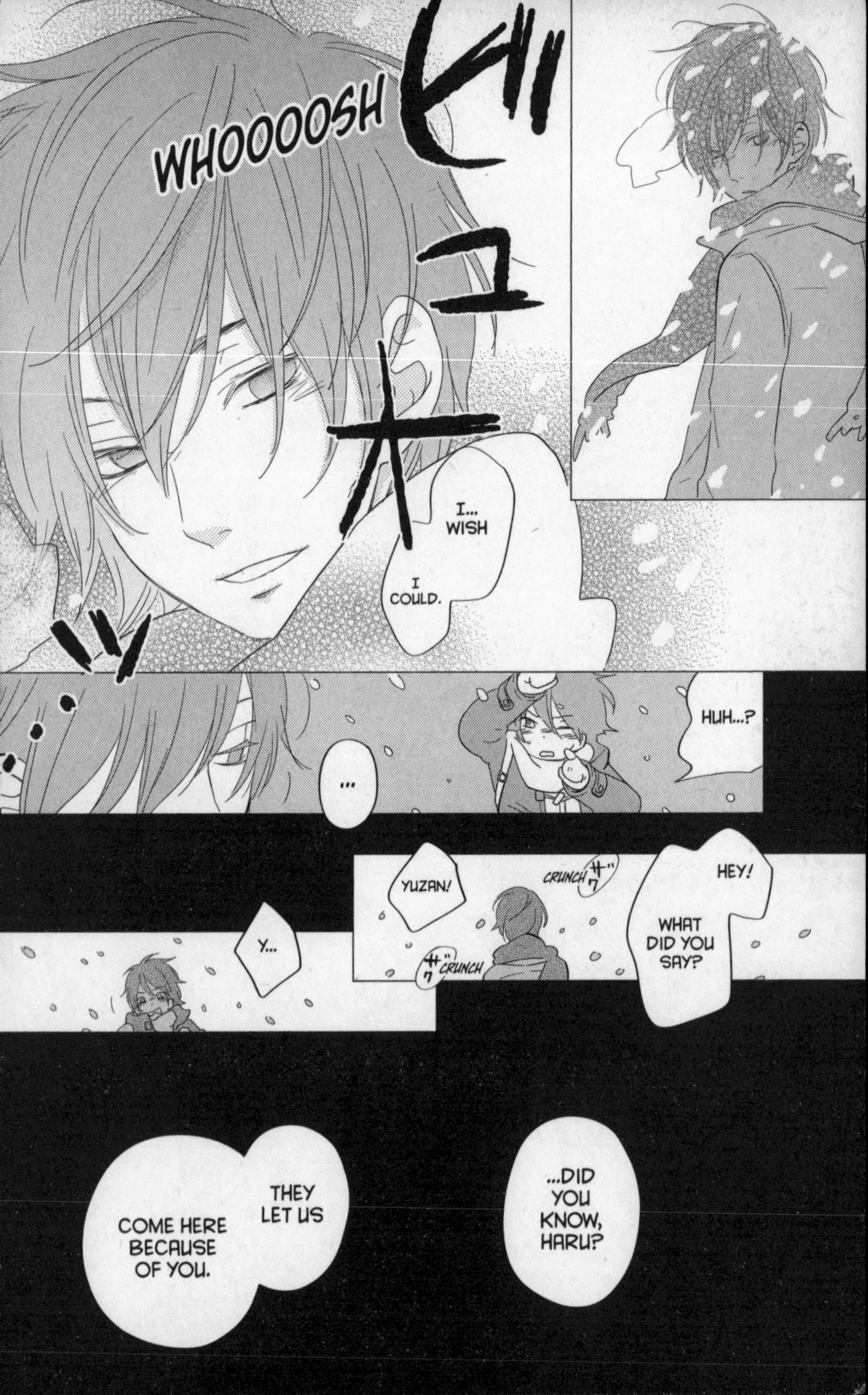
WHOOOOSH
I... WISH
I COULD.
HUH...?
...
HEY!
WHAT DID YOU SAY?
CRUNCH
YUZAN!
CRUNCH
Y...
...DID YOU KNOW, HARU?
THEY LET US
COME HERE BECAUSE OF YOU.

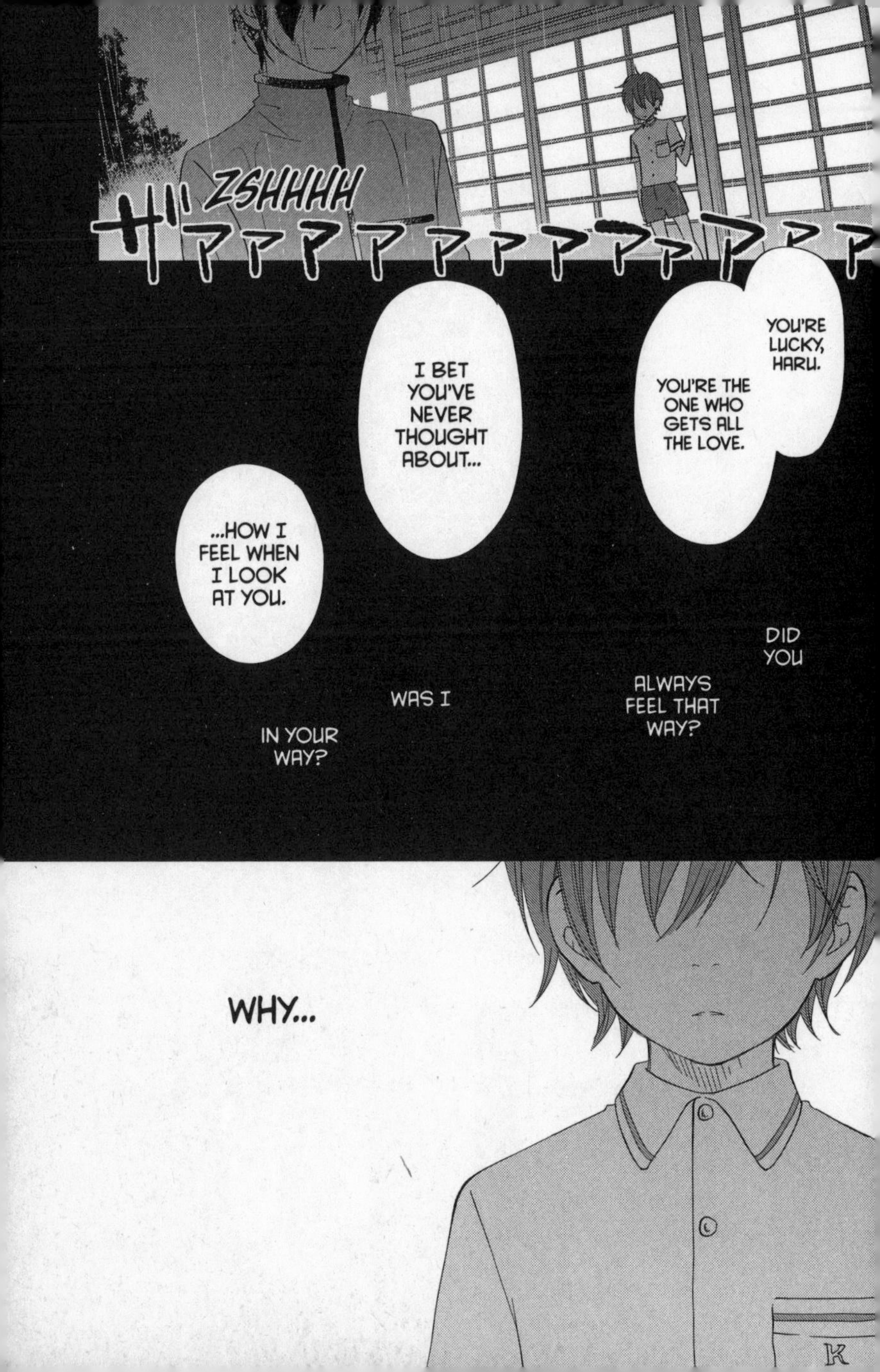
ZSHHHH
YOU'RE LUCKY, HARU.
YOU'RE THE ONE WHO GETS ALL THE LOVE.
I BET YOU'VE NEVER THOUGHT ABOUT...
...HOW I FEEL WHEN I LOOK AT YOU.
DID YOU
ALWAYS FEEL THAT WAY?
WAS I
IN YOUR WAY?
WHY...

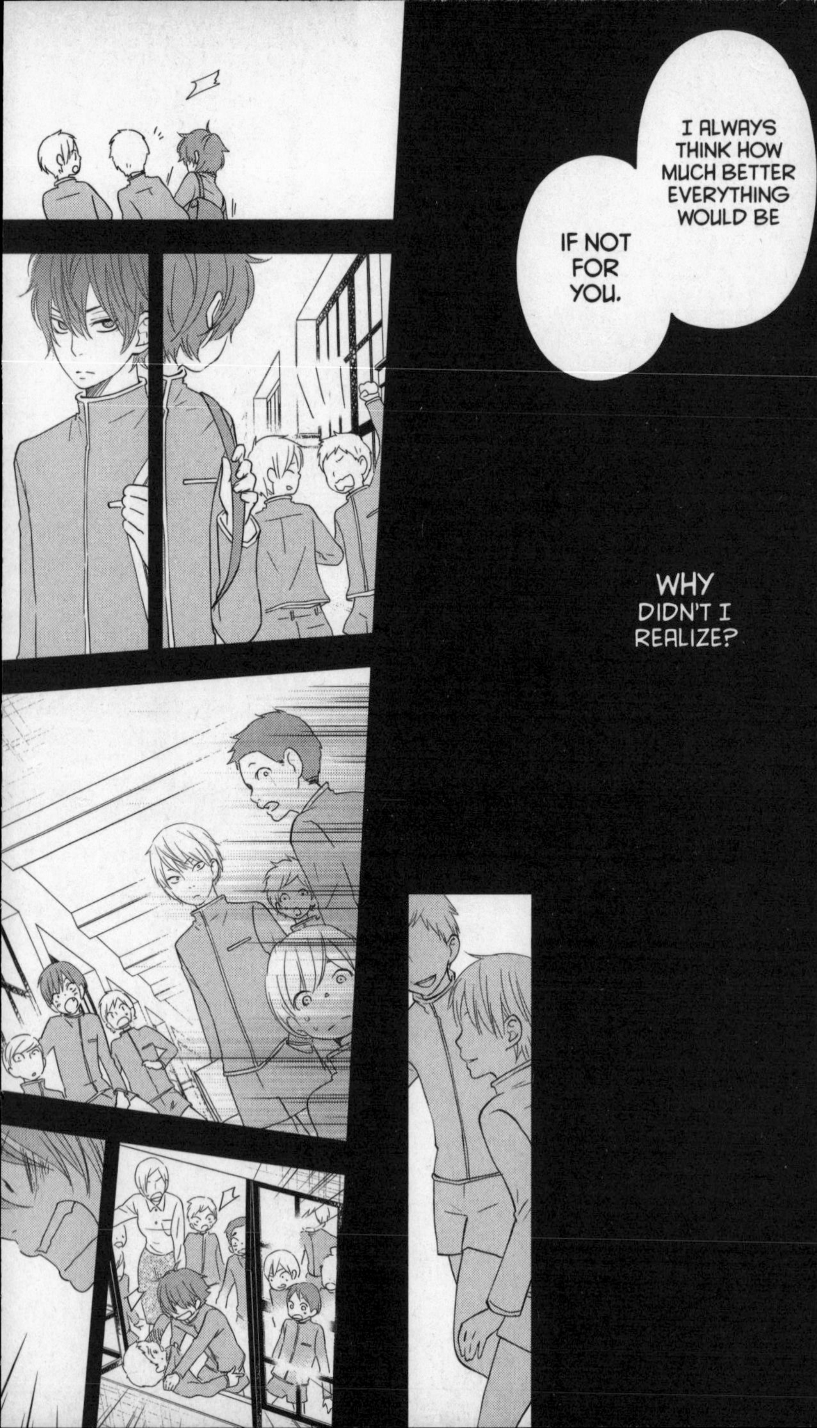
I ALWAYS THINK HOW MUCH BETTER EVERYTHING WOULD BE
IF NOT FOR YOU.
WHY DIDN'T I REALIZE?

み゛ー
BUZZZZZZ BUZZ BUZZ BUZZZZZZZ
み゛み゛み゛ー
YOU CAN'T DO THAT, HARU.
YOU CAN'T GET INTO FIGHTS WITH YOUR FRIENDS.

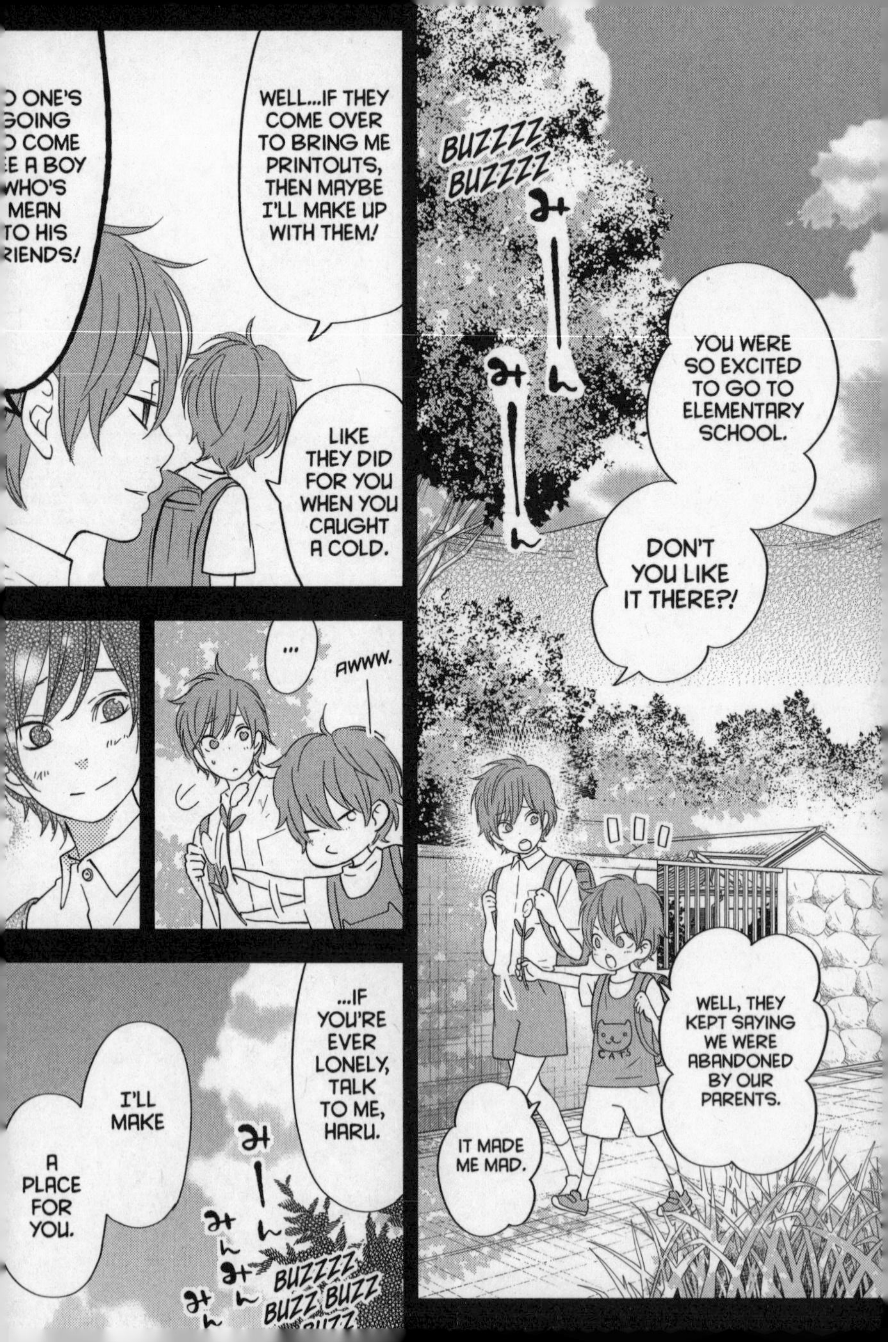
BUZZZZ BUZZZZ
みーん
みーん
YOU WERE SO EXCITED TO GO TO ELEMENTARY SCHOOL.
DON'T YOU LIKE IT THERE?!
!!!
WELL, THEY KEPT SAYING WE WERE ABANDONED BY OUR PARENTS.
IT MADE ME MAD.
WELL...IF THEY COME OVER TO BRING ME PRINTOUTS, THEN MAYBE I'LL MAKE UP WITH THEM!
LIKE THEY DID FOR YOU WHEN YOU CAUGHT A COLD.
O ONE'S GOING O COME E A BOY WHO'S MEAN TO HIS RIENDS!
...
AWWW.
...IF YOU'RE EVER LONELY, TALK TO ME, HARU.
I'LL MAKE A PLACE FOR YOU.
みーん みーん みーん みーん
BUZZZZ BUZZ BUZZ

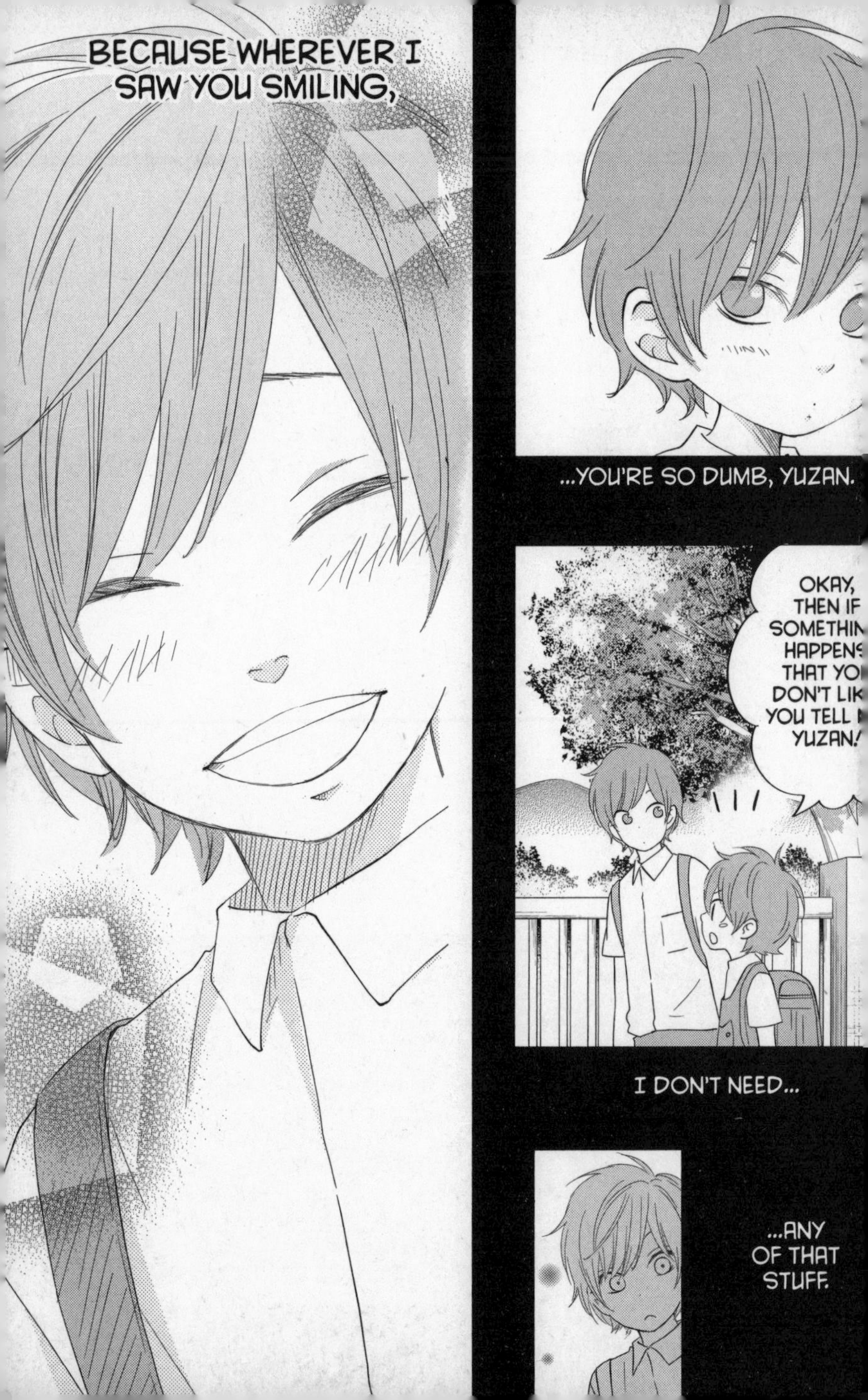
...YOU'RE SO DUMB, YUZAN.
OKAY, THEN IF SOMETHIN HAPPENS THAT YO DON'T LIK YOU TELL YUZAN!
I DON'T NEED...
...ANY OF THAT STUFF.
BECAUSE WHEREVER I SAW YOU SMILING,

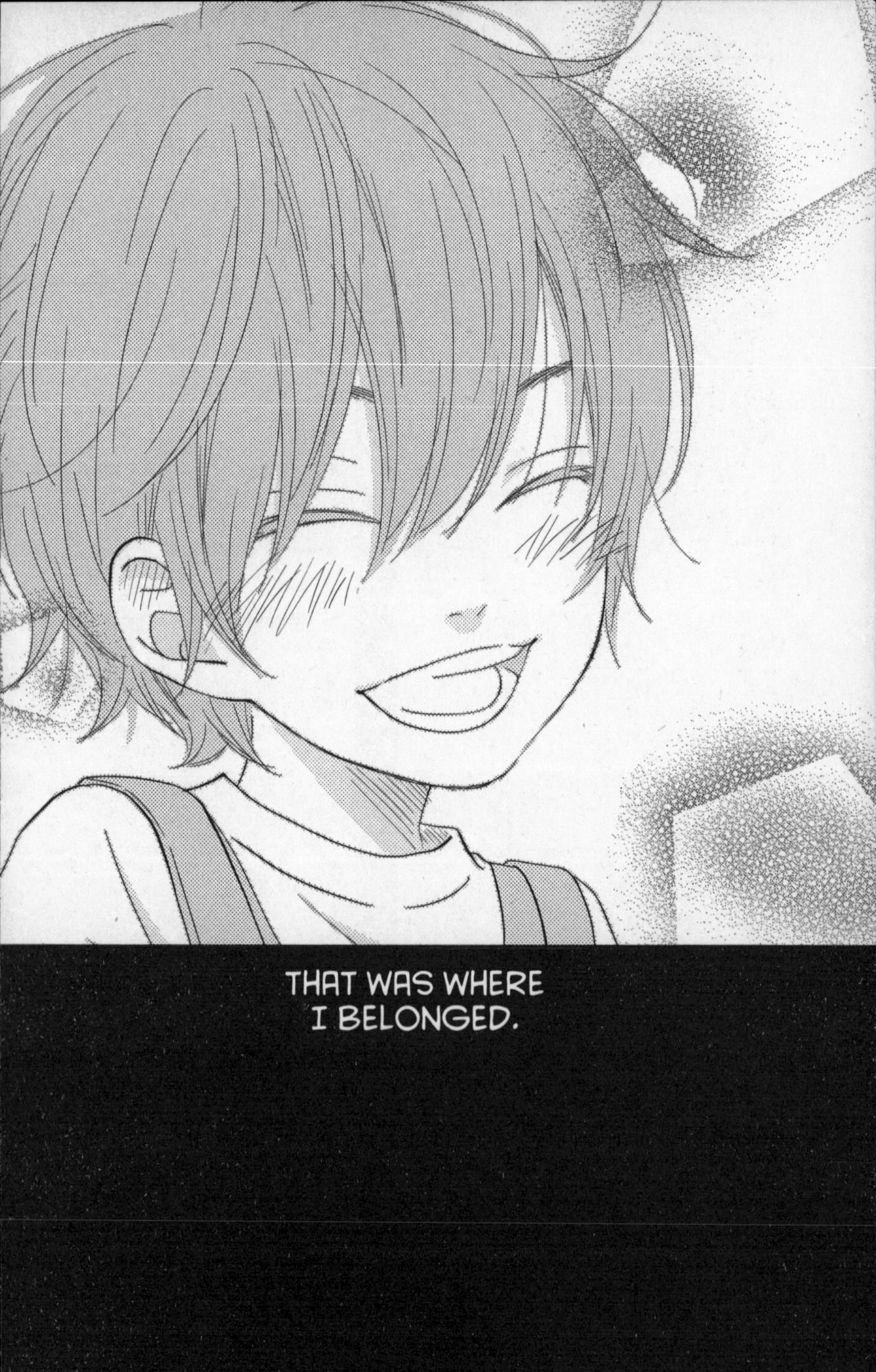

THAT WAS WHERE
I BELONGED.

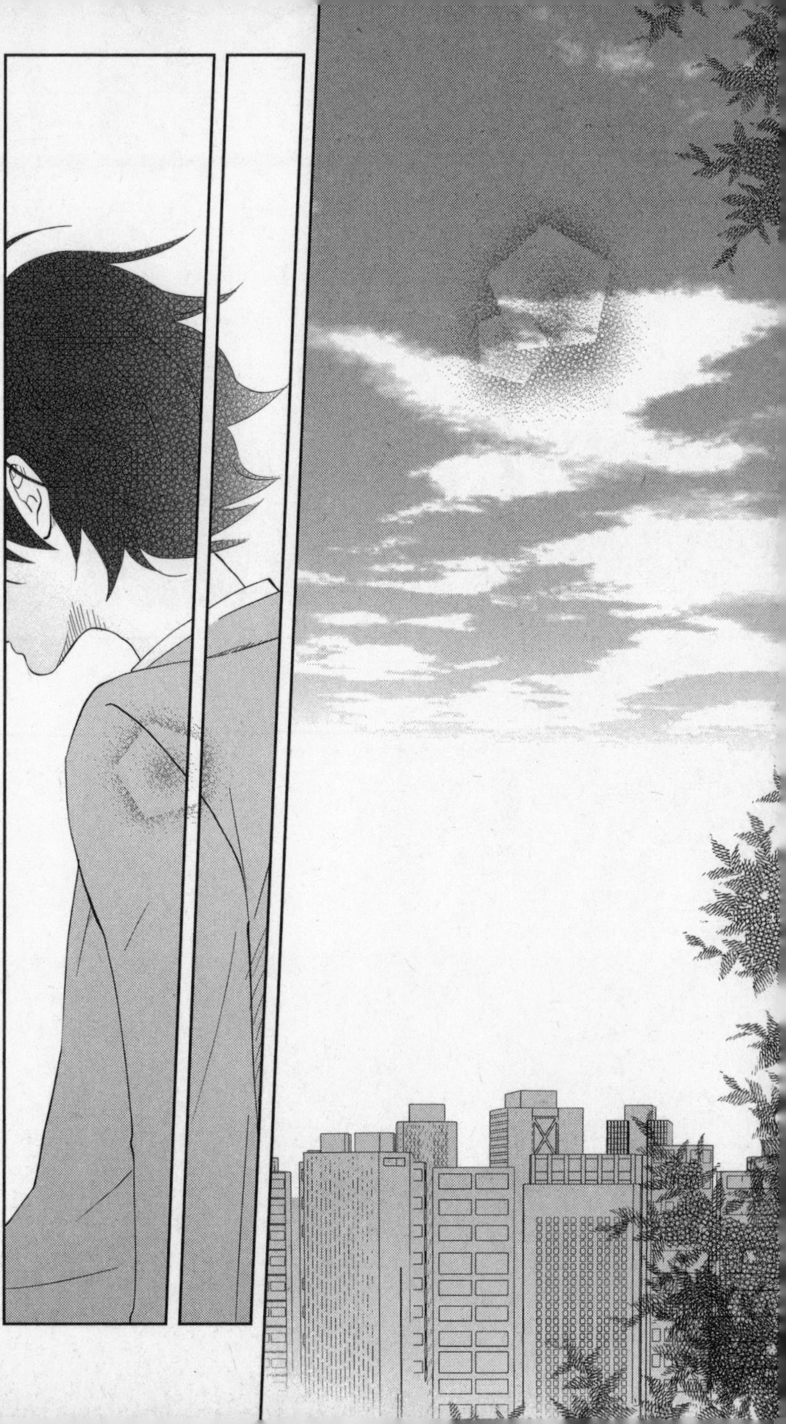

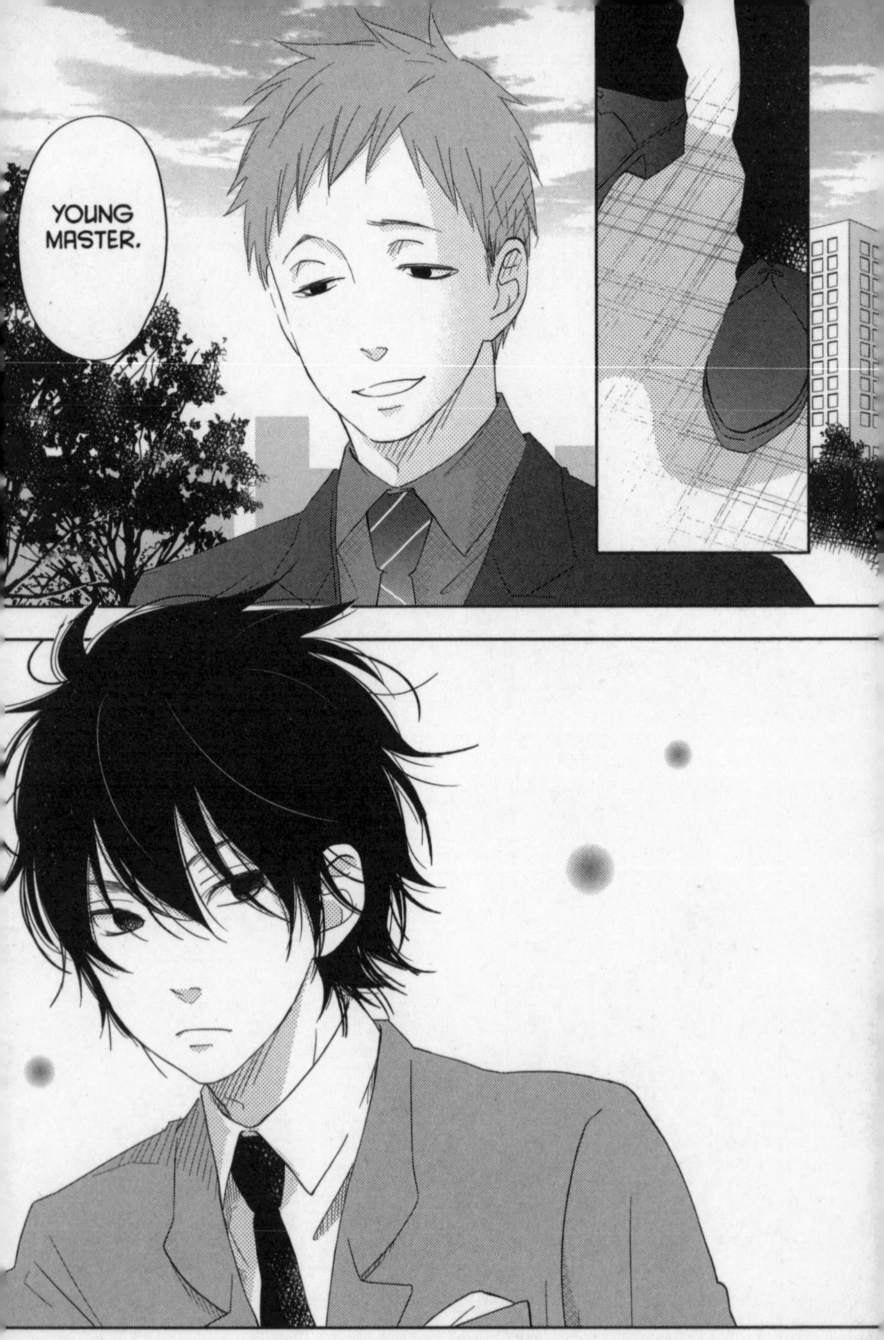
YOUNG MASTER.

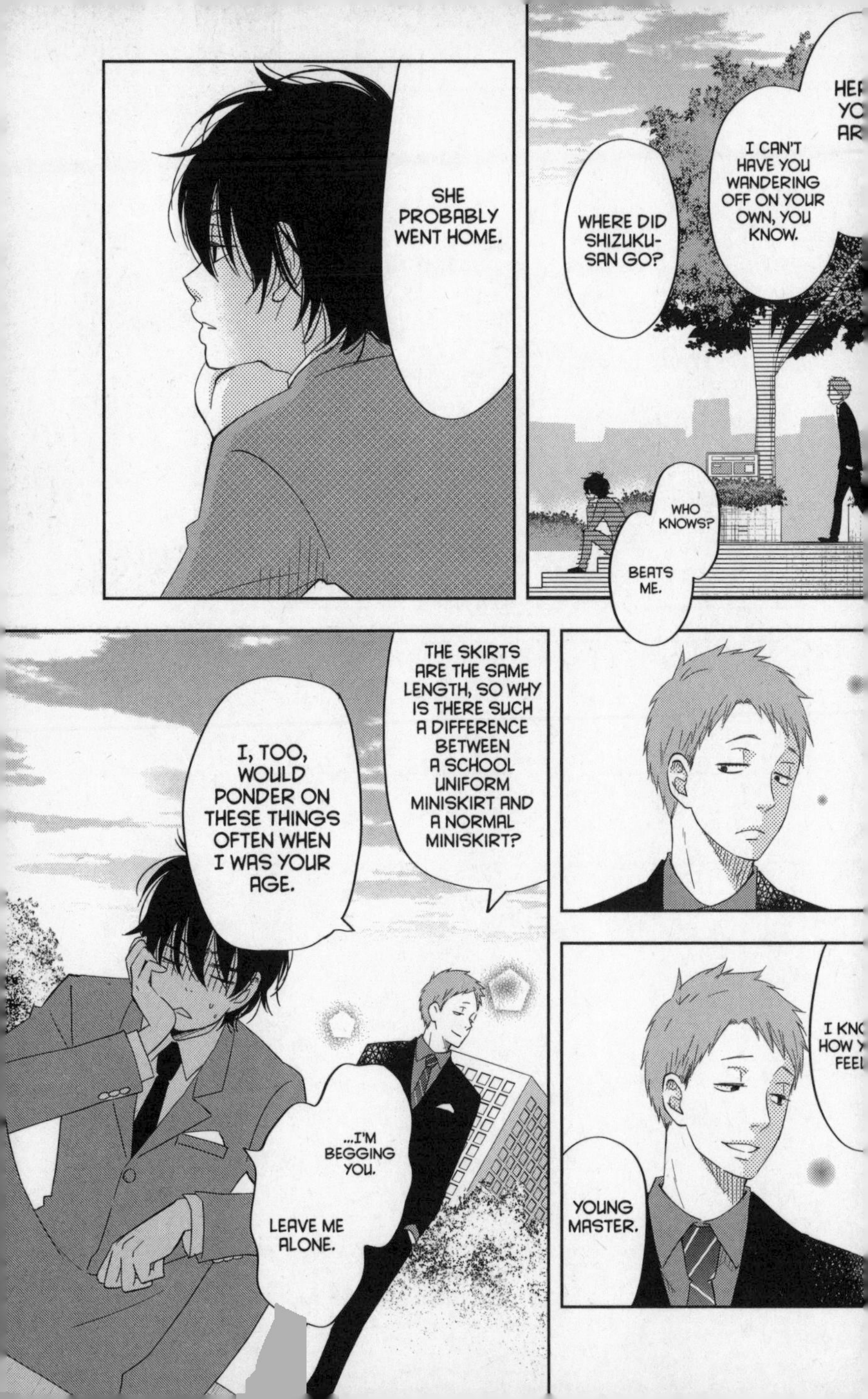
I CAN'T HAVE YOU WANDERING OFF ON YOUR OWN, YOU KNOW.
WHERE DID SHIZUKU-SAN GO?
WHO KNOWS?
BEATS ME.
SHE PROBABLY WENT HOME.
YOUNG MASTER.
THE SKIRTS ARE THE SAME LENGTH, SO WHY IS THERE SUCH A DIFFERENCE BETWEEN A SCHOOL UNIFORM MINISKIRT AND A NORMAL MINISKIRT?
I, TOO, WOULD PONDER ON THESE THINGS OFTEN WHEN I WAS YOUR AGE.
...I'M BEGGING YOU.
LEAVE ME ALONE.

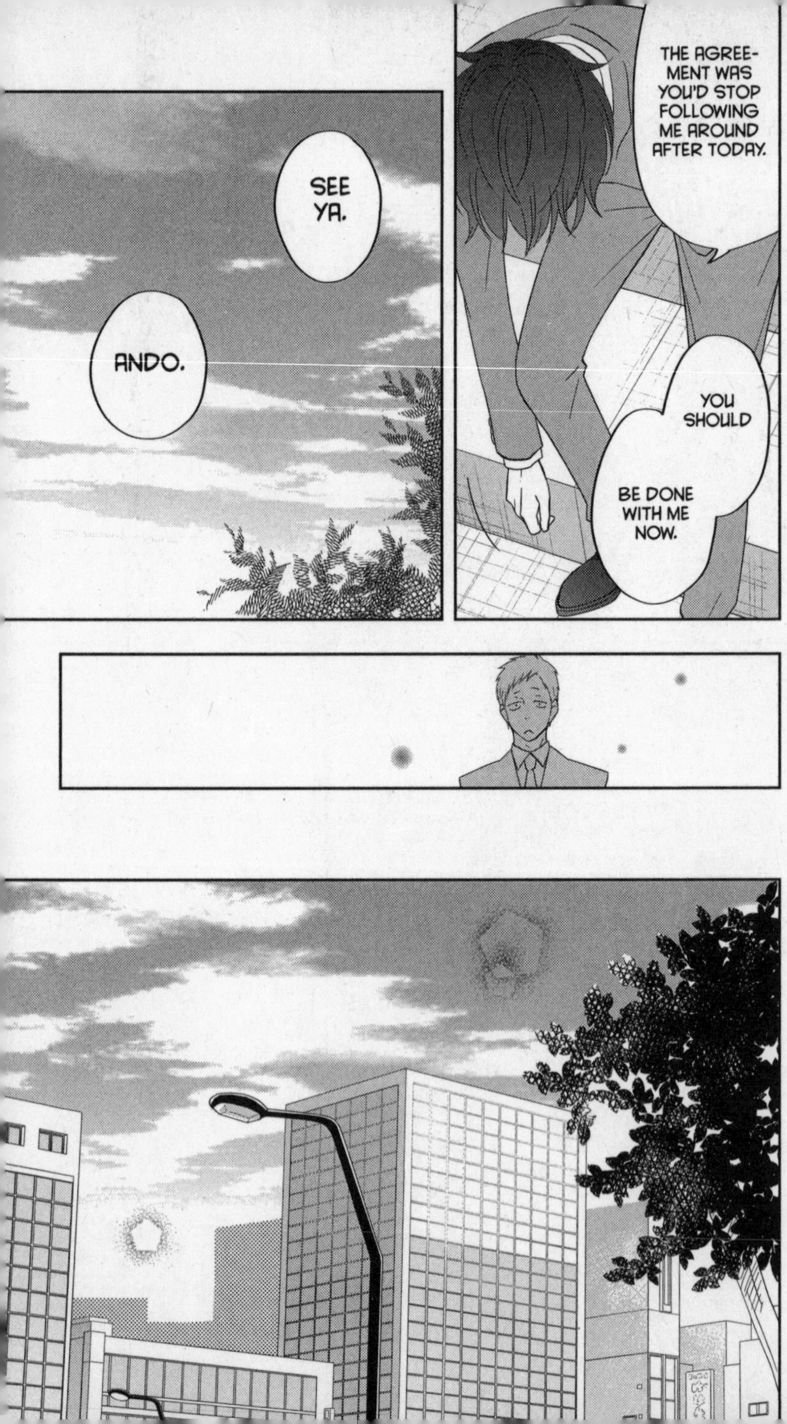
THE AGREEMENT WAS YOU'D STOP FOLLOWING ME AROUND AFTER TODAY.
YOU SHOULD
BE DONE WITH ME NOW.
SEE YA.
ANDO.

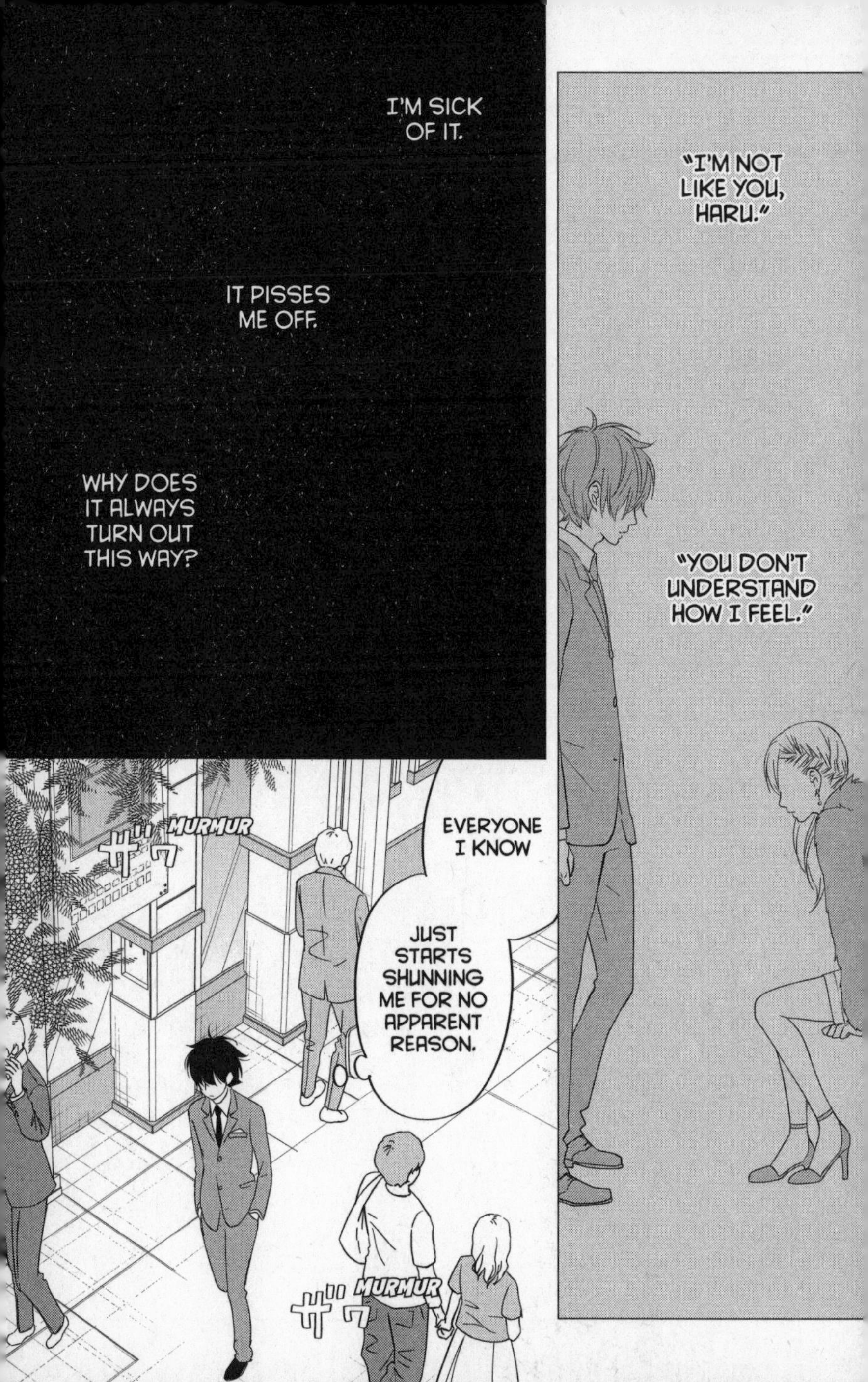
"I'M NOT LIKE YOU, HARU."
"YOU DON'T UNDERSTAND HOW I FEEL."
I'M SICK OF IT.
IT PISSES ME OFF.
WHY DOES IT ALWAYS TURN OUT THIS WAY?
EVERYONE I KNOW
JUST STARTS SHUNNING ME FOR NO APPARENT REASON.
ザワ MURMUR
ザワ MURMUR

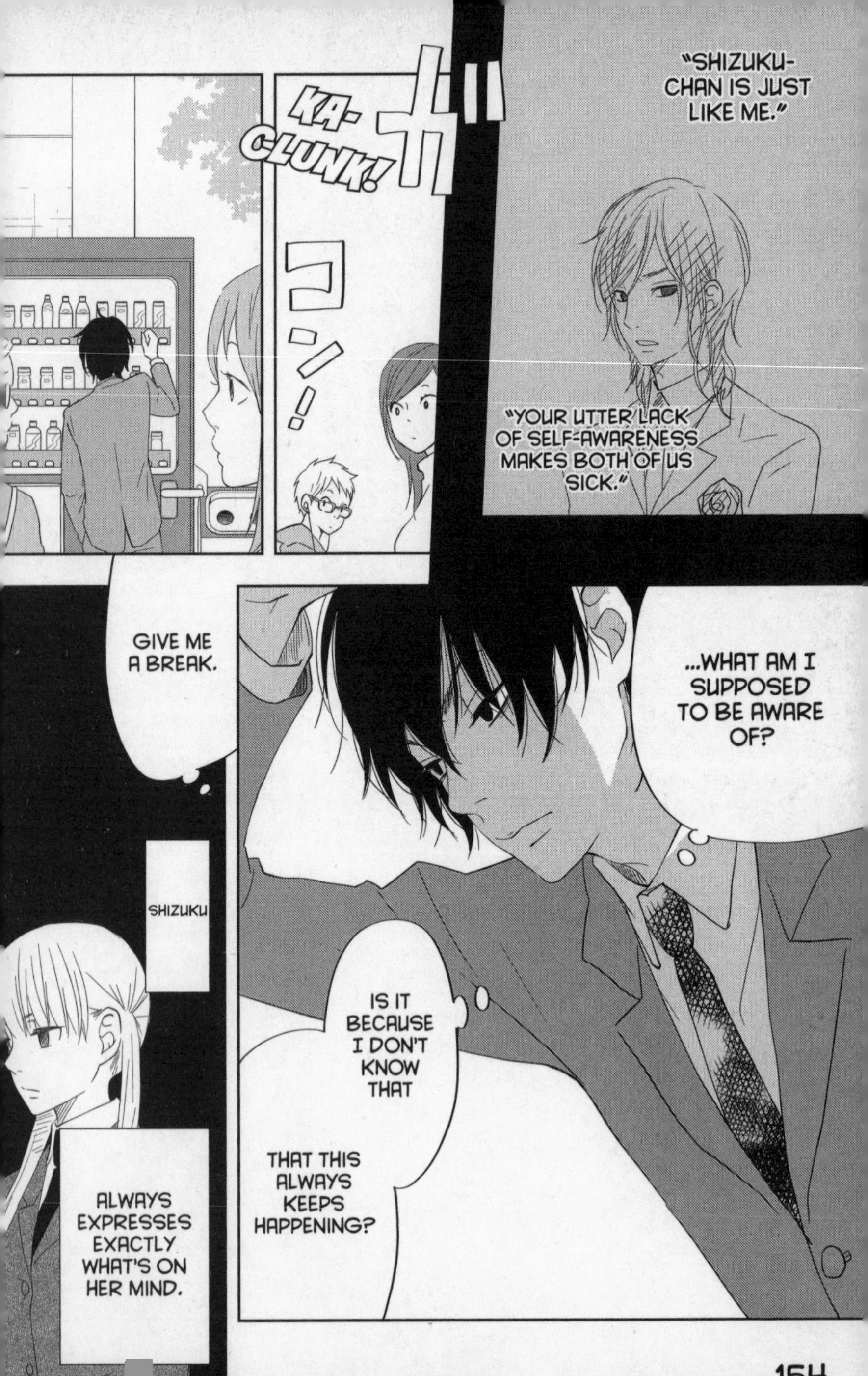
"SHIZUKU-CHAN IS JUST LIKE ME."
"YOUR UTTER LACK OF SELF-AWARENESS MAKES BOTH OF US SICK."
KA-CLUNK!
...WHAT AM I SUPPOSED TO BE AWARE OF?
GIVE ME A BREAK.
IS IT BECAUSE I DON'T KNOW THAT
THAT THIS ALWAYS KEEPS HAPPENING?
SHIZUKU
ALWAYS EXPRESSES EXACTLY WHAT'S ON HER MIND.

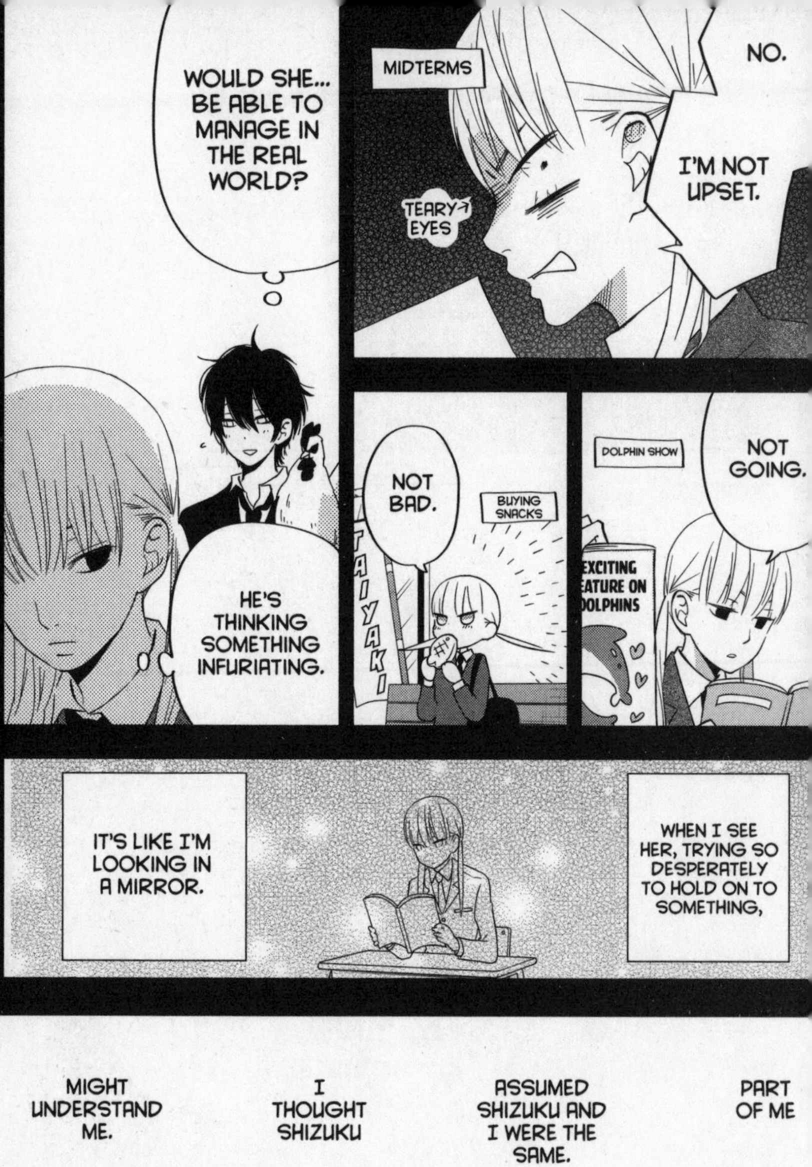
NO.
I'M NOT UPSET.
MIDTERMS
TEARY EYES
NOT GOING.
DOLPHIN SHOW
EXCITING EATURE ON OLPHINS
BUYING SNACKS
NOT BAD.
TAIYAKI
WOULD SHE... BE ABLE TO MANAGE IN THE REAL WORLD?
HE'S THINKING SOMETHING INFURIATING.
WHEN I SEE HER, TRYING SO DESPERATELY TO HOLD ON TO SOMETHING,
IT'S LIKE I'M LOOKING IN A MIRROR.
PART OF ME
ASSUMED SHIZUKU AND I WERE THE SAME.
I THOUGHT SHIZUKU
MIGHT UNDERSTAND ME.

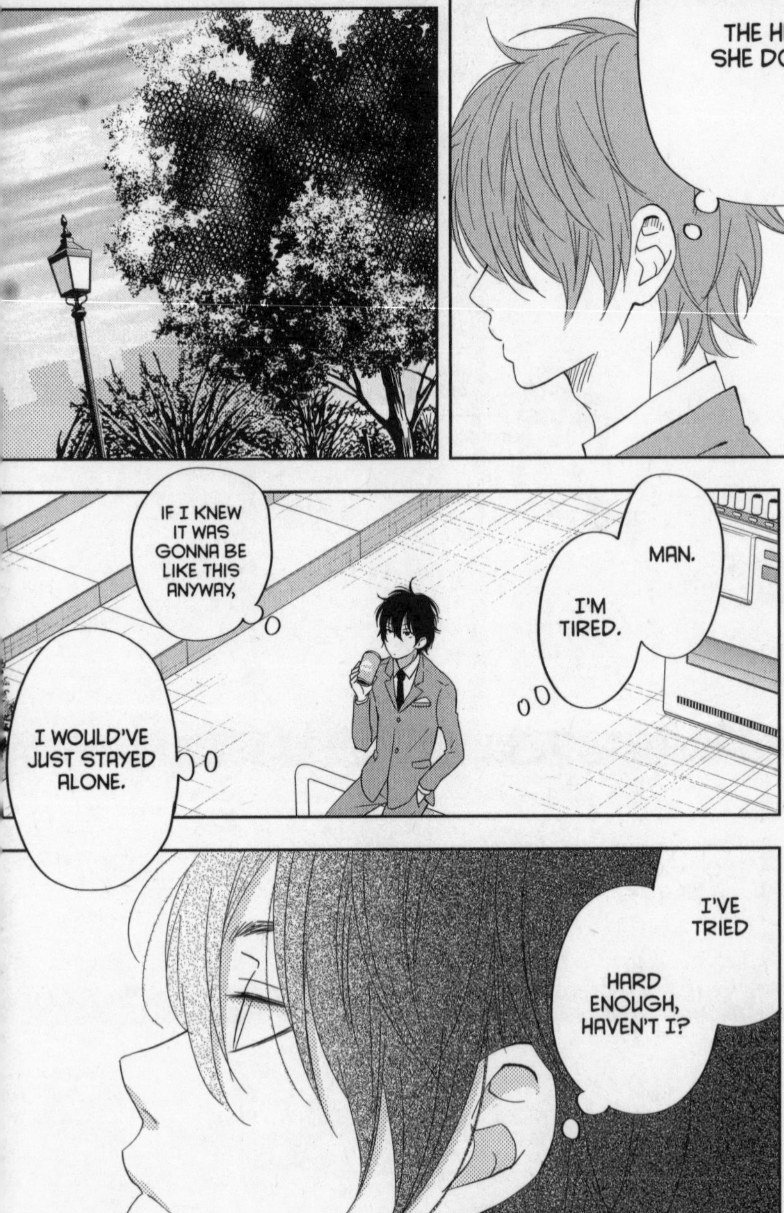
THE HELL SHE DOES.
MAN.
I'M TIRED.
IF I KNEW IT WAS GONNA BE LIKE THIS ANYWAY,
I WOULD'VE JUST STAYED ALONE.
I'VE TRIED
HARD ENOUGH, HAVEN'T I?

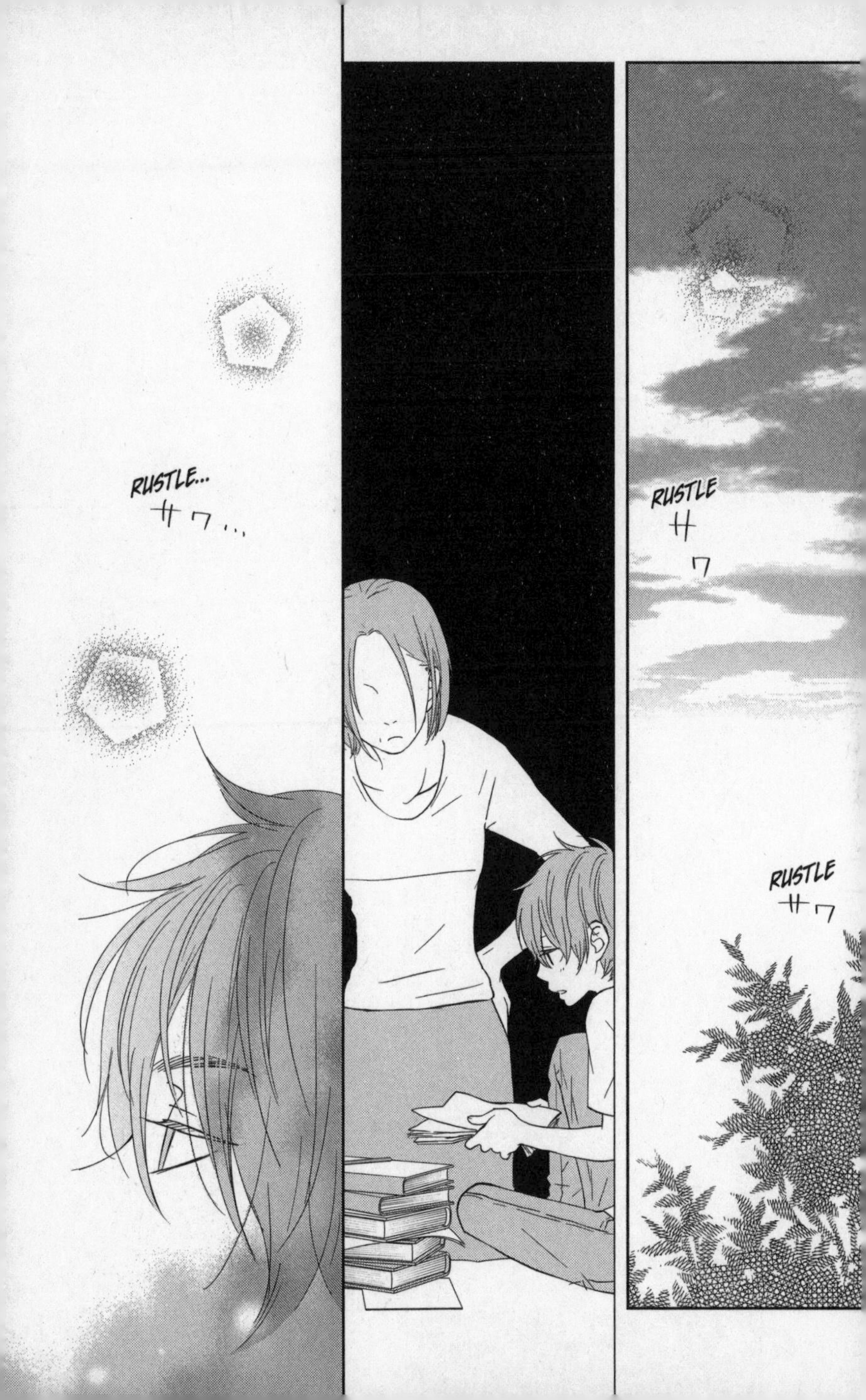
RUSTLE
サワ
RUSTLE
サワ
RUSTLE...
サワ…

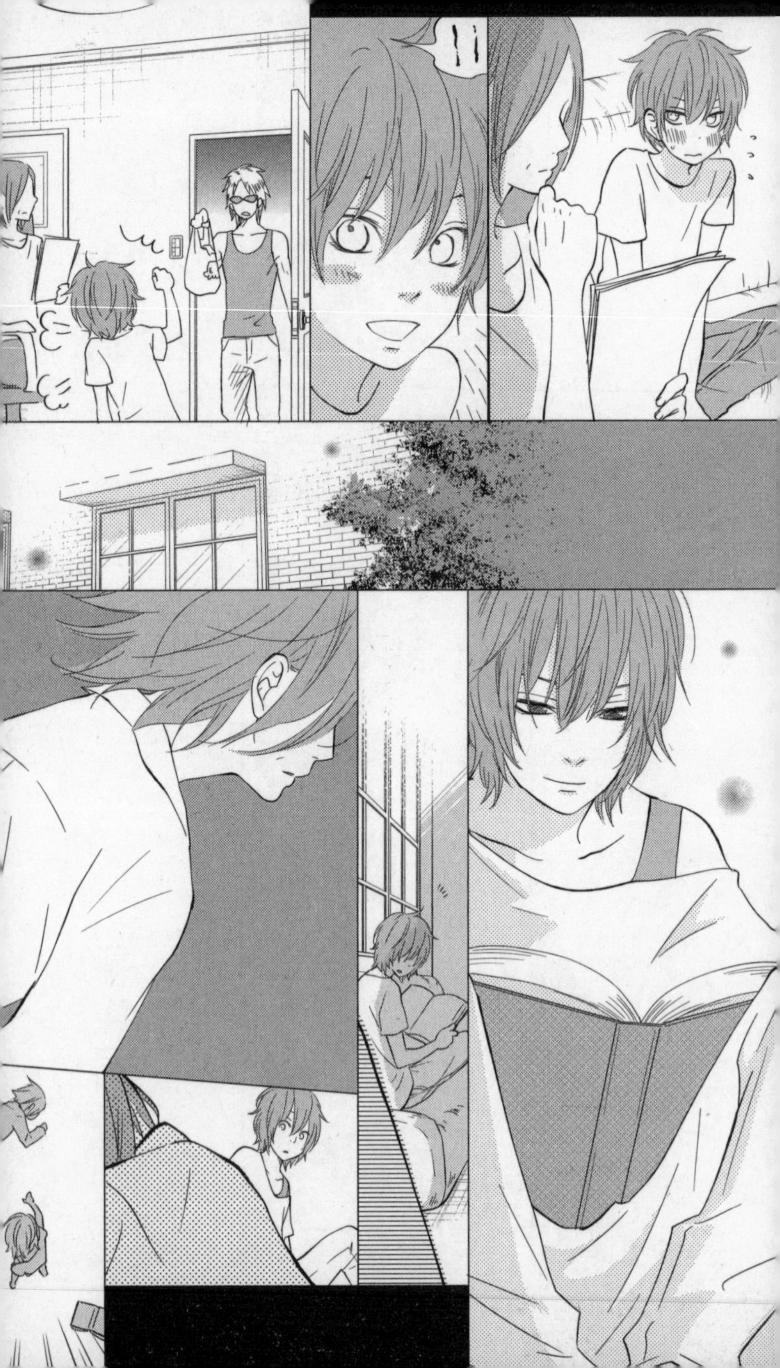
!!

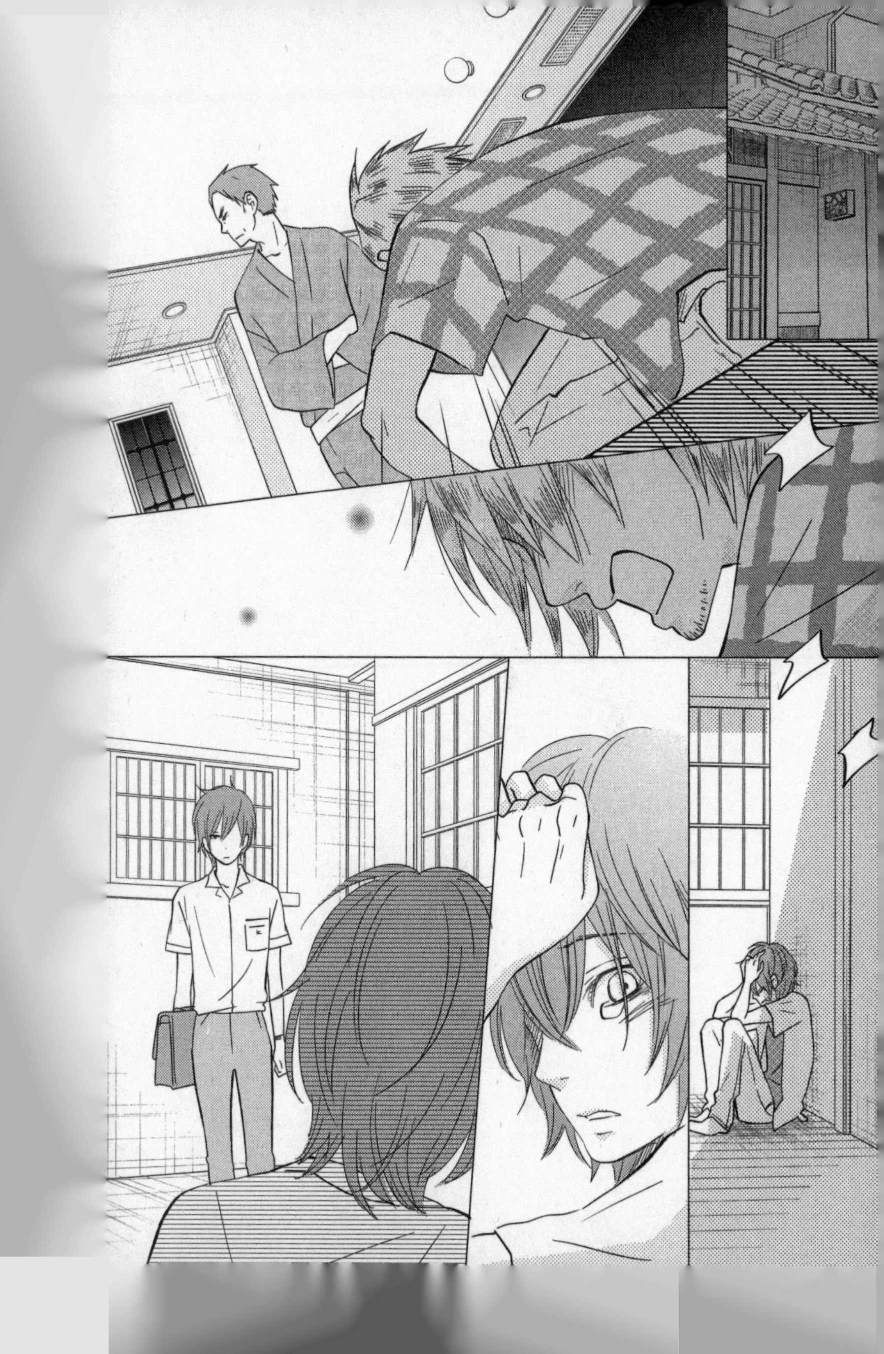

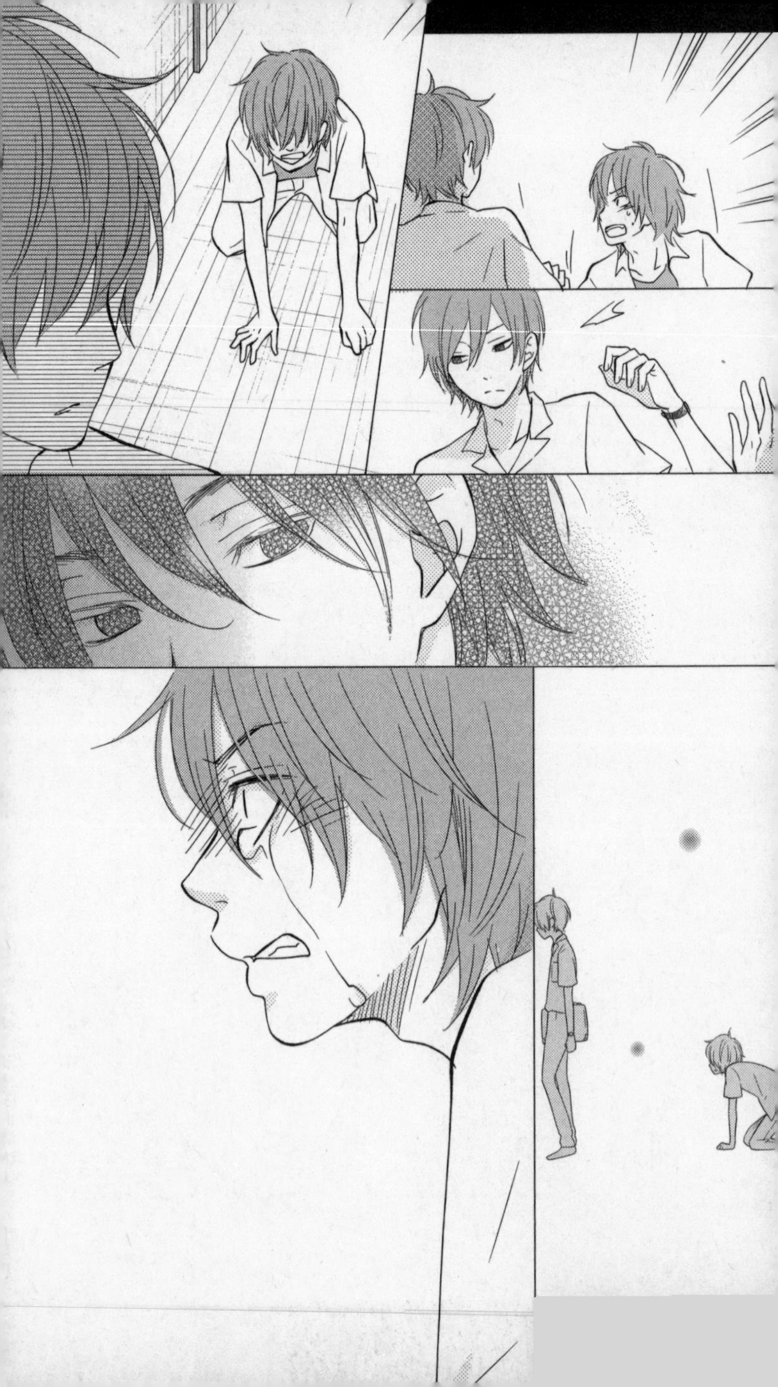

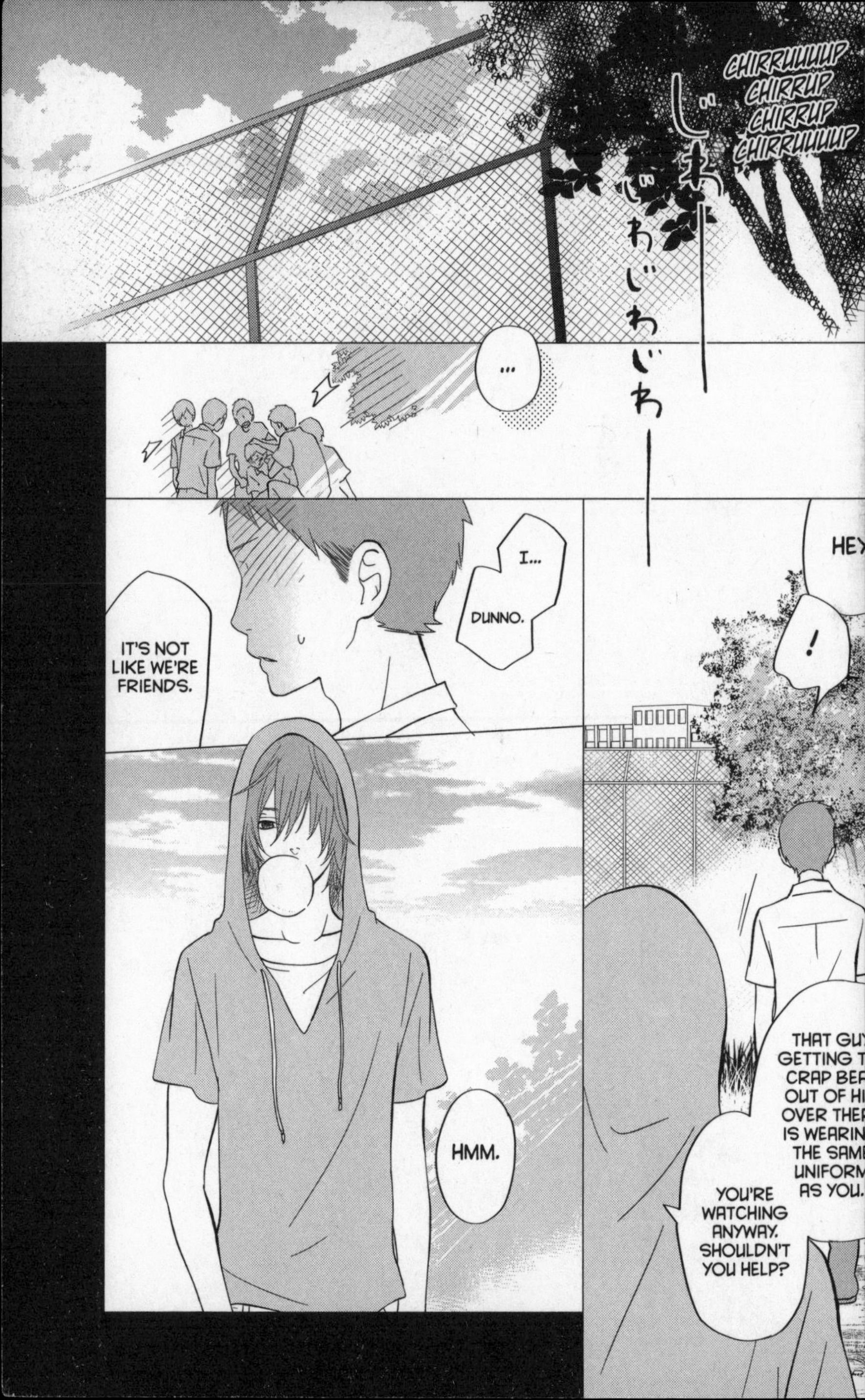
CHIRRUUUUP CHIRRUP CHIRRUP CHIRRUUUUP
...
HEY
!
THAT GU GETTING T CRAP BEA OUT OF HI OVER THE IS WEARIN THE SAM UNIFORM AS YOU.
YOU'RE WATCHING ANYWAY. SHOULDN'T YOU HELP?
I... DUNNO.
IT'S NOT LIKE WE'RE FRIENDS.
HMM.

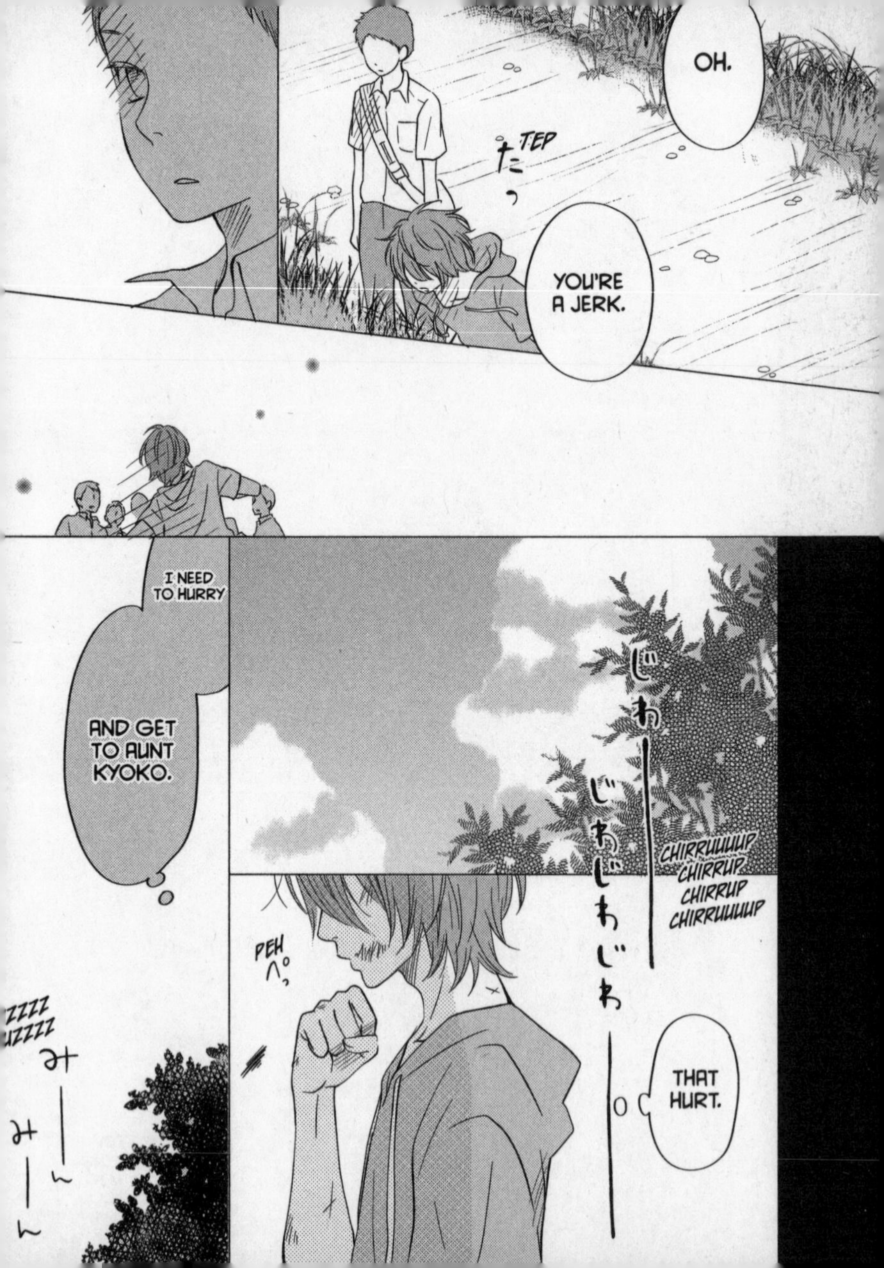
OH.
YOU'RE A JERK.
TEP
たっ
じわーじわじわじわー
CHIRRUUUP CHIRRUP CHIRRUP CHIRRUUUP
THAT HURT.
PEH
ぺっ
I NEED TO HURRY
AND GET TO AUNT KYOKO.
ZZZZ ZZZZ
みーんみーん

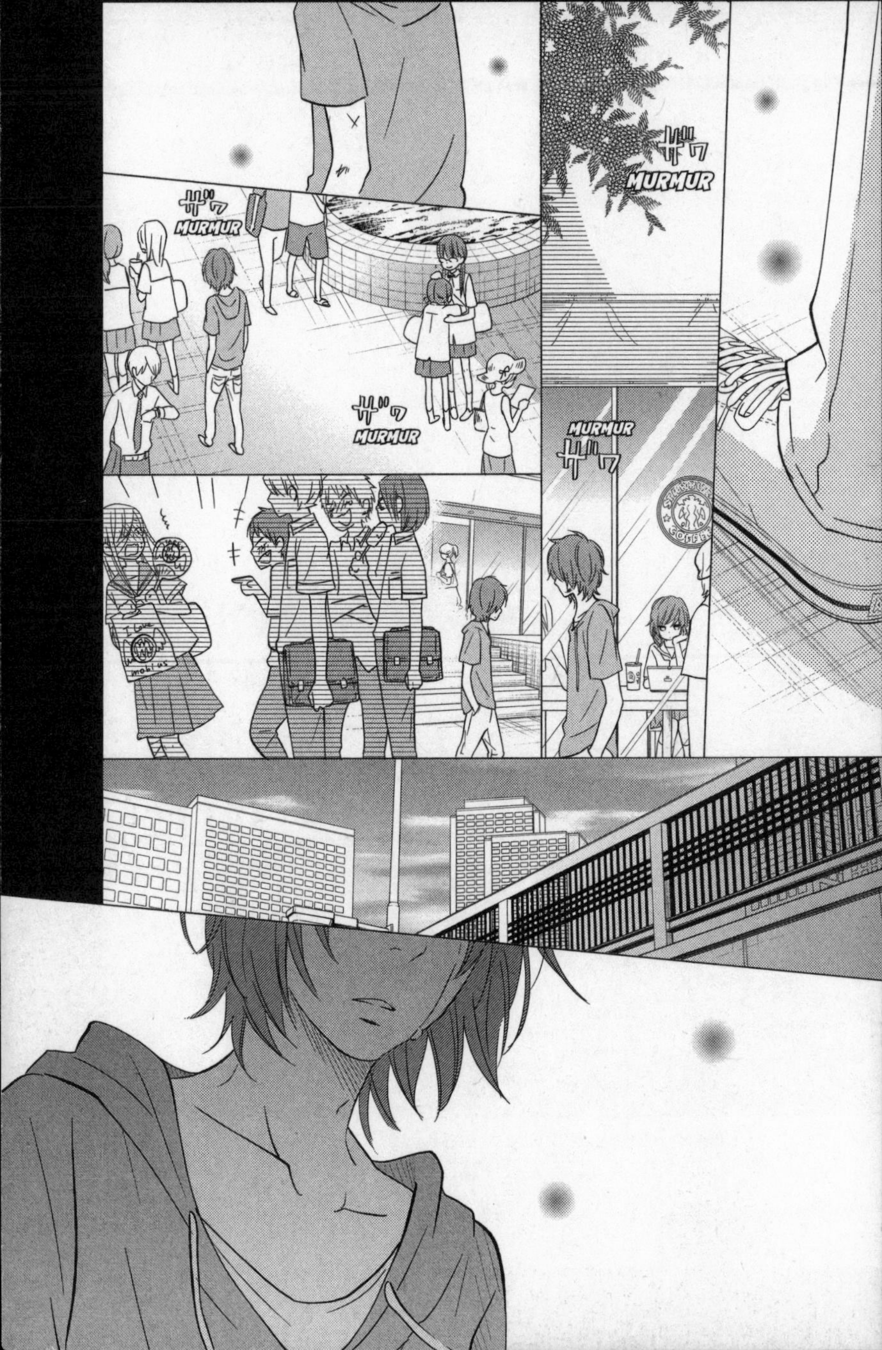

ザワ
MURMUR
MURMUR
ザワ
COFFEE
ザワ
MURMUR
ザワ
MURMUR
I Love
mobius

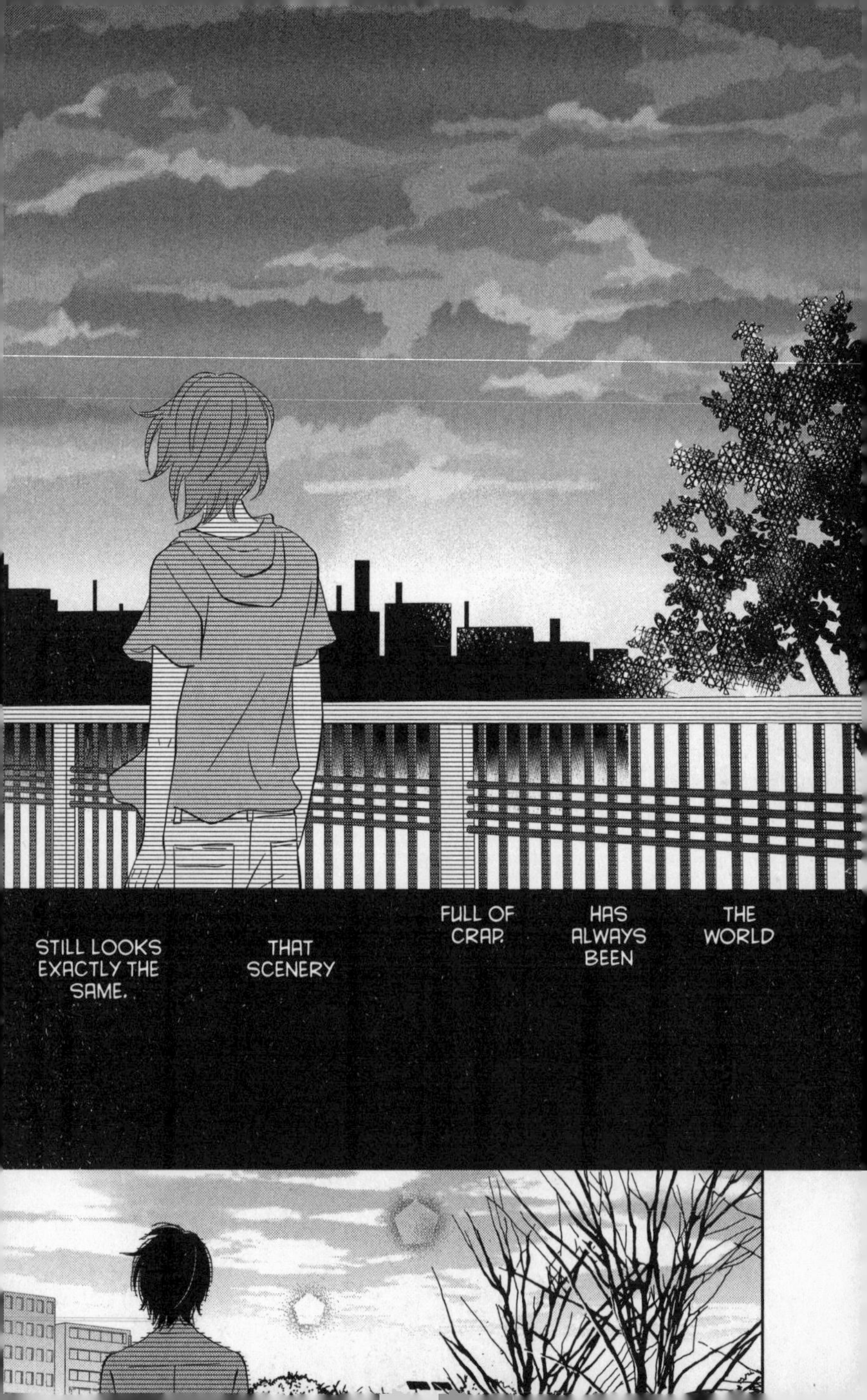
THE WORLD
HAS ALWAYS BEEN
FULL OF CRAP.
THAT SCENERY
STILL LOOKS EXACTLY THE SAME.

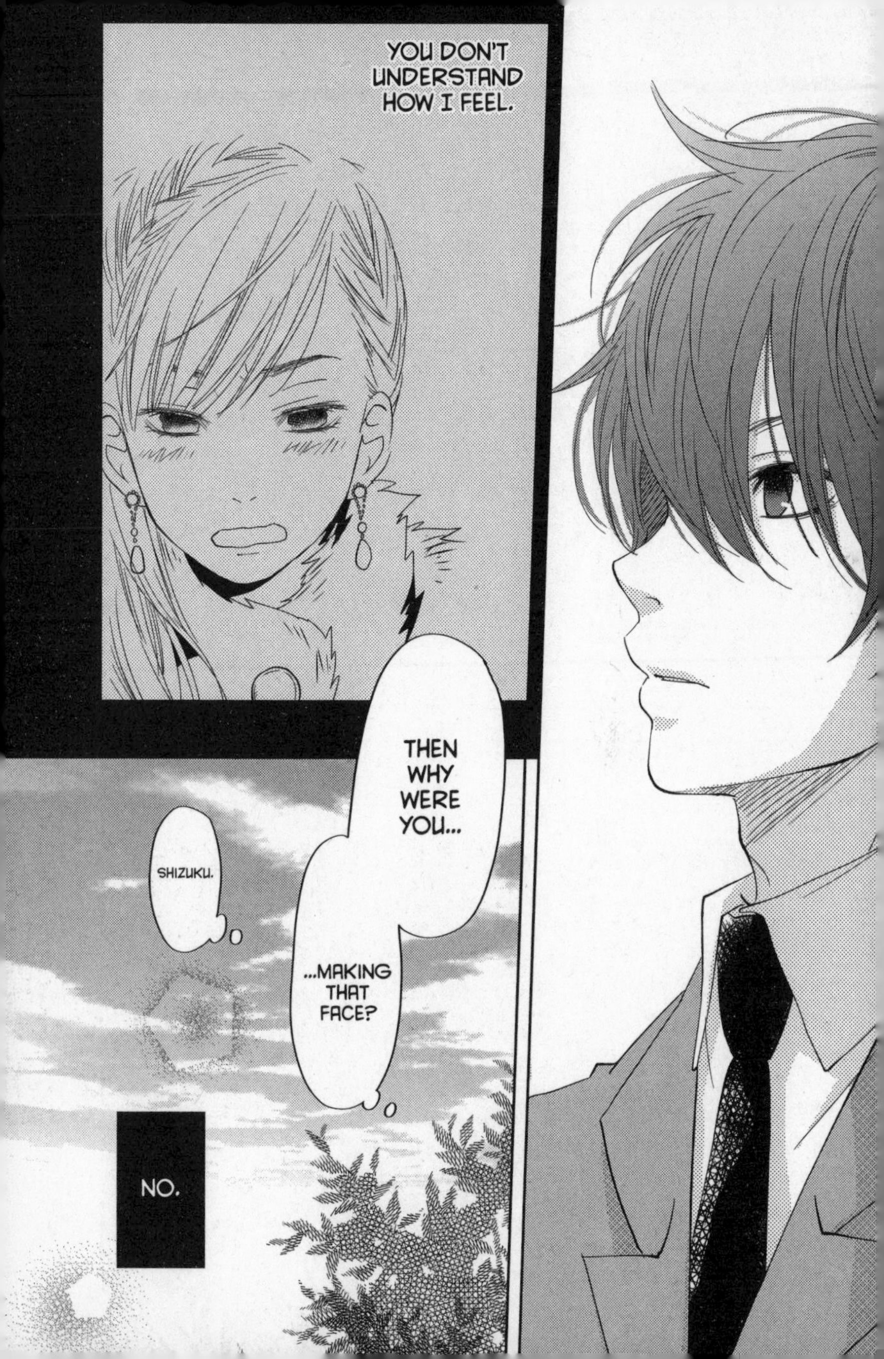
THEN WHY WERE YOU...
...MAKING THAT FACE?
YOU DON'T UNDERSTAND HOW I FEEL.
SHIZUKU.
NO.

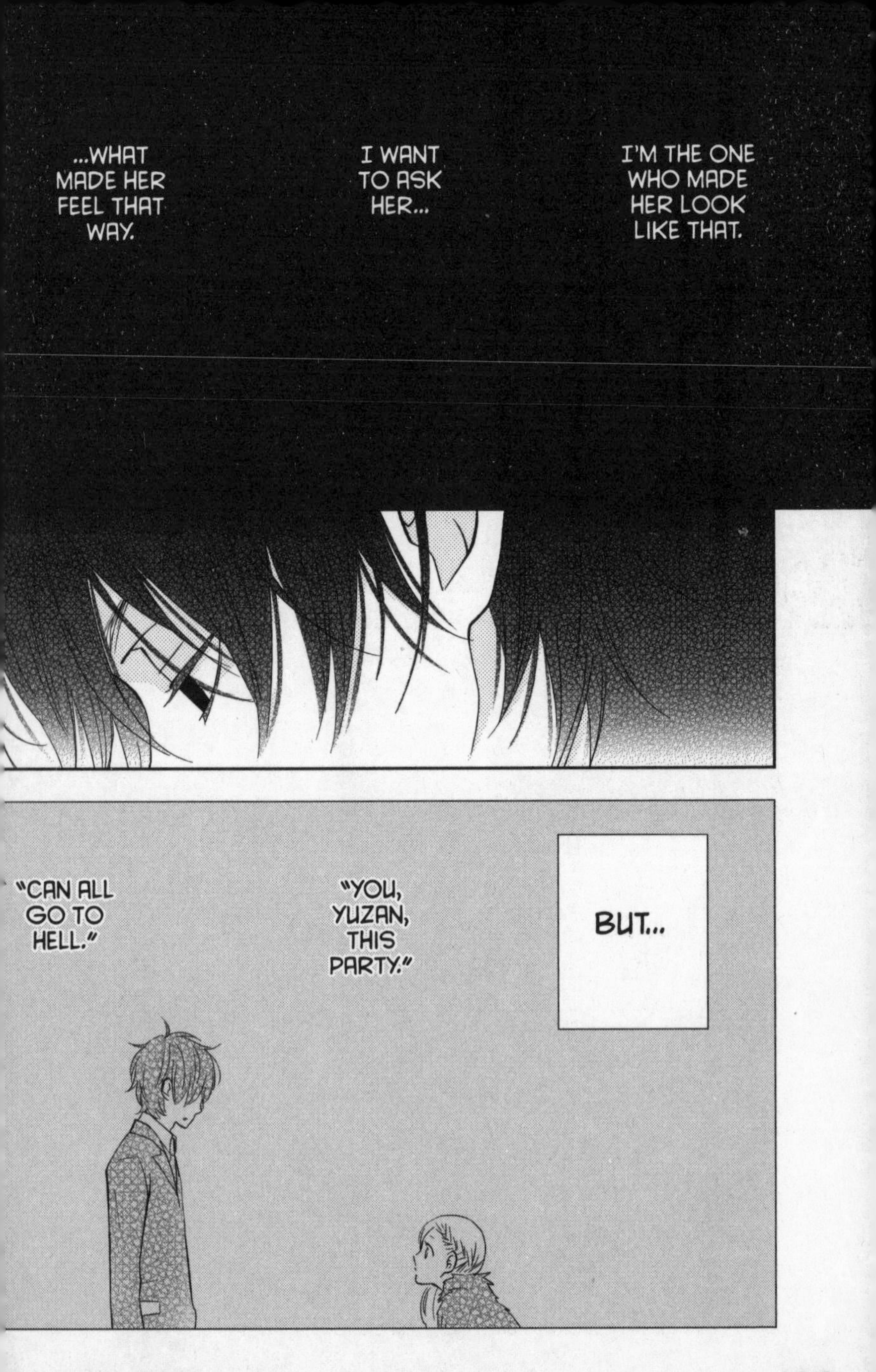
I'M THE ONE WHO MADE HER LOOK LIKE THAT.
I WANT TO ASK HER...
...WHAT MADE HER FEEL THAT WAY.
BUT...
"YOU, YUZAN, THIS PARTY."
"CAN ALL GO TO HELL."

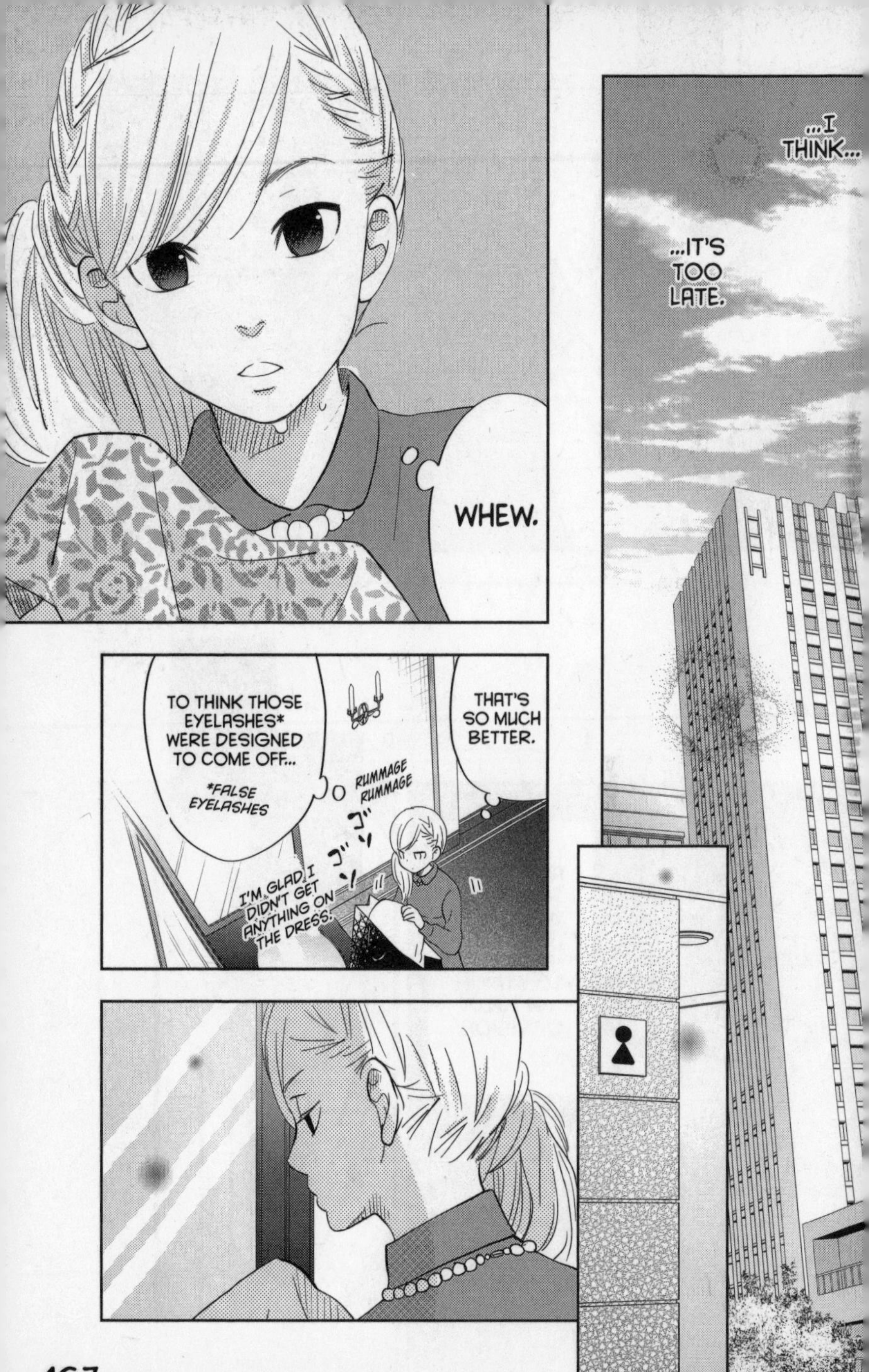
...I THINK...
...IT'S TOO LATE.
WHEW.
THAT'S SO MUCH BETTER.
RUMMAGE RUMMAGE
TO THINK THOSE EYELASHES* WERE DESIGNED TO COME OFF...
*FALSE EYELASHES
ゴソ ゴソ
I'M GLAD I DIDN'T GET ANYTHING ON THE DRESS.

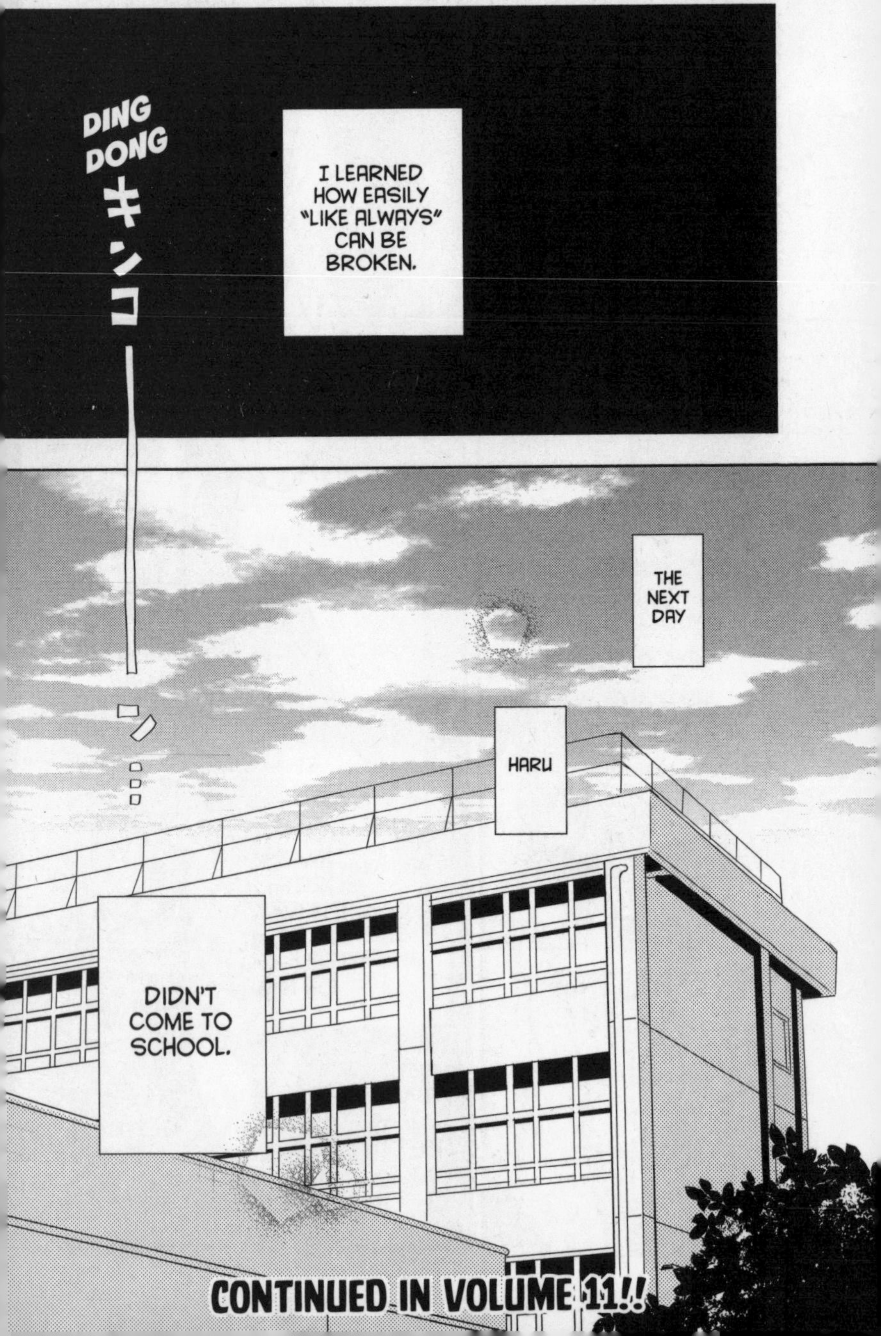
I LEARNED HOW EASILY "LIKE ALWAYS" CAN BE BROKEN.
DING DONG
キンコーン…
THE NEXT DAY
HARU
DIDN'T COME TO SCHOOL.
CONTINUED IN VOLUME 11!!

YOUNG BROTHERS, PART 1

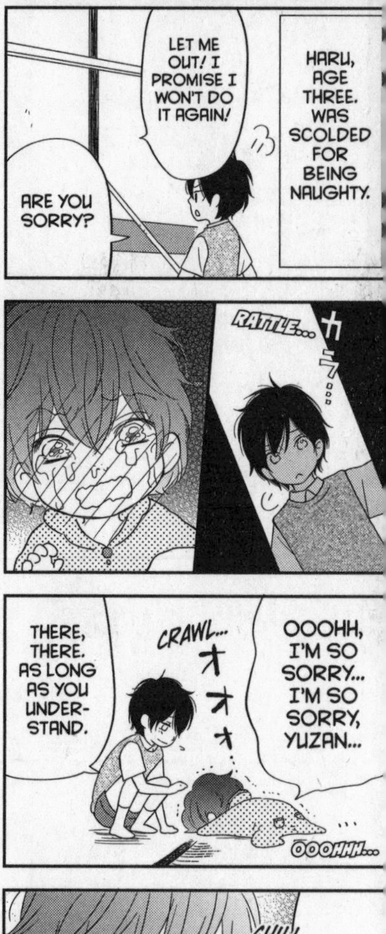
HARU, AGE THREE. WAS SCOLDED FOR BEING NAUGHTY.
LET ME OUT! I PROMISE I WON'T DO IT AGAIN!
ARE YOU SORRY?
RATTLE...
OOOHH, I'M SO SORRY... I'M SO SORRY, YUZAN...
CRAWL...
THERE, THERE. AS LONG AS YOU UNDER-STAND.
OOOHHH...
CHILL
OOO-OHHH... HE'S SO CUTE...

YOUNG BROTHERS, PART 2

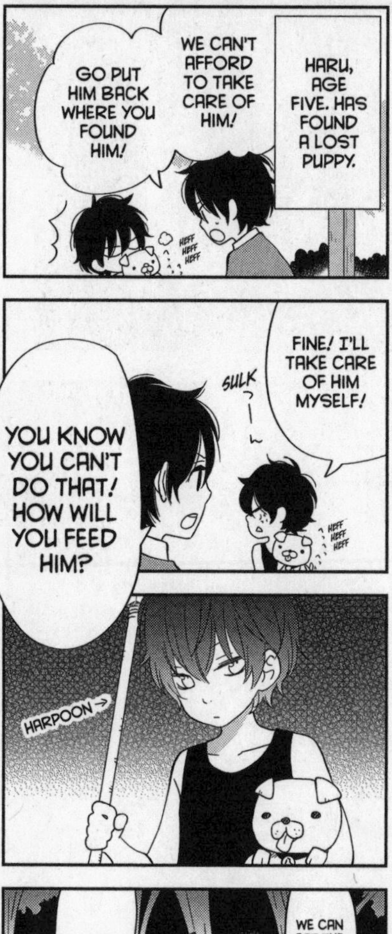
HARU, AGE FIVE. HAS FOUND A LOST PUPPY.
WE CAN'T AFFORD TO TAKE CARE OF HIM!
GO PUT HIM BACK WHERE YOU FOUND HIM!
HEFF HEFF HEFF
FINE! I'LL TAKE CARE OF HIM MYSELF!
SULK
HEFF HEFF HEFF
YOU KNOW YOU CAN'T DO THAT! HOW WILL YOU FEED HIM?
HARPOON→
WE CAN EAT THE GRASS, TOO!
CRACKLE CRACKLE
OH, NO... HARU'S DEVOLVING INTO A WILD MAN.
I'LL HAVE TO TAKE HIM HOME AND TAME HIM.
WORRY WORRY

★ END OF VOLUME BONUS MANGA ★

KENJI AND HARU

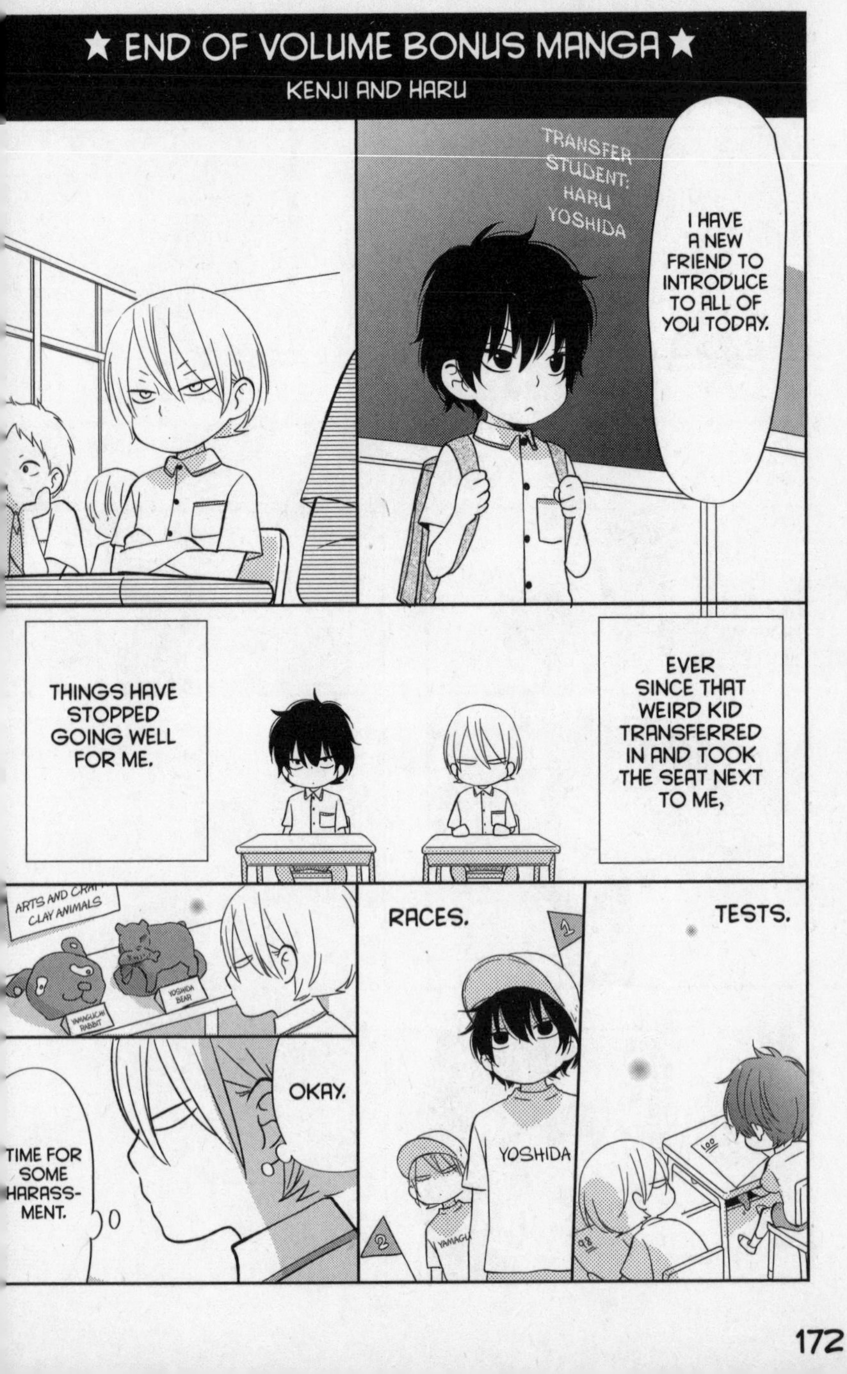
TRANSFER STUDENT: HARU YOSHIDA
I HAVE A NEW FRIEND TO INTRODUCE TO ALL OF YOU TODAY.
EVER SINCE THAT WEIRD KID TRANSFERRED IN AND TOOK THE SEAT NEXT TO ME,
THINGS HAVE STOPPED GOING WELL FOR ME.
TESTS.
RACES.
YOSHIDA
YAMAGU
ARTS AND CRAFT CLAY ANIMALS
YOSHIDA BEAR
YAMAGUCHI RABBIT
OKAY.
TIME FOR SOME HARASS- MENT.

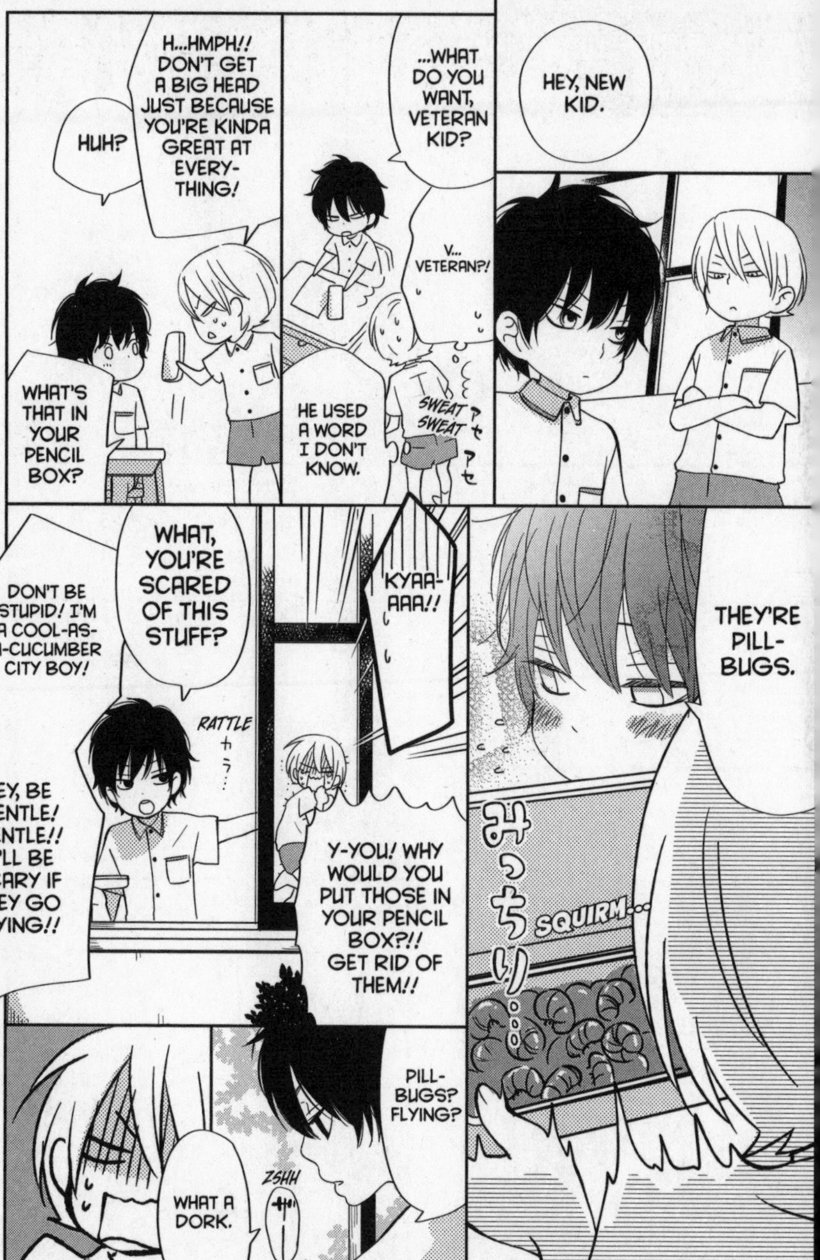
HEY, NEW KID.
...WHAT DO YOU WANT, VETERAN KID?
V... VETERAN?!
SWEAT SWEAT アセアセ
HE USED A WORD I DON'T KNOW.
H...HMPH!! DON'T GET A BIG HEAD JUST BECAUSE YOU'RE KINDA GREAT AT EVERY-THING!
HUH?
WHAT'S THAT IN YOUR PENCIL BOX?
THEY'RE PILL-BUGS.
SQUIRM...
みっちり…
KYAA-AAA!!
Y-YOU! WHY WOULD YOU PUT THOSE IN YOUR PENCIL BOX?!! GET RID OF THEM!!
WHAT, YOU'RE SCARED OF THIS STUFF?
DON'T BE STUPID! I'M A COOL-AS-A-CUCUMBER CITY BOY!
RATTLE カラ…
HEY, BE GENTLE! GENTLE!! IT'LL BE SCARY IF THEY GO FLYING!!
PILL-BUGS? FLYING?
ZSHH
WHAT A DORK.

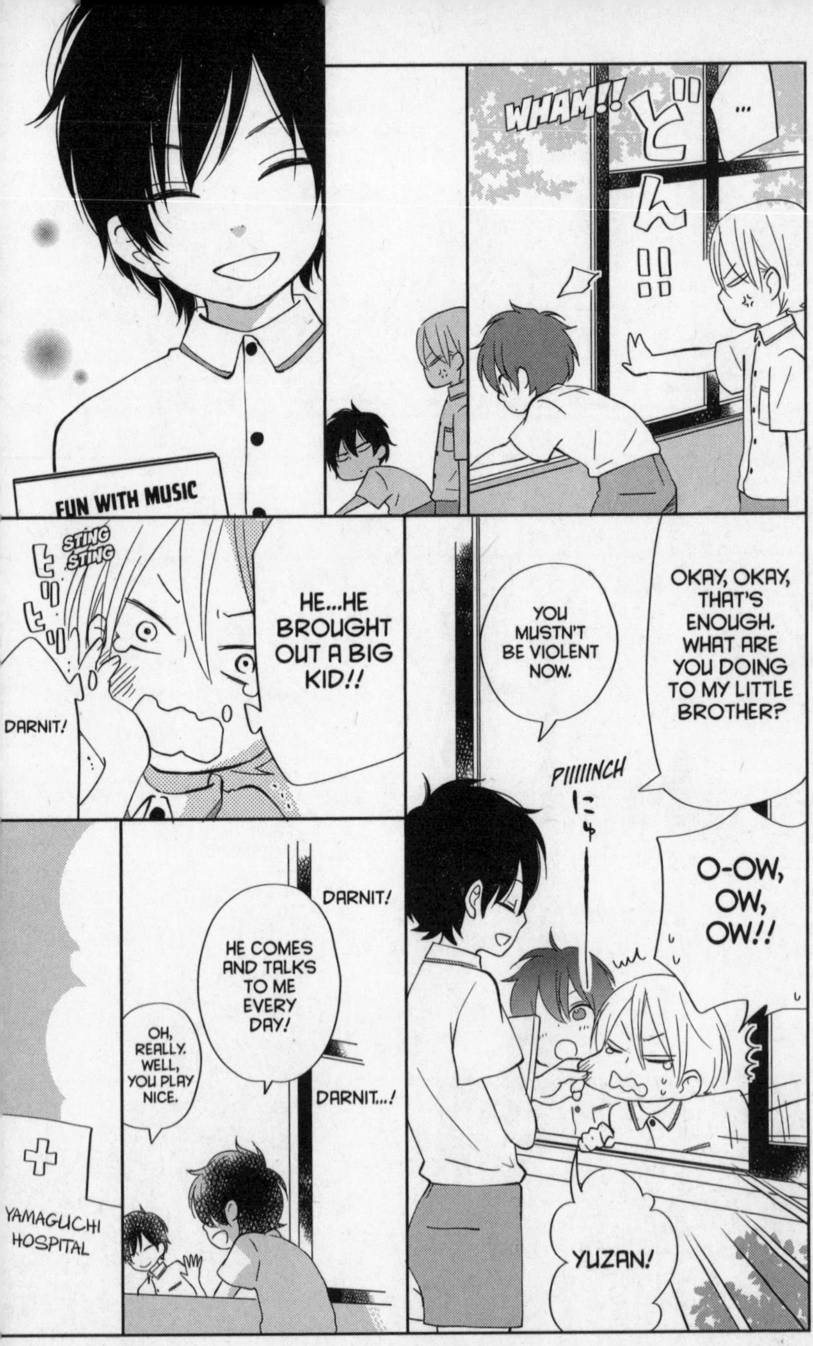
...
WHAM!!
どん!!
FUN WITH MUSIC
OKAY, OKAY, THAT'S ENOUGH. WHAT ARE YOU DOING TO MY LITTLE BROTHER?
YOU MUSTN'T BE VIOLENT NOW.
PIIIIINCH
にゅー
O-OW, OW, OW!!
YUZAN!
HE...HE BROUGHT OUT A BIG KID!!
STING STING
ヒリ ヒリ
DARNIT!
DARNIT!
HE COMES AND TALKS TO ME EVERY DAY!
DARNIT...!
OH, REALLY. WELL, YOU PLAY NICE.
YAMAGUCHI HOSPITAL

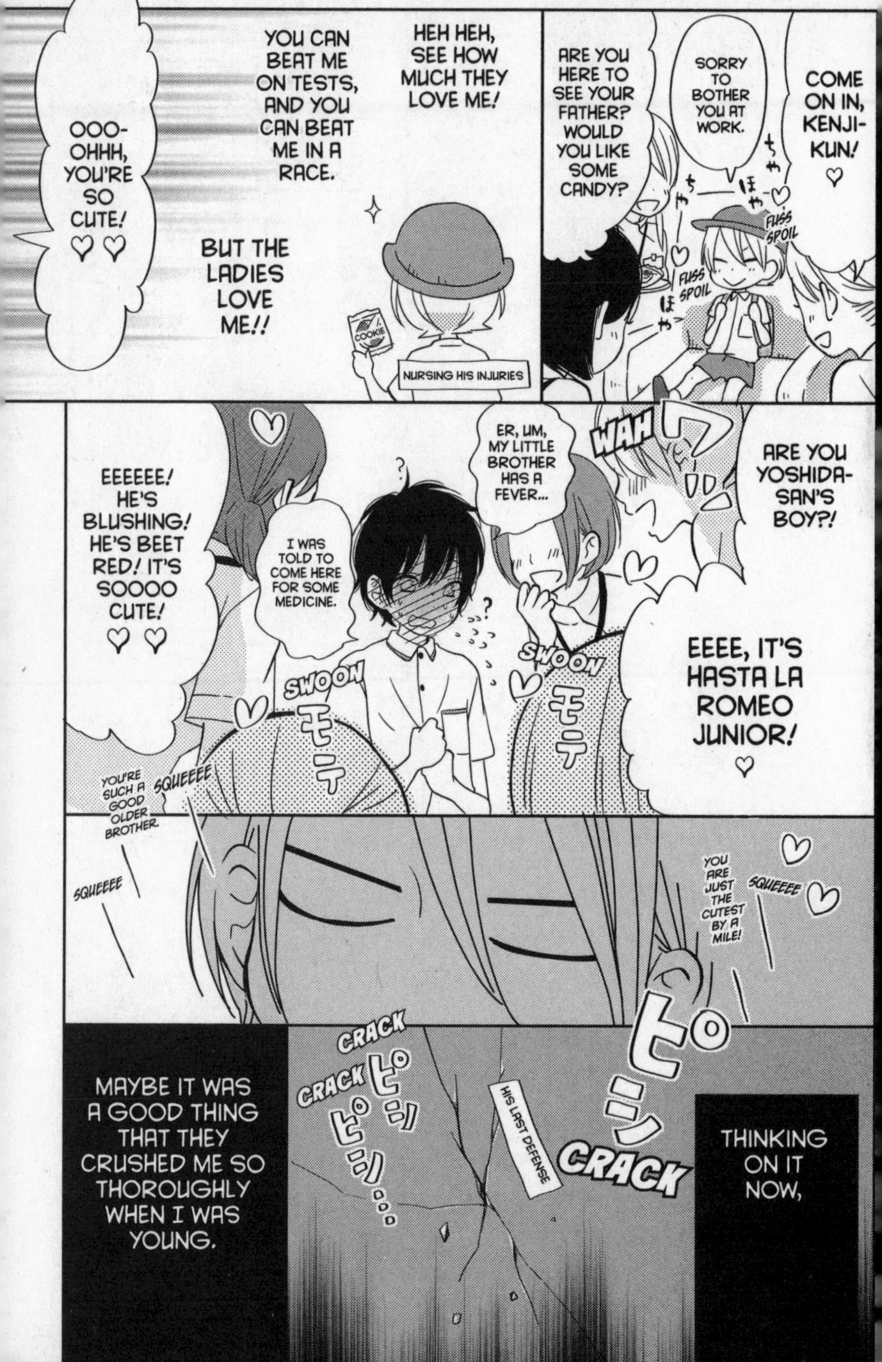
COME ON IN, KENJI-KUN! ♡
SORRY TO BOTHER YOU AT WORK.
ARE YOU HERE TO SEE YOUR FATHER? WOULD YOU LIKE SOME CANDY?
FUSS SPOIL
FUSS SPOIL
HEH HEH, SEE HOW MUCH THEY LOVE ME!
YOU CAN BEAT ME ON TESTS, AND YOU CAN BEAT ME IN A RACE.
BUT THE LADIES LOVE ME!!
COOKIE
NURSING HIS INJURIES
OOO-OHHH, YOU'RE SO CUTE! ♡ ♡
ARE YOU YOSHIDA-SAN'S BOY?!
WAH
ER, UM, MY LITTLE BROTHER HAS A FEVER...
EEEE, IT'S HASTA LA ROMEO JUNIOR! ♡
SWOON
I WAS TOLD TO COME HERE FOR SOME MEDICINE.
EEEEEE! HE'S BLUSHING! HE'S BEET RED! IT'S SOOOO CUTE! ♡ ♡
SWOON
SQUEEEEE
YOU'RE SUCH A GOOD OLDER BROTHER.
SQUEEEEE
YOU ARE JUST THE CUTEST BY A MILE!
SQUEEEE
THINKING ON IT NOW,
CRACK
HIS LAST DEFENSE
CRACK
CRACK
MAYBE IT WAS A GOOD THING THAT THEY CRUSHED ME SO THOROUGHLY WHEN I WAS YOUNG.

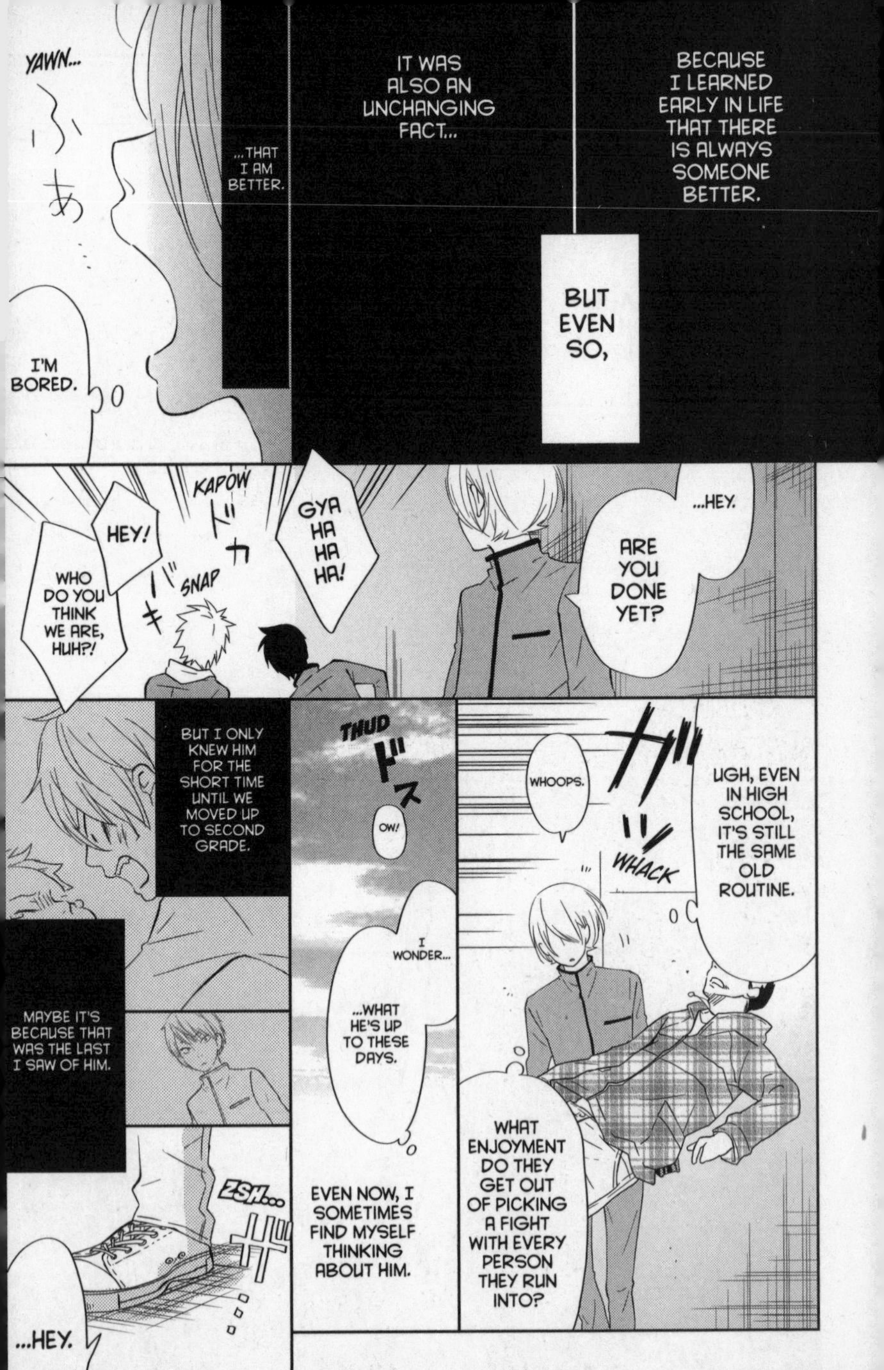
BECAUSE I LEARNED EARLY IN LIFE THAT THERE IS ALWAYS SOMEONE BETTER.
BUT EVEN SO,
IT WAS ALSO AN UNCHANGING FACT...
...THAT I AM BETTER.
YAWN...
ふあ
I'M BORED.
...HEY.
ARE YOU DONE YET?
GYA HA HA HA!
KAPOW
ドカ
HEY!
WHO DO YOU THINK WE ARE, HUH?!
SNAP
バキ
UGH, EVEN IN HIGH SCHOOL, IT'S STILL THE SAME OLD ROUTINE.
WHOOPS.
ガツ
WHACK
WHAT ENJOYMENT DO THEY GET OUT OF PICKING A FIGHT WITH EVERY PERSON THEY RUN INTO?
THUD
ドス
OW!
I WONDER...
...WHAT HE'S UP TO THESE DAYS.
EVEN NOW, I SOMETIMES FIND MYSELF THINKING ABOUT HIM.
BUT I ONLY KNEW HIM FOR THE SHORT TIME UNTIL WE MOVED UP TO SECOND GRADE.
MAYBE IT'S BECAUSE THAT WAS THE LAST I SAW OF HIM.
ZSH...
ザ
...HEY.

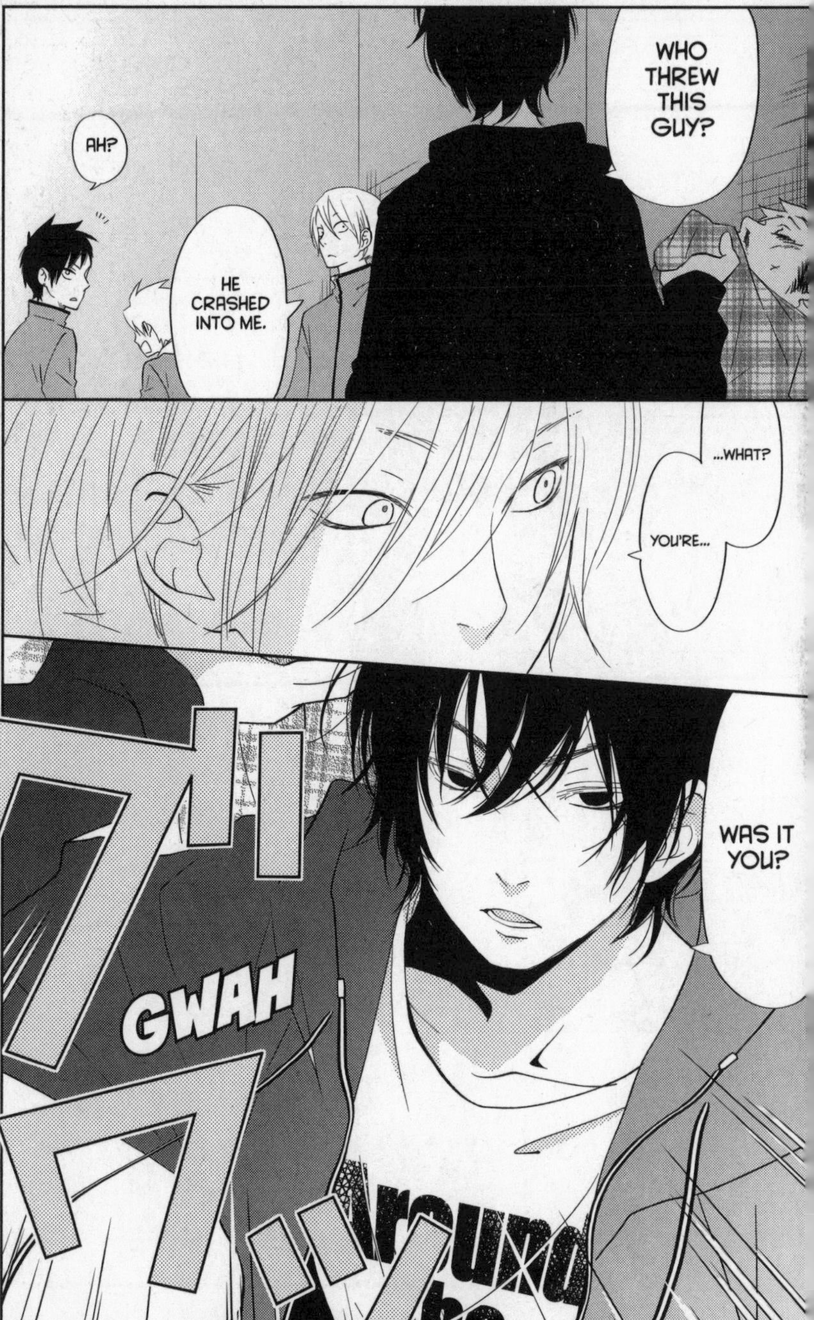
WHO THREW THIS GUY?
AH?
HE CRASHED INTO ME.
...WHAT?
YOU'RE...
WAS IT YOU?
GWAH

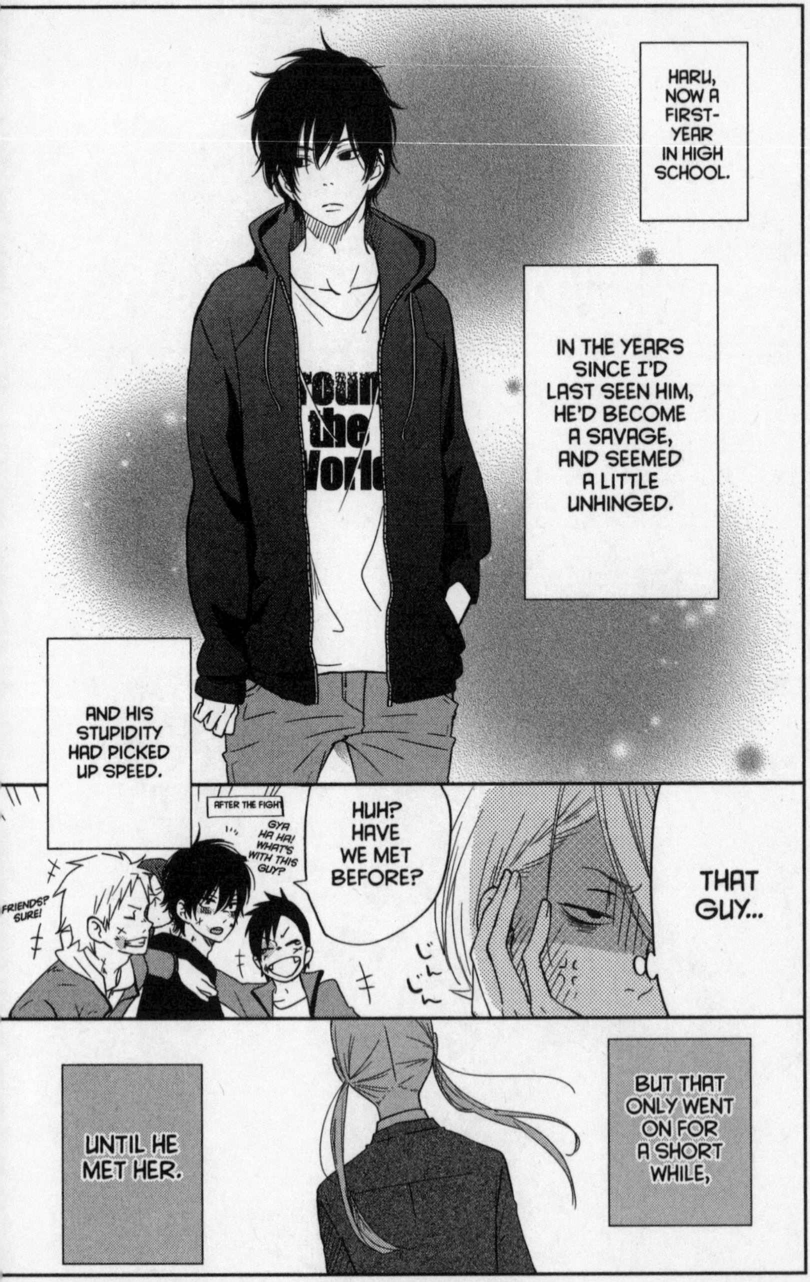
HARU, NOW A FIRST-YEAR IN HIGH SCHOOL.
IN THE YEARS SINCE I'D LAST SEEN HIM, HE'D BECOME A SAVAGE, AND SEEMED A LITTLE UNHINGED.
AND HIS STUPIDITY HAD PICKED UP SPEED.
THAT GUY...
じんじん
HUH? HAVE WE MET BEFORE?
AFTER THE FIGHT
GYA HA HA! WHAT'S WITH THIS GUY?
FRIENDS? SURE!
BUT THAT ONLY WENT ON FOR A SHORT WHILE,
UNTIL HE MET HER.

COMMENT

Robico

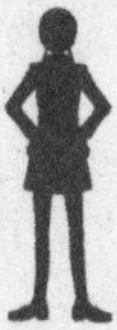

This is volume 10. It's like I woke up and suddenly the series is 10 volumes long. I'll do my best. I hope you enjoyed volume 10.

MY LITTLE MONSTER

UNDER-THE-SLIPCOVER SPECIAL BONUS MANGA: "MY SISTER"

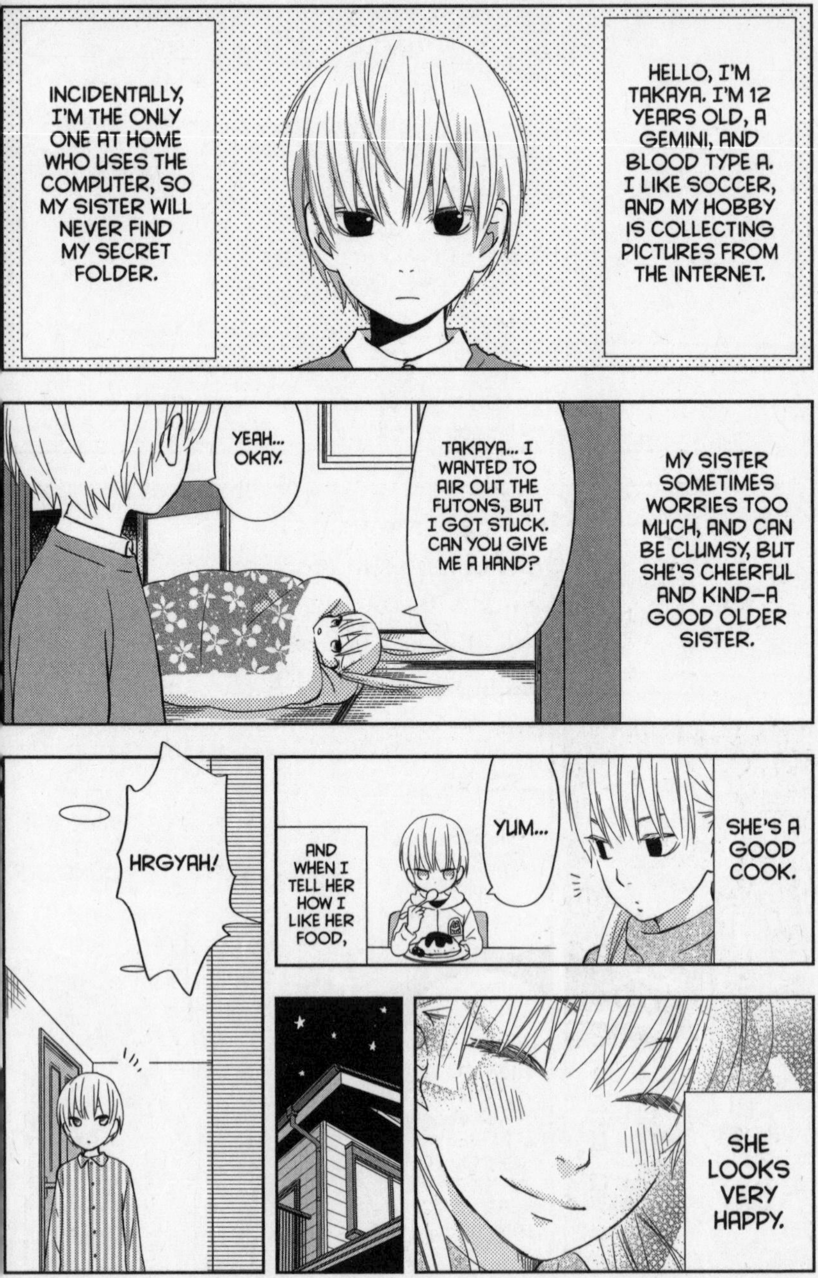

HELLO, I'M TAKAYA. I'M 12 YEARS OLD, A GEMINI, AND BLOOD TYPE A. I LIKE SOCCER, AND MY HOBBY IS COLLECTING PICTURES FROM THE INTERNET.
INCIDENTALLY, I'M THE ONLY ONE AT HOME WHO USES THE COMPUTER, SO MY SISTER WILL NEVER FIND MY SECRET FOLDER.
MY SISTER SOMETIMES WORRIES TOO MUCH, AND CAN BE CLUMSY, BUT SHE'S CHEERFUL AND KIND—A GOOD OLDER SISTER.
TAKAYA... I WANTED TO AIR OUT THE FUTONS, BUT I GOT STUCK. CAN YOU GIVE ME A HAND?
YEAH... OKAY.
SHE'S A GOOD COOK.
YUM...
AND WHEN I TELL HER HOW I LIKE HER FOOD,
SHE LOOKS VERY HAPPY.
HRGYAH!

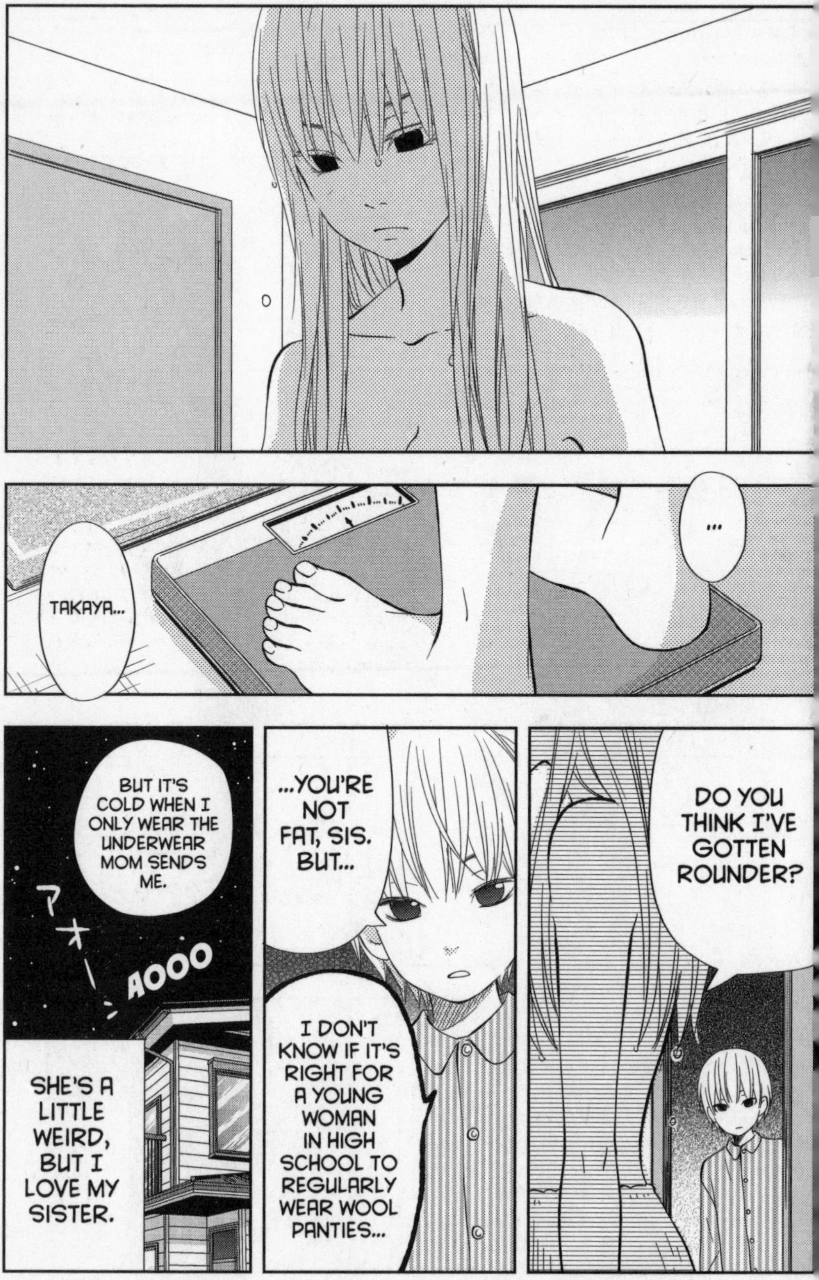
...
TAKAYA...
DO YOU THINK I'VE GOTTEN ROUNDER?
...YOU'RE NOT FAT, SIS. BUT...
I DON'T KNOW IF IT'S RIGHT FOR A YOUNG WOMAN IN HIGH SCHOOL TO REGULARLY WEAR WOOL PANTIES...
BUT IT'S COLD WHEN I ONLY WEAR THE UNDERWEAR MOM SENDS ME.
アオー
AOOO
SHE'S A LITTLE WEIRD, BUT I LOVE MY SISTER.

My Little Monster 10 Translation Notes

apanese is a tricky language for most Westerners, and translation is often more art ıan science. For your edification and reading pleasure, here are notes on some of ıe places where we could have gone in a different direction in our translation of ıe work, or where a Japanese cultural reference is used.

oming of age, page 13

Japan, a person legally reaches dulthood when he or she turns 20. Since s such a big year, it is a cause for special elebration, and if Taizo Yoshida throws party for his son, it can show the public at he is a family man after all.

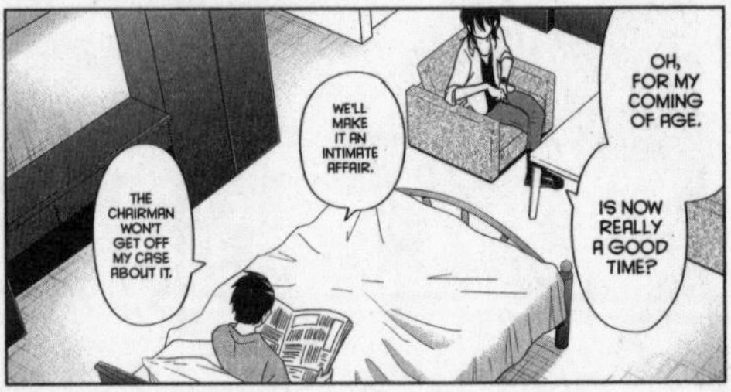
OH, FOR MY COMING OF AGE.
IS NOW REALLY A GOOD TIME?
WE'LL MAKE IT AN INTIMATE AFFAIR.
THE CHAIRMAN WON'T GET OFF MY CASE ABOUT IT.

The Cave of the Sun Goddess, page 57

Amano-Iwato, or "The Cave of the Sun Goddess", is a traditional tale from Japanese mythology. According to legend, Amaterasu, the Sun Goddess was harassed by Susano-O, the God of Storms, into hiding herself in a cave, thus bringing darkness to the world. The other gods lure her out of hiding with treasures and a party.

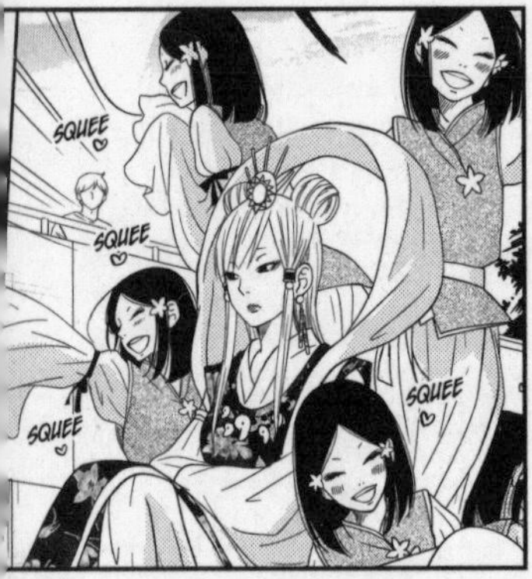
SQUEE
SQUEE
SQUEE
SQUEE

Sasayan's high school debut, page 66

The change from junior high to high school in Japan can be a very big one, because, instead of just going on to the local public high school, students can choose a high school from anywhere in the country—as long as they pass the required entrance exam. This makes it a good opportunity to make a new start, by changing your look, going to a school where know one knows you, etc. This is called a high school debut. But Sasayan doesn't answer the question, so the truth as to whether or not he wanted to make a high school debut remains a mystery.

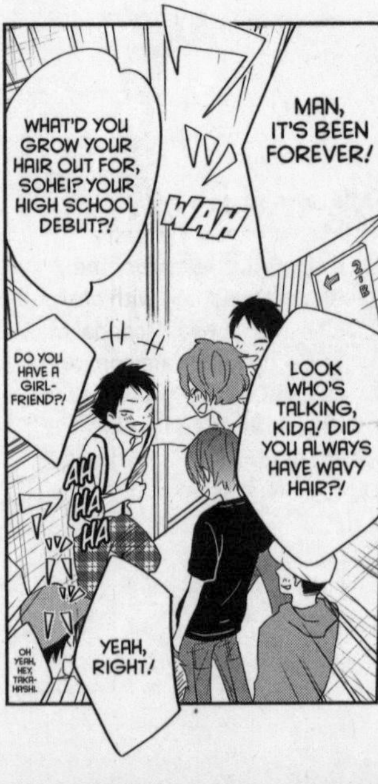
MAN, IT'S BEEN FOREVER!
WHAT'D YOU GROW YOUR HAIR OUT FOR, SOHEI? YOUR HIGH SCHOOL DEBUT?!
WAH
LOOK WHO'S TALKING, KIDA! DID YOU ALWAYS HAVE WAVY HAIR?!
DO YOU HAVE A GIRL-FRIEND?!
AH HA HA
YEAH, RIGHT!
OH YEAH, HEY, TAKA-HASHI.

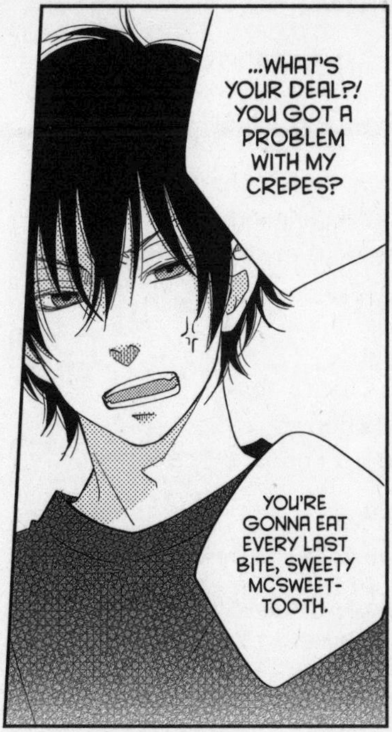
...WHAT'S YOUR DEAL?! YOU GOT A PROBLEM WITH MY CREPES?
YOU'RE GONNA EAT EVERY LAST BITE, SWEETY MCSWEET-TOOTH.

Sweety McSweet-tooth, page 70

As the reader may have guessed, this is not what Haru called Yuzan in the original Japanese text. He called him "suiitsu yaro", which translates to "sweets guy", but the translation doesn't pack the same punch as the intended nuance of the Japanese, so the translators attempted to make the insult more insulting.

Hasta la Romeo, page 129

Taizo Yoshida has earned himself a nickname that combines part of the word *tsuyadane* (love affair) with *otoko* (man). In other words, he is "scandal man". When the kanji characters are combined, they are pronounced ade-osu, or "adios". The translators attempted to retain the "goodbye" in his lady-killer nickname by rendering it as Hasta la Romeo

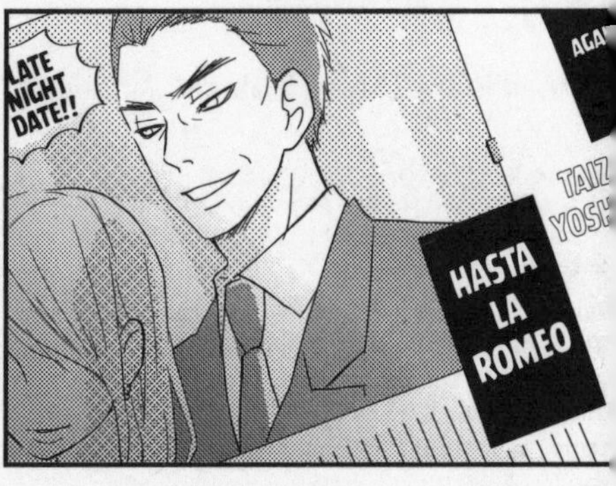
LATE NIGHT DATE!!
HASTA LA ROMEO

A Kodansha Comics Trade Paperback Original.

My Little Monster volume 10 copyright © 2012 Robico
English translation copyright © 2015 Robico

Published in the United States by Kodansha Comics, an imprint of Kodansha USA Publishing, LLC, New York.

Publication rights for this English edition arranged through Kodansha Ltd., Tokyo.

First published in Japan in 2012 by Kodansha Ltd., Tokyo as *Tonari no Kaibutsu-kun*, volume 10.

ISBN 978-1-63236-106-6

Printed in the United States of America.

www.kodanshacomics.com

9 8 7 6 5 4 3 2 1

Translator: Alethea Nibley & Athena Nibley
Lettering: Paige Pumphrey